The Archaeology of Frontiers and Boundaries

This is a volume in

STUDIES IN ARCHAEOLOGY

A complete list of titles in this series appears at the end of this volume.

The Archaeology of
Frontiers and Boundaries

Edited by

STANTON W. GREEN
Department of Anthropology
University of South Carolina
Columbia, South Carolina

STEPHEN M. PERLMAN
Sovran Bank, N.A.
Richmond, Virginia

1985

ACADEMIC PRESS, INC.

(Harcourt Brace Jovanovich, Publishers)

Orlando   San Diego   New York   London
Toronto   Montreal   Sydney   Tokyo

ACADEMIC PRESS, INC.
Orlando, Florida 32887

United Kingdom Edition published by
ACADEMIC PRESS INC. (LONDON) LTD.
24–28 Oval Road, London NW1 7DX

Library of Congress Cataloging in Publication Data

Main entry under title:

The Archaeology of frontiers and boundaries.

 (Studies in archaeology)
 Includes index.
 1. Anthropo-geography--Addresses, essays, lectures.
2. Social archaeology--Addresses, essays, lectures.
3. Frontier and pioneer life--Addresses, essays, lectures.
4. Social structure--Addresses, essays, lectures.
I. Green, Stanton W. II. Perlman, Stephen M.
III. Series.
GF53.A73 1984   304.2   84-9325
ISBN 0-12-298780-2 (alk. paper)

PRINTED IN THE UNITED STATES OF AMERICA

85 86 87 88   9 8 7 6 5 4 3 2 1

*To my mother and the beloved memory
of my father; and to my wife, Claudia.*
Stanton W. Green

*To my wife, Judith, and children, Naomi,
Benjamin, and Lara, and to those events
that shape our lives.*
Stephen M. Perlman

CONTENTS

Part II. Foragers, Pastoralists, and Subsistence Farmers

Part III.   Complex Society

13. Baptists and Boundaries: Lessons from Baptist Material Culture

Gordon Bronitsky, Alan Marks, and Cindy Burleson

CONTRIBUTORS

Numbers in parentheses indicate the pages on which the authors' contributions begin.

GORDON BRONITSKY (325), Department of Sociology and Anthropology, University of Arizona, Tucson, Arizona 85721

CINDY BURLESON (325), University of Texas of the Permian Basin, Odessa, Texas 76762

ROBIN DENNELL (113), Department of Prehistory and Archaeology, University of Sheffield, Sheffield S10 2TN, England

STANTON W. GREEN (3), Department of Anthropology, University of South Carolina, Columbia, South Carolina 29208

STEVEN HAMPSON (15), School of Social Sciences, University of California, Irvine, Irvine, California 92717

DONALD HARDESTY (213), Department of Anthropology, University of Nevada, Reno, Nevada 89557–0006

IAN HODDER (141), Department of Archaeology, University of Cambridge, Cambridge CB2 3DZ, England

JOHN JUSTESON (15), 22 Caywood Place, Hyde Park, New York 12538

KENNETH E. LEWIS (251), Department of Anthropology, Michigan State University, East Lansing, Michigan 48824

ALAN MARKS (325), Department of Psychology, University of Texas of the Permin Basin, Odessa, Texas 79762

THOMAS McGOVERN (275), Department of Anthropology, Hunter College, City University of New York, New York, New York 10021

JAMES A. MOORE (93), Department of Anthropology, Queens College and the Graduate Center, City University of New York, Flushing, New York 11367

ROBERT W. PAYNTER (163), Department of Anthropology, University of Massachusetts, Amherst, Massachusetts 01003

STEPHEN M. PERLMAN (3,33), Sovran Bank, N.A., Richmond, Virginia 23261

PATRICIA E. RUBERSTONE (231), Department of Anthropology, Brown University, Providence, Rhode Island 02912

PETER THORBAHN (231), Public Archaeology Laboratory, Inc., 217 Angell Street, Providence, Rhode Island 02906

DAVID R. YESNER (51), Department of Geography–Anthropology, University of Southern Maine, Gorham, Maine 04038

PREFACE

The present volume, like many edited books, is derived from an organized attempt of like-minded individuals. The inspiration in this case was a symposium organized by us for the 1978 meetings of the Society for American Archaeology in Tucson, Arizona (on the frontier for us easterners). The discussion generated by this session made it clear to us that many of our colleagues were working on similar problems, and a commonality of these inquiries began to emerge: frontiers and boundaries were used as a focus for studying perhaps the most slippery of anthropological constructs—social process. More specifically, the margins of social systems were seen as a place to begin the study of the openness of human society. A wide range of theoretical and methodological approaches was brought to bear on this area of study, within an equally wide range of prehistoric, historic, and contemporary contexts. Instead of working within the assumed bounds of the traditional pristine closed model of human society and culture, frontier and boundary researchers were trying to build theory and develop method for interpreting the ways societies are interconnected.

Motivated by these considerations, we pursued the revision of the original papers (four of which appear in this volume), and the solicitation of complementary chapters (a total of nine new chapters are included in the volume). The result of this effort is this book: a diverse and innovative set of case studies that address fundamental questions concerning social change through the study of anthropological archaeology. All of the original chapters have been revised and updated (Lewis, Perlman, Paynter, and Moore), and the other chapters represent original research.

The concept of social systems as open systems is not original in theory. However, its explicit incorporation into an archaeological frame of reference is, we believe, quite innovative, perhaps because it is methodologically difficult to break away from closed models of human behavior. While we do not pursue here the specifically methodological angle, we do strongly believe that the frontier and boundary approach provides a viable and powerful means for incorporating open systems notions into the study of social process and change.

The overall theoretical contribution of this volume derives from each author's attempt to free him or herself from the necessarily closed anthropological models used in the study of culture process. The methods used range from the analysis of prehistoric and historic artifactual and biological remains, through ethnohistory, ethnoarchaeology, and the study of contemporary U.S. material culture. Temporal contexts range from the Mesolithic period through the twentieth century; geographic representation includes Africa, Europe, Greenland, and North America. This diversity in theory, method, and data underlies the volume's strength in making a case for frontier and boundary research in archaeology.

The book is, in fact, organized in such a manner as to promote the evaluation of our open system's proposition. The table of contents resembles a traditional culture-evolutionary sequence (in simplified form). The intent is to encourage comparison within and between broad categories of sociocultural scale to demonstrate the notion that at all levels of complexity social systems are open systems. In the end we hope this encourages all archaeologists to bear in mind the open system's model in whatever context they work.

The book is divided into three parts with a total of 13 chapters. Part I includes 2 introductory chapters that are respectively a presentation of our frontier and boundary approach and introduction to the other chapters, and a discussion of the methodological difficulties of modeling open systems. Part II includes 5 chapters on foraging, pastoral, and nonindustrial farming societies. Of these, Moore presents a theoretical treatise on forager-farmer interaction using simulation experiments, Perlman and Dennell deal primarily with prehistoric materials, Yesner includes ethnohistoric records with his archaeological evidence, and Hodder bases his work on ethnoarchaeology. Part III includes 6 chapters on complex, world-system societies. Paynter, Hardesty, Lewis, and Rubertone and Thorbahn present case studies on the historic archaeology of the Anglo-American world system, McGovern studies the aboriginal populations of Greenland within the context of Norse expansion, and Bronitsky, Marks, and Burleson present a study of contemporary behavior and material culture among American Baptists.

The diversity of these case studies provides a powerful first evaluation of an open system's approach within archaeology. We believe that a critical reading of this volume will lay a convincing foundation for the study of frontiers and boundaries and bear important insights for the anthropological study of social process.

ACKNOWLEDGMENTS

Acknowledgments, we think, have two purposes. They should, of course, give credit to individuals who have substantively contributed to the project. They can also make known the conditions under which the project was completed.

We begin with the second type of acknowledgment. Both of the editors began this volume with the support of our academic institutions. Initially, the University of South Carolina encouraged both of us to pursue our project, first through the development of the symposium on frontiers and boundaries at the 1978 Society for American Archaeology meetings, and then, after Perlman left that Institution for Virginia Commonwealth University, through the pursuit of its publication. Green would like to thank the Department of Anthropology at the University of South Carolina for its continued support during the development and completion of the project. Edited volumes are often considered second-class citizens in the world of publish or perish, but in Green's case this project was respected by his colleagues and acknowledged fairly within tenure and promotion concerns. Green would especially like to thank Karl Heider, Leland Ferguson, Morgan MacLachlan, and Stanley South for their support.

Perlman's experiences were somewhat different. Rather than review them all, a summary statement will suffice. Anthropology has almost been eliminated at Virginia Commonwealth University. This loss is even greater because we are at a time when anthropology's importance to the academic and nonacademic world should be increasing. Instead, a poor vision by academia of existing and future educational and behavioral needs is creating a trend in the opposite direction. Interestingly, the same appears not to be true for the nonacademic side.

The speed with which Perlman found employment, first as Vice President and Director of Administrative and Operations Training at Wheat, First Securities, Inc., and presently as a Training Officer at Sovran Bank, N.A., indicates that the business community can understand the value of anthropological training. Of course, the product must be "packaged" and "marketed" correctly. Therein lies the challenge to academic anthropology.

Focusing on Perlman's own recent experiences, he wants to thank F. C. Tiller, Chief Executive Officer, Marcia Haight, Senior Vice President, Bill Fields, Executive Vice President, and Brenda Watts, Vice President, all at Wheat, First Securities, Inc., and Bob Hamilton, Vice President, and Bob Blake, First Vice President at Sovran Bank, N.A., among others, for facilitating a most important personal transition. Thanks to you all.

With regard to specific substantive contributions, we first wish to thank all of the participants in the symposium and volume for their hard work and patience. Martin Wobst and Mike Schiffer provided constructive and divergent critiques of the symposium to get us off to a good start. Stanley South read through early drafts of many of the papers and encouraged our pursing publication. John Justeson offered comments of great import, specifically on our introductory chapter. Also, we want to thank the editors and staff of Academic Press, who have guided this volume through publication.

Finally, emotional support from our families has made this project possible. Our wives Claudia and Judy certainly deserve their fair share of whatever credits result from this effort for their patience and indulgence. And, both authors would like to acknowledge the never-ending loyalty and quadrupedal support of Tammy and her son Marz; their incredible ability to run around in circles has minimized the editors' need to do the same.

PART I

An Approach to the Archaeological Study of Frontiers and Boundaries

CHAPTER 1

Frontiers, Boundaries, and Open Social Systems

STANTON W. GREEN

Department of Anthropology
University of South Carolina
Columbia, South Carolina

STEPHEN M. PERLMAN

Sovran Bank, N.A.
Richmond, Virginia

> *Something there is that doesn't love a wall, That sends the*
> *frozen-ground-swell under it, And spills the upper boulders*
> *in the sun; And makes gaps even two can pass abreast.*
> "Mending Wall," Robert Frost, 1912

> *The world of humankind constitutes a manifold, a totality*
> *of interconnected processes, and inquiries that disassemble*
> *this totality into bits and pieces and then fail to reassemble*
> *it falsify reality. Concepts like "nation," "society" and*
> *"culture" name bits and threaten to turn names into things.*
> *Only by understanding these names as bundles of rela-*
> *tionships, and by placing them back into the field from*
> *which they were abstracted, can we hope to avoid mislead-*
> *ing inferences and increase our share of understanding.*

> *Europe and the People without History*, Eric R. Wolf, 1982

INTRODUCTION

As students of human behavior, anthropologists are forced to "construct walls" around social activities in order to define workable units of study. In such a manner, ethnographic cultures are created from observations of living peoples, and archaeological cultures are derived from the remains of past societies. At the same time, anthropologists are aware that the bounding of human behavior can be artificial and can lead to closed conceptions of culture. In archaeology this boundary problem involves the definitions of types and patterns: artifact types and settlement patterns, for example, rest upon theoretical and empirical considerations concerning behavior, material culture, and their expression in the archaeological record. The problem in anthropology and archaeology has been how to overcome the inability to examine open social process within the limitations of closed analytic models.

A partial solution is to assess the openness of human systems through the study of frontiers and boundaries. A *frontier* is defined quite literally as "the front tier" of a society; and "that part of a country which fronts another country" (*Oxford English Dictionary:566*). As the "front," the frontier defines a *cultural boundary*.

Obviously, the concepts of frontiers and boundaries are very closely related. Frontier studies direct their attention to the peripheries or edges of particular societies, and the characteristics of the groups occupying that space. As a complement, boundary studies examine the interactions that occur at these societal edges. On the one hand, frontier research addresses questions about the causes of political and economic expansion into new habitats, and its effects on indigenous societies and ecological systems. Boundary research such as the study of trade, on the other hand, focuses on the social, political, and economic factors that guide the interaction between societies. Clearly, frontiers and boundaries provide complementary foci for the examination of the edges of social systems. This distinction is of analytic importance.

Our position builds upon this analytic difference by emphasizing its most significant implication: local events are not solely the product of local conditions. One society's changing frontier can, for example, require another society to make changes. Likewise, exchanges between two societies underscore their interdependence. In both cases, local conditions and history are influenced by external factors. By bringing these external factors under examination, frontier and boundary studies can help us develop more open models of society and build toward more realistic theories of cultural change. This volume provides a demonstration of the utility of the frontier and boundary to the study of open social systems.

PATTERN AND PROCESS IN ARCHAEOLOGY

Anthropological archaeology has had to grapple with the problem of developing an operational definition for the term *process*. One anthropologist's formal definition is "the interaction of causal factors which produce a given condition" (Bee 1974:3). These conditions are expressed as behavioral or material traits and patterns.

A social-scientific example in which *process* and *pattern* are clearly distinguished is Hudson's (1967) modeling of agricultural colonization. Hudson's hypothesized colonization process delineates the way in which settlers move into a previously unfarmed area. From this, he predicts a series of measurable settlement patterns. The initial settlement of a previously unfarmed, uninhabited, and unknown region involves an unpredictable placement of settlers resulting in a random pattern of farms. Some farmers may settle along the nearest edge of the frontier in order to minimize their distance to the homeland, hence minimizing the costs of social and economic interaction. Other farmers may risk the costs and dangers of distance in order to maximize their landholdings by purchasing inexpensive lands away from the previous frontier. Initial growth within the region—the second of Hudson's process-stages—involves a cloning process in which a new generation of farms develops from the initial farmsteads. A new generation of farmers maintains contact with family and community support by staying close to their original farmsteads. This leads to a clustered pattern of settlement. Finally, population growth ultimately fills up the region which in turn leads to land competition and some farm abandonment. The end result of this process is a systematic or regular pattern of farms in the region. Operationally, this work simply describes *how* a human activity is expected to occur (process) and *what* the observable outcome of this activity will be (pattern). This colonization process is used to account for settlement pattern changes.

A general problem for archaeologists has been where to begin one's study—by modeling process or by identifying pattern. The archaeologist's general inability to directly observe the human activities that produce the archaeological record has led in the past to a reliance on pattern recognition as the first stage of archaeological interpretation. Typological study, however, is guided by several assumptions. First, we assume that a limited set of patterns will be found. Second, some underlying assumptions about the function of the archaeological artifacts, features, and so on must be made. No interpretation of an archaeological observation is possible without some notion of the activity that created or used it, otherwise, it would be impossible to delimit a set of observations for study from the multitude of possibilities. Pattern and process, therefore, are logically and empirically bound: thinking about and measuring one always involves the other. The way in which one approaches this complementarity, we would argue, has important implications for how one considers culture in general. More specifically, pattern-oriented study implies a closed conception of culture; in contrast to a process-oriented approach that strives toward developing open models of culture.

This contrast is exemplified in Kroeber's (1948) early discussion of process, pattern, and the nature of culture. Kroeber defined *pattern* as "a rough plan of convenience for the preliminary ordering of facts awaiting description or interpretation" (Kroeber 1948:120). Interpretation requires a move to *process:* "those factors which operate either toward the stabilization and preservation of cultures and their parts, or toward growth and change" (Kroeber 1948:148). Such process, Kroeber notes, results in the movement of cultural patterns within and between cultures and through time. Although Kroeber's view of spatial diffusion and culture change is probably more trait oriented than many current archaeologists would feel comfortable with, his view of process and pattern clearly implies that culture be viewed as an open phenomenon: Pattern perseveres or changes through time and space as the result of underlying cultural processes.

Kroeber's definitions of pattern and process help us understand some of the current difficulty with well-established concepts used in archaeological typology such as archaeological cultures (Childe 1956), traditions, phases, horizons, and components (Willey and Phillips 1958). Typological concepts define *temporal* and *spatial patterning* in the archaeological record as "rough plans of convenience for the preliminary ordering of facts." However, they are problematic because they implicitly carry a closed concept of culture—a concept that frustrates the study of spatial process and culture change. Once an archaeological culture (or an ethnographic culture, for that matter) is defined, it carries with it the theoretical implication of closure. As an example we refer to the difficulties of explaining cultural evolution using typologies of cultural complexity (Fried 1967; Sahlins 1963; Service 1962). Even though band society theoretically could evolve to tribal society, and then to chiefdom and state, the closed conception of each of these levels of social complexity makes it difficult to model change from one level to another. Each is defined unto itself, hence evolutionary openness is logically frustrated.

Stated differently, pattern-oriented studies focus on standardizing behavior and material culture into phases, traditions, and types. Process-oriented studies focus on the ways in which behavior and material culture vary over space and through time. As such, process study forces one to deal with the fact that human behavior is not always bounded in time and space, and that it is not always packageable into type units.

OPEN SOCIAL SYSTEMS

The notion of culture as an open system is amply supported in the anthropological literature. A combination of theoretical discussion and empirical studies indicate that social systems at all levels of complexity are more open and flexible than they are often considered in archaeological and ethnographic models.

Studies of desert-foraging societies have identified the tremendous variability that exists in group sizes and their distributions (Lee 1980; Steward 1938). These changes on both local and regional scales are associated with geographic and seasonal shifts in net productivity patterns (Harpending and Davis 1977). Often this variability affects group size and distribution. While the movements of groups and particularly individuals suggest that foraging systems are quite open, the areal extent of the networks has not been identified. Quite possibly, the spatial extent of this movement is greater than the ethnographer can observe. This point is suggested by Wobst's (1974) simulations of band mating networks. For bands, a mate is rarely found in one cohabitating group. Low population densities and small group sizes require contact over areas several times greater than one group's settlement pattern.

This is not to say that all foragers live in boundless plains with uniform costs. In some instances, contact over great areas is inhibited by cultural and geographic boundaries. In such cases, the boundary processes at work must be studied in order to understand how they affect the local group movements and general regional adaptations. The boundary can be, in effect, an external factor that can stimulate local change. As an example, Yesner (Chapter 4, this volume) documents a 4000-year boundary (3000 B.C. to A.D. 1000) between Aleuts and Eskimos. Tracing the activities on both sides of this boundary, through archaeological, ethnohistoric, and paleoenvironmental study, Yesner concludes that in this case the boundary area was a resource-poor zone that served to insulate the Aleuts and Eskimos. Neither group found it useful to exploit this area since its resources were neither as rich nor diverse as the surrounding habitats. In an important sense, then, the boundary zone was a dynamic factor in the cultural history of the region— its ecological characteristics actively shaped the cultural development of the area.

Perlman's study (Chapter 3) discusses how mobility costs, particularly those associated with subsistence, affect and even limit the size of hunter–gatherer groups. The limits set by mobility vary over time and space. As a result any changes in hunter–gatherer group size and site location must be evaluated with respect to changes in mobility. As an example, Perlman discusses the implications of his model for the archaeological record from the Archaic period in New England and the mid-Atlantic regions. Settlement patterns seem to reflect the changing mobility patterns commensurate with at least two environmental processes—rising sea level and increased interior productivity. Constriction back toward the coast and major rivers during this period reflect changes in the use of the distribution of subsistence resources and the limits mobility costs place on hunter–gatherer group size.

Tribes and nation-states have also been shown to be open social systems. A *tribe*, traditionally defined as a group sharing a specific set of cultural traits, appears to be based on an oversimplified model. The distribution of linguistic, subsistence, kinship, and other traits are not spatially coter-minous (Fried 1975). Noninterdependent trait distributions indicate un-bounded social systems; that is, a continuum of social links between a series of social groups. The tribe as a closed system, then, can be an artifact of ethnographic analysis.

Hodder and Bronitsky's essays in this volume (Chapters 7 and 13) dem-onstrate the complex relationships between ethnicity, group identity, and other sociocultural and material traits. One-to-one relationships between these are not clear. Hodder's work among African pastoralists and farmers shows that the stylistic boundaries that exist between the Tugen and the Njemps relate to the differences in women's roles in these societies. The material evidence of social boundaries between these tribal groups reflects internal social organizational differences; that is, in the ways social things are done, and not simply differences in group identity or ethnicity.

In Bronitsky's study of Texas Baptists (Chapter 13), ethnicity is expected to be associated with church affiliation; however, the material culture of the various Baptist sects (church furniture, ritual paraphenalia) seems to suggest socioeconomic class. The boundaries of social activities are multidimen-sional; they can manifest themselves differently in the behavioral and mate-rial worlds.

As noted above, nation-states, most notably those based on complex market economies, are affected by long distance processes (Wallerstein 1977). World system processes create and maintain differences between the central and frontier areas. Paynter's and McGovern's studies in this volume (Chapters 8 and 12) illustrate the extent to which world system processes can effect local and regional events, and how these processes can be moni-tored archaeologically.

Paynter's essay (Chapter 8) offers a discussion of the long distance eco-nomic interactions that affected agricultural settlement in the nineteenth century Connecticut River valley. He utilizes a world system model to pro-pose implications for a frontier settlement pattern. His essential contribu-tion is a model of how economic surplus at the frontier shapes the economic landscape. The way in which economic surplus funds move from the fron-tier to the regional elite and homeland underlies much of the spatial and temporal patterning of the Anglo-American world system.

McGovern's study (Chapter 12) of the relationship between Norse settle-ments in Greenland and their Norwegian homeland brings to light the extremes to which world system processes can shape local adaptations. To maintain essential long distance economic, social, and political links with

Norway, the Norse settlers developed the dangerous and expensive *Nordrestur* hunt for walrus and other Arctic fauna. These hunting trips required hundreds of miles of travel and can only be explained when nonlocal factors are included in the foraging model of the frontier settlers. Moreover, the colony's eventual extinction can be tied to the tenuous core–periphery relationship between the colonizers of the island and the home base in Norway. The retraction of home base support for this Scandinavian frontier produced archaeologically observable consequences that affected both the colonizing and aboriginal populations.

Clearly, at all levels of complexity, social systems are open. The study of frontiers and boundaries, therefore, has broad implications because it can and should, we argue, be a focus for the study of the entire range of past and present society. We now discuss some specific problem areas in which frontier and boundary research can help archaeologists with the study of open social systems.

FRONTIERS AND BOUNDARIES AS FOCI FOR OPEN SYSTEM RESEARCH

Frontier and boundary studies recognize that societies are open. By so doing, they can contribute insights into the processes that produce the spatial, temporal, and organizational variability observed in the archaeological record. First, they open prehistoric and historic archaeology to a systematic study of noncentral places and the links between these and the traditionally studied central place sites. The archaeological intrigue with central places probably reflects the high visibility and rich artifact inventories of large sites. It might be argued, however, that this bias is also importantly underlain by the *assumption* that since large sites may contain examples of a wide range of a society's material culture, these sites can be used to typify the society at large. The central place of the X society, in the material sense, becomes a standard for the entire X culture. However, the interest in culture process and organization minimizes the importance of identifying typical assemblages. For example, organizational context can only be determined if the full range of sites and functional tool kits are studied within their temporal (seasonal), spatial (microenvironmental), and cultural (social group) contexts. Frontier settlements, then, take on importance because they are a part of the archaeological variability that is tied in with this range of contexts. This reason alone makes frontier and boundary studies critical elements in the analysis of social systems.

Second, broad historical patterns have taught us that social change often is most visible, and in some cases most active, on the peripheries of social systems. The spread of agriculture into previously unfarmed habitats serves as a classic illustration. The questions most pondered by archaeologists interested in the so-called Mesolithic–Neolithic transition (a typological bind in itself) concern the relationships between Mesolithic foragers and Neolithic farmers, and the ecological responses of the primary forest to agricultural colonization. These questions are naturally suited for a frontier framework (see Ammerman and Cavalli-Sforza 1972; Green 1980; Moore, Chapter 5, this volume; Dennell, Chapter 6, this volume). In essence, the initial spread of agriculture during the Neolithic period can be modeled as a frontiering or pioneering process that created social boundaries between farmer and forager (ultimately expressed as archaeological patterns), and ecological boundaries between farmers and forests (as expressed in the paleoecological record). Note that while we still must cope with our typological categories of Mesolithic and Neolithic for chronological control, we can now begin to frame behavioral questions concerning frontier demography (Lefferts 1977), frontier settlement (Hudson 1967), frontier ecology (Clapham 1975; Green 1979, 1980), and frontier culture (Thompson 1973). We can also begin to examine how the forager–farmer frontier itself generated culture change. Moore and Dennell each provide examples of this type of study.

Moore's essay (Chapter 5) discusses the role information flow plays in shaping the activities of foragers and farmers on the agricultural frontier. The amount of information a foraging group has about the location of other settlements affects settlement movement efficiency and social organization. Moore's simulation experiments demonstrate why forager groups on agricultural boundaries might choose to involve farmers in their conflict resolution. Foragers are faced with higher costs of fission and fusion when farmers infringe on their territory. Also, sedentism and trade with farmers may provide a mechanism for counteracting the higher mobility costs on the frontier. It is important to note that neither social interaction nor trade between foragers and farmers necessarily results from pressure on local resources. Moore's thesis suggests that one possible process leading to agricultural diffusion resides in the very nature of the boundary between farming and foraging societies.

Dennell (Chapter 6) extends and in some ways operationalizes Moore's work through a discussion of the types of boundaries that can exist between foragers and farmers. Using the test case of Mesolithic and early Neolithic temperate Europe, he posits several models of farmer–forager interaction which, in turn, generate multiple working hypotheses and implications for ethnographic and archaeological evidence. Most importantly, he discusses the respective roles of farmers and foragers in the adoption of agricultural technology and economy within the context of the social and demographic interaction between these groups. Foragers, he notes, have too long been considered as the passive party in agricultural development. The spread of agriculture may well have been generated by the actual interaction between farmer and forager—reiterating the point Moore makes in his theoretical discourse.

Finally, frontier studies are a natural and perhaps necessary element for the study of long distance spatial process. The recent development of world systems models (Wallerstein 1977) is the most prominent case in point. Here, long distance political and economic processes are essential elements in explanations of local, regional, and worldwide social process. Such a superregional approach promises to breed a new generation of models for the evolution of complex social systems.

In addition to Paynter's and McGovern's essays discussed previously, we have several important world system's type studies in this volume. Rubertone and Thorbahn (Chapter 10) explore the processes underlying the urban–hinterland frontier surrounding Providence, Rhode Island, from 1689 to 1865. They begin by rejecting the notion of the city as a bounded unit, and model it as a part of a settlement network and continuous landscape. They proceed to study the urbanization process at the frontier as a continuous spatial phenomenon using Thünen land-use models. By applying these models to diachronic land clearance and population density data, the authors interpret the complex relationship between the urban–hinterland and aspects of the frontier.

Lewis's study (Chapter 11) of the South Carolina frontier extends the archaeology of world systems to the political realm—a much-needed area of study to complement the economic emphases of Paynter, McGovern, Rubertone, and Thorbahn. The colonial South Carolina frontier is examined with respect to the political and economic dimensions of state level systems and how these affect frontier settlement patterns. Lewis's accounting of the variability in settlement functions and structures in the South Carolina core and frontier is tested using a combination of historic documents and archaeological data.

Finally, Hardesty's study (Chapter 9) of the industrial frontier of the American west uses the widest range of sociocultural factors to account for frontier change. He uses a variety of demographic, cognitive, technological, and ecological models to account for the different patterns of social change on the mining and agrarian frontiers in the western desert. Long-distance factors turn out to effect a "boom–bust" pattern for the settlement of the industrial frontier. Unlike agrarian frontiers, for example, the colonization of the mining frontier took place in sudden spurts associated with labor strikes and at times sudden subsequent abandonment. Rapid social change on the mining frontier was enhanced by the mass importation of urban and industrial society during a "boom" period; an equally rapid severing of these relationships took place during a "bust." The implications of the models for understanding variability among nineteenth- and early twentieth-century archaeological sites in the region are also discussed, with special reference to the Cortex, Bullfrog, and Comstock mining districts in Nevada. With this example, we begin to see the variability of world system frontiers and the factors underlying it.

CONCLUDING REMARKS

We have argued that the study of cultural process and change through time and over space requires a concept of an open social system. This parts from the usual ethnographic and archaeological models of culture that must often assume closed social systems. The studies in this volume offer the frontier and boundary approach as a means for the study of open social systems. These studies also offer several approaches for the study of long-term culture change. They bring a wide range of theoretical approaches and methodologies to frontier and boundary research. The approaches, in fact, are sometimes drawn from rival schools of thought; yet the common goal is to overcome the analytic bounds of closed models to move toward an understanding of the spatial and temporal fluidity of human history and prehistory. As individual studies, these contributions signify the utility and power of the open systems approach. As an aggregate volume, they provide a comparative data base which reflects the general applicability of this approach for the study of social process.

REFERENCES

Ammerman, A., and L. Cavalli-Sforza
    1972   Measuring the rate of spread of early farming in Europe. *Man* 6:674–688.
Bee, R.
    1974   *Pattern and process.* Free Press, New York.
Childe, V. G.
    1956   *A short introduction to archaeology.* Collier Books, New York.
Clapham, E.
    1975   An approach to quantifying the exploitability of human ecosystems. *Human Ecology* 4:1–31.
Fried, M.
    1967   *The evolution of political society.* Random House, New York.
    1975   *The notion of tribe.* Cummings, Menlo Park, California.
Green, S. W.
    1979   The agricultural colonization of temperate forest habitats: an ecological model. In

The frontier: comparative studies (Vol. 2), edited by W. Savage and S. Thompson. University of Oklahoma Press, Norman.

1980 Toward general model of agricultural systems. In *Advances in method and theory in archaeology* (Vol. 3), edited by M. Schiffer. Academic Press, New York.

Harpending, H., and H. Davis
1977 Some implications for hunter–gatherer ecology derived from the spatial structure of resources. *World Archaeology* 8:275–286.

Hudson, J.
1967 A location theory for rural settlement. *Annals of the Association for American Geographers* 58:356–381.

Kroeber, A. L.
1948 *Culture pattern and processes.* Harcourt, Brace, New York.

Lee, R.
1980 *The !Kung San: men, women and work in a foraging society.* Harvard University Press, Cambridge.

Lefferts, L.
1977 Frontier demography: an introduction. In *The frontier: comparative studies* (Vol. 1), edited by D. H. Miller and J. O. Steffen. University of Oklahoma Press, Norman.

Sahlins, M.
1963 Poor man, rich man, chief: Political types in Melanesia and Polynesia. Comparative Studies in Society and History 5:285–303.

Service, E.
1962 *Primitive social organization.* Random House, New York.

Steward, J.
1938 Basin–plateau aboriginal sociopolitical groups. *Bureau of American Ethnology Bulletin* 120, Washington, D.C.

Thompson, S.
1973 Pioneer colonization: a cross-cultural view. *Addison-Wesley Module in Anthropology,* No. 33.

Wallerstein, I.
1977 *The modern world system.* Academic Press, New York.

Willey, G., and P. Phillips
1958 *Method and theory in American archaeology.* University of Chicago Press, Chicago.

Wobst, M.
1974 Boundary conditions for paleolithic social systems: a simulation approach. *American Antiquity* 39(2):147–178.

ables and complex interactions among them, and this was cited (e.g., by Flannery 1972 and especially 1973) as the major advantage of attempts to study whole-system behavior synthetically rather than focusing on individual processes analytically (e.g., by deducing constraints on state transitions from constraints on the co-occurrence of defining features of states).

Explicit modeling of social systems was a direct outgrowth of this recognition. To account for the behavior of complex systems, interrelations among a large number of major variables had to be defined more precisely than had been done in previous archaeological work, and in the interaction among those variables a correspondingly greater number of additional variables had to be recognized as intervening. Since our capacity to conceive the effects of this complex of interactions decreases as the number of variables and interactions increases, explicit models are required to describe system structure in a way that renders overall system behavior accessible to the scientist.

Construction of formal models is relatively straightforward in the case of a closed system. Such a system consists of a set of variables interacting without "outside" influence; matter, energy, and information are retained in and obtained from the system itself. Indeed, it is just because of this isolation from contact that we can easily identify just what the system is: since it has impermeable boundaries, these zones of no interaction serve to define the perimeters of the system. To model a closed system, one need only specify the list of variables, the form of interaction among those variables, and the values those variables can assume.

Modeling open systems is more problematic. An *open system* is one in which matter, energy, and information are exchanged between elements inside and elements outside the system. These systems have semipermeable boundaries—zones of low interaction rather than no interaction. Just what is considered to be "inside" the system is in part a matter of analytic convenience, but due to the semipermeability of the system's boundaries it must consist either of an indefinite number of variables interacting or of an indefinite number of kinds of interaction among them. Since these two sets of indefinites are formally equivalent, an open system is formally one in which an infinite number of variables are interacting.

Cultural systems are open systems: semipermeable boundaries separate them from one another and from noncultural systems. In contrast, any explicit model must be closed, since it must incorporate a definite number of variables and must specify the relationships among them. The anthropologist is therefore faced with the problem of effectively modeling an open system as though it were closed. The remainder of this essay considers the consequences of such modeling in terms of system and model boundaries—a crucial focus inasmuch as the impermeability of its boundary is

Closed Models of Open Systems: Boundary Considerations

JOHN JUSTESON

Department of Anthropology
Vassar College
Poughkeepsie, New York

STEVEN HAMPSON

Department of Information and Computer Science
University of California, Irvine
Irvine, California

> *"An infinite number of variables should be considered, but due to limitations on space I can consider only a few."*
>
> From a student exam

SOCIAL SYSTEMS AND THEIR MODELS

The conceptual framework of general systems theory was introduced into archaeological research in 1968, in influential works by Buckley (1968), Clarke (1968), and Flannery (1968). Since then, cultural processes have increasingly come to be thought of in terms of the quantitative effects of interaction among variables, much as they are in biological and physical systems. In the intervening years, systems theory has become an important facet of archaeological attempts to understand and describe social systems.

From the first, the recognition that social systems are quite complex led to assumptions that a large number of variables intervene between environmental variation and the higher-level structure of extrasomatic responses to it; and, since many of these variables are interrelated, that causal variables are not clearly distinguishable from effect variables. Yet the systems framework seemed capable, in principle, of handling both large numbers of vari-

The Archaeology of Frontiers and Boundaries   **15**

what closes a system's model. This focus suggests the methodological importance of a topical focus on the frontiers of social systems.

Orientation of model construction to a particular problem or class of problems is basic to the discussion, and further motivates the salience of a focus on boundaries. As formal description became necessary in archaeological attempts to understand social systems synthetically, modelers confronted a variety of formalizations by which to express system structure. Social systems are complex enough that their models entail substantial simplification, and thereby become inaccurate or misleading in some circumstances. Alternative models are apt to have contrasting weaknesses (cf. Zubrow 1973:250–254), and these determine their relative utility for exploring a given problem.

In open systems, the definition and location of the boundaries are inherently relative, problem-related constructs, and are therefore of central importance in settling on a productive modeling strategy. For some spatial applications, boundaries might be defined by population densities; for others, by economic interaction densities. Such definitions need not coincide. Consequently, under some problem definitions the boundaries are much larger than the central zones; this is often the case with frontier adaptations. Even given a single general problem area, different boundaries may be defined at different levels of analysis. For example, resource utilization in society may be modeled with a boundary at the gross level of supply of raw materials or manufactured goods to the society at large; households making use of various classes of goods have boundaries at a finer level of analysis. Boundary location is thereby also problem-related; for, as a zone of low average interaction among variables, the position of the boundary is defined relative to relations existing elsewhere among other variables in the system, and relative to the period over which data measurements are made.

In what follows we distinguish two classes of orientation to problems and two corresponding approaches to the modeling of system boundaries: (1) attempts to understand the causes of system stability and change with regard to a given class of variables versus attempts to predict system behavior under the assumption of system stability; and (2) modeling by incorporating system boundary variables into the central portions of the model, and vice versa, versus an equation of system boundaries with model boundaries.

BOUNDARY MODELS AND SYSTEM CHANGE

Anthropologists typically model stable systems by focusing on the processes and variables in the central zones of high interaction; change is normally modeled by looking at sequences of stable adaptations. Models of change, then, are not treated as fundamentally different from models of stability. We contend that stability and change in a system can both be observed from the same model, under appropriately varying conditions, only in the case of models focused on system change; models of stable systems, focused on zones of relatively high interaction, put model boundaries at system boundaries. A focus on change requires a focus on boundary processes, as in frontier studies, so that model boundaries must be situated elsewhere; here especially, it is inappropriate to model zones of relatively low interaction (system boundaries) as zones of no interaction (model boundaries).

Fundamental change in models can occur in six ways: (1) the values of variables may shift, (2) the definitions of variables may shift, (3) variables may be added or deleted, (4) the level of interaction among variables may shift, (5) the form of interaction among variables may shift, and (6) interactions among variables may be added or deleted. Notice, however, that changes of types (2) and (3) are limiting cases of type (1) changes, and changes of types (5) and (6) are limiting cases of type (4) changes. This is readily demonstrated. With the addition of a variable, the interaction of that variable with some others shifts from zero to a positive amount. This shows that change (2) is a special case of change (1). Likewise, the gradual shift in the definition of a variable normally involves the retention of some former defining features and the addition of some new defining features; in changing circumstances, the new defining features become more important determinants of interaction than are some of the old. The gradually shifting definition may therefore be reduced to addition and deletion of these defining features, which are effectively the underlying variables on which the model is based. Change (3) therefore involves shifts from positive to zero and/or zero to positive interaction of some of the underlying variables with others, and thus again is a special case of change (1). Changes (4)–(6) involve the interactions among variables, interactions that have to be specified by mathematical functions. Functions applying in anthropological situations are normally smooth, continuous curves, which can be approximated with arbitrarily close precision by Taylor polynomials (see Courant and John 1965:445–453). Multiplication of a given function by a constant or addition of a constant to such a formula is sufficient to shift its value from effectively zero to a positive amount and conversely, so that change (6) is a special case of change (4). The form of the Taylor approximation to a function can be changed by shifting the values of the constant coefficients of the terms of the Taylor polynomial, so that change (5) is also a case of shifts in the values of these (no longer constant) underlying variables.

To an anthropologist focusing on the structure of a stable system, it may seem ad hoc analytic chicanery to incorporate variables into the model of an early system which only appear to become pertinent in a later phase of that system's operation; such modeling appears to impute foreknowledge of the future to the system itself, a peculiar kind of "superorganic" concept.

In fact, such variables are generally pertinent at the earlier phases of system behavior as well; however, when the total interaction among the remaining variables is such that the value or interaction level of the seemingly ad hoc variable is optimally zero (or otherwise constant), the variable makes no *apparent* contribution to system behavior. For example, unexploited food resources may not be modeled if stable adaptation is the focus of research; however, as Perlman (Chapter 3, this volume) argues, those resources are not exploited because it is economically advantageous to exploit others to the exclusion of these. The patterns of exploitation and nonexploitation should both be explainable from the same basic socioeconomic variables; it is really the extent of exploitation of all environmentally available resources that these variables are meant to explain. Shifts in the values of those variables should result in shifts in which resources are exploited, and in how extensively they are exploited (change types 2 and 3, recognized by Perlman as actually change type 1).

In sum, the variables to be incorporated in a later phase of a system's model are normally part of the total adaptation in the real world; they are a part which is not directly utilized given local conditions, but these conditions are subject to change. Abrupt, qualitative changes appear to be features, not of systems as Glasgow (1972) argues, but of models designed to describe structural relations in stable systems.

To model change in a chosen aspect of a system, one must focus explicitly on the processes of that change. The variables and relationships incorporated in a model are a classification that an analyst imposes; the classification is imposed, one assumes, on the basis of its pertinence to a particular problem. Problems concerning system change always entail features that do not appear pertinent to the modeling of stable systems. They accordingly require a focus on features that are tangential in a stable model, a focus on variables that have little interaction with those considered in modeling stable systems. This means a focus on boundaries.

The utility of such a focus is exemplified by Wobst's (1977) discussion of phases and phase transitions in Palaeolithic times. The classic phases are defined temporally in accord with the centers of glacial and interglacial periods. The trends in adaptation under conditions of cooling and glaciation in the first half of the period are thereby lumped with trends in response to warming and glacial retreat. By treating the prehistoric record in terms of broad periods of glacials alternating with interglacials, fictitiously stable pictures are adopted which obscure temporally and behaviorally distinct processes of adaptation. In contrast, by centering analytic phases on the temporal centers of transitions between glacial and interglacial periods, distinct adaptive trends are more likely to be distinguished clearly; this, in turn, should permit a more realistic picture of the stable outcome of such trends at glacial maximum and minimum. In short, models based on the assumption of stability obscure the understanding both of the operation of stable systems and of the processes of change which ultimately lead to them. Assumed-stable models have their boundaries fixed in positions different from those of the actual systems being modeled.

Accordingly, understanding change and stability requires different kinds of models than are used to understand a system whose stability is simply assumed. In the latter, a definitional, classificatory scheme is maintained; model stability has no basis beyond analytical convenience. If the models are testable, those focused on boundaries can be used to verify why changes took place, or did not take place. Thus, the conditions maintaining stability can only be understood in this way—by modeling factors leading to change.

Assumed-stable models work, to the extent they do, because of homeostatic mechanisms in the system which are not explicitly modeled or even recognized. In everyday life, for example, rocks are normally modeled as stationary objects, ignoring the considerable activity of the stone at the atomic and molecular levels which happen to conspire toward macroscopic stability in position. Biological and cultural systems have many powerful homeostatic mechanisms which require active inputs of energy (work) to maintain. Since this unmodeled work is susceptible to disruption or change, like other organized behavior explicitly incorporated into an assumed-stable model, the effects being taken for granted are actually crucial to the understanding of system stability. The behavior of the real-world system is therefore achieved by different means than those by which the model generates its analogue of that behavior. Furthermore, since the results of the model are consistent with the data on system operation, the modeler fails both to understand the process by which stability is achieved and to recognize this ignorance.

The problem is that our models may appear to work correctly when we have not understood the processes involved in the operations of the systems they model; thus, they tend to perpetuate our ignorance through success. This is not as much a problem in the more dynamic, boundary-oriented models discussed here. Failure to incorporate system variables is tantamount to treating them as constants; in systems that are changing, tacit incorporation of constant variables is not usually a source of spurious change coincidentally mimicking changes observed in real-world systems.[1]

MODEL BOUNDARIES OF STABLE SYSTEMS

While models focused on stability and change are useful for investigating the effects of particular processes on system structure, models in which stability is assumed are useful for investigating the effects of system structure on system behavior. Here, then, it is precisely the zones of relatively high interaction that are the proper focus of concern. In such cases, model boundaries are properly equated with system boundaries; the methodological goal is thereby simply to minimize the error that results from modeling zones of low interaction as zones of no interaction.

We recognize three modeling strategies for approaching this goal, applicable also, in varying degrees, for the boundaries of models of stability and change. (1) Nonzero interactions at the boundary of the actual system may be approximated by inputing a parametric estimate at the boundary of the model. (2) The model may be applied toward the understanding of system behavior only under conditions in which the low interactions are near zero; the model approximates the system when external linkages are most justifiably ignored. (3) The boundaries of the system can be modeled at great distance from the primary variables whose behavior is of interest. There are constraints on the usefulness of each of these strategies.

Autonomous Input Parameters

Input parameters are perhaps the most prominent of the devices used in mathematical models of the behavior of biological and social systems. Such parameters are autonomous from the model in that they have no feedback connections to any explicitly modeled system variables.

Decisions about the proper parameters to input, and about the form of such inputs, depend on the use to which the model will be put. Insofar as causal roles are being attributed to the external inputs to the system, there is little difficulty in designing an adequate input strategy. In attempting to relate variability in system behavior to variability in the external inputs to the system, any series of values might be input that fall within the range of values typically attested, particularly if in rough proportion to their attested frequency; in econometric research, input parameters are almost always normally distributed random variables. Alternatively, where a reliable input history is available for the system under study, one simply inputs parameters mimicking the actual input history of the external linkages of the system and compares model response with the history of the system's response. Attribution of a causal role to external inputs is typical of models of stability and change, but is also consistent with studies of the effects of system structure on system behavior; variability in the inputs simply conditions those effects.

In models assuming stability, however, the objective is typically to understand normal system behavior from a system-internal perspective. The interest is in typical behavior of a system or systems of a given structure rather than in the relationship of system behavior to external inputs. Since the inputs to the model are autonomous from it, they cannot reflect causal relationships between input variables and variables which are explicitly modeled. This can be unproblematic in models of very small systems, but seldom in models of social systems since, in general, the larger the system the greater its potential effects on its environment. The inputs to a social system are normally contingent on the outputs from it, to say nothing of the possible contingent relationships intervening between system-internal variables. A typical example of anthropological concern is long-distance trade; in Rathje's (1971, 1973a,b) model of Classic Lowland Maya society, trade items input to and output from the Lowland system were crucially linked, and were also important in governing the relationships between social classes and even the symbolic manifestations of social differences. Modeling trade as an autonomous input parameter in such a system could result in model behavior that was atypical at best and quite possibly unrealistic since the inputs that drive the system are related to the model in unrealistic ways.

Another artifact of modeling objectives may serve to counterbalance this deviant model behavior, however. Insofar as system stability is assumed, and insofar as the relationship of the social system to its unmodeled environment is therefore likely to be homeostatic, the input–output link may be assumed homeostatic; given a reasonable lag in effects on system activity, a normal distribution for the inputs may not yield such unrealistic effects if the model output is also normal—on the average, increases are balanced by decreases in these distributions which therefore roughly mimic a homeostatic response over a large enough period. Likewise, alternative and empirically derived curves for parameter histories, with or without normal error terms, might be input where relatively strong and direct correlations between input and output levels can be demonstrated. The use of such empirical formulae is more appropriate for some parameters than for others: they should either respond primarily to a single overriding factor or be sensitive enough to fluctuations in the unmodeled variables that they are reliably described by simple curves. These are fragile solutions, however, since the input history of the model need not reflect the unanalyzed causal relationships of the inputs to the unmodeled variables, relationships which are assuring the stability which the model takes for granted (see discussion of homeostatic processes and assumed-stable models, p. 20). This is all the more likely in the case of the empirical formulae, since they are constructed under conditions which are typically unknown to the analyst inducing them, and which are thereby often conditions of reduced variability; inputing such data into a model involves a pretension to knowledge exactly where uncertainties are greatest.

Modeling with Boundaries at Increasing Distance

Paradoxically, then, input parameters are less problematic in cases of causal models designed to test causal theories than in models designed to mimic normal system behavior without concern for the causal role of the input variables; the seemingly more ambitious goal is virtually a prerequisite to reliable attainment of the more limited objective.[2] To circumvent the difficulties associated with the use of input parameters that are autonomous from the modeled variables one may therefore attempt to model the processes underlying them. This involves adding enough variables to mimic the behavior of the parameter being estimated rather than simply basing its input to the model on an empirically derived curve whose fundamental controls are unknown or on a normal distribution which in effect bypasses those controls. Autonomous parameters must still be input to the submodel devised, and the number of parameters being input to the system is thereby increased. The goal in such models is to replace a parameter whose behavior is complex by a model requiring parameters whose behavior is simpler; in this case, there are normally a number of interacting processes involved in the determination of the behavior of the complex input. For the fiction of autonomy of the new parameters input to the submodel to be substantially more realistic, at least in terms of its effects on the variables in the central portion of the model, the inputs should be removed an extra level in the hierarchical organization of the processes modeled. For example, interaction among cells in muscle tissue is so far removed from the level of analysis appropriate to subsistence economics that it would seldom be a problem for modelers—in spite of the fact that there are ultimately causal linkages between such variables.

In some instances, direct modeling of such higher-level processes in terms of processes at a lower hierarchical level becomes impractical because the structure of interaction at the higher level is simply the statistical effect of a mass of individual interactions at the lower level whose results are difficult to anticipate directly, and even to simulate directly because of the sheer number of individual interactions involved. For example, Kasakoff and Adams (1977) demonstrate that Tikopian marriage choice was at least largely determined by distance according to a "social gravity" model; inferentially, the extent of interaction between groups directly determines the extent of marriage between those groups. Such a relationship could be simulated directly given reliable initial data for a small island, but in zones with larger populations it would quickly become unmanageable. Mathematical research in physics has led to the development of renormalization theory to handle just this problem, drastically reducing the number of units necessary for direct treatment in the model (see Amit 1978 for a recent synthesis).

Increasing the distance between the central processes in a model and the boundary of the model can therefore be done efficiently within hierarchical structures either across a sufficiently large number of levels, or given a mass interaction problem across a single level—at least in principle. The logical extension would be to model the boundary, not at increasing distance, but at an infinite distance from the center. In this case the zero-interaction zones would provoke no contradiction with the boundaries in the system itself, since at infinite distance the interaction is indeed nonexistent. Infinite modeling, of course, is impractical in a traditional simulation. As discussed above, it amounts to modeling an infinite number of variables or an infinite number of interactions among variables; neither can be defined explicitly unless, e.g., recursively, in terms of a finite number of more basic variables which would therefore be at finite distance from the model boundaries.

Infinite models are possible at the conceptual level, however, insofar as it is possible to determine the effects of the failure to model unspecified variables of the open system; such determinations depend on mathematical regularities concerning partial correlation effects. Some correlations among modeled variables covertly depend on the effects of unmodeled variables; should the value of the unmodeled variable change, novel correlations may result. This is particularly true in the case of an unmodeled variable whose constancy is tacitly assumed, or whose tacitly assumed range of variation is at least reduced from its actual range.

An information-theoretic example illustrates this possibility. Receipt of information concerning one variable normally cannot increase the uncertainty concerning the value of another variable—an intuitively plausible restriction corresponding to a theorem (formula 2.3.9 of Gallager 1968) of information theory. The theorem only holds, however, when uncertainty levels are calculated with the complete probability distributions for both variables (Aczél and Daróczy 1975:35). When one of the distributions is incomplete—as in the case of a variable assumed constant—then the receipt of information about one of the variables *can* increase uncertainty about the other; more picturesquely, information about one variable may destroy information about another. Behaviorally, this is more realistic. For example, unexpected behavior by a supposed military ally may increase uncertainty concerning the assistance that that ally plans to render in an upcoming conflict. This effect is not surprising; the point is that it can be traced to the incompleteness and closure of models, whether those of anthropologists or those of the U.S. Senate Foreign Relations Committee.

Such effects can be incorporated into theoretical constructs. If an increase in the number of information sources being monitored by an information-processing hierarchy selects for vertical or horizontal expansion of that hierarchy, as suggested for example by Wright (1969), Flannery (1972), Peebles and Kus (1977), and Johnson (1978), then error and malfunction can result directly in the strengthening of that hierarchy rather than, as otherwise expected and frequently assumed in discussions of the Classic Maya collapse, in its debilitation or demise. It is important to determine the conditions under which each alternative becomes likely; in the present case, expansion is to be expected most readily in religious hierarchy, which exercises control by monitoring and manipulating control variables uncorrelated with the behavior of the controlled variables (Justeson n.d.).

Ignoring External Linkages

Although a system boundary is an area of low average interaction, it may increase the concentration of one variable near it or the interactions among variables near it, by inhibiting flow and interaction across it. This makes threshold effects possible: a zone of low average interaction may sporadically be a zone of great interaction while being of *very* low interaction over long intervals.[3] By studying a system during a period in which the low average interaction contains few if any spikes of high interaction, the zero-interaction characterization of the open boundary is made more realistic.

An obvious difficulty with this approach is that it involves a failure to account for the range of variability in the actual operation of the system. Beyond this, however, it is difficult to know just when to study the system. Even presuming that it is possible to determine when the periods of low interaction occur in the system so as to collect data for a test of the model, variables linking directly to the low-level inputs may be linked to other variables by lag effects; in a complex social system they surely are. Accordingly, low-level system inputs may occur together with system responses to prior, higher-level inputs, while high-level system inputs may occur together with system responses to prior, lower-level inputs. Without understanding the processes which create the patterns of low and high interaction, the response patterns of the system are not apt to function as they would were the system, like the model, to involve only near-zero interaction at the boundary.

Furthermore, systems research that has implicitly followed this strategy has sometimes led to results overgeneralized from the context of their validity; in effect, they have mistaken model behavior for system behavior. Conclusions derived from closed models are susceptible to proof as mathematical theorems, and since the assumption of closure is often implicit rather than explicitly stated, their logical dependence on this assumption is not apparent from the phrasing of the theorem. What should apply only under very limited conditions in the world of real behavior—a world in which systems respond to variability in the inputs from the environment defined as external to them—comes to be applied as a universal law of system behavior.

Such overgeneralization can be illustrated by W. Ross Ashby's law of requisite variety. Ashby formulated a model of a regulatory system, stated and proved his theorem, or law, and concluded: "The law states that certain events are impossible. . . . It has nothing to do with the properties of the [regulatory] machine" (Ashby 1968:136).

The law of requisite variety states that the variety in the potential decisions of a regulatory system must be at least equal to the variety of potential outputs of the system being regulated if a particular desired outcome is to be assured. A strictly formal law, it has been applied to the cultural evolution of information-processing systems in general and of hierarchical organization in particular (Gero and Moore 1975; Johnson 1978; Peebles and Kus 1977; Rathje 1973b).

The law is in fact a special case of one of the coding theorems of information theory (Justeson, in preparation). The theorem, however, is only valid for cases in which one has a complete probability distribution of the system's variables; and in an open system there is an infinite number of variables or values of variables. An accurate model of the open regulatory system, with a finite number of variable values, demands a model utilizing an incomplete probability distribution: that is, one which does not sum to unity; the theorem, however, is not valid for incomplete distributions. Accordingly, the law of requisite variety is crucially dependent on the closure of the regulatory system—and the assumption of closure is always present, at least tacitly, in the creation of an explicit (hence finite) model.

TESTING

While susceptibility to empirical test has been one of the features by which we have been considering conditions on the appropriateness of various modeling strategies, it must be admitted that realistically complex models of social systems are seldom capable of adequate testing from the archaeological record alone. Any social system model will incorporate a large proportion of variables for which direct archaeological measures are not utilized. Yet any model incorporating both deviation-amplifying and deviation-counteracting processes must incorporate the mathematical form of all relationships between variables—not simply their classification as deviation-amplifying or deviation-counteracting—as well as the initial values of those variables if even qualitative behavior of the system is to be reliably reflected by the model. If the model is a fair approximation to an actual behavioral system, the strength of some relationships and perhaps initial values of some variables may be determined by collecting archaeological data reflecting the input, output, and internal states of the system; the problem for the rest is simply calibration. But even if the model is *not* accurate, it will very likely be possible to calibrate if a large number of deviation-counteracting relationships occur in the model: the values of modeled variables for which direct data exists can be adjusted in the model in either direction, the power of preceding and following deviation-counteracting loops being adjusted subsequently so as to maintain the archaeologically determined values. Given a fixed range of data for a test, the testability of the model declines rapidly with increasing numbers of deviation-counteracting loops incorporated, and more slowly with increasing numbers of deviation-amplifying loops; the additions reduced the degrees of freedom of the model. Furthermore, the input parameters utilized in most explicit archaeological models are relatively near in hierarchical level to the variables that are central to the model; for example, carrying capacity versus population. Accordingly, causal linkages between the modeled variables and the input parameters are apt to be relatively strong, and even when the input history of the system is reliably known, the model will not respond to it in a realistic fashion, and the maintenance of the input history itself inhibits proper testing since, in an adequate model, that history would be affected and thus systematically different inputs with correspondingly different responses would be expected. Conversely, discrepancies might well appear in an adequate model of this sort, discrepancies which should differ given different initial value conditions or forms or strengths of relationship, since the feedback relations which should have existed between the dependent and modeled variables are not incorporated. Accordingly, the alternative discrepancies noted by Zubrow (1973:250–254) for alternative rate parameters in his simulations of population growth across different resource zones in the Hay Hollow Valley are to be expected in an adequate central model of its degree of refinement.

Clearly, a great deal of the effort in testing simulation models of the behavior of social systems must come from other than archaeological evidence. So, if such models are to be constructed to account for the history of more than a limited period of a few societies favored by a wealth of documentation of various kinds, that evidence will have to be comparative rather than culture-specific. Whole-system synthetic treatments must differ in structure from one society to another, so that such analysis can only be handled tractably by the complementary approach of analyzing individual processes. As discussed in Note 2, the empirical relationship between variables can be reliably incorporated into models only when guided by a theory concerning the processes by which the empirical relationship is produced; this, too, depends upon analytic treatment of individual processes. Accordingly, the complementary approaches of individual process analysis and whole-system synthesis within processual archaeology will both be required as explicit mathematical models of social systems begin to replace the largely discursive models characteristic of most current archaeological work. It is precisely this sort of convergence that began to be anticipated some years ago (Flannery 1973:53), and toward which beginnings have already been made (e.g., in Zubrow 1974).

NOTES

1. An important example in which this *can* occur is when the system variable being treated as a constant is a parameter of a function relating population size and time. If the function has deviation-amplifying effects only for certain parameter values, it is possible to have a tacit constant resulting in qualitative change of the sort observed in the system's behavior. However, the quantitative and directional (increase/decrease) characteristics of the change are unlikely to agree with real-world system behavior in such cases, and this quantitative disagreement is a clue allowing identification of the deficiency of the model. This is not the case in models assuming stability, since the variables which are of concern are then not even modeled; in models of change, the variables have to be modeled for the constant to effect a change of the proper kind even by accident, so that the necessary changes are more easily located and incorporated.

2. This is true not only when the causal role being tested is that of the input variables, but also when dealing with relationships between system-internal variables. For example, suppose that one is modeling the variables involved in the acquisition and utilization of food resources among agricultural groups in nonstate societies. Social and spatial priorities in the utilization of the resources might be determined from economic records for certain of these societies. An empirical relation between the production and utilization of foodstuffs could be plotted based on this priority schedule in complete ignorance of, for example, whether the induced priority system was the result of or a control over the production and utilization of these foodstuffs. Such different bases for the empirical priority formulae can have quite different relationships with the remaining modeled variables; ignorance of the processes determining the priority schedule affects the predictive power of the model under conditions different from those special conditions, again of reduced variability, under which empirical curves were constructed. Use of empirical formulae, then, can be unreliable unless their incorporation into the model is guided by a theory concerning the processes by which the empirical relationship is produced.

3. Such spikes also appear at boundaries of quantitative models as an undesireable side effect of discrete-time modeling of continuous-time processes (see Loomis *et al.* 1979).

ACKNOWLEDGMENTS

We thank Stanton Green and Stephen Perlman for their discussion of this essay at its first writing (1978), and Green for further feedback in the course of its main revision (1979). A previous version was presented at the annual meeting of the Society for American Archaeology in May, 1978, at Tucson, Arizona; we thank Christopher Peebles, Michael Schiffer, and Norman Yoffee for comments at that time.

REFERENCES

Aczél, Janus and Z. Daróczy
    1975   *On entropy measures and their characterizations.* Academic Press, New York.

Amit, Daniel J.
   1978   *Field theory, the renormalization group, and critical phenomena.* McGraw-Hill, Inc., London.
Ashby, W. Ross
   1968   Variety, constraint, and the Law of Requisite Variety. In *Modern systems research for the behavioral scientist,* edited by Walter F. Buckley. Aldine, Chicago.
Buckley, Walter F. (ed.)
   1968   *Modern systems research for the behavioral scientist.* Aldine, Chicago.
Clarke, David L.
   1968   *Analytical archaeology.* Methuen, London.
Courant, Richard, and Fritz John
   1965   *Introduction to calculus and analysis,* Volume 1. Interscience, New York.
Flannery, Kent V.
   1968   Archaeological systems theory and early Mesoamerica. In *Anthropological archaeology in the Americas,* edited by Betty J. Meggers. Anthropological Society of Washington, Washington, D.C.
   1972   The cultural evolutions of civilizations. *Annual Review of Ecology and Systematics* 3:399–426.
   1973   Archaeology with a capital "S". In *Research and theory in current archeology.* edited by Charles L. Redman. John Wiley and Sons, New York.
Gallager, Robert G.
   1968   *Information theory and reliable communication.* John Wiley and Sons, New York.
Gero, Joan M., and James A. Moore
   1975   The role of requisite variety in prehistoric Southwestern societies. Manuscript on file, Department of Anthropology, University of South Carolina.
Glassow, Michael A.
   1972   Changes in adaptations of Southwestern Basketmakers: a systems perspective. In *Contemporary archaeology,* edited by Mark P. Leone. Southern Illinois University Press, Carbondale.
Johnson, Gregory A.
   1978   Information sources and the development of decision-making organizations. In *Social archaeology: beyond subsistence and dating,* edited by Charles L. Redman, Mary Jane Berman, Edward V. Curtin, William T. Langhorne, Jr., Nina M. Versaggi, and Jeffry C. Wanser. Academic Press, New York.
Justeson, John S.
   n.d.   Predicting change in information-processing systems. Manuscript.
   in preparation   The Law of Requisite Variety and the open regulatory system.
Kasakoff, Alice Bee, and John W. Adams
   1977   Spatial location and social organization: An analysis of Tikopian patterns. *Man* 11:48–64.
Loomis, Robert S., R. Rabbinge, and Edward Ng
   1979   Explanatory models in crop physiology. *Annual Review of Plant Physiology* 30:339–367.
Peebles, Christopher S., and Susan M. Kus
   1977   Some archaeological correlates of ranked society. *American Antiquity* 42:421–448.
Rathje, William L.
   1971   The origin and development of Lowland Classic Maya civilization. *American Antiquity* 36:275–285.
   1973a   Classic Maya development and denouement: A research design. In *The Classic*

Maya collapse, edited by T. Patrick Culbert. University of New Mexico Press, Albuquerque.

1973b Models for mobile Maya: A variety of constraints. In *The explanation of culture change,* edited by Colin Renfrew. Gerald Duckworth and Co., Ltd., London.

Wobst, H. Martin

1977 Pet peeves in Palaeolithic prehistory. Colloquium at the Department of Anthropology, University of South Carolina.

Wright, Henry T.

1969 *The administration of rural production in an early Mesopotamian town.* Anthropological Papers, Museum of Anthropology, University of Michigan, 38.

Zubrow, Ezra B. W.

1973 Adequacy criteria and prediction in archaeological models. In *Research and theory in current archaeology.* edited by Charles L. Redman. John Wiley and Sons, New York.

1974 *Prehistoric carrying capacity: A model.* Cummings Publishing Co., Menlo Park.

PART II

Foragers, Pastoralists, and Subsistence Farmers

Group Size and Mobility Costs

STEPHEN M. PERLMAN

Sovran Bank, N.A.
Richmond, Virginia

INTRODUCTION

Archaeologists have usually considered hunter–gatherer settlement patterns a response to local resource conditions. The density, distribution, and diversity of resources are used to explain the size and location of hunter–gatherer camps as they change through the seasons (Lee 1967; Silberbauer 1972; Steward 1938) or over long periods of time (Jochim 1976; Perlman 1976). In essence, this approach treats the behavior of foraging groups as a closed system, holding constant external and nonsubsistence factors. This essay discusses and demonstrates the importance of bringing such factors as long distance social interaction and group movement (mobility) into the analysis of hunter–gatherer settlement patterns (Smith 1981).

Both local and long distance aspects of hunter–gatherer networks are affected by mobility and group size processes; mobility costs, in particular, have nonlocal implications. For example, if we assume that the maximum mobility cost a group can absorb from a location is set by the existing transportation technology, than any costs above this threshold would require either an adjustment in settlement location, the development of a new technology, or the costs would have to be transferred to other variables. A transfer of costs, however, extends the influence of one limiting factor—a technology in this case—to others. This study investigates how mobility costs, specifically subsistence-related mobility costs, can be extended to and, as a result, can limit hunter–gatherer group sizes.

Foraging theory provides the foundation for this research (Emlen 1966; Schoener 1971). By combining this theoretical base with four assumptions, utilitylike curves are constructed that identify the maximum group sizes for various hunter–gatherer population densities. These curves are then used to develop implications for hunter–gatherer behavior in stable and changing environments. Finally, a brief test of these expectations are made by comparing them to the ethnographic record and to Archaic population distributions for the region from South Carolina to Massachusetts.

The discussions and tests suggest a series of conclusions:

1. hunter–gatherer behavior is affected by mobility costs;
2. hunter–gatherer group sizes can be limited by mobility costs;
3. ethnographically observed hunter–gatherer group sizes, which average around a "magic" 25, could be a product of mobility cost limitations;
4. variability in hunter–gatherer group sizes over time could be a product of the changing relationship between group size and mobility costs as the environment shifts;
5. cultural evolutionary models that assume modern small hunter–gatherer groups to be representative of the optimal social organization might be in error; and
6. mobility costs and other limiting variables can have nonlocal consequences; in other words, human social systems are open systems.

MOBILITY COSTS

Most discussions of hunter–gatherer mobility have emphasized its benefits. For example, mobility can alleviate resource depletion and scheduling problems through seasonal changes in group sizes (moving individuals around) and/or settlement relocation (moving the whole group). The capacity to move about has even been presented as a mechanism for alleviating social stress (Lee 1972). Although not ignored, the costs of mobility have received less explicit study. For example, the time required to forage a specific area from a site sets a limit on the catchment zone's size and the resources that can be acquired. Recent work by Hawkes and O'Connell (1981) has identified how the cost of getting to the resource limits its value and sets a limit on group size. In the following sections, I examine the question, To what extent do subsistence-related mobility costs limit hunter–gatherer group sizes? To answer this question, the factors influencing subsistence-related mobility costs and their systematic effects on hunter–gatherer group sizes will be identified.

Subsistence-Related Mobility Costs and Group Size

Any mobility cost can be measured by the energy or time spent during an activity. Subsistence-related mobility costs are those time or energy expenditures associated with the search, pursuit, and travel required to capture a prey (MacArthur and Pianka 1966). In this study, time provides the measure.

Search and pursuit costs are incurred within the habitat, or patch, of the prey being sought; travel costs are incurred reaching the prey's patch and returning to the home base. As any of these increase, the total cost of acquiring the selected resource increases. For example, if search and pursuit times are held constant, then the exploitation of more distant patches increases travel time and reduces the probability of acquiring the resource (MacArthur and Pianka 1966). At some point the margin is attained for obtaining that resource from the home base. The time required becomes too great.

Two potential solutions are clear. A population can either remain where they are and select a new diet (Emlen 1966) or choose a new location closer to the prey. This second option involves another mobility cost: the time required to change and reestablish a settlement. Obviously, these options can also be combined.

Regardless of the strategy selected, the new one would require a greater expenditure of time. This assumes that the resources and the locations with the highest returns are selected first, and that the time cost associated with a settlement shift is added to the new location's return rates. While the relocation costs would become negligible over long periods of time, they would help maintain a lower return rate from the new location.

These examples identify the negative effects of mobility costs on return rates. The initial diet from a location reached its margin because of increasing mobility costs; the lower return rates associated with the new diet are a consequence of the initial diet's increasing mobility costs; and finally, if a change in settlement location should occur, the mobility and residential costs associated with the move would further reduce the return rates from the new location.

An alternative strategy to dietary and locational changes would be to reduce the group's size. Smaller groups would require fewer captures or less time to provide sufficient sustenance. More time could be spent at one place before a move or a change in diet would be necessary. In other words, by varying group size, hunter–gatherers can control the impact that increasing mobility costs have on their strategy. While this is a viable option, varying group size, particularly the selection of smaller groups, is not necessarily a panacea. Smaller groups have been associated with higher social (Coraco and Wolf 1975) and even foraging costs (Cody 1974; Hirsh 1977) of non-human groups. Various lines of evidence indicate that small group sizes have similar effects on hunter–gatherer social and subsistence-related costs (Perlman 1981).

For the time being, human settlement and foraging decisions will be viewed as a product of the interplay between group size and mobility cost considerations. For some environments, the decisions might vary seasonally. To counteract the effect of a resource availability pattern, group size might be emphasized during one season, mobility cost during another. Regardless, in any environment, the range of compromises is limited by the effect mobility costs have on the capacity to both acquire resources and to form group sizes that minimize social costs.

Mobility Costs and Hunter–Gatherer Group Size Potential

Theoretical works have established that a general relationship does exist between the size and distribution of subsistence resource patches (factors influencing search, pursuit, and travel costs) and the size and distribution of human groups (Harpending and Davis 1977; Smith 1981; Wilmsen 1973). These studies, however, only identify the general relationships; they do not specify what the potential sizes of these groups might be. By creating utlitylike curves, potential group sizes can be estimated. These curves indicate whether a particular group size is possible given resource availability and catchment size. This estimation can be improved by identifying the effect of topographic variability on group size potential. For example, what happens to group size potential when catchments are not circular and not flat?

The construction of these group size curves requires three supporting assumptions. These assumptions establish the effect technology is expected to have on group size potential; the expected range of hunter–gatherer population densities; and the maximum distance a group can travel from a location before a new camp location is required.

First, how does technology affect mobility costs? Technology affects mobility costs by influencing the time required to reach the prey's habitat and to search for and pursue the prey. However, technology also has its costs. For example, the production time for a hunting implement is a time cost and should be included in the total time required to acquire the selected resource; therefore, groups should try to minimize the technological costs required for their sustenance. This leads to the first assumption: all hunter–

Table 3.1

Approximate Number of Hours per Capture for Temperate Forest Species

Species	Return per hour	Hours per capture
Deer	.09 individuals	11.1
Bear	.01 individuals	100
Shellfish	.4 bushels	2.5 bushels/hour
Fish	5.1 pounds	Depends on fish species
Turkey	.1 individuals	11
Beaver	.14 individuals	7.1
Raccoon	.2 individuals	5
Small game	.06 individuals	16.6

gatherer technologies are available to all hunter–gatherers with the selection of a specific technology determined by the subsistence demands. As a result, hunter–gatherer group size is not limited by the lack of a more effective technology.

Second, what is the expected range of hunter–gatherer population densities? The range for modern hunter–gatherers is quite wide (Hassan 1975). In addition, densities higher than the .01 and .1 per square mile of low-productivity environments are oftentimes associated with more productive environments (e.g., riverine and estuarine environments [Perlman 1981]). Since these latter environments are known to have existed in the past, a reasonable assumption would be that the range for prehistoric hunter–gatherers could have been the same. [2]

Finally, at what distances do mobility costs become excessive and require a move to a second camp if the same resource is to be pursued? The distance should vary for each resource; particularly with their search and pursuit times. For example, while Lee has reported a 6-mile one-way limit for nut collection, search and pursuit times for nuts are low. Once it is known where nuts are available, they are easy to find and acquire. In contrast, the combined search and pursuit value of 10 hours for deer in temperate forests (based upon 20 deer per square mile [Perlman 1976 and 1981]) would require second camps for most distances to the deer's habitat. The hours per capture for other temperate resources are provided in Table 3.1. Secondary camps would be common for most of these resources as well.

Since the maximum round-trip distances for all resources cannot be identified, a constant will be used. The available hunter–gatherer literature indicates a maximum one-way walking distance from a camp of less than 10 miles (Table 3.2). In fact, Lee's maximum figure of 6 miles is probably close to the absolute maximum. Remember, the resource Lee is referring to has a

Table 3.2
Catchment Distances from Ethnographic Data

Group	Distance	Source
!Kung bushmen	6 miles (maximum)	Lee 1967
G/wi San bushmen	10–30 km (6–19 miles) round trip	Tanaka 1980
Mistassini Cree	8-mile radius	Rogers 1973
Ainu	1.5–4 miles	Watanabe 1972
G/wi bushmen	5 miles	Silberbauer 1972

high return and minimal search and pursuit times; nuts can absorb large travel costs before reaching its margin. Most other resources, even those with equal returns, have higher search and pursuit times; their distance margin will be reached faster. To minimize the potential error of using a constant distance value, a 10-mile one-way value is used. Any distance greater than 10 miles requires a second camp.

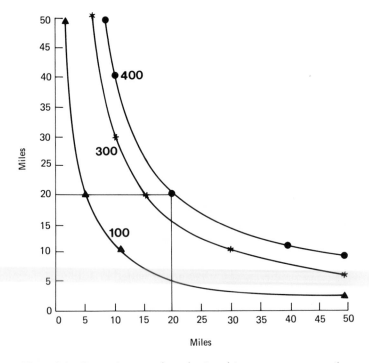

Figure 3.1   Group size curve for a density of 1 person per square mile.

Group Size Curves and Potential Hunter–Gatherer Group Sizes

Utility-like curves can be constructed that identify how mobility costs, set by a 10-mile distance threshold, establish limits on the sizes of sedentary camps. While hexagonal and circular catchments are most common in the literature, many environments (river valleys, hilly areas, coastal strips, etc.) do not permit these shapes. Therefore, these curves identify the potential village sizes for right-angled quadralateral catchment areas (Figures 3.1– 3.4). The x and y axes are distance indicators and, except for one small distortion, the small box circumscribes all the possible shapes that can exist with a maximum length of 20 miles (a 10-mile trip from the camp in two directions). The distortion is that the upper right corner of the square represents a distance of greater than 20 miles. Village size curves that touch this corner are not actually possible. Anything within the square will be considered a potential village. As an example, a village of 50, when population density is 1 per square mile, requires a catchment area of 50 square miles.

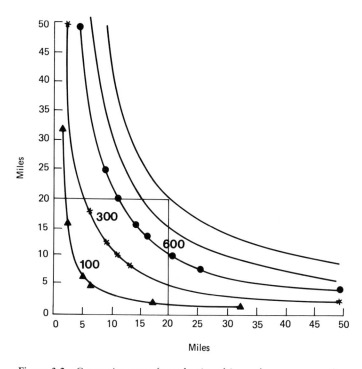

Figure 3.2 Group size curve for a density of 3 people per square mile.

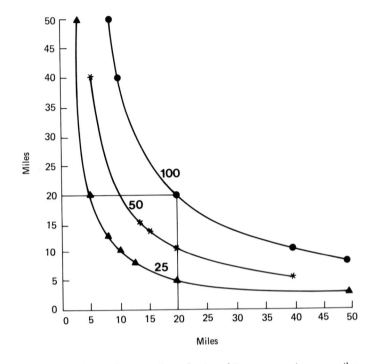

Figure 3.3   Group size curve for a density of 1 person per 4 square miles.

This village size is possible as long as the maximum distance to the edge of the catchment does not exceed 10 miles, or a maximum catchment length of 20 miles. For a rectangular catchment, any width of less than 2.5 miles would require a length of greater than 20 miles. Curves are provided for densities of 1/1, 3/1, 1/4, 1/10 square miles (Figures 3.1–3.4).

◦ The curves indicate that sedentism is unlikely for hunter–gatherer populations living in environments supporting less than one-tenth person per square mile. Sedentism is also unlikely for certain catchment shapes and group sizes at higher densities. Only the widest environments could maintain a sedentary group of 25 at 1 person per 10 square miles. A village of 50 is impossible. Sedentary villages of 25 are more likely when the potential density reaches .25 person per square mile. Villages of 50 and 100 are only possible in broad-plain environments. Sedentary villages of 100 are more likely to occur at a density of 1 per square mile (see Figure 3.1).

* The curves also identify two simple relationships. First, as expected, the size of potential sedentary villages increases with a rise in population density. Second and more important, as catchments of the same areas become less

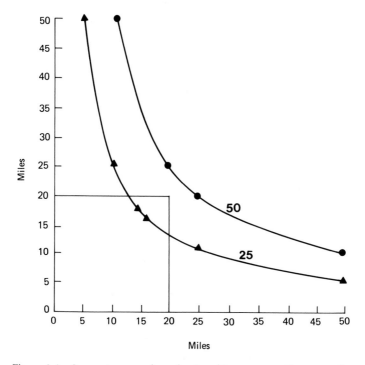

Figure 3.4 Group size curve for a density of 1 person per 10 square miles.

symmetrical, the potential village sizes become smaller. This second relationship also has implications for the third dimension of a catchment area, the variation in the local topography.

Since movement over 10 miles of uneven ground takes more time than movement across flat terrain, uneven landforms will create unequal-length radii from a center. Therefore, uneven terrain will reduce the sizes of both the catchment area and the potential sedentary village. Terrell's (1977) Bougainville land-use study makes these relationships explicit. High-relief zone pathways are limited to the ridges, while in lower-relief areas, like valley bottoms and coastal plains, the pathways are less restricted by topography. Furthermore, as the relief changes from a plain to a ridge formation, the catchment zones and the settlements become smaller. The settlements are also clustered in the coastal plain and dispersed along the ridges.

Finally, high-relief areas often have lower productivities than flatter terrains in the same region (Perlman 1981). Their lower productivities would further limit group sizes by reducing the potential hunter–gatherer population densities—less food suggesting fewer people. Therefore, high-relief zones restrict group sizes in two ways: by restricting the size of the catchment area that can be searched in the time it takes to walk 10 miles on a flat surface; and by reducing the number of people that can be supported.

THE HUNTER–GATHERER GROUP SIZE CURVES AND OPEN SYSTEMS

Mobility cost curves have implications for both hunter–gatherer group sizes and the existence of open hunter–gatherer systems. As shown, mobility costs set limits on hunter–gatherer group size. Most often the largest potentially sedentary group sizes are relatively small. At 1 person per square mile—a fairly high hunter–gatherer density for extant groups—the largest groups would be between 100 and 300 people. When these figures are compared to other group size requirements, it becomes clear why many hunter–gatherer groups cannot form closed systems.

• Mating network simulations and empirical studies have identified the minimum number of individuals required to provide sufficient mates (Adams and Kasakoff 1976; Wobst 1976). The second study identifies that 80% of a group's mates could be obtained from the local pool if that pool contained 100 people. Closed mating systems require groups of approximately 300–500 persons (Wobst 1976). The group size curves indicate that the 80% closure could be achieved in some high-density environments; completely closed mating systems are unlikely.

An implication of the general existence of open hunter–gatherer systems is that major changes in local productivity would have nonlocal consequences. If productivity should increase, then larger and more sedentary groups might be selected. These groups would be formed by consolidating existing groups. The redistribution of the population, through the existing open system, would require adjustments by groups removed from the source of the change.

The archaeological significance of this implication is of particular importance to studies in the eastern United States. Are any of the hunter–gatherer changes identified in the coastal eastern United States archaeological record a product of changes in group size potential? Or are all the changes due to population growth or other demographic pressures? We will return to this question later.

In summary, by placing limitations on hunter–gatherer group sizes, mobility costs play a role in creating open hunter–gatherer systems. As these limitations are lifted, due to increasing local productivity, larger groups could be selected and some closure of hunter–gatherer systems would result. While complete closure is not expected, observed changes in hunter–

gatherer behavior must take into consideration changes in group size restrictions.

MOBILITY COSTS AND HUNTER–GATHERER ETHNOGRAPHY

The ethnographic data indicate that mobility costs do play a significant role in determining subsistence- and nonsubsistence-related behaviors for hunter–gatherers. These include the structure of the regional settlement system and the size of hunter–gatherer groups.

Smith (1981:47) cites mobility costs as one of the factors that affect group sizes: "The geometry of foraging may be hypothesized to affect optimum coresident group size by setting a limit on the area exploited from the home base, depending on mobility costs and resource densities." Some of Smith's other comments foreshadow the objective of this work; specifically, do mobility costs set limits that are operationalized? The group size curves suggest that they do. For example, transhumant behavior could be a bene- ✓ fit—a way of alleviating stress—or the operative side of mobility costs in low-density, seasonal, and/or unpredictable environments (see Testart's [1982] review of the ethnographic literature). Binford's (1980) hunter–gatherer settlement system typology uses logistics as the mechanism for distinguishing between his two types. In fact, his data fit neatly with the implications of the curves and an earlier work (Perlman 1981). Hunter–gatherer groups in higher-productivity temperate environments are more sedentary. Some ethnographic examples are even more specific: subsistence-related mobility costs do effect the amount of transhumance.

Both Lee (1967) and Silberbauer (1972) have identified the effect of mobility costs on subsistence returns and on decisions to relocate. Six miles is the maximum one-way distance a person will walk to gather nuts. Beyond it, a change in settlement location is more efficient than incurring greater travel costs from the original campsite (Lee 1967). The G/wi bushmen (Silberbauer 1972) camp locations appear to minimize travel costs. A number of resource zones or patches can be exploited from one camp (Silberbauer 1972: Fig. 7-7 through 7-11). The camp is not located within the confines of a patch until patch productivity is so high that other areas do not need to be exploited for a number of gathering episodes. The high patch productivity also permits the group to select greater sedentism.

Besides the greater sedentism associated with high-productivity patches, Steward (1938) and Harpending and Davis (1977) state that these groups are oftentimes larger; occasionally, as many as 150–200 people. These larger and more sedentary groups raise an additional question: How large would hunter–gatherer groups become if they were not limited by mobility costs? The actual optimal size cannot be identified at this time; however, two points should be kept in mind. First, empirical and theoretical evidence abounds that small groups (e.g., 25 persons) might not be the optimal size. In fact, a number of studies for humans and nonhumans indicate advantages are associated with the formation of larger groups (Perlman 1981). Second, the question of the optimal group size is not a mundane one. If we are to use the archaeological record to test our hypotheses about the "why" of cultural evolution, we need to have a better understanding of the factors influencing the changes observed in that record. Again, are the changes in hunter–gatherer behavior all products of various stresses or are some the products of limitations being lifted? If we observe an increase in group size and even social complexity, does this necessarily indicate a response to stress? The group size curves demonstrate that such is not necessarily the case.

GROUP SIZES IN STABLE AND CHANGING ENVIRONMENTS AND THEIR ARCHAEOLOGICAL IMPLICATIONS

What are the implications of the group sizes for environments with changing elevations and what expectations do they produce for group sizes in stable and changing environments? First, for a stable environment, the expectation is simple: as topographic relief increases and gross and net productivities are reduced, group sizes will become smaller.

Second, when considering the effects of environmental change, two types of change need to be distinguished: changes in physiography versus changes in local productivity. If local physiography should change, then the potential sizes and distribution of settlements could change as well. As an example, consider a river that shifts its location in the floodplain. Such a change could alter the sizes of both the catchment areas and the settlements. Obviously, even with a constant local productivity pattern, the sizes as well as the distribution of human settlements would not necessarily remain the same. A change in local productivity could have similar effects.

These potential changes for stable and changing environments can be restated as expectations for the archaeological record. By readjusting the population distributions to mimic the changes in resource availability, the number of sites observed in each zone will vary over time. For example, if coastal productivity decreases relative to the uplands, then the latter becomes a relatively more inviting habitat. More people moving into this environment would increase site counts because potential group sizes are restricted by the smaller catchment zones. If the coastal zone's productivity should increase, then the population readjustment would be toward that habitat. If larger groups are possible on a coastal plain, then site counts might drop in both the upland and coastal zones. If group sizes are at the optimum—that is larger groups are selected against—then site counts would increase in the coastal zone and the lowered demand for upland habitat would reduce the site counts there.

CHANGING ARCHAIC POPULATION DISTRIBUTIONS FROM SOUTH CAROLINA TO MASSACHUSETTS

Major changes in resource availability have occurred in the eastern United States during the Holocene. Sea level rose approximately 400 feet (Emery and Milliman 1970), major vegetation zones migrated northwards (Edwards and Merrill 1977), and as a result, nut, deer, and fish productivities were altered, but not necessarily in unison.

The rise in sea level both reduced the land area available for habitation and inundated the most productive inhabitable space: coastal bays and estuaries. Even a constant population, in a stable environment, occupying a decreasing land area would have been forced to select a more intensive exploitation of the remaining resources and resource zones. Contemporary hunter–gatherers would have formed larger groups in what remains of the original occupied space and/or increased the exploitation of previously unoccupied or less occupied space. Along the eastern United States coast and its adjacent interior, sea level rise alone would have increased the demand for interior, or upland, habitat.

Changes in the availability and distribution of key resources—nuts, deer, and anadromous fish—would have affected the distribution of the contemporary human population. Pollen records for most of the eastern United States coast indicate a change to more temperate forests, followed by a slight return to a more northern climate and forest cover after the fourth millennium B.P. (Edwards and Merrill 1977). Associated with these changes, one would expect increases and then decreases in the relative abundance of nut and non-nut bearing trees. While the actual timing of these changes varies with latitude—later for the increase and slightly earlier for the decrease further north—the general pattern remains the same. For example, oak reaches its peak slightly before hickory. At Dismal Swamp, oak reaches a peak at approximately 9000 years B.P. and hickory at 7000 years B.P. (Whitehead 1972). Further north at Rogers Lake in Connecticut, peaks for oak and hickory pollen are attained at approximately 7000 and after 5000 years B.P. respectively (Davis 1969). As the temperature cooled, hickory began to drop out of the pollen record about 4000 years ago.

The initial development of nut-bearing forests would have increased the food value of upland zones. If pressure on coastal and riverine populations was increasing due to loss of land, the contemporary increase in upland production would have relieved some of the pressure; after 4000 years B.P., the loss of upland nut resources would have reversed the trend. Individuals occupying the upland zones would have required alternative sources of subsistence.

Deer productivity would have responded in a similar fashion to the changes in climate and nut productivity (McCullough 1970). The changes in deer density would have enhanced the population readjustment trends: the development and exploitation of more productive uplands followed by the loss of this upland resource and the reduction in the use of that zone.

Finally, eastern United States coastal fisheries were increasing in productivity as these others were decreasing. This conclusion is based upon the assumption that a positive correlation exists between marsh or estuarine primary productivity and fish productivity (Perlman 1981). This assumption is supported by the link between major estuarine systems and/or upwelling zones and major commercial fisheries (Cushing 1975). Approximately 4000 years ago the rate of relative sea level rise slowed and local sedimentation rates appear to have surpassed it. The sedimentation provided a foundation for the expansion of existing estuarine marshes (Kraft and Margules 1971; Redfield 1972), and an assumed subsequent increase in fish productivity. Given the return rates of anadromous fish and the importance of this resource to many hunter–gatherers (Perlman 1981), the expansion of the marshes would have had profound effects on comtemporary social systems.

The combined effects of these changes was to alter the subsistence strategy of Archaic hunter–gatherers along the western Atlantic coast and to change the potential sizes of some hunter–gatherer groups. As sea level rise eliminated much of the coastal plain, greater utilization of upland environments would have developed. The smaller catchments of the upland environments would have required smaller group sizes, probably smaller sites, and a greater number of sites. As anadromous fish productivity increased, greater emphasis would be placed on this resource; possibly concentrating hunter–gatherer subsistence activities in the riverine and estuarine zones. Still, the continued loss of coastal land to rising relative sea level after 4000 years ago would have maintained some pressure due to an increasing man/land ratio. In other words, loss of coastal land might have required continued occupation of upland areas. However, the increasing returns from anadromous fish exploitation about 4000 years ago could have (and is expected to have) produced an observable shift in the relative utilization of upland versus estuarine and riverine zones, and also an increase in site size as groups consolidated on the broader and flatter coastal environments.

Presently, only the spatial changes in site distribution can be adequately compared to the archaeological record. From South Carolina to the Charles River basin in Massachusetts, these expectations are supported by site survey results (Dincauze 1974; Gardner 1978; Goodyear *et al.* 1979; Swigart 1978). Early Archaic remains (approximately 9000 years B.P.) are found primarily in the river valleys. During the middle and late Archaic (until 4000 B.P.), population redistributions occurred and utilization of the uplands increased. In addition, as is true of the forest development, these redistributions occurred earlier in South Carolina and Virginia than further north. After 4000 B.P. and roughly contemporary with Savannah River or similar projectile point types, a second shift occurred. People began to move back into the river valleys.

While the record is spotty, evidence does exist that supports the other expectations. Larger groups and possibly more complex forms of social organization were developing in estuarine and riverine zones around 4000 B.P. In the Southeast massive shell rings occur on the coast and deep middens containing highly decorated bone pins and early pottery are found along the major drainages. In Virginia our initial research indicates the formation of larger and highly structured sites. A large central hearth was identified at one site surrounded by smaller hearths. At the same site the large number of axes found could indicate substantial clearing—the clearing associated with and required for longer occupations and larger groups. In another excavation a similar large hearth was found associated with Savannah River materials. Furthermore, an increase in riverine and estuarine sedimentation rates reported for various southeastern coastal localities (Carbone, personal communication, 1982) suggests that an increase in clearing could have been a more general occurrence—a possible outcome of larger numbers of people concentrating in the riverine zone. In many areas large steatite bowls were produced. The probability that these were curated suggests the formation of base camps. Finally, changes in social networks are indicated by the combination of a new lithic technology and a consistency in point style found from Georgia to Massachusetts after 4000 B.P. Furthermore, these Savannal River like points are often associated with the adoption of a new lithic material for biface production; another change that suggests altered social networks.

The period about 4000 B.P. and shortly thereafter was a time of rapid changes in this region. That these changes were a response to the lifting of group size limitations cannot be rejected at this time. In fact, this explanation is easier to accept than the more common one of demographic stress. This latter explanation runs counter to site distribution evidence. Site counts should not drop in the uplands under conditions of stress. Furthermore, why did population growth create these changes at a time when a major resource—anadromous fish—was increasing, probably dramatically, in availability? The explanation offered here does not run counter to the archaeological evidence, and the mobility cost curves demonstrate how changes in resource availability can lift group size limitations.

SUMMARY AND CONCLUSIONS

Mobility costs play a role in dietary and population distribution decisions. A brief discussion of the general parameters that generate this conclusion were presented and was followed by the construction of group size curves. These curves, by identifying the restrictions mobility costs place on hunter–gatherer group sizes, suggest a number of conclusions. First, in many environments, these restrictions contribute to the openness of hunter–gatherer social systems. Potential group sizes are insufficient to permit the formation of closed systems. Still, the potential for larger groups did exist in higher-productivity environments. This possibility, and its implications, were compared briefly to both the ethnographic data for modern hunter–gatherers and the archaeological record for the Archaic period of the western Atlantic coast. Both records indicate that larger and even sedentary hunter–gatherer groups could and might have formed when the opportunity arose. As a result, the comparisons support the contention that modern small group hunter–gatherers might not identify the optimum group size for hunter–gatherers in general. Furthermore, these larger groups might have required more complex social organizations, as some do today. Both of these possibilities must be considered when utilizing the Holocene archaeological record to test models of cultural evolution. Some changes might be a response to the lifting of group size restrictions rather than a forced response to demographic stress.

REFERENCES

Adams, J. W., and A. B. Kasakoff
    1976   Factors underlying endoquamous group size. In *Regional analysis: social systems*,
           edited by C. A. Smith. Academic Press, New York.
Binford, L. R.
    1980   Willow smoke and dogs' tails: hunter–gatherer settlement systems and archae-
           ological site formation. *American Antiquity* 45:4–20.
Cody, M. L.
    1974   Optimization in ecology. *Science* 183:1156–1164.
Coraco, T., and L. L. Wolf
    1975   Ecological determinants of group sizes of foraging lions. *The American Naturalist*
           109:343–352.

Cushing, D. H.
1975 *Marine ecology and fisheries.* Cambridge University Press, New York.
Davis, M. B.
1969 Climatic changes is southern Connecticut recorded by pollen and deposition at Rogers Lake. *Ecology* 50:409–428.
Dincauze, D. F.
1974 An introduction to archaeology in the greater Boston area. *Archaeology of Eastern North America* 2:39–67.
Edwards, R. L., and A. S. Merrill
1977 A reconstruction of the continental shelf areas of eastern North America for the times 9,500 B.P. and 12,500 B.P. *Archaeology of Eastern North America* 5:1–43.
Emery, K. O., and J. D. Milliman
1970 Quaternary sediments of the Atlantic continental shelf of the United States. *Quaternaria* 12:3–18.
Emlen, J. M.
1966 The role of time and energy in food preference. *The American Naturalist* 100:611–617.
Gardner, W.
1978 *Comparison of ridge and valley, blue ridge, piedmont, and coastal plain Archaic period site distribution: an idealized transect.* Paper presented at the 1978 Middle Atlantic Conference,
Goodyear, A. G., J. H. House, and N. W. Ackerly
1979 *Laurens-Anderson: An archaeological study of the inter-rivrine piedmont.* Institute of Archaeology and Anthropology, Anthropological Studies 4, Columbia, South Carolina.
Harpending, H., and H. Davis
1977 Some implications for hunter–gatherer ecology derived from the spatial structure of resources. *World Archaeology* 8:275–286.
Hassan, F. A.
1975 Determination of the size density and growth rate of hunting–gathering populations. In *Population, Ecology, and Social Evolution,* edited by Steven Folgar. Aldine Press, Chicago.
Hawkes, K., and J. F. O'Connell
1981 Affluent hunters? Some comments in light of the Alyawara case. *American Anthropologist* 83:622–626.
Hirsh, D. H.
1977 *Social behavior of white-tailed deer in relation to habitat.* Wildlife Monograph, No. 53.
Jochim, M. A.
1976 *Hunter–gatherer subsistence and settlement: a predictive model.* Academic Press, New York.
Kraft, J. C., and G. Margules
1971 Sediment patterns, physical characters of the water mass and foraminiferida distribution in Indial River Bay, coastal Delaware. *Southeastern Geology* 12:223–250.
Lee, R. B.
1967 !Kung bushmen subsistence: An input–output analysis. In *Environment and cultural behavior,* edited by Andrew P. Wayda. Natural History Press, New York.
1972 The intensification of social life among the !Kung bushman. In *Population growth: anthropological implications,* edited by Brian Spooner. Massachusetts Institute of Technology Press, Cambridge.

MacArthur, R. H., and E. R. Pianka
    1966   An optimal use of a patchy environment. *American Naturalist* 100:603–609.
McCullough, D. R.
    1970   Secondary production of birds and mammals. In *Analysis of temperate forest ecosystems,* edited by David E. Reichle. Springer-Verlag, New York.
Perlman, S. M.
    1976   Optimum diet models and prehistoric hunter–gatherer: a test on Martha's Vineyard Island. Unpublished Ph.D. dissertation, Amherst, University of Massachusetts,
    1981   An optimum diet model, coastal variability, and hunter–gatherer behavior. In *Advances in archaeological method and theory* (Vol. 3), edited by M. Schiffer. Academic Press, New York.
Redfield, A. C.
    1972   Development of a New England salt marsh. *Ecological Monographs* 42:201–237.
Rogers, E. S.
    1973   *The quest for food and furs: the Misstassini Cree, 1953–1954.* National Museums of Canada, Publication in Ethnology, No. 5, Ottawa.
Schoener, T. W.
    1971   Theory of feeding strategies. *Annual Review of Ecology and Systematics* 2:369–404.
Silberbauer, G. B.
    1972   The G/wi bushmen. In *Hunter–gatherers today,* edited by M. G. Bicchieri. Holt, Rinehart, and Winston, New York.
Smith, E. A.
    1981   The application of optimal foraging theory to the analysis of hunter–gatherer group size. In *Hunter–gatherer foraging strategies,* edited by B. Winterhalder and E. A. Smith. University of Chicago Press, Chicago.
Steward, J.
    1938   Basin plateau aboriginal sociopolitical groups. *Bureau of American Ethnology Bulletin* 120, Washington, D.C.
Swigart, E. K.
    1978   The ecological placement of western Connecticut sites. *Archaeology of Eastern North America* 5:61–73.
Tanaka, J.
    1980   *The San: hunter–gatherers of the Kalahari.* University of Tokyo Press, Tokyo.
Terrell, J.
    1977   Geographic systems and human diversity in the North Solomons. *World Archaeology* 9:62–81.
Testart, A.
    1982   The significance of food storage among hunter–gatherers: residence patterns, population densities, and social inequalities. *Current Anthropology* 23:523–530.
Watanabe, H.
    1972   *The Ainu ecosystem.* University of Washington Press, Seattle.
Wilmsen, E. N.
    1973   Interaction, spacing behavior, and the organization of hunting bands. *Journal of Anthropological Research* 29:1–31.
Wobst, H. M.
    1976   Locational relationships in Paleolithic society. In *The demographic evolution of human populations,* edited by R. H. Ward and K. M. Weiss. Academic Press, New York.

CHAPTER 4

Cultural Boundaries and Ecological Frontiers in Coastal Regions: An Example from the Alaska Peninsula

DAVID R. YESNER

Department of Geography–Anthropology
University of Southern Maine
Gorham, Maine

INTRODUCTION

"Systemic" views of cultural change adopted by archaeologists generally emphasize the processes underlying cultural change rather than the structure of the social units undergoing transformation.[1] Even synchronic analyses of cultural adaptation tend to focus more on relationships *between* individual social units than on the boundaries that separate and maintain them. Although it has been nearly 30 years since Barth (1956) described the ecology of ethnic boundaries in northern Pakistan, archaeologists have been slow to recognize the importance of boundary maintenance in the survival of prehistoric human populations.

The original analyses of social boundaries by Barth (1956), Despres (1969), Haaland (1969), and others emphasized the development of boundaries under conditions in which potentially competing populations were able to coexist through both spatial and temporal partitioning of the exploitation of a habitat, becoming resource "specialists" in a fashion akin to competitive exclusion among sympatric animal species. However, these authors were not dealing with hunter–gatherers who forage within spatially discrete home ranges in common with other anthropoids. For these populations, the study of social boundary maintenance can inform us greatly on how prehistoric human adaptations were organized over relatively short distances, that is, on the scale of individual cultural units.

Social boundaries have evidently been an important part of the adaptive framework of human populations since the early Pleistocene (Wobst 1974, 1975). However, there is some evidence to suggest that their importance has increased during the course of human evolution. During the late Pleistocene, human populations grew on a worldwide basis (Butzer 1971), filling preferred ecological niches (Cohen 1977). Niche saturation probably resulted in the development of more localized territories (Yesner 1982), and would have increased the social distance between groups. Boundary maintenance would have increased in order to ensure the survival of individual cultural units.

At the same time, new "broad spectrum" subsistence strategies were being developed by human populations, including more use of wild (and eventually domesticated) plants as well as aquatic resources (Binford 1968; Osborn 1977). These subsistence changes allowed for more sedentary lifeways. At the same time, regionally dense populations developed among intensive plant gatherers (and early farmers) as a result of local resource abundance, while among groups dependent upon aquatic resources—particularly maritime hunter–gatherers—similarly dense populations resulted from resource diversity and stability as well as abundance (Yesner 1977a, 1980, 1983a, 1984; Perlman 1980a, 1980b). As Abruzzi (1982) noted, it is precisely under the latter conditions (sedentary populations in diverse, stable environments) that distinct strategies of resource exploitation are likely to evolve and to be maintained by social boundaries.

This does not necessarily mean, however, that social boundaries were only structured by competition over valuable resources—those resources that have low cost–benefit ratios or that are spatiotemporally aggregated (cf. Perlman, Chapter 3, this volume). Alternatively, *boundaries* may be seen as structures that promote the efficient exploitation of resource clusters by human populations in environments (such as coastal regions) in which the resources themselves are "tightly packed," guaranteeing access of populations to resources. The existence of social boundaries would then relate more to efficient exploitation of tightly packed resource clusters than to competition over individually valuable resources, although in both cases the resources might be spatially circumscribed. How, then, might we distinguish between the test implications of these hypotheses? If competition over valuable resources is the primary cause of boundary maintenance, then we might expect to find boundaries located in resource-rich zones with population centers relatively close to the boundary zones. If, however, the alternate hypothesis is true, then we might expect to find boundaries located in resource-poor or even uninhabited areas.

Hardesty (1982) has additionally suggested that social boundaries might result simply from a history of geographical isolation of groups and associated "cultural drift." However, this cannot be a general explanation of how social boundaries are maintained as adaptive features, since not all groups that are divided by social boundaries are also geographically isolated. Instead, this should be seen as an explanation of how cultural boundaries become established, but even here it is not totally satisfying because we are left wondering what caused the populations in question to become isolated originally. For example, did population differentiation occur as a opportunistic response to the opening up of new ecological niches created by environmental change or did it occur because of group fissioning resulting from resource scarcity (involving environmental change, population growth, or both)? Alternatively, social boundaries might be created solely as the result of the immigration of a new group into the area, either to take advantage of newly available opportunities, to compete with already established groups, or both. Hardesty's hypothesis is also essentially tautological, since cultural drift is as much a consequence as it is a cause of cultural boundary formation. Furthermore, cultural drift will occur whether or not boundary maintenance results from competition or adaptive efficiency (although group isolation might be expected to be more complete in the latter case). Nevertheless, the degree of cultural drift between populations—as measured by differences in material culture—is probably a good index of the fixity and strength of the boundary between groups at any given point in time; while the frequency with which changes in material culture takes place along a common boundary would appear to be a good index of the relative stability and permeability of that boundary over time.

This study examines how social boundaries become established between populations that focus on the exploitation of marine resources. Although the origins of such boundaries are discussed, the main focus is on how they are maintained through time. In the process, the null hypothesis suggested earlier—that competition over resources is the primary force maintaining social boundaries—is tested. To accomplish this goal, distinct social systems must be identifiable archaeologically. This identification is of course troublesome at best; few archaeologists totally agree on the technological or stylistic criteria necessary to define such systems (Fitzhugh 1972, 1975), and the ethnographic record does not help much in this regard. Thus, it is not necessarily assumed here that larger amounts of information on the distinctiveness of social units are embedded in any one technological system (i.e., chipped stone, ground stone, bone, ceramics, or metal). However, during this discussion, some evaluation of the cultural specificity of these technological systems is offered.

THE ALEUT/ESKIMO BOUNDARY

The region selected for this study is in southwestern Alaska, where archaeological and ethnohistoric data suggest that substantial population flux has been occurring for at least the last 4000 years. It is also the area of Alaska with the highest aboriginal population density. Paradoxically, geological (Black 1975, 1976), palynological (Heusser 1963, 1973), and faunal (Yesner 1977b) evidence suggest that the region was generally ecologically stable during the same period (the last 4000 years). As an area of rich marine resources—particularly sea mammals and anadromous fish—southwestern Alaska has attracted diverse populations whose cultures have been transformed by the richness of the marine environment, as well as by contact with previously established cultures. Within the southwestern Alaskan region, an apparent geographical continuum existed so that at either end of the region—the Aleutian Islands to the south and Cook Inlet to the north— long-standing traditions developed with only gradual internal change (Laughlin 1963; Workman 1980), while in the intermediate region of the Alaska Peninsula and Kodiak Island, substantial population flux occurred. This pattern continued well into historic times, and is therefore reflected in both the archaeological and ethnohistoric record, culminating in the modern Eskimo and Aleut populations of the region.

The *Aleuts* have historically occupied the Aleutian Islands and western portions of the Alaska Peninsula, while *Eskimos* have inhabited the eastern peninsula, Kodiak Island, and other portions of the southwestern Alaskan mainland, as well as northern Alaska, adjacent Siberia, Canada, and Greenland. The core of the Aleut population was always centered in the Aleutian Islands, a stormy archipelago that was nevertheless extremely rich in food resources. Those resources included the following:

1. Sea mammals, including resident harbor seals, sea lions, and sea otters, as well as migratory fur seals and whales.
2. Fish, including anadromous salmon (five species) and trout, as well as deep-sea cod, halibut, and intertidal rockfish.
3. Seabirds, including more pelagic forms such as shearwaters and alcids, as well as near-shore and lacustrine waterfowl.
4. Invertebrates, including shellfish, sea urchins, and octopus.

Among the factors responsible for this embarrassment of riches are the following:

1. Nutrient upwelling systems of the eastern Aleutian passes where the warm, deep waters of the Pacific mix with the cold, shallow waters of the Bering Sea shelf. This upwelling supports both migratory sea mammals (fur seals and whales) and seabirds (shearwaters/fulmars and albatrosses) in the eastern Aleutian passes, which in turn supported a particularly large number of Aleuts in the eastern islands (Turner *et al.* 1975; Yesner 1977c).
2. A lack of winter ice, which allows the development of a significant intertidal fauna, particularly sea urchins and various species of shellfish, as well as the sea otters that depend on them.
3. A complex, rocky coastline offering potential habitat for breeding sea lions and seabirds of various types.

This diversity of faunal resources is reflected in the numerous Aleutian midden sites formed during the past 4000 years (Yesner 1977c, 1982).

No such facile analysis can be made for the Alaska Peninsula region to the north and east of the Aleutian Islands (Figure 4.1). Substantial population flux occurred in this region during both prehistoric and historic times, yet a long-term boundary zone was maintained between the Aleuts and the Eskimo groups of the upper peninsula region. The balance of this paper focuses on this boundary between the Eskimos and Aleuts on the Alaska Peninsula, using a mix of archaeological, ethnohistoric, and biological data to attempt to answer the following questions:

1. Can we indeed verify the existence of an Eskimo/Aleut boundary on the Alaska Peninsula for both prehistoric and historic times?
2. What factors account for the original divergence between Aleut and Eskimo populations?
3. What factors helped to maintain the boundary over time?
4. Did the location of the boundary shift over time?
5. Was the boundary located in a resource-rich or resource-poor zone? What resources were abundant or scarce in the area?

After answering these questions, it will be possible to test the hypotheses on boundary maintenance specified earlier. In order to do so, the prehistoric and historic record of the Alaska Peninsula will be reviewed, followed by an examination of biological data in order to develop an ecological model to explain the existence and maintenance of the Aleut/Eskimo boundary.

ALEUT/ESKIMO ORIGINS

Modern Eskimos and Aleuts are descendants of prehistoric populations that originally inhabited the Bering Land Bridge region during late Pleistocene times, populations that have been labeled Bering Sea Mongoloids (Aigner 1978; Laughlin 1963, 1975, 1980). The length of separation of these two major linguistic stocks of the larger EskAleut language family is somewhat a subject of debate, but an antiquity of 6000 years or so may be defensible on linguistic grounds as well as archaeological ones (cf. Dumond 1965, 1968). Evidence that might be offered in support of the latter would be the apparent divergence from a common Paleoarctic core-and-blade tradition ancestor (dating back some 9000 years in the region) to a possibly proto-Eskimo Ocean Bay tradition of Kodiak Island and the Pacific coast of the Alaska Peninsula (D. W. Clark 1974, 1979), and a proto-Aleut "transitional industry" of the eastern Aleutian Islands (Aigner *et al.* 1976; Laughlin 1975) by around 5000–6000 years ago. Both of these tool industries (Ocean Bay and the Aleutian transitional industry) contain elements suggesting their common derivation from earlier core-and-blade industries, as well as similar large, ovate to lanceolate shaped bifacial knives, contracting-stem points, and corelike scrapers (G. H. Clark 1974). Differences, however, involve both stone projectile points and bone harpoon styles, as well as the early appearance (in the Ocean Bay industry) of polished slate artifacts—a classic Eskimo trait—although such polished stone artifacts did not become prevalent until at least Ocean Bay II times (around 4500 years ago).

Accepting this thesis, however, requires that the later, clearly Eskimo materials of southwestern Alaska and elsewhere be confidently accepted as descendants of the somewhat enigmatic Ocean Bay industry (D. W. Clark 1975, 1976, 1979). As an alternative explanation, a separate, later migration from eastern Siberia could have introduced the so-called Arctic Small Tool tradition ("Denbigh" variety) into northwestern Alaska. This tradition, which most scholars agree leads directly to modern Eskimos, appeared in Alaska around 4000–5000 years ago, possibly in response to changing climatic conditions.

A second major question about Eskimo/Aleut origins is have both of these populations always been essentially maritime adapted, or has Eskimo maritime dependence increased over time? Dumond (1975), for example, has suggested that Eskimos began with more of a riverine, mixed economy involving a combination of fishing, caribou hunting, and seasonal sea-mammal hunting; Eskimo prehistory, according to this model, is one of continually increasing focus on marine resources. The distinction between these two models is very much related to the distinction between the Denbigh and pre-Denbigh models of Eskimo origins because, according to some, the later Denbigh culture may have been less maritime oriented than the earlier Ocean Bay culture. Thus, a view that sees Eskimo origins as taking place earlier and further south—among the Ocean Bay people—would also tend to favor a greater antiquity for maritime adaptation among Eskimos. The opposite point of view would not see Eskimo/Aleut contact and boundary formation occurring until at least 4000–5000 years ago on the Alaska Peninsula. Clearly, however, since Thule times (post-A.D. 1000), Eskimos have had a strong maritime orientation involving a focus on sea-mammal hunting and fishing, although not as exclusively maritime oriented as the Aleuts.

LATER ARCHAEOLOGICAL SEQUENCES ON THE UPPER ALASKA PENINSULA

The upper Alaska Peninsula (Figure 4.1) includes the part of the Peninsula subsumed by the three major river drainages of the Bristol Bay coast (the Naknek, Egegik, and Ugashik rivers) and the part of the Pacific coast from Shelikof Strait northward. The archaeology of this area is well known as the result of two decades of research by Don Dumond (University of Oregon) and his students. In this region numerous elements of the Ocean Bay tradition apparently persisted in the form of the Brooks River Strand Phase of the Naknek River drainage—to about 2000 B.C. (Dumond 1981)—and the Takli Period or Pacific Period of the upper Pacific coast of the peninsula— possibly to as late as around 1300 B.C. (G. H. Clark 1977). After this point in time, the Arctic Small Tool tradition makes its appearance in the Naknek and Ugashik river drainages in the form of the Brooks River Gravels Phase and the Ugashik Hilltop Phase, respectively (Dumond et al. 1976; Henn 1978). This was followed successively in both areas by Norton tradition materials after 400 B.C., and western Thule tradition materials after approximately A.D. 1000.[2] As Henn (1978) has cogently pointed out, it is only after about 2000 B.C., when the Arctic Small Tool tradition penetrates the upper peninsula, that the culture history of the peninsula begins to diverge strongly from that of the Aleutian Islands, as represented at the long-occupied Chaluka site. For a time (ca. A.D. 200–1000), the culture history of the upper Pacific coast of the peninsula—in common with Kodiak Island—also took on its own pattern, showing affinities with the Kachemak Bay tradition to the northeast, particularly in the form of bone points and stone lamps. After A.D. 1000 a kind of cultural homogenization apparently occurred throughout the upper peninsula and Kodiak Island regions, as all of these areas took on a western Thule appearance (e.g., as reflected in the widespread use of ground stone).

It is noteworthy that these cultural transitions apparently were correlated with changes in exploitation patterns. On the basis of site locations, artifacts, and fragmentary faunal remains from both the Naknek and Ugashik drainages, it is possible to conclude that the earliest inhabitants of the

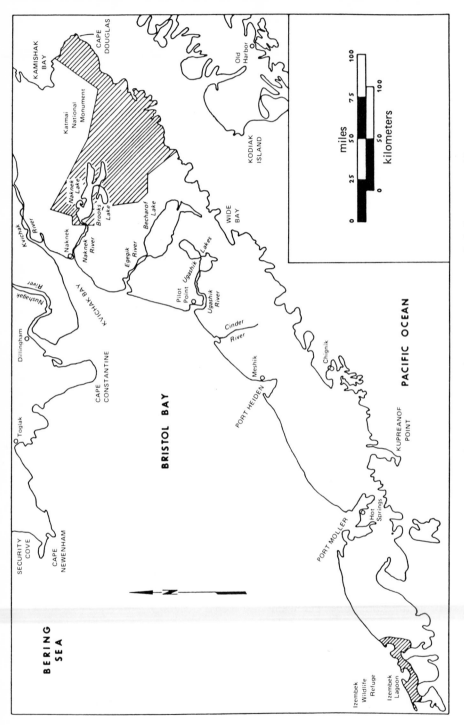

Figure 4.1   The Alaska Peninsula and vicinity. (Copyright © 1976, University of Alaska Press; used by permission).

peninsula were primarily caribou hunters (Dumond 1981). Similar evidence suggests that local Arctic Small Tool populations were the first to focus intensively on fishing, while Norton populations may have been the first to focus intensively on sea-mammal hunting, with a shift in site locations toward the modern coast. This is evidently even more true of the succeeding Thule period.

ARCHAEOLOGICAL MATERIALS OF THE LOWER ALASKA PENINSULA

The archaeology of the lower Alaska Peninsula—as befits a boundary zone—is difficult to place within either the classical Eskimo framework of the upper peninsula or the Aleutian tradition that postdates 2000 B.C. Unfortunately, there are no sites in the lower peninsula that predate this period of clear peninsula/Aleutian cultural divergence. Sites that have been excavated often were occupied during vastly different time spans. In fact, there are few sites in general in the lower Peninsula region (the reasons for which should be evident shortly). Perhaps even more frustrating is the fact that many of the archaeological assemblages that do exist are essentially noncomparable; for example, the important sequences from Izembek and Chignik (at the base of the peninsula) have little or no preservation of bone.

With this proviso in mind, the known archaeology from surveys and excavations on the lower Alaska Peninsula can be summarized by area in terms of cultural affiliations, beginning with the base of the peninsula and proceeding eastward. It should be noted that surveys and excavations in the region have generally been spotty rather than systematic, and the resulting uneven coverage tends to reflect the few areas of specific interest to archaeologists who have worked there.

Izembek

McCartney (1974) excavated some 2300 stone artifacts (exclusive of débitage) from a series of house pits on Izembek Lagoon, on the Bering Sea coast at the base of the peninsula (Figure 4.1). More than 10% of all of the artifacts at the site were weights or sinkers (McCartney 1974), testifying to the importance of fishing in this large shallow bay. The site, which dates to about A.D. 1000, is linked with the upper peninsula sites in terms of the prevalence of ground slate (approximately 30% of the collection). The use of ground slate during this time period is characteristic of the peninsular region in general, and of the easternmost Aleutian Islands (e.g., at Akun; see Turner and Turner 1974). Also found in both Izembek and the upper peninsula sites—but not in the Aleutians—is coarse, gravel-tempered pottery (Yarborough 1974). On the other hand, the artifacts made of chipped rather than ground stone—including a variety of knife and projectile point syles— are more similar to those from the eastern Aleutians than the upper peninsula. House depressions suggesting temporary (skin?) shelters appear to be unique to the region, but an excavated circular house with whalebone rafters seems to be more related to a number of similar houses known from the Aleutians (e.g., Aigner 1978) than to anything known from the peninsula. An exception here is that the bone house excavated by McCartney had an interior hearth, a pattern well known from the upper peninsula but uncharacteristic of the Aleutians.

Chignik

Dumond *et al.* (1976) excavated two sites of differing age from the Chignik region of the Pacific coast, east of Izembek (Figure 4.2). The earlier of these two sites, dating to circa 200 B.C., produced a number of projectile point styles such as fishtail points that have their closest similarities to the Izembek materials. However, the site lacks pottery or ground stone (as well as bone). The more recent site, dating to around A.D. 1400, did produce a number of ground-stone items.

Port Moller

Excavations have been undertaken at the Hot Springs site near Port Moller (Figure 4.2) since 1928 by both American and Japanese teams (Okada 1980; Okada and Okada 1974; Weyer 1930; Workman 1966). The bulk of the occupation here apparently spanned the period from 1600 to 1000 B.C., but there are components that date as late as A.D. 1340. Although the sample of materials postdating A.D. 500 is smaller, some of the differences from the earlier period are significant: an increase in fishing weights and sinkers, as well as the appearance of toggling harpoons and slit salmon-spear barbs, all testify to an increased importance of fishing. Ground stome implements also make their appearance—albeit in a limited fashion—during this period. Chipped stone materials from the site show their strongest affinities to the earlier of the two Chignik sites, but the salmon spears, leister prongs, and toggling harpoons suggest that linkages to Thule materials from the north are also strong (McCartney 1969). As at Izembek, dwellings at Port Moller show affinities both with Aleutian and Eskimo house styles. They have stone-lined shallow "drains" like Aleutian houses (Aigner 1978), but also have clay bowls like upper peninsula Eskimo houses (Okada 1980).

Port Heiden

During the summer of 1981, the author undertook an archaeological survey of the Port Heiden region of the north-central peninsula, the only major invagination of the northern peninsula coastline between Port Moller and the upper peninsula drainages (Figure 4.1). Two sites were examined in detail: one at the current village of Meshik or Port Heiden; the other at Reindeer Creek, known locally as North River (Figure 4.2). The site at Meshik village contained a relatively thin archaeological horizon above dune sand, volcanic ash, and pumice deposits (Figure 4.3), which produced a number of prehistoric bone tools as well as obviously historic metal and ceramic items. A large amount of seal and caribou bone was also recovered (Table 4.1). Unfortunately, no stone materials were uncovered except for a few basalt flakes. The bone tools (Figure 4.4) included a number of harpoons that show a striking similarity to those recovered by Dumond from the late prehistoric (A.D. 1470 to 1720) Pavik Phase of the Paugvik site at the mouth of the Naknek River, particularly items identified as fishing harpoons (Figure 4.5A). The slotted harpoon (Figure 4.5B) shows some similarity to items both from Paugvik (Pavik Phase) as well as late materials from Port Moller (Okada 1980: Fig. 3). Other bone items with strong linkages to the north include bipointed pins and bone spoons with handles and incised decorations; similar items appeared at Paugvik and in the River Phase materials from the Ugashik River mouth, dated to 335 ± 60 years B.P. (A.D. 1650 ± 60) (Dumond et al. 1976; Henn 1978). These materials can all easily be encompassed within a late Western Thule horizon, while their Aleutian affinities are less obvious.

At North River, a 5 × 5 m pentagonally shaped house depression was discovered that had an eroding but still visible entranceway feature composed of charred logs and postholes (Figure 4.5). Also found were two storage (?) pits and an interior hearth containing a large amount of charred seal and caribou bone (Figure 4.6). The house—which dated to A.D. 1490 ± 50 (Beta 4241)—is more similar to Dumond's Brooks River Bluff Phase houses from the Naknek drainage of about the same date. Overall, the closest similarities of these two sites—in terms of both artifacts and house styles—are to late prehistoric materials from the Naknek drainages.

Unangashik

Related to the Port Heiden materials are some collected just below Port Heiden at Unangashik, near the mouth of the Unangashik River, south of Cape Stroganoff. Like Meshik, this was a village that was abandoned after

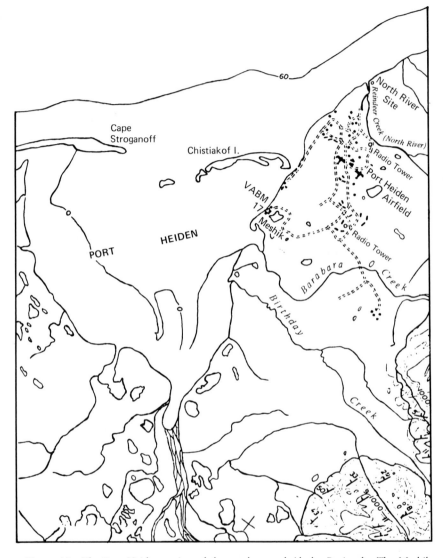

Figure 4.2 The Port Heiden region of the north-central Alaska Peninsula. The Meshik village site is located at the notation "VABM" to the west of Meshik village. The North River site is located at the mouth of North River or Reindeer Creek, north of the Port Heiden Airfield.

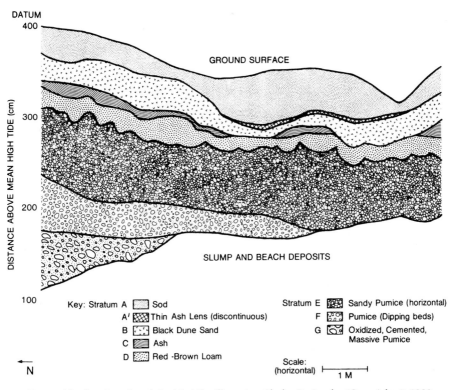

Figure 4.3 Stratigraphy of the Meshik village site, Alaska Peninsula. (Copyright © 1983, Atechiston, Inc.; used by permission.)

an epidemic, but 100 years earlier (in 1819). Much of the material collected here by Dumond was apparently undiagnostic (Alaska State Files n.d.), but overall the historic/prehistoric mixed assemblage is probably related to that of Meshik itself. Between Unangashik and Port Moller is practically an archaeologist's no-man's land, with only small, late historic settlements located at the mouth of the Illnek and Bear Rivers (although a larger site may be present at the mouth of Bear Lake; see Okada 1980).

Finally, it is necessary to look at the available biological data for prehistoric northern peninsula populations. The only skeletal series excavated so far have come from the Hot Springs site at Port Moller. Primarily on the basis of discrete osteological features, Laughlin (1966) identified two crania from the site as "Paleo-Aleuts," while Okada and Yamaguchi (1975, 1976)—using similar criteria—have identified five additional crania as more closely related to Eskimo than Aleut. The north-central Alaska Peninsula population therefore appears to have been transitional in both material culture and morphological traits.

Table 4.1
Faunal Remains at Meshik Village

	Rank order	Numbers of specimens	Percentage of total
Species			
Harbor seal	1	94	27.1
Caribou	2	51	14.7
Fox (*Vulpes*)	3	18	5.2
Walrus	4	14	4.0
Porpoise/orca	5	7	2.0
Beaver	6	5	1.4
Moose	7	4	1.2
Whale (species unidentified)	8	3	0.9
Sea lion (*Eumetopias*)	9	2	0.6
Bear (*U. arctos*)	10	1	0.3
Identified mammalian remains		199	57.3
Small mammal fragments		45	13.0
Large mammal fragments		45	13.0
Unidentified mammalian remains		90	26.0
Subtotal: mammal bone remains		289	83.3
Subtotal: bird bone remains		58	16.7
Total bone remains		347	100.0

In sum, early Eskimo penetrations into the upper peninsula region by Arctic Small Tool populations seem not to have affected the lower peninsula region at all. The Norton tradition penetration of the area was only slightly more extensive, as possibly reflected in some similarities in chipped stone projectile point styles with the lower peninsula. Not until the second millennium A.D., however, did Eskimo culture definitely penetrate the lower peninsula, as reflected in the archaeology of Izembek, Chignik, Port Moller, and Port Heiden. When this occurred, a certain degree of cultural homogenization took place, so that it is difficult to discriminate statistically between late prehistoric cultural assemblages of the Alaska Peninsula and areas immediately to the north and west (Dumond *et al.* 1975). However, while the lower peninsula did partake in some fashion of the Thule influence, it is equally clear that such influences only imperfectly penetrated the region and possibly did not reach beyond the easternmost Aleutian Islands until just before contact times. While the boundary obviously allowed a certain degree of penetration, the wonder is that it remained so strong throughout prehistoric times (Henn 1978).

A final comment needs to be made concerning the possible role of various geological factors on site distribution and preservation. Although, as noted, environmental stability was generally true of the region during the last few

thousand years, some degree of coastal erosion has been continuously occurring, particularly in the low-lying north-central peninsula region. This is
probably not a great factor in interpreting the earlier prehistoric record
since, as Dumond has argued, occupation of the coast was itself apparently
rather late, at least in the norther upper peninsula region. However, few
inland settlements of earlier periods have yet been located (although a new

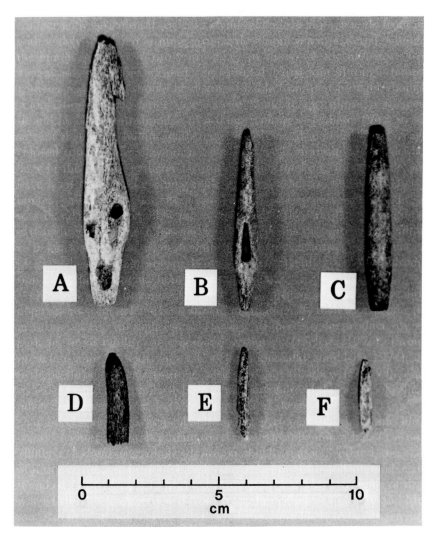

Figure 4.4 Bone tools from the Meshik village site, Alaska Peninsula. A, slit-barbed fishing
harpoon; B, slotted harpoon; C, D, simple bone points; E, F, bipointed pins.

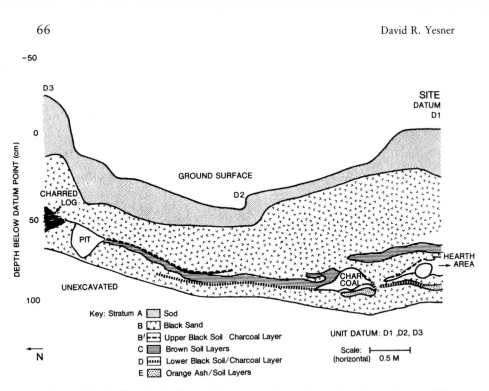

Figure 4.5 Profile of the North River site, Alaska Peninsula. (Copyright © 1983, Atechiston, Inc.; used by permission.)

site on Bear Lake north of Port Moller may be an exception; see Okada 1980). Even for more recent periods, it is unlikely that erosional factors are so different along the north coast of the peninsula as to have produced the observed site distribution pattern, particularly since it does appear to correlate with historic demographic data. Another possibility is that chronic regional vulcanism may have obscured sites, producing the observed distribution pattern. Although there were certainly many prehistoric volcanic eruptions in the northern peninsula area as indicated by various ash horizons, most of the latter are relatively thin, and thus the obscuring of sites by ashfall is unlikely. Massive pumice deposits are also found throughout the area, but these are generally quite ancient and have been reworked by marine, riverine, and even glacial mechanisms.

If geological factors such as vulcanism have not obscured the archaeological record, did they affect the prehistoric inhabitants enough to create a no-man's land at different time periods (such as just before Russian contact)? Dumond's (1979) data suggest that even the tremendous explosion at Katmai in 1912 did not do more than temporarily affect local wildlife; it apparently did not even substantially affect local salmon runs. However, it

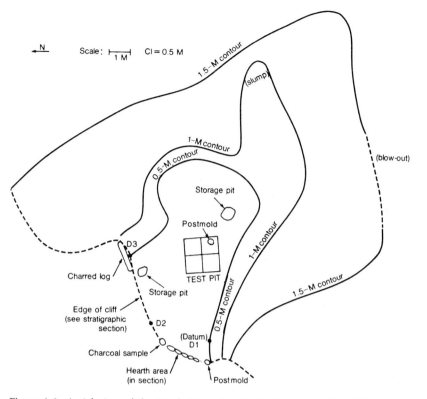

Figure 4.6 Aerial view of the North River site, Alaska Peninsula. (Copyright © 1983, Atechiston, Inc.; used by permission.)

did result in the displacement and southward movement of the historic Eskimo village of Katmai to its present location at Perryville (south of Chignik)—an area that was formerly Aleut! On the Bristol Bay side of the peninsula, the effects of vulcanism may have been more muted because of being a greater distance from the volcanoes and a greater likelihood of westerly winds; relatively thin ash horizons are found in the Meshik site stratigraphy, for example. However, these effects cannot be discounted, and should probably be integrated into the ecological model so that it incompasses more than just resource densities and distributions.

ETHNOHISTORY

Although place names are indicated on maps as early as 1791, the earliest apparent record of ethnic distributions on the Alaska Peninsula is an 1863 map by Wehrman, a Russian naval officer, found in Tikhmenev (1863) and recently reproduced with the previously unpublished notes of Klebnikov (Lyapunova and Federova 1979). This map shows a boundary just east of Port Moller on the north coast of the Peninsula—at 160° west longitude—connecting across the peninsula to Kupreanof Point on the south coast—at about 159° west longitude. This basically corresponds to Pinart's (1873) conclusion that the easternmost Aleut settlement on the south coast was just east of Kupreanof Point, west of Kuiukta Bay, while the westernmost Eskimo settlement was just west of the same bay. Dall's (1870) map also places the Eskimo/Aleut boundary at 159° west longitude, which was reiterated by Hodge (1907) and more recently by Dumond (1979) (Figure 4.7). Petroff (1884) and Schanz (1893) apparently placed the official U.S. census boundary closer to the Ugashik drainage on the northern coast of the peninsula. However, these authors are remarkably consistent in their attribution of the boundary position and may in fact be drawing on the same sources.

Above the Aleut/Eskimo boundary, Wehrman's 1863 map apparently differentiates a Peninsular Eskimo group that lived as far north as Cook Inlet along the Pacific coast, but was found on the Bristol Bay coast only as far north as the Egegik River drainage. Above this—occupying the Naknek River drainage, for example—were Aglegmiut Eskimos, a separate group clearly identified in the Russian records and known to have had extensive interrelations with the Russians. Davydov (1807) also speaks of the natives of the Ugashik River drainage—the "Ugashintzy"—as a distinct group from those farther north, and Tikhmenev (1863) refers to a "Ugashik" tribe. Schanz (1893:93) also refers to the "Aleut half-bred type found in the neighborhood of Ugashik, a people who speak a language with marked dialectic differences from the Eskimo, and who show the peculiar domestic traits which characterize the inhabitants of the Aleutian Islands." Furthermore, Dumond (n.d.) reports that while Alaskan Russian church records suggest that the settlements at the mouth of the Naknek and Egegik River drainages were both approximately 75% Aglegmiut, the Ugashik River mouth settlement was identified as being only 10% Aglegmiut but approximately 85% "Aleut" (probably in this case referring to original Peninsular Eskimos of the "Ugashintzy" variety), echoing an earlier statements by Petroff (1884).[3] Dall (1870), however, drawing on Holmberg (1856), places the Aglegmiut all the way west to the 159° boundary. Part of the problem here is one of historic migration. Wrangell (1839) and Klebnikov (Lyapunova and Federova 1979) indicate that the Aglegmiut had moved on to the northern peninsula as part of a southward expansion out of their original homeland, displacing southward the original inhabitants of the Naknek–Kvichak–Nushagak River region, who then became the "Ugashintzy" of Davydov. Unfortunately there is also a terminological confusion in some of the early nineteenth-century records between the "Ougagook" (now Egegik) and "Oogazhik" rivers.

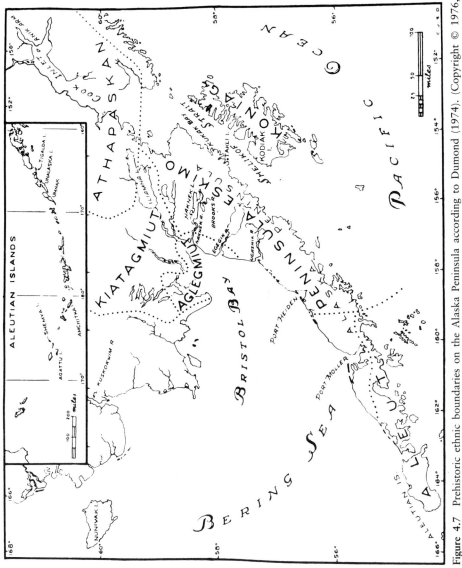

Figure 4.7 Prehistoric ethnic boundaries on the Alaska Peninsula according to Dumond (1974). (Copyright © 1976, University of Alaska Press; used by permission.)

Table 4.2

Size of Northern Alaska Peninsula Villages

Native villages	Maximum population (1869–1888)	Average population (1869–1888)
Aglegmiut villages		
Paugvik (Naknek River)	255	180
Egegik	120	80
Peninsular Eskimo villages		
Ugashik	252	190
Savonoski	162	135
Unangashik	190	94
Meshik	74	38

Source: Dumond n.d.; Petroff 1884; Schanz 1893.

In reviewing all of the evidence, Dumond (1974) suggested that the area of the northern peninsula coast west of Port Heiden (i.e., Meshik and Unangashik) was essentially devoid of human population at the time of European (Russian) contact. This does appear to be supported by one of the earliest maps of the peninsula region (Efimov 1791) that shows the westernmost (permanent?) settlement on the northern coast at the mouth of the Ugashik River. This would appear to substantiate the lack of very late prehistoric (post A.D. 1350) dates at Port Moller, as well as McCartney's (1974) contention that Izembek was not utilized during the last few hundred years before contact. Even nineteenth-century demographic data (Dumond n.d.; Petroff 1884; Schanz 1893) suggest that villages closer to the boundary zone (Meshik, Unangashik) were on the average one-fourth to one-half the size of villages at the head of the bay (Paugvik, Ugashik) (Table 4.2). By the early twentieth century, however, small sites had been established west of Port Heiden at the mouths of the Ilnik and Bear rivers (Alaska State Files n.d.).

In sum, ethnohistoric data from the Alaska Peninsula suggest that a definite boundary existed between Eskimo and Aleut peoples, although its exact position may have varied somewhat. On the northern coast of the peninsula, there was apparently substantial population density east of the boundary, while only scanty populations may have occupied or even exploited (perhaps on a seasonal basis) areas to the west of the boundary. Why this may have been the case will be examined subsequently. Although most archaeologists have doubted that a highly fixed Eskimo/Aleut boundary existed, it must be admitted that (1) Peninsular populations have retained a surprising degree of geographical coherence, and that (2) Aleuts and (surviving?) Eskimos are linguistically distinct. Both points suggest that the boundary was real, although they do not indicate what factors may have been responsible for maintaining that boundary.

As a final note, it is interesting to observe that much of these relationships within the Alaska Peninsula are maintained today (cf. Yesner 1983b). For example, genealogical data from Port Heiden (Brelsford n.d.) suggest that its strongest linkage by marriage is with Aleuts of the Port Moller/Nelson Lagoon region, as well as with Chignik across the pass, while it has only secondary (although evidently increasing) linkages to the north with Eskimo settlements at Pilot Point (at the Ugashik mouth) and Egegik (at the mouth of the Egegik River).

MODELING THE NORTHERN PENINSULA

By now it should be clear that on the northern Alaska Peninsula a broad transitional zone existed between the Aleut and Eskimo population systems—the boundaries of which cannot be precisely defined in space and were variable over time. The Aleut population system to the west was almost exclusively maritime in orientation (Laughlin 1972; McCartney 1975), while Eskimo population systems of the upper peninsula and beyond exploited a diverse mix of marine, riverine, and terrestrial fauna. In what way did ecological factors, then, affect—if not determine—the nature of the boundary between the two population systems? An answer requires a detailed analysis of the ecological features of the northern peninsula region, including the oceanic, terrestrial, and riverine/lacustrine environmental systems.

Oceanic System

The southeastern Bering Sea shelf is one of the richest marine zones in the world, with primary productivity ranging up to 200 mgC/m³/day in summer. The productivity of this zone greatly affected the subsistence base of both the northern Alaska Peninsula and eastern Aleutian Islands (where most prehistoric settlements were on the north, or Bering Sea, side of the islands). Faunal evidence from prehistoric sites in the eastern Aleutians (Yesner 1977a) and Cook Inlet to the north (Yesner 1977b) suggests that the regional marine system may have been relatively stable for the last few thousand years, with only limited environmental change having taken place. However, there is substantial variation in the productivity of the marine ecosystem even within the southeastern Bering Sea/Bristol Bay region.

The inner portion of Bristol Bay—roughly inside a line connecting Port Heiden on the Peninsula with Cape Newenham (Figure 4.1)—is dominated by estuarine phenomena, while the outer bay has a much more oceanic character. Differences in circulation patterns within the bay become well established during the summer (ice-free season), when the outer bay is dominated by a simple, counterclockwise gyre that brings in an eastward flow of nutrient-rich waters from the mixing systems of the eastern Aleutian passes (Straty 1977). Northeast of Port Heiden, the circulation becomes much more complex, with the eastern segment of the gyre mixing with the brackish waters of the estuarine inner bay (Figure 4.1). Here there is considerable freshwater inflow, estimated at 112×10^9 m^3/yr (USACE 1974). These two systems meet east of Port Heiden (Straty 1977). In general, as one proceeds northeastward, the nutrient flow from the eastern Aleutian region drops off, to be replaced by a different flow of nutrients from the suspended fine-grained sediment load carried by runoff from the three major river systems of the upper peninsula region. This occurs even during the winter, when freshwater ice emptied into the bay carries considerable sediment loads. In the north-central peninsula region (i.e., between the Ugashik River and Port Moller), neither nutrient source prevails (although lagoons and minor bays contribute somewhat to local productivities and result in relatively distinctive local waters) (Straty 1977). In addition, the tidal range of the north-central peninsula is from 2.3 m to 2.6 m while that of the inner bay region between the Ugahsik and Naknek rivers ranges from about 4 to 6 m (AOCS 1981); thus tidal effects, which further increase productivity, are much more pronounced in the inner bay. To compound this, the tidal current in the north-central peninsula averages only about 50 cm/sec, being stronger both in the outer bay (ca. 100 cm/sec) and in the inner bay (ca. 130 cm/sec) (USACE 1974). This occurs largely because of the juxtaposition of the coast with the Bristol Bay–Nushagak Lowlands in this region between the Ugashik River and Port Moller (USACE 1974). The net result of all of the foregoing is that coastal productivities are relatively more limited in the north-central peninsular region than on either side of it. These central waters are probably more variable in productivity as well.

During winter ice forms in Bristol Bay, up to a maximum of 70% ice coverage (USACE 1974). Bristol Bay lies at the southern boundary of true seasonal ice. However, the ice coverage is, again, very unevenly distributed in the bay. In the inner bay ice coverage (from December through April) ranges from 50 to 70% (USACE 1974). At the same time, the outer bay is generally ice-free (i.e., less than 10%) with only scattered ice floes found as far south as Port Moller. The north-central peninsula, however, is a highly variable "tension zone" that fluctuates between 10% and 40% ice coverage (30-year records). While tidal amplitudes are often sufficient to break up shore-fast ice, solid floes and drift-pack ice do occur at least as far south as Port Heiden (USACE 1974). It is estimated that 1 out of every 5 years is a "heavy ice" year in which ice coverage along the north-central peninsula is substantially increased. This year-to-year variability in the southern extent of the Bering Sea ice pack has been attributed to a 3°C range in annual mean sea–surface temperature in the southern Bering Sea (Niebauer 1981) as well as to variability in the pattern of fall and winter storm tracks in the southern Bering Sea (Overland 1981). Often heavy or light ice years occur in at least pairs because they result from longer-than-1-year climatic fluctuations (Niebauer 1981; Overland 1981). Clearly, wave action and wind stress as well as temperature are involved in determining the actual position of the southern margin of the ice; these are highly variable in the northern peninsula area, though persistent winds of 35–75 km/hr (20–40 knots) are frequently the case.

These oceanographic patterns have consequences for the abundance and distribution of marine biota in the northern peninsula region. For example, while the average standing stock (the amount of organic matter in the form of phytoplankton measureable at any point in time) is approximately 1.25 mg/m^3 of chlorophyll for all of Bristol Bay, that for the inner bay is 3.25 mg/m^3 of chlorophyll. Furthermore, during the late spring—as the growing season begins—the inner bay additionally benefits from phytoplankton blooms that develop near the bottom surface of the sea ice. This provides a significant addition to the production where ice conditions are consistent from year to year (i.e., in the upper reaches of the bay). On the other hand, the far outer bay contains a greater biomass of zooplankton. Summer zooplankton volumes (in m^3/m^3 sea water) average .2 for the inner bay, but .5 for the outer bay (USACE 1974).

What consequences do these patterns have for the marine biota that humans can exploit for food? The latter fall into four main categories: intertidal invertebrates, marine mammals, seabirds, and ocean fish (anadromous fish will be discussed later under the "Riverine/Lacustrine Zone"). Of these, the first two categories are by far the most important.

Intertidal Invertebrates

As was suggested, the ice-free Aleutians provide an ideal environment for the development of intertidal invertebrates, including mollusks and echinoderms (sea urchins). The same is true of the lower portion of the Bristol Bay coast of the peninsula, although the mud flats and sand beaches of this region support razor claims (*Siliqua patula*), giant cockles (*Clinocardium nuttalii*), butter clams (*Saxidomus giganteus*), surf clams (*Spisula polynyma*), and littleneck clams (*Protothaca staminea*) rather than the sea urchins, limpets, mussels, and chitons of the rocky Aleutian shore (USACE 1974). The former species are all well represented at the Hot Springs site near Port Moller (Kotani 1980), but are not prevalent in sites north of this region. This is because as one moves north into the zone of solid winter ice, the scouring effect of shorefast ice on tidal flats and coastal lagoons both abrades any attached marine organisms and erodes the mudflats and sand beaches where burrowing mollusks might be able to persist. Low temperatures and sunlight penetration also play a role here. In the north-central peninsula some shellfish species survive (butter clams, surf clams, and the shoft-shell clam, *Mya arenaria*), but in general both species' abundance and diversity are reduced; and the variability in both the extent of winter ice and summer coastal productivity make this resource unpredictable at best (Hughes and Nelson 1979). At the same time, echinoderm biomass drops off from about 50 g/m^2 to essentially zero north of Port Moller (Ivanov 1964).

Sea Mammals

Undoubtedly more important to human subsistence in the region than shellfish are sea mammals, but many of the same factors apply to understanding their abundance and distribution.

Sea Otters

Sea otters, while prevalent throughout the Aleutians, are found on the northern Alaska Peninsula only as far north as Port Moller, where densities are only about 4 individuals km^2 (USACE 1974). Two factors seem to prevent their distribution north of Port Moller: the absence of offshore strandflats and kelp beds necessary both for the production of sea urchins (one of their primary foods) and for their reproduction; and the presence of winter ice, of which they are evidently intolerant.

Walrus, Spotted Seals, Ribbon Seals

In contrast to the sea otter, these three species are generally tied to the edge of the seasonal sea-ice pack, and are associated with the southern portion of the ice front between fringe and pack ice. Their abundance is therefore limited to the area along the northern coast of the peninsula south of the pack-ice region, and is highly variable, depending on the extent and timing of sea-ice formation in given years. This is particularly true of walrus, the southern terminus whose distribution is along the north peninsula coast. However, walrus were a significant (if minor) component of the sea-mammal portion of the faunal assemblages at both the Port Moller and Port Heiden sites. The Nushagagmiut of northern Bristol Bay—and to some degree the Aglegmiut—were known to be involved with walrus hunting (Lyapunova and Federova 1979).

Fur Seals and Baleen Whales

These migratory species tend to remain only in the outer portion of the bay because of their dependency on the nutrient upwelling deriving from the shelfbreak and particularly the eastern Aleutian passes. In addition, only two species of baleen whales—the gray and minke whales—are tolerant of the shallow, turbid Bristol Bay shelf waters, and other species tend to remain in the outer bay (Braham and Dalheim 1982).

Sea Lions

The Steller sea lion (*Eumetopias jubata*) is also largely confined to the outer bay, south of Nelson Lagoon, however, there is a different reason: the lack of rocky habitat for "hauling grounds" north of this region. The absence of such haul-outs presents the seal lions from wintering in the region and from establishing breeding rookeries (Braham and Dalheim 1982).

Harbor Seals

The harbor seal (*Phoca vitulina*) is both highly abundant and ubiquitous throughout the bay, with no essential differences in distribution. Largest concentrations are found on sand bars and islands (Everitt and Braham 1979).

Seabirds

Seabirds show a somewhat similar trend to sea mammals. The alcids (murres, murrelets, auklets, guillemots, puffins) and gulls (including kittwakes) are the most numerous seabirds in the region and are distributed throughout the north peninsula coastal region (Sowls *et al.* 1978). The third and fourth largest groups, however—the petrels and shearwater/fulmars— are found almost exclusively west of Port Moller since they are dependent upon the enormous phytoplankton generated by the eastern Aleutian upwelling systems (Bartonek and Gibson 1972). The same was probably true of the short-tailed albatross, an important bird in prehistoric times (Yesner 1976) but now locally extinct. Oystercatchers—which depend on both shellfish and rocky habitat—are also rare above the Izembek region of the peninsula. One reflection of these trends is found in the faunal record of north peninsula coast archaeological sites. For example, while the Hot Springs site at Port Moller contains nearly equal frequencies of seabirds and waterfowl—the former including significant numbers of shearwaters and fulmars as well as alcids and gulls (Yesner, unpublished data, 1978)—the Meshik village site at Port Heiden shows predominantly waterfowl, with seabirds being primarily alcids. Obviously, the diversity of seabird resources is more limited in this region, and the waterfowl that are harvested are generally only a seasonal, migratory resource.

Interior Zone

The second of the major habitat zones for peninsular populations was the interior, an area virtually unexploited in the Aleutians. Caribou, moose, and brown bear—the three most important terrestrial species on the peninsula—are found only on Unimak Island in the Aleutians. Even on the peninsula, however, the distribution of these species is by no means uniform. Moose (*Alces alces*), for example, are found quite extensively in the upper peninsula region, but their distribution extends only as far south as Port Moller, and they are relatively scanty south of the Ugashik region. The same is also generally true of beaver (*Castor canadensis*) and marten (*Martes martes*), basically boreal species. Caribou (*Rangifer tarandus*) are distributed throughout the area, but their major herds are concentrated in the Egegik River region to the north, and in the area south of Port Moller (AOCS 1981). Migratory caribou are found in the Port Heiden region of the Peninsula, for example, but can usually be exploited only at a distance from the coast.

Riverine/Lacustrine Zone

By far the most important resource in the Bristol Bay region—today as in the past—is anadromous fish, primarily five species of salmon (*Oncorhynchus* spp.). These species spawn in large numbers in the streams at the headwaters of the bay, but the different migratory pattern of each species determines its availability in the larger region of the Bristol Bay coast. Table 4.3 shows the distribution of fish runs by river system on the northern peninsula coast, while Tables 4.4 and 4.5 indicate the average escapement of salmon into each of those river systems over a 15-year period.

King (Chinook) Salmon

This large species is probably the most evenly distributed on the northern peninsula. Major spawning systems are found in the Naknek River and Nelson Lagoon, while minor systems are found in the Port Heiden, Bear River, and Izembek Lagoon regions (Tables 4.3, 4.5). However, the minor systems show a zero escapement on the average of once every 3 years (Table 4.6) so that king salmon are not a totally reliable resource in the north-central peninsula region (ADFG 1977).

Red (Sockeye) Salmon

This smaller species is the most abundant and reliable in the Bristol Bay region. Nearly 70% of these fish spawn in the Naknek and Egegik river

Table 4.3

Distribution of Major Salmon Runs on the Northern Alaska Peninsula

Drainage area	King salmon	Red salmon	Chum salmon	Pink salmon	Silver salmon
Naknek River	X	X		X	
Egegik River		X			
Ugashik River		X			
Port Heiden	X				X
Ilnik					X
Bear River	X	X			
Port Moller			X		X
Nelson Lagoon	X	X	X		X
Izembek Lagoon	X		X		

Source: ADFG 1977; Straty 1975, 1977.

systems of the upper peninsula (Straty 1975) (Table 4.4). Another important spawning area is the Bear River region; smaller runs are found at Ugashik River and Nelson Lagoon. Red salmon are, however, not harvestable in any quantity in the north-central peninsula region between the Ugashik and Bear rivers; even today, residents of Port Heiden go north to Pilot Point (Ugashik) or Egegik to fish for red salmon.

Dog (Chum) Salmon

This species is not as abundant in the region in general, and only runs for about three weeks. None of the major river systems of the upper peninsula

Table 4.4

Average Escapement for Red (Sockeye) Salmon, Alaska Peninsula
(1960–1975)

Drainage area	Number of fish (thousands)	Percentage of total
Naknek River	930	35.8
Egegik River	850	32.7
Ugashik River	490	18.8
Cinder River	3.6	0.1
Port Heiden	11.3	0.4
Ilnik	23.3	0.9
Bear River	221.7	8.5
Port Moller	—	—
Nelson Lagoon	60.5	2.3
Izembek Lagoon	13.4	0.5
Total	ca. 2600	

Source: ADFG 1977.

Table 4.5

Average Escapement for King and Chum Salmon, Alaska Peninsula (1961–1975)

Drainage area	King salmon (thousands)	Percentage of total	Chum salmon (thousands)	Percentage of total
Naknek River	3.8	27.4	—	—
Cinder River	1.3	9.4	2.3	1.9
Port Heiden	1.1	8.0	7.2	6.0
Ilnik	0.1	0.7	2.3	1.9
Bear River	1.4	10.1	1.8	1.5
Port Moller	—	—	23.7	19.7
Nelson Lagoon	5.0	35.7	13.1	10.9
Izembek Lagoon	1.2	8.6	69.8	58.1
Total	13.9		120.2	

Source: ADFG 1977.

have significant runs of chum salmon (Table 4.3). Small numbers are produced in the Port Moller region and in the outlying areas of Nelson and
Izembek lagoons (ADFG 1977). They are essentially unavailable in the
north-central peninsula streams—representing only 11.3% of the total
run—(Table 4.5) and show a zero escapement on an average of once every 5
years (Table 4.6).

Pink (Humpback) Salmon

This species is even more poorly represented in the Bristol Bay region.
Approximately 90% of the fish are found in the Bechevin Bay region at the
southwestern tip of the peninsula (Straty 1975). The exception is the
Naknek River region of the upper peninsula, where significant pink salmon
runs are found in even-numbered years.

Silver (Coho) Salmon

This species is harvested late in the season. The most productive area for
this species is in the Port Moller/Nelson Lagoon region, although the Port
Heiden/Ilnik region also has a secondary run, and much smaller runs are
present in the Naknek, Egegik, and Ugashik river drainages.

Clearly, these data show that the Naknek River on the upper peninsula
and the Port Moller region of the lower peninsula have both the most
productive and diverse fisheries. Lower-species diversity and smaller escape-
ments tend to be the rule for the rivers of the north-central peninsula
(Cinder River, Port Heiden, Ilnik, Bear River).

Table 4.6

Percentage of Years with Escapement of Less than 1000 Fish
(1961–1975)

Drainage	King salmon	Chum salmon
Cinder River	33.3	25.0%
Port Heiden	13.3	12.5
Ilnik	66.7	43.8
Bear River	13.3	6.3
Nelson Lagoon	—	—
Izembek Lagoon	46.7	—

Source: ADFG 1977.

In sum, the ecological data from the northern Alaska Peninsula (Table 4.7) suggest the following:

1. While nutrients from large river systems are pumped into the head of Bristol Bay, and Aleutian upwelling adds to the nutrients in the western portion of the peninsula, the north-central peninsula does not particularly benefit from either source, at least in a predictable fashion. This has an effect on summer phytoplankton blooms, in turn affecting the availability of anadromous fish, seabirds, and some sea mammals (e.g., fur seals and whales).

2. While the head of the bay has 50–70% winter ice coverage and its associated populations of walrus (and some ribbon and spotted seals), the lower peninsula did not benefit from this resource. However, ice scouring in the intertidal zone would have limited shellfish resources in the upper peninsula while this would not have been the case in the lower peninsula. In the intermediate zone of the north-central peninsula, the availability of both types of resources (walrus and shellfish) would have been again largely unpredictable.

3. The lack of a complex, rocky coastline in the upper peninsula reduced the availability of habitat for both sea otters and sea lions in this area, while the shallowness of the Bering Sea shelf prohibited immigration of all but two species of baleen whales into inner Bristol Bay.

4. Caribou herds were concentrated in the upper and lower peninsula regions, with only smaller herds in the central peninsula, while more boreal species such as moose and beaver were found primarily on the upper peninsula.

Of all the potentially available resources, then, only harbor seals (*Phoca vitulina*) and king salmon were both abundant and reasonably predictable

Table 4.7

Summary of Resource Availability, Northern Alaska Peninsula

Lower Peninsula	North-central Peninsula	Upper Peninsula
Some shellfish	Few shellfish, low diversity	Fewer shellfish, lower diversity
Sea otters present	Occasional sea otter	No sea otters
No walrus	Occasional walrus	Walrus available
No ribbon or spotted seal	Few ribbon or spotted seals	Few ribbon or spotted seals
Sea lions present	No sea lions	No sea lions
Fur seals present	No fur seals	No fur seals
Harbor seals present	Harbor seals present	Harbor seals present
Baleen whales present	Gray/minke whales only	Gray/minke whales only
Caribou herd	Some migratory caribou	Small caribou herd
No moose	Few moose	Moose abundant
Few beaver	Few beaver	Beaver abundant
Shearwaters/fulmars/ albatrosses/petrels	No shearwaters/fulmars/ albatrosses/petrels	No shearwaters/fulmars/ albatrosses/petrels
King salmon abundant	King salmon available	King salmon abundant (Naknek River only)
Red salmon abundant	Red salmon present, low numbers	Red salmon abundant
Chum salmon abundant	Chum salmon present, low numbers	No chum salmon
Silver salmon available	Silver salmon available	Few silver salmon

in the north-central peninsula boundary zone. Of these, the king salmon is strictly seasonal in its migration. "Second bets" would have included caribou, red salmon, waterfowl, shellfish, and coho salmon, while least reliable—but possible—as subsistence items would have been walrus, moose, chum salmon, sea otter, and various seabirds.

In fact, these differences in environmental resource potential are quite well reflected in the prehistoric faunal record from the northern peninsula. For example, the Hot Springs site at Port Moller (Okada and Okada 1974; Okada 1980) contains a very diverse fauna, including the following: 6 species of sea mammals (harbor seal, ringed seal, bearded seal, fur seal, sea lion, and walrus); 7 species of fish; 10 species of shellfish; 35 species of birds (15 of them common); and caribou (comprising only about 5% of the collection). In contrast, the smaller Port Heiden faunal assemblage is markedly less diverse (Table 4.1), and shows an apparent concentration (in terms of minimum numbers of individuals) on harbor seals, caribou, seabirds, waterfowl, and shellfish, in that order. Unfortunately, however, no fish bones were preserved at either the Meshik or North river sites.

In sum, while the boundary zone between Eskimos and Aleuts on the north-central peninsula cannot quite be characterized as a no-man's land, it does appear to have been somewhat of an "ecological frontier" when compared to the extremely rich coastal zones of the inner bay and the Aleutians, particularly in terms of resource *predictability* (rather than abundance per se). Thus, the observed demographic patterns on the Alaska Peninsula—suggesting smaller villages and perhaps more ephemeral occupation on the north-central peninsula in both prehistoric and historic times—seem to correspond to the ecological data from the peninsula region as summarized previously.

DISCUSSION

Establishment of a boundary zone between Aleuts and Eskimos on the Alaska Peninsula seems to have occurred approximately 4000–5000 years ago, when Denbighlike materials made their appearance on the upper peninsula. The archaeological data suggest that some differentiation between Aleutian and Peninsular archaeological assemblages had begun even by 5000–6000 years ago. This was probably correlated with changes in the environment, as the coastline stabilized, as Holocene upwelling systems, ice distributions, and river sedimentation patterns became established, and as modern fish runs, shellfish beds, and sea-mammal migration patterns developed. Whether significant cultural differentiation (affecting biology and/or language) was associated with these early archaeological developments is a moot issue. With the development of the Arctic Small Tool tradition, however—whatever its roots—a boundary had developed between populations that appear to be more distinct in material culture, and perhaps language as well.

For the next several thousand years (until the emergence of the Thule tradition around A.D. 1000) a boundary zone apparently continued to exist between Eskimo and Aleut populations on the Alaska Peninsula. How was this Eskimo/Aleut boundary maintained? It seems clear that the boundary zone separating these groups was an ecological frontier in which resources were generally less predictable, less abundant, and less diverse than those in the biomes on either side. Of the resources most valuable to the southwestern Alaskan populations (sea mammals, salmon, and caribou/moose), none were probably sufficiently abundant to attract permanent settlement to the area. In fact, it could be argued that long-term settlement in the boundary zone would have been risky for any group, primarily because of a lack of resource predictability. On this basis, it seems possible to reject the null hypothesis suggested earlier—that competition for resources was directly responsible for the location and persistence of the boundary zone.

⨎(Clearly, resources of the boundary zone were of little interest to populations living on either side of it. This situation conflicts with a model proposed by Hickerson (1965) and Wattrall (1968), which suggests that boundary zones often have a direct adaptive role in the sense that they serve as "reservoirs" for maintaining animal populations (and thereby also maintain the human populations that depend on them for food).)These models seem to have a better fit with interior regions of lower environmental diversity in which both groups divided by a boundary zone would be likely to have a similar subsistence base, or at least consider the same species valuable. They would not tend to fit as well with coastal regions of more substantial environmental diversity.)In addition, the Hickerson–Wattrall models probably fit better with interior environmental zones for the reason that resource overexploitation may have been more likely in such zones, where the development of cultural devices that act to limit such overexploitation might be to the selective advantage of any groups concerned.

If the "frontier model" espoused here is valid, however, then how does one go about explaining the records of warfare between Aleuts and various other Peninsular groups? For example, the missionary Veniaminov (1840) recorded warfare between the Aleuts and the Aglegmiut, Kodiak Islanders, and Shumagin Islanders. McCartney (1974) has even suggested that the paucity of settlement in the boundary zone may have been the *result* of chronic warfare. Perhaps it is true in some ultimate sense that competition between these densely populated coastal peoples underlay the chronic warfare between them, but even if so, the resources of the boundary zone itself were clearly irrelevant to that warfare.(Perhaps this warfare is best seen as a *boundary maintenance device* that actually allowed conflict to take place with little detrimental effect to the resource base of either side.[4])

(Assuming that the frontier model is correct, then, it follows that once the Aleut and Eskimo population systems became separated, the lack of attractive features in the boundary zone may have kept them culturally isolated. From that point, local settling in would have created behavioral differences, resulting in cultural drift (following the model proposed by Hardesty). Furthermore,(additional immigration from outside the system was directed into the upper peninsula only. It was probably this one-directional population flow system, rather than continued selection for living in distinct environments, that primarily underlay continuing differentiation between populations on either side of the boundary zone.)

None of the foregoing, however, helps to explain why the boundary zone was apparently not penetrated until Thule times. As noted earlier, the Denbigh and Norton tradition peoples had a mixed economy that focused on caribou as much as on fish or sea mammals. For these populations in particular, the lower peninsula region would have harbored an insufficient abundance of the more valuable terrestrial species, and the marine resources would have been too unpredictable. By the time of the Thule migration, however, the coastline had stabilized, allowing fish, shellfish, and sea-mammal resources greater predictability. More intensive use of marine resources by Thule populations is reflected by shifts in settlement patterns toward the coast throughout the northern peninsula (Dumond 1975), and by changes in the technological inventory, particularly in the bone harpoons and ground stone tools. The greater efficiency of the Thule peoples as sea-mammal hunters, in particular, has been argued on a wider basis as responsible for their widespread penetration of much of the Arctic soon after A.D. 1000. However, it should be clear that the frequently repeated general model of Thule success based on efficiency at hunting large baleen whales probably will not work on the northern peninsula, where these whales could not have been an important food resource. An alternative model might be that population pressure among increasingly densely populated groups in southwestern Alaska, as suggested by Dumond (1975), finally necessitated the exploitation of the marginal area of the lower peninsula, in a fashion analogous to coastal peoples elsewhere (Perlman 1980a; Yesner 1980). This population increase may have had an effect on interior species such as caribou, perhaps reducing their abundance to the point where less valuable marine resources became the focus of attention. This interpretation would fit well not only with the increasing interest in the coastline during late prehistoric and historic times, but also with the historic pattern of southward movement of Eskimo groups onto the northern peninsula, displacing earlier populations. This phenomenon could well have resulted from some form of population pressure on existing resources. At the very least, the Alaska Peninsula data suggest that we must begin to rethink the whole question of the nature of the Thule adaptation, paying careful attention to the relative roles of changes in the environment, technology, and population density.

Even though the Thule peoples finally penetrated the older Eskimo/Aleut boundary, it is worth noting that their penetration into the lower peninsula was still imperfect. The result was that, although there was some apparent "Thule-ization" of lower peninsular and eastern Aleutian cultures— marked particularly by widespread homogenization in bone technology (Dumond et al. 1975)—materials such as ground-stone tools tend to show the development of a "clinal" distribution from the mid-peninsula to the western Fox Islands (eastern Aleutians).[5] As one moves farther west from the boundary zone into the eastern Aleutians, the more dramatic the late shift in technology appears. Final penetration of diagnostic materials (such as ground slate) into the western Fox Islands seems to have been quite late, perhaps only slightly predating Russian contact. The relative recency of penetration of the boundary may also help to explain the strong differentiation between modern Aleut and Peninsular Eskimo speech. On the other hand, as McCartney (1974) has emphasized, we may have overemphasized the linguistic differences between the two groups since the original (pre-Aglegmiut) Peninsular Eskimo speech is so difficult to reconstruct.

CONCLUSION

The boundary zone between Eskimo and Aleut populations on the Alaska Peninsula was not a resource-rich buffer zone, but a (relatively) resource-poor zone that acted as an isolating barrier between two relatively richer resource zones—one nearly exclusively maritime (the Aleutian Islands and lower peninsula) and one providing a mixed coastal/riverine/tundra suite of resources traditionally exploited by Eskimos (the upper peninsula). Once established, the boundary between these two regions remained relatively stable over a long period until the Thule peoples—either because of environmental change, increased technological efficiency, or population pressure—were finally able to penetrate the boundary. Thus, the Alaska Peninsula data suggest that, even in regions with relatively rich coastal resources and dense human populations, ecological frontiers may serve as boundary zones to structure access to resources by human groups.

NOTES

1. In this essay, the terms *social unit* and *cultural unit* are used to refer to spatially bounded cultural entities above the level of individual bands. These units are thought of as fundamentally distinct in language, biology, and material culture, although the degree to which they differ according to any of these criteria remains unspecified.

2. However, the patterns of culture change in all cases appear to be clearer in the Naknek than in the Ugashik drainage. This may be in part a result of the larger sample size of archaeological materials from the Naknek region, but also may reflect the depth of various cultural penetrations into the peninsular area from outside. Unfortunately, no systematic archaeological work has yet been done on the Egegik drainage between the Naknek and Ugashik.

3. On this score, however, Petroff (1884) is somewhat confusing. On the one hand, he states (p. 24) that Aleuts occupied both Port Moller and Ugashik, with warring parties going as far north as the Naknek River, and (p. 136) credits the Aglegmiut with occupation of the northern peninsula down to the Ugashik River. Later, however, he suggests (p. 146) that the Aleuts occupied the northern peninsula west of Cape Stroganoff (near Port Heiden). Clearly, he seems to be including the (non-Aglegmiut) Peninsular Eskimos as "Aleuts," at least in the first version. Part of the problem in all of these cases is the unfortunate tendency of the Russians to refer (rather inconsistently) to the Peninsular Eskimos as "Aleuts," a practice continued to the present day as reflected in the manner in which these people often refer to themselves.

4. It may also be true that the warfare between the "Aleuts" (Peninsular Eskimos?) and the

Aglegmiut was a relatively recent event, in retribution for the southward movement of the Aglegmiut and seizure of river-mouth areas of the upper peninsula in historic times. However, one would suspect that the pre-Thule inhabitants of the peninsula would have greeted Thule peoples immigrating from the north in a similar fashion.

5. Given this situation, multivariate analyses of tool assemblages (Dumond *et al.* 1975) tell us little about cultural change; at least in the peninsular case, "diagnostic" tools of various sorts appear to reveal more about both the nature and direction of cultural change.

ACKNOWLEDGMENTS

Archaeological fieldwork in the Port Heiden region of the Alaska Peninsula was undertaken during 1981 by the author and K. J. Crossen of the Institute for Quaternary Studies, University of Main at Orono (now Department of Geological Sciences, University of Washington), who contributed ideas on the geology of the Alaska Peninsula and helped in editing the manuscript. The research was supported by grants from the Faculty Senate of the University of Southern Maine, and from the Office of History and Archaeology, Alaska Department of Natural Resources. Earlier versions of this essay were reviewed by W. B. Workman and A. P. Mc-Cartney. Don Dumond generously shared some of his unpublished data on Alaska Peninsula archaeology and ethnohistory. Interpretation of the ethnohistoric record was enabled by detailed discussions with D. W. Veltre, L. Black, and especially R. A. Pierce, who shared unpublished material and allowed access to early historic maps as well as helping with Russian translations. I would also like to thank Steve Perlman for originally suggesting the idea for this manuscript, and the staff of Academic Press for understanding of production schedules. Figures were provided by Media Services at McGill University during my 1981–1982 sabbatical. Deepest thanks go to the people of Meshik Village (Port Heiden) who provided hospitality and helped in so many ways.

REFERENCES

Abruzzi, W. S.
    1982   Ecological theory and ethnic differentiation among human populations. *Current Anthropology* 23: 13–35.

Aigner, J. S.
    1978   Activity zonation in a 4000-year-old Aleut house, Chaluka village, Umnak Island, Alaska. *Anthropological Papers of the University of Alaska* 19: 11–25.
    1982   Early Holocene maritime adaptation in the Aleutian Islands. In *Peopling of the new world* (Edited by J. E. Ericson *et al.* Ballena Press, Los Altos, California.

Aigner, J. S., B. Fullem, D. Veltre, and M. Veltre
    1976   Preliminary report on remains from Sandy Beach Bay, a 4300–5600 B.P. Aleut village. *Arctic Anthropology* 13(2): 83–90.

Alaska Department of Fish and Game (ADFG)
    1977   *A fish and wildlife resource inventory of the Alaska Peninsula, Aleutian Islands, and Bristol Bay areas,* (Vol. 2: Fisheries). ADFG, Juneau, Alaska.

Alaska Outer Continental Shelf Office (AOCS)
    1981   *Draft environmental impact statement, proposed oil and gas lease sale, St. George Basin.* U.S. Department of the Interior, Washington, D.C.

Alaska State Files, Office of History and Archaeology
    n.d.   Data on Chignik and Unangashik sites. Alaska Department of Natural Resources,
            Anchorage.
Barth, F.
    1956   Ecological relationships of ethnic groups in Swat, North Pakistan. *American An-
            thropologist* 58: 1079–1089.
Bartonek, J. C., and D. D. Gibson
    1972   Summer distribution of pelagic birds in Bristol Bay, Alaska. *Condor* 74: 416–422.
Binford, L. R.
    1968   Post-Pleistocene adaptations. In *New perspectives in archaeology*, edited by S. R.
            Binford and L. R. Binford. Aldine, Chicago.
Black, R. F.
    1975   Late Quaternary geomorphic processes: effects on the ancient Aleuts of Umnak
            Island in the Aleutians. *Arctic* 28: 159–169.
    1976   Influence of Holocene climatic changes on Aleut expansion into the Aleutian Is-
            lands, Alaska. *Anthropological Papers of the University of Alaska* 18: 31–42.
Braham, H. W., and M. E. Dalheim
    1982   Marine mammals. In *Marine resources of the St. George Basin, Bering Sea, Alaska,*
            edited by S. Zimmerman. Alaska Outer Continetal Shelf Office, Juneau.
Brelsford, T.
    n.d.   Summary of genealogical data from Port Heiden, Alaska Peninsula. Unpublished
            paper, Department of Anthropology, University of Alaska, Anchorage.
Butzer, K. W.
    1971   *Environment and archaeology.* Aldine-Atherton, Chicago.
Clark, D. W.
    1974   Koniag prehistory. *Tübingen monographien zur Urgeschichte* 1. University of
            Tübingen, Stuttgart.
    1975   Technological continuity and change within a persistent maritime adaptation,
            Kodiak Island, Alaska. In *Maritime adaptations of the circumpolar zone,* edited by
            W. W. Fitzhugh. Mouton, The Hague.
    1976   *Pacific origin of Eskimos.* Paper presented to the Alaska Anthropological Associa-
            tion, Anchorage.
    1979   *Ocean Bay: an early north pacific maritime culture.* National Museum of Man,
            Archaeological Survey of Canada Mercury Series, No. 86, Ottawa.
Clark, G. H.
    1974   *Prehistory of the Pacific Coast of the Katmai National Monument.* University
            Microfilms, Ann Arbor.
    1977   Archaeology on the Alaska Peninsula: the coast of Shelikof Strait. *University of
            Oregon Anthropological Papers,* No. 13, Eugene.
Cohen, M. N.
    1977   *The food crisis in prehistory.* Yale University Press, New Haven.
Dall, W. H.
    1870   *Alaska and its resources.* Lee and Shepard, Boston.
Davydov, G. I.
    1807   *Two voyages to Russian America.* Translated by R. A. Pierce. Limestone Press,
            Kingston, Ontario.
Despres, L. A.
    1969   Differential adaptations and micro-cultural evolution in Guyana. *Southwestern
            Journal of Anthropology* 25: 14–44.

Dumond, D. E.
    1965 On Eskaleutian linguistics, archaeology, and prehistory. *American Anthropologist*
          67: 1231–1257.
    1968 Prehistoric cultural contacts in southwestern Alaska. *Science* 166:1108–1115.
    1974 Prehistoric ethnic boundaries on the Alaska Peninsula. *Anthropological Papers of
          the University of Alaska* 16: 1–7.
    1975 Coastal adaptation and cultural change in Alaska Eskimo prehistory. In *Prehistoric
          maritime adaptations of the circumpolar zone,* edited by W. W. Fitzhugh. Mouton,
          The Hague.
    1979 People and pumice on the Alaska Peninsula. In *Volcanic Activity and Human
          Ecology,* edited by P. D. Sheets and D. K. Grayson. Academic Press, New York.
    1981 Archaeology on the Alaska Peninsula: the Naknek region, 1960–1975. *University
          of Oregon Anthropological Papers,* No. 21, Eugene.
    n.d. Demographic data from Russian church archives, Alaska Peninsula. Unpublished
          paper, Department of Anthropology, University of Oregon, Eugene.
Dumond, D. E., L. Conton, and H. M. Shields
    1975 Eskimos and Aleuts on the Alaska Peninsula: a reappraisal of Port Moller affinities.
          Arctic Anthropology 12: 49–67.
Dumond, D. E., W. Henn, and R. Stuckenrath
    1976 Archaeology and prehistory on the Alaska Peninsula. *Anthropological Papers of
          the University of Alaska* 18: 17–29.
Efimov, A. V.
    1791 *Atlas of geographical discoveries in Siberia and Northwestern America in the 17th
          and 18th centuries.* St. Petersburg.
Everitt, R. D., and H. W. Braham
    1979 Harbor seal distribution and abundance in the Bering Sea: Alaska Peninsula and
          Fox Islands. *Proceedings of the 29th Alaska Science Conference,* University of
          Alaska, Fairbanks.
Fitzhugh, W. W.
    1972 Environmental archaeology and cultural systems in Hamilton Inlet, Labrador.
          Smithsonian Contributions to Anthropology, No. 16. Smithsonian Institution
          Press, Washington, D.C.
    1975 A comparative approach to northern maritime adaptations. In *Prehistoric mar-
          itime adaptations of the circumpolar zone,* edited by W. W. Fitzhugh. Mouton, The
          Hague.
Haaland, G.
    1969 Economic determinants in ethnic processes. In *Ethnic groups and boundaries* edit-
          ed by F. Barth. Little, Brown, Boston.
Hardesty, D.
    1982 Comments on Abruzzi's "Ecology and ethnic differentiation." *Current An-
          thropology* 23: 23.
Henn, W.
    1978 Archaeology on the Alaska Peninsula: the Ugashik drainage, 1973–1975. *Univer-
          sity of Oregon Anthropological Papers,* No. 14, Eugene.
Heusser, C. J.
    1963 Postglacial palynology and archaeology in the Naknek River drainage area, Alas-
          ka. *American Antiquity* 29: 74–81.
    1973 Postglacial vegetation on Umnak Island, Aleutian Islands, Alaska. *Review of Pal-
          eobotany and Palynology* 15: 277–285.

Hickerson, H.
    1965 The Virginia deer and intertribal buffer zones in the upper Mississippi valley. In *Man, culture, and animals,* edited by A. Leeds. American Association for the Advancement of Science, Publication No. 78. Washington, D.C.

Hodge, F. W. (editor)
    1907 *Handbook of North American Indians.* Bureau of American Ethnology, Bulletin No. 30, Washington, D.C.

Holmberg, H. J.
    1856 Ethnographische skizzen uber die volker des Russischen Amerika. *Acta Societatis Scientierum Fennicae* 4: 281–421 (Helsinki).

Hughes, S. E., and R. W. Nelson
    1979 *Distribution, abundance, quality, and production studies on the surf clam in the southeastern Bering Sea.* U.S. Department of Commerce, National Marine Fisheries, Seattle.

Ivanov, B. G.
    1964 Quantitative distribution of echinodermata on the shelf of the eastern Bering Sea. In *Soviet fisheries investigations in the* North Pacific, edited by P. A. Moiseev. Israel Program for Scientific Translations, Jerusalem.

Kotani, Y.
    1980 Paleoecology of the Alaska Peninsula as seen from the Hot Springs site, Port Moller. In *Alaska native culture and history,* edited by Y. Kotani and W. B. Workman. National Museum of Ethnology, Senri Ethnological Studies, No. 4, Osaka.

Laughlin, W. S.
    1963 Eskimos and Aleuts: their origins and evolution. *Science* 142: 633–645.
    1966 Paleo-Aleut crania from Port Moller, Alaska Peninsula. *Arctic Anthropology* 3: 154.
    1972 Ecology and population structure in the arctic. In *The structure of human populations,* edited by G. Harrison and A. J. Boyce. Clarendon Press, Oxford.
    1975 Aleuts: ecosystem, Holocene history and Siberian origin. *Science* 189: 507–515.
    1980 *Aleuts: survivors of the Bering land bridge.* Holt, Rinehart and Winston, New York.

Lyapunova, P. G., and S. G. Federova
    1979 *Russian America in the unpublished notes of K. T. Klebnikov* (in Russian). Nauka, Leningrad.

McCartney, A. P.
    1969 Prehistoric Aleut influences at Port Moller, Alaska. *Anthropological Papers of the University of Alaska* 14: 1–16.
    1974 Prehistoric cultural integration along the Alaska Peninsula. *Anthropological Papers of the University of Alaska* 16: 59–84.
    1975 Maritime adaptations on the North Pacific rim. *Arctic Anthropology* 11 (suppl.): 153–162.

Niebauer, H. J.
    1981 Recent fluctuations in sea-ice distribution. In *The eastern Bering Sea shelf,* edited by D. W. Hood and J. A. Calder. U.S. Government Printing Office, Washington, D.C.

Okada, H.
    1980 Prehistory of the Alaska Peninsula as seen from the Hot Springs site, Port Moller. In *Alaska native culture and history,* edited by, Y. Kotani and W. B. Workman. National Museum of Ethnology, Senri Ethnological Studies, No. 4, Osaka.

Okada, H., and A. Okada
  1974 Preliminary report of excavations at Port Moller, Alaska. *Arctic Anthropology* 11
          (Supplement): 112–124.
Okada, H., and B. Yamaguchi
  1975 Human skeletal remains excavated at the Hot Springs village site, Port Moller,
          Alaska Peninsula, in 1972. *National Science Museum Bulletin*, Series D (An-
          thropology), 1:27–40 (Tokyo).
  1976 Further human cranial remains excavated in 1974 at the Hot Springs village site,
          Port Moller, Alaska Peninsula. *National Science Museum Bulletin,* Series D (An-
          thropology), 2:25–35 (Tokyo).
Osborn, A. J.
  1977 Strandloopers, mermaids, and other fairy tales: ecological determinants of marine
          resource utilization. In For theory building in archaeology, edited by L. R. Binford.
          Academic Press, New York.
Overland, J. E.
  1981 Marine climatology of the Bering Sea. In *The eastern Bering Sea shelf,* edited by D.
          W. Hood and J. A. Calder. U.S. Government Printing Office, Washington, D.C.
Perlman, M.
  1980a An optimum diet model, coattal variability, and hunter–gatherer behavior. In
          Advances in Archaeological Method and Theory, Volume 3, edited by M. B.
          Schiffer. Academic Press, New York.
  1980b The relative stability of Coastal and Interior Environments. Paper presented to the
          Society for American Archaeology, Philadelphia.
Petroff, I.
  1884 *Report on population, industries, and resources of Alaska.* U.S. Census Office,
          Washington, D.C.
Pinart, A. L.
  1873 Voyage a la cote nord-ouest d'Amerique d'Ounalashka a Kadiak. *Societe de Geog-
          raphie Bulletin* 6: 561–580 (Paris).
Schanz, A. B.
  1893 The fourth or Nushagak district. In *Report on population and resources of Alaska,*
          edited by R. P. Porter. U.S. Census Office, Washington, D.C.
Sowls, A. L., S. A. Hatch, and C. J. Lensink
  1978 *Catalog of Alaskan seabird colonies.* U.S. Department of the Interior, Fish and
          Wildlife Service, Washington, D.C.
Straty, R. R.
  1975 *Migratory routes of adult sockeye salmon in the eastern Bering Sea and Bristol
          Bay.* U.S. Department of Commerce Technical Report, National Marine Fisheries
          Service, Washington, D.C.
  1977 *Current patterns and distribution of river waters in inner Bristol Bay, Alaska.* U.S.
          Department of Commerce Technical Report, National Marine Fisheries Service,
          Washington,D.C.
Tikhmenev, P. A.
  1863 Historical review of the formation of the Russian-American Company and its
          activity up to the present time (map). Translated by R. A. Pierce. Limestone Press,
          Kingston, Ontario.
Turner, C. G. II, and J. A. Turner
  1974 Progress report on evolutionary anthropological study of Akun Strait district,
          eastern Aleutians, Alaska, 1970–1971. *Anthropological Papers of the University
          of Alaska* 16(1):27–57.

Turner, C. G. II, J. A. Turner, and L. R. Richards
  1975 *Aleut population size and its relation to seasonality of marine fauna.* Paper present-
        ed to the International Congress of Americanists, Mexico.
U.S. Army Corps of Engineers, Alaska District (USACE)
  1974 *The Bristol Bay environment: a background study of available knowledge.*
        USACE, Anchorage.
Veniaminov, I.
  1840 *Notes on the islands of the Unalaska district.* Translated by the Human Relations
        Area Files. Russian-American Co., St. Petersburg.
Wattrall, C. R.
  1968 Virginia deer and the buffer zone in the late prehistoric/early protohistoric periods
        in Minnesota. *Plains Anthropologist* 13: 81–86.
Weyer, E. M.
  1930 Archaeological material from the village site at Hot Springs, Port Moller Alaska.
        Anthropological Papers of the American Museum of Natural History 31: 239–
        279.
Wobst, M.
  1974 Boundary conditions for Paleolithic social systems: a simulation approach. *Ameri-
        can Antiquity* 39: 147–178.
  1975 Locational relationships in Paleolithic society. In *Demographic evolution of human
        populations,* edited by R. H. Ward and K. M. Weiss. Academic Press, New York.
Workman, W. B.
  1966 Prehistory at Port Moller, Alaska Peninsula, in light of fieldwork in 1960. *Arctic
        Anthropology* 3:132–153.
  1980 Continuity and change in the prehistoric record from southern Alaska. In *Alaska
        native culture and history* edited by Y. Kotani and W. B. Workman. National
        Museum of Ethnology, Senri Ethnological Studies, No. 4, Osaka.
Wrangell, F. P.
  1839 *Russian America: statistical and ethnographic information.* Translated by M.
        Sadouski; edited by R. A. Pierce. Limestone Press, Kingston, Ontario.
Yarborough, M. R.
  1974 Analysis of pottery from the western Alaska Peninsula. *Anthropological Papers of
        the University of Alaska* 16: 85–89.
Yesner, D. R.
  1976 Aleutian Island albatrosses: a population history. *Auk* 93: 263–280.
  1977a Resource diversity and population stability among hunter-gatherers. *Western Ca-
        nadian Journal of Anthropology* 7: 18–59.
  1977b Avian exploitation, occupational seasonality, and paleoecology of the Chugachik
        Island site. *Anthropological Papers of the University of Alaska* 18: 23–30.
  1977c *Prehistoric subsistence and settlement in the Aleutian Islands.* University Micro-
        films, Ann Arbor.
  1978 Avian remains from the Hot Springs site, Port Moller, Alaska Peninsula. Un-
        published manuscript, University of Southern Maine, Gorham.
  1980 Maritime hunter-gatherers: ecology and prehistory. *Current Anthropology* 21:
        727–750.
  1982 Archaeological applications of optimal foraging theory: Harvest Strategies of Aleut
        hunter–gatherers. In *Hunter–gatherer foraging strategies,* edited by B. Win-
        terhalder and E. Smith. University of Chicago Press, Chicago.
  1983a On explaining changes in prehistoric coastal economies. In *The Evolution of mar-*

itime cultures on the Northeast and Northwest Coasts of North America, edited by R. J. Nash. Simon Fraser University, Department of Archaeology No. 11.

1983b Archaeological theory, ethnohistory, and cultural resource management: some notes from the Alaska Peninsula. *Contract Abstracts and CRM Archaeology* 3: 109–116.

1984 Population pressure in coastal environments: An archaeological test. *World Archaeology* 16: 108–127.

CHAPTER 5

Forager/Farmer Interactions: Information, Social Organization, and the Frontier

JAMES A. MOORE

Department of Anthropology
Queens College and the Graduate Center
City University of New York
Flushing, New York

INTRODUCTION

Sitting between societies with differing patterns of energy, matter, and information flow, frontiers provide anthropologists with both provocative history and crucial laboratories for the study of social change. Unfortunately, the interest in "pristine" societies and their pristine cultural process has lead us to overlook the valuable insights into cultural change that frontier research offers. Along the frontier we find cultural systems operating not only at their geographical limits, but often at their systemic limits as well. The forces forming and transforming social relations are often visible in ways that are otherwise rarely apparent in our idealized pristine societies. On the frontier the reproduction of social relations occurs in a delicate and unstable dynamic. Material constraints are modified. The continuation of familiar relations are stymied. New social and economic resources spring up over the cultural landscape. When two societies are thrown against each other, we learn from the results of the collision what was required for the reproduction of those societies and how conflicts among these processes can create a dynamic toward social transformation.

This discussion of the frontier focuses on a single type of frontier and a single issue: on a sedentary farmer/mobile-forager frontier—a cultural mosaic of interspersed communities with varying subsistence and settlement requirements—what effect do sedentary agricultural settlements have on the hunting and gathering groups? This question has often been asked with the notion that competition for land or other strategic resources drives the territorial displacement we expect to take place along the frontier. This perspective, however, with it's all-other-things-being-equal assumption, overlooks the all-too-different organizational requirements of these two settlement strategies. Initially, this study concentrates on the effects of the frontier on the seasonal movement patterns of the foraging groups, but the effects are hardly so narrowly contained. Mobility, a central feature of hunter–gatherer social life, has its prerequisites, costs, and benefits. An examination of the social requirements and implications of mobility, moreover, reveals how the different organizational requirements of transhumant hunter–gatherer's and sedentary farmers create a social dynamic that has been largely misconceived and undertheorized by anthropologists.

The concept of *frontier,* when defined as a mosaic, suggests that the settlement, subsistence, and social strategies of sedentary farmers and mobile hunter–gatherer's may unintentionally interfere with each other and that this meddling can lead to rapid social transformation or cultural disintegration. Archaeologists often have viewed this disruption as the result of geographical displacement driven by superior subsistence techniques, population growth, and, implicitly, greater coercive force. The competitive advantage of farming communities is so generally assumed that agricultural expansion is understood as a given—hunter–gatherers retreat in the face of "superior" farming communities (Jarman 1972; Welinder 1975), or agriculturalists expand into a seemingly uninhabited region (Ammerman and Cavalli-Sforza 1971, 1973; Binford 1968; Madsen 1982). It is unfortunate then that our tidy archaeological assumptions are harassed by inconvenient ethnographic facts. It is simply not the case that agriculturalists necessarily displace hunter–gatherers the M'buti live in close contact with Bantu farmers (Abruzzi 1979, 1980; Harako 1981; Turnbull 1965), complex exchange relationships tie together foraging and farming populations in the Torres Strait region (Harris 1977, 1979), and similar observations are plentiful for India (Williams 1975), the Philippines (Peterson 1978), and the American Southwest (Ford 1972). The social dynamics of the farmer/forager frontier are not likely to be as simple as we would like to assume. In the mosaic landscape of the frontier, there are more subtle and, I will argue, more powerful forces at work. Simple notions of subsistence efficiency, maximization, or optimization will not effectively chart either the course or the dynamics of cultural change. Sedentary agricultural settlements modify the social landscape of hunter–gatherer groups: they impose limitations and create new economic, social, political, and religious opportunities. The question we must face is why does this new social landscape at times seemingly lead to stable social boundaries and at other times lead to the rapid social transformations conventionally called frontiers? To make the distinction between "moving frontiers" and stationary cultural boundaries, as has often been done, simply answers the question with a typological obstruction that obscures the fundamental problem (Alexander 1977).

INFORMATION AND THE FRONTIER

The cultural systems of hunter–gatherers, or low-level agriculturalists for that matter, are usually modeled as flows of matter and energy with there generally being little formal consideration given to the crucial role information sharing plays in the coordination of social behavior (Flannery 1972; Johnson 1973, 1978). This focus on matter and energy draws archaeologists to concentrate their research efforts in two areas: energy-producing subsistence activities and matter-moving exchange activities. It should not be surprising then that the archaeology of the frontier is characterized by these same two concerns: the frontier is viewed as an area of competing subsistence systems demonstrating competitive exclusion (Jarman 1972; Welinder 1975), or alternatively, it is viewed as an area where the exchange processes and mechanisms of one society disrupt the economic equilibrium of another (Sharp 1952). Each of these focuses tend to emphasize different scales of analysis. Subsistence competition is local; exchange is often interregional. These two different orientations fail to note that differently organized societies may require different amounts of information in order to coordinate, to some extent, the subsistence, locational, and exchange dimensions of social life. In both scales of analysis, the problems of meshing and practical and cultural behavior of two different forms of social organization in the regional mosaic of the frontier sit off-stage, poorly illuminated by the ecological or long distance exchange models.

The role of information sharing and its social requirements has only recently been explicitly integrated into archaeological modeling. More typically, models of hunter–gatherer subsistence strategies, exchange networks, mating patterns, and settlement systems share a common (and at times nearly invisible) assumption: decisions are made by a coldly rational, all-knowing, unerring economic being. It is a corollary of this assumption that all decision makers, being omniscient, have the same knowledge and so no information needs to be shared. In short, there is no information flow and the quality, quantity, and structure of information channels in the social network is neither the result nor the prerequisite of any particular form of social organization. The assumption of an omniscient decision maker robs an important dynamic from our models of social change by treating information sharing, social organization, and the quality of decision making as separate research domains. Furthermore, this moves us closer to a position where the effects of everyday social acts cannot escape from the realm of the intentional, so change is regarded as necessarily exogeneous to the society studied, driven by long distance exchange or local ecological factors.

Although it is argued that the omniscient decision maker is merely a convenient heuristic, it may be time to question assumptions that remove fundamental organizational issues from the realm of archaeological research. Biologically, the human brain is a poor computational device unable to give full and proper consideration to even limited amounts of information (Pred 1967; Salop 1978). Moreover, socially, the quality of decision making and the manner in which an individual participates in society is to a large extent determined by the quality and quantity of the information available to that individual (Hagerstrand 1953, 1957; Reynolds 1978). Ignorance and error further complicate decision making. All decisions involve the sorting out of lies, half-truths, and outdated information to select an effective, risk-averting strategy: it is likely that a good deal of social behavior can be attributed to strategies for either validating information or circumventing these validity tests (Moore 1983). We should go beyond Binford's behavioralist assumption (Binford 1962) that individuals differentially participate in cultural systems as a tenet of contemporary archaeology. We need to ask what factors structure this unequal participation in social life, how it is held in check, and how it is amplified.

Furthermore, decision making is not a timeless, changeless part of social life. Decision making is by its nature contextual: enmeshed in historic as well as social processes. Previous decisions establish constraints and limit the range of future actions. Once a decision is made and an action taken, the social context has been altered, and the range of future options is expanded or constricted by these changed conditions. The point of anthropological studies of information processing, however, is not to study the effects of the unique and idiosyncratic factors that influence decisions, but to understand how structural aspects of information networks limit and constrain the range of options open to the decision makers and how these constraints and opportunities set into motion new social dynamics.

Many anthropological studies of settlement process have borrowed heavily from among the concepts and theories of normative locational geography. In particular, hexagonal lattice models of settlement packing have come to be archaeology's dominant heuristic model for locational analysis. In these lattice models, the settlement pattern is generated through a process of unerring decision making based on complete and perfect information

(Kant 1951; Losch 1954). This model has been an unmitigated disaster for hunter–gatherer studies and our notions of the social dynamics of the frontier. The hexagonal lattice, by assuming the solution, hides from view the problems of regional coordination and competition present in all settlement systems, and by doing so obscures the impact that the social organization of information flows has on the operation of the settlement system.

SIMULATION EXPERIMENTS

This study uses computer simulation techniques to integrate the capacities and limitations of information-sharing networks with the mosiaic character of farmer/forager frontiers. These two concerns meet in many of the daily concerns of social life—from the pursuit of subsistence activities to the creation and maintenance of alliances. Yet one archaeologically and ethnohistorically tangible effect of the interaction of information sharing and the mosaic character of the frontier is likely to be the change in locational patterning. The working hypothesis for this research is simply that each social form has different information-processing capacities, each settlement system requires different amounts of locational information, and that each social form responds differently when thrown against another in the cultural mosaic of the frontier.

Toward this end, two computer simulation experiments are proposed. The simulations operate on a regional level to incorporate a frequently overlooked yet important information requirement—that the effectiveness of the locational process is dependent on both the knowledge of suitable locations and knowledge of the locational plans of the other groups in the region. The first simulation model explores the effect of limited information flow on the locational choice of hunter–gatherer groups and on the resulting settlement behavior. In the second simulation, the effects of sedentary agricultural groups on the locational decision making and the seasonal locational costs of hunter–gatherer groups are examined. With these alternative models of the settlement process available for comparison, it may become easier to understand, first, the role of information in settlement behavior, second, what organizational alternatives to information sharing exist, and third, how the presence of sedentary agriculturalists in a mosaic frontier necessitate new responses by hunter–gatherers.

Simulation Rules

It should be apparent that this study intends to call into question many of the implicitly held assumptions about hunter–gatherers and simple farmers, and the nature of their interaction along the frontier. The simulation rules governing locational behavior are surprisingly few and simple. Admittedly, the simulation rules are incomplete abstracts of the complex rules applied in real-world decision making, but the purpose of the simulations is not to replicate reality, but to attempt to trace the dynamics generated by a simple and completely controlled set of assumptions. The resulting aggregate behavior is sufficiently complex, however, to warrant the apparent simplicity. A more complex simulation could be constructed (and the results might indeed provide a more faithful mimic of reality), but the price of such complexity would be a loss of understanding of the driving force common to farmer/forager frontiers (Levins 1966).

The simulations operate under two sets of rules: the first set defines the acceptable range of seasonal settlement locations, while the second set covers the types of information shared and the pattern of information exchange.

Locational Rules

The locational criteria used in these models are derived from ecological models of optimal foraging behavior. In their simplest form, these models state that in a strongly heterogeneous environment, the optimal foraging strategy would maximize the energy return or the time spent feeding in patches of dense resources, while minimizing risk or the time spent traveling between resource patches (Cody 1974; MacArthur and Pianka 1966; Schoener 1971; Smith and Winterhalder 1981; Wiens 1977; Winterhalder 1981). Among centrally based foragers, groups settle in or near to clustered resources to maximize their foraging efficiency (Anderson 1979; Orians and Pearson 1979). Besides the clustered resources, it is assumed that other resources are required to supplement the clustered resource. It is further assumed that the region has a homogeneous distribution of these supplemental resources. Applying optimal foraging theory to this resource distribution generates a circular-use area around the settlements located at the main resource cluster. Attempts to feed at the same resource clusters, or foraging rounds that lead to the overlapping of the circular catchments, will lead to reduced energy return rates for the time spent in the shared areas. Under these constraints, optimal settlement locations will not share resource clusters nor will catchment areas overlap.

The effect of these settlement requirements on locational choice depends entirely on the food resource distribution (cf. Jochim 1976; Smith 1974). If the major food clusters are distributed in a perfect lattice with a distance between the clusters equal to or greater than the diameter of the circular area visited during foraging, there is no chance for overlap of the catchment areas and the opportunity for the settlements to "get in each other's way" is greatly reduced. Under these circumstances, the penalties for poor locational choice are more infrequent, and the benefits of information sharing are proportionally reduced. Working our way through similar lines of argument for random and clustered distributions of food clusters reveals that the opportunity for locational interference increases as we move from regular through random to clustered distributions. To hold the ecological environment constant, and to create a comparative benchmark, it is assumed:

1. that the resource clusters will be distributed randomly through the simulated environment;
2. that all resource clusters are calorically equal;
3. that the foraging rounds move through calorically equivalent areas and so result in catchment areas of equal radii.

Information-Sharing Rules

The second set of rules—the rules for information sharing—is similarly abstracted and simplified. There are two types of information required for locational choice. The first type of information, information concerning the distribution of resources, is assumed to be perfectly shared among all the groups of the region. This assumption is not as much as simplification as it might first appear; the ethnographic record indicates that among hunter–gatherer groups, the locations of clustered resources are known over large areas of the region (Lee 1979; Rogers and Rogers 1959; Silberbauer 1981; Winterhalder 1977, 1981).

The second category of information shared is the seasonal movement plan for each of the groups. This is a type of information rarely considered in the ethnographic record, and even more rarely given consideration in archaeological models of seasonal settlement patterns (cf. Steward 1938). The implicit assumption of anthropological/archaeological models of seasonal subsistence and settlement systems can be stated in two different but equivalent forms:

1. there is only one group in region—optimization is not hindered by possible overlap of use areas with other groups, or
2. the groups in the region have perfect knowledge of the seasonal movement plans of all the other groups in the region so that overlapping catchment areas can be avoided.

It is this oversimplification of the foragers' social environment that permits and encourages researchers to ignore information gathering, processing, and distribution. The justification usually given for this assumption claims that the lack of perfect knowledge will not result in significantly different behavioral patterns. Earlier simulations revealed that information about the location of food clusters and the patterns of information sharing strongly affected the costs of various seasonal settlement strategies (Moore 1977, 1981).

(In these simulations, it is assumed that there is no sharing of seasonal movement plans among the groups. Each group selects a location and attempts to settle there without any knowledge of the distribution of other groups in the region. It is unlikely that this assumption is ever totally true, but again, the ethnographic record indicates that the assumption is not as great a distortion as might be believed (Leacock 1954; Lee 1979; Silberbauer 1981; Williams 1975). (There is strong evidence to believe that within camps, foragers have effective means for distributing information; however, between camps both the quality, quantity, and rate of information sharing drops off sharply (Johnson 1978, 1982; Lee 1979; Marshall 1976; Meggett 1962; Wiessner 1982; Wobst 1978).

The Simulation Arena

The simulation region consists of a square area measuring 100 units by 100 units. The circular catchment areas of each settlement have a radius of four units. Thus each settlement occupies approximately .5% of the total area of the region. The number of clustered resources is high in relation to the size of the region. With 500 resource clusters in the region, on the average, each circular catchment area has 2.5 clusters. As this distribution approximates a Poisson distribution, the variance is also 2.5 clusters. The resource level is held at this relatively high level throughout the simulation. These conditions are deliberately established to ensure that resource availability will not be the limiting factor in determining the density of settlement or the locational costs. The limits on the settlement process are the result of the randomness of the resource cluster distribution, and by the limited ability to share locational plans.)

The Cost of Seasonal Mobility among
Hunter–Gatherers

In this simulation, the rules previously outlined are applied to the seasonal movements of foraging groups. Before the seasonal shifts in settlement, groups are randomly distributed over the region. To begin the seasonal movement, a group is randomly selected and moved to the closest known food cluster to attempt to settle at this location. If the food cluster is not already being used by another community, and if the catchment area around the clustered resource does not overlap with an already in-use catchment, then settlement is permitted. If these conditions are not met, a record of the unsuccessful attempt is made. After the first round of movements, all the

Table 5.1

Settlement Costs for Hunter–Gatherers
(measured as unsuccessful settlement attempts)[a]

Number of settled groups	Percentage of region settled	Mean cumulative costs	Marginal cost of settlement	Standard deviation cumulative costs
10	4.4	.3	.03	.45
20	8.9	3.2	.29	1.82
30	13.4	9.8	.66	2.91
40	17.9	23.9	1.41	8.92
50	22.4	48.0	2.41	10.33
60	26.8	84.8	3.68	18.23
70	31.3	148.3	6.35	25.97
80	35.8	276.5	12.62	42.29
90	40.3	562.2	28.57	91.36
100	44.7	2523.3	196.10	637.31
110	49.2	9966.7	744.35	3041.75

[a] $N = 10$ simulation repetitions.

groups that failed to successfully settle are randomly selected to examine new clusters for settlement. Unsuccessful locational attempts continued to be tallied as costs, and the settlement process continues until the predetermined number of settlements successfully reach their seasonal camp locations. Throughout this series of simulation experiments, the unsuccessful move is used as the standard unit of measurement to gauge locational costs.

It is not surprising that the results of the first simulation experiment indicate that settlement systems that operate with extremely limited patterns of information sharing are inefficient when measured by the total percentage of the region that can be brought into utilization, and also in terms of the movement costs. Table 5.1 indicates that while the costs incurred by the first group's seasonal movements are low, the costs for groups attempting later seasonal resettlement rise at an ever-increasing rate. By the time that 50% of the region is occupied by the seasonal settlements of 100 groups, the total cost approaches nearly 10,000 unsuccessful locational attempts. Examining the cost involved in adding each additional seasonal camp clearly reveals that costs also increase at an accelerating rate (Table 5.1). Under the rules specified, the cost of seasonal movement increases dramatically with the addition of each group to the region. The settlement of the first 4.4% of the region by the first 10 groups costs on the average .3 unsuccessful attempts for each settlement, while the addition of each seasonal camp from the sixty-first to seventieth group costs, on the average, 63.5 unsuccessful attempts. Yet with the addition of the seventieth camp, a total of only 32.2% of the region is in use. With limited information sharing and no learning, transhumance can become costly at even low settlement densities.

Location Costs along the Farmer/Forager Frontier

What implications do these results have for the dynamics of a regional mosaic of hunter–gatherer and agricultural settlements? To gain some insight into the interactions of interspersed agricultural and hunter–gatherer communities, a simple model of sedentary farming settlement will be combined with the model of seasonally scheduled foraging activities. In this second simulation experiment, the agricultural groups are fully sedentary, and although the subsistence activity is primarily based on farming, it will be assumed that an exploitation area around the settlement is required to supply additional resources—supplemental foraging and hunting, grazing land, and fodder. Given these locational requirements, this simulation experiment asks, What effects do farming communities have on the locational costs of a transhumant settlement system?

The locational rules and the information-sharing rules in the second experiment remain identical to the first simulation; that is, settlement criteria remain the same: a resource cluster and a catchment area are required to meet each foraging camp's subsistence requirements. And again, the groups know the distribution of all resources in the region, but the hunter–gatherer groups do not share information. The only difference between the two sets of simulations is the presence of farming groups which are randomly located over the region before the foragers begin their seasonal settlement shift. As the hunter–gatherers shift settlements, they must avoid locations where the catchment areas overlap with the exploitation zones of the farmers. Any locational attempt that does overlap is recorded as unsuccessful, and the foraging group continues to search until it finds a site meeting all the locational requirements.

For the purposes of the simulation, it was arbitrarily decided to populate the region with 40 hunter–gatherer groups. The number of farming settlements is systematically increased during the simulation to explore the impact of increasing numbers of sedentary groups. In isolation, the 40 hunter–gatherer groups with limited information sharing would average 23.9 unsuccessful attempts as their total avoidable settlement cost (Table 5.2). If 10 sedentary farming communities are assumed to be present in the region prior to the beginning of the forager seasonal settlement shift, the average cost of settlement for the 40 groups increases to 46.7 unsuccessful attempts. A further increment of 10 sedentary agricultural settlements in the region increases the average total avoidable locational cost to 81.9 attempts. It

Table 5.2

Regional Settlement Costs for Forager/Farmer Frontiers
(measured as unsuccessful settlement attempts)[a,b]

Number of hunter–gatherer settlements	Number of farming settlements				
	0	10	20	30	40
0	0	0	0	0	0
	(0.0)	(4.4)	(8.9)	(13.4)	(17.9)
10	0.3	2.9	6.6	14.1	24.1
	(4.4)	(8.9)	(13.4)	(17.9)	(22.4)
20	3.2	9.5	20.7	38.2	60.9
	(8.9)	(13.4)	(17.9)	(22.4)	(26.8)
30	9.8	23.6	44.8	75.0	124.4
	(13.4)	(17.9)	(22.4)	(26.8)	(31.3)
40	23.9	46.7	81.2	148.5	252.6
	(17.9)	(22.4)	(26.8)	(31.3)	(35.8)

[a]$N = 10$ simulation repetitions.

[b]The costs are borne solely by the hunter–gatherers and are measured as unsuccessful locational attempts. The figures in parentheses indicate the percentage of the region occupied by the combined forager/farmer settlements.

should be kept in mind that during this experiment the total area used by the foraging groups remains constant: the increased locational costs are driven entirely by the increase in sedentary settlements. Each additional farming community creates accelerating increases in the hunter–gatherer locational costs.

A close examination of the results (Tables 5.1 and 5.2) confirms the nonlinear relationship between the use of space/food resources and locational costs. The 40 forager groups in isolation use 17.9% of the region at a cost of 23.9 attempts. In other words, 82.1% of the region is not actively used. With the presence of 20 sedentary groups occupying 8.9% of the region, the location costs for the transhumant groups jump to 81.9 attempts even though 73.1% of the region is not yet effectively used. Clearly, even a small number of interspersed sedentary settlements disrupt the seasonal settlement shifts of hunter–gatherer groups. And this disruption is not simply proportional to the amount of land occupied or food resources consumed. Sedentary farmers increase the foragers' information costs and this may in turn influence the shape, size, and content of the hunter–gatherers' information network. Agriculturalists do not directly threaten the subsistence base of hunter–gatherer groups. They do however meddle in and muddle the patterns of mobility on which the knowledge of the ecological and social environment is based—a direct threat to the social relations that organize the performance of subsistence activities and the distribution of necessary resources.)

DISCUSSION

The points to be gleaned from these simulation experiments are not that flesh-and-blood hunter–gatherers in any way respond to increasing population or colonization by sedentary groups by necessarily spending ever greater amounts of time searching the region for adequate settlement locations. We have little right to expect the cultureless creatures of the simulations to reflect the *cultural* responses of real foraging groups. The simulations do however map out the growing complexity of the social environment and the pressures this complexity creates for social change. In particular, mobility— characterized by many anthropologists as the fundamental characteristic of the hunting–gathering *band*—is clearly revealed in the simulation to be the locus of tensions in the forager/farmer mosaic.

Forager Simulations

Turning to the first set of simulations, we can see that the increase in the number of groups in the region greatly complicates the issue of seasonal settlement. A second point to be drawn from the simulation experiment relates to the general expectations that many demographically oriented anthropologists hold about the relation of population size to the resource base of the region. For many of these anthropologists, there is the expectation that population levels are in some manner directly regulated by the abundance of calories or proteins in the region. Population pressure is thus observable by changes in the diet selection toward items with less favorable cost/benefit indexes (Cohen 1975:472, 1977). While the results of the simulations do not directly contradict these hypotheses, the results do suggest several alternate man/land relationships.

1. Population growth may not be felt initially as food-item scarcity or lower cost/benefit indexes. The simulation indicates that as the regional population increases, the costs of seasonal settlement shifts increase dramatically. It is likely that the increasing mobility costs and the greater complexity of the social landscape may simply "feel" socially crowded long before food items become scarce. The hexagonal lattice settlement model (by obscuring the relationship between the regional resource base, regional population size, and regional settlement processes) has focused research at a scale much smaller than that experienced by foraging groups. Mobility

spreads costs and benefits from the local to the regional scale of interaction (Moore 1981).

If population pressure did exist, rather than suffer the increasing costs of preferred diet items, groups could put more effort into searching for settlement locations. If this occurred, neither the faunal or floral assemblages of the sites would change nor would the habitat preferences demonstrated by the sites change. In these cases, population pressure would be archaeologically invisible. This is not a solution to the problem of increased costs however, it is merely an alternate means for allocating the increased costs.

2. Alternatively, if increasing settlement density is felt as high locational costs, one response to population growth would be a reduction in the frequency of seasonal movement. In other words, population pressure would create a slight pressure toward reducing the number of seasonal stations on the annual rounds. Archaeologically, there would be a shift toward a less optimal diet, but it should also be accompanied by changes in the scheduling of subsistence activities and evidence of reduced mobility. This alternative could lower costs; however, it seems likely that such a solution would interfere with the standard method of dispute settlement among hunter–gatherers—fission and fusion. Increases in ritual activity may provide an alternate means of easing social tensions (Gross 1979; Johnson 1982).

3. Finally, increases in information sharing and increased coordination of seasonal settlement movements should lower the locational costs significantly. Changes in social organization that increase information-processing capacities (Johnson 1978, 1982; Moore 1977, 1981) will significantly reduce subsistence and settlement costs and permit increased settlement density. Amplification of seasonal aggregation and dispersal creates a sequential information-processing structure (Johnson 1982) where increased information flows during periods of aggregation lead to more effective and lower cost dispersals (Moore 1981). If population pressure felt as increased locational costs leads to changes in social organization and increased information-processing capacities, we may expect to see increased settlement density and increased seasonal differentiation of structural poses. This can take place without any significant change in technology or subsistence patterning.

Farmer/Forager Simulations

Formally, there is little to distinguish the operation of the pristine hunter–gatherer simulation from the frontier simulation. In each case the addition of a group increases the total regional costs of settlement by an ever-accelerating amount. But such a perspective ignores that the social environment is constituted by more than the simple occupation of space. There are two factors that sharply differentiate the pristine hunter–gatherer situation from the context of the frontier. First, there is the allocation of movement costs which the farmers shift to the foragers. Second, it should not go unnoticed that the farmers are a social resource for the foraging groups.

To start by stating the obvious, one critical difference between farmers and foragers, as modeled in the simulation, is the role that mobility plays in the mode of production. Among hunter–gatherers, mobility represents the means by which open access to basic resources is maintained. When hunter–gatherers "vote with their feet," they vote the egalitarian ticket. Among farmers the relations of land, labor, and subsistence are not nearly as direct, but one clear effect is the reduced role of mobility in the relations of production. Along the frontier, the increased information costs created by the sedentary farmers are in effect a transfer of mobility costs from the whole of the region to hunter–gatherers. The costs of the increasingly complex social landscape are carried primarily by the foragers.

This brings us to the second point. The farming settlements are social resources for the foragers. In the mosaic of the frontier, the hunting–gatherering groups do not attempt to solve the problems of increasing mobility costs in the manner outlined previously for pristine foragers. The presence of farming settlements offer opportunities to fashion more effective responses to the increasing costs of mobility.

Exchange

There is a widespread pattern of subsistence goods being exchanged along forager/farmer frontiers. This exchange usually takes the form of meat for grain or root staples. While this form of exchange is widely reported, several curious aspects of the exchange escape analysis.

1. Barter exchange of foodstuffs among hunter–gatherers is nearly unheard of. Why is it so frequent on the frontier?

2. It is widely reported that meat is highly valued among hunter–gatherers even during periods of no nutritional stress. Reciprocal exchange of meat is often seen as a social lubricant, easing tensions and increasing solidarity. Why then is meat offered in barter exchange, in effect changing the allocation of resources in the realm of social reproduction? Does this shift in the patterns of exchange from meat reciprocity to meat barter fracture internal social ties to create (a) even greater "social flexibility" as disputes increase and (b) ever smaller social units as social production is drained from the hunter–gatherers (cf. Bender 1978)?

3. The economic organization of hunter–gatherers is universally described as following a sexual division of labor. Males hunt, females gather vegetables and small prey. Frontier exchange, for the foragers, represents

the exchange of the products of male labor for those that females would be producing. Why are males increasing their productive efforts to lower the susbistence efforts of their wives? How does this affect the status of women?

Many anthropologists have suggested that small village farmers desire meat because their own livestock production falls short of their wants. This may explain why farmers desire to trade for meat; it does not however explain why hunter–gatherers appropriate extra meat for exchange. Demand does not necessarily provoke supply. The attraction for the hunter–gatherers is that exchange offers a means of lowering the increasing mobility costs of the frontier. The foragers become more sedentary, and while the local production costs of vegative calories increase, hunting for exchange permits groups to import calories.

Conflict Resolution

It is known that hunter–gatherers turned to their sedentary neighbors to help them end disputes. This is often reported as if the foragers were relieved to finally have a means to settle disputes. The pastoralists' relationship with the San and the Bantu's role for the M'buti come quickly to mind, but the literature is peppered with such references. These instances are often cited as if to demonstrate the inadequacy of the hunter–gatherers means of dispute settlement. However, two points need to be emphasized. First, the presence of sedentary groups by diverting social production may be responsible for increases in the frequency of disputes. Second, the effects of the mosaic frontier on mobility costs have not been considered when arriving at this conclusion. The use of farmers as mediators is related to the increased mobility costs of fission and fusion. There are two dimensions to the increased costs. First, there is the direct effect of the cost of finding an additional food cluster and foraging catchment for settlement. Additionally, there is the cost of moving away from the locus of the farmer/forager exchange. Given the alternatives of prolonged feuds or additional increases in already higher mobility costs, the acceptance of an outside arbitrator becomes a reasonable strategy of conflict resolution. Finally, it must be noted that the sedentary groups are not providing some sort of *pro bono* legal service. By offering mediation and settling disputes, the sedentary groups prevent disputes from disrupting their access to exchange partners and labor. The constraints in mobility and information sharing found along the frontier are circumvented through the creation of new social relations.

Information Processing

There are inherent limits in the amount of information that can be distributed through egalitarian dyadic relations. A simple and relatively egalitarian solution is to centralize information either socially or spatially. Sedentary agricultural communities offer an opportunity for the spatial centralization of information for mobile hunter–gatherers. This can increase the information processing rate, improve the quality of decision making, and reduce mobility costs. But also, serving as "community bulletin boards," collecting and distributing information for hunter–gatherers, agriculturalists take a further step toward asymmetrical patron–client relations.

CONCLUSION

There are three major conclusions resulting from this study. First, the central and vulnerable role of mobility in hunter–gatherer relations of production has been emphasized. Several major features of forager social life serve to maintain access to ecological and social resources by maintaining and encouraging mobility. Visiting, reciprocity, gift-giving, ritual aggregation, and fission/fusion all create social relations that permit future mobility. While the mobility creates direct access to resources and organizes both the allocation of effort among the tasks of subsistence production and the distribution of products, mobility is both the sensitive barometer and the vulnerable point of hunter–gatherer band organization.

Second, the notion of the mosaic frontier reveals the threat to mobility found on the farmer/forager frontier. Subsistence as well as social and political activities are modified as the costs of mobility increase. It is increasingly found that social relations mediate the access to resources and become a substitute for mobility. Information on the social and ecological environment that previously would have been gathered directly is increasingly socially distributed and socially processed as information-handling and conflict-resolving specialists emerge. Furthermore, these specialists arise outside of the hunter–gatherer community. The reduction in mobility creates social opportunities in both the sedentry and mobile groups, and the new social ties fuse the groups into a single cultural system with aspects of hunter–gatherer exchange, dispute settlment, and information processing being handled by agriculturalists.

Third, the simulations indicate that many features of hunter–gatherer band organization thought to be remnants of pristine social forms are actually the results of mosaic frontiers and the internal dynamics of changing social relations caused by the increased mobility costs of mosaic settlement systems. We should take to heart the notion that ethnographic and archaeological studies of hunter–gatherers have often dealt with partial societies. However, we should not mourn the loss of our pristine band models, and attempts to model these social fragments as cultural wholes should be treated as suspect. Rather the discovery of social processes generated by the conflicting requirements of transhumant and sedentary social organizations adds new dynamics to our understanding of social transformations.

REFERENCES

Abruzzi, W. S.
  1979 Population pressure and subsistence strategies among the Mbuti Pygmies. *Human Ecology* 7:183–189.
  1980 Flux among the Mbuti Pygmies of the Iture forest: an ecological interpretation. In *Beyond the myths of culture: essays in cultural materialism,* edited by E. B. Ross. Academic Press, New York.
Alexander, John
  1977 The frontier concept in prehistory: the end of the moving frontier. In *Hunters, gatherers and first farmers beyond europe,* edited by J. V. S. Megaw. Leicester University Press.
Ammerman, Albert J., and L. L. Cavalli-Sforza
  1971 Measuring the rate of spread of early farming in Europe. *Man* 6:674–688.
  1973 A population model for the diffusion of early farming in Europe. In *The explanation of culture change: models in prehistory,* edited by C. Renfrew. Duckworth Publishers, London.
Andersson, Malte
  1979 Optimal foraging area: size and allocation of search effort. *Journal of Theoretical Population Biology* 13:397–409.
Bender, Barbara
  1978 Gatherer–hunter to farmer: a social perspective. *World Archaeology* 10:204–222.
  1981 Gatherer–hunter intensification. In *Economic archaeology: towards an integration of ecological and social approaches,* edited by A. Sheridan and G. Bailey. British Archaeological Reports International Series 96, Oxford.
Binford, Lewis R.
  1962 Archaeology as anthropology. *American Antiquity* 28:217–225.
  1968 Post-Pleistocene adaptations. In *New perspectives in archaeology,* edited by S. R. Binford and L. R. Binford. Aldine, Chicago.
Cody, Martin L.
  1974 Optimization in ecology. *Science* 183:1156–1164.
Cohen, Mark N.
  1975 Archaeological evidence for population pressure in pre-agricultural societies. *American Antiquity* 40:471–476.
  1977 *The food crisis in prehistory.* Yale University Press, New Haven.
Flannery, Kent V.
  1972 The cultural evolution of civilizations. *Annual Review of Ecology and Systematics* 3:399–426.
Ford, Richard I.
  1972 Barter, gift or violence. In *Social exchange and interaction,* edited by E. N. Wilmsen. University of Michigan Museum of Anthropology, Anthropological Papers 46, Ann Arbor.
Gross, D. R.
  1979 New approach to central Brazilian social organization. In *Brazil: anthropological*

    perspectives: essays in honor of Charles Wagely, edited by M. L. Margolis and W. E. Carter. Columbia University Press, New York.

Hagerstrand, Torsten
    1953 *Innovationsforloppet ur korologisk synpunkt.* Gleerup, Lund, Sweden.
    1957 Migration and area. In *Migration in Sweden,* edited by D. Hannerberg, T. Hagerstrand, and O. Odeving. Lund Series in Geography, Series B, No. 13.

Harako, Reizo
    1981 The cultural ecology of hunting behavior among Mbuti Pygmies in the Ituri Forest, Zaire. In *Omnivorous primates,* edited by R. S. O. Harding and Geza Teleki. Columbia University Press, New York.

Harris, David R.
    1977 Subsistence strategies across Torres Strait. In *Sunda and Sahul: prehistoric studies in southeast Asia, Melanesia and Australia,* edited by J. Allen, J. Golson, and R. Jones. Academic Press, London.
    1979 Foragers and farmers in the western Torres Strait Islands: an historical analysis of economic, demographic and spatial differentiation. In *social and ecological systems,* edited by P. C. Burnham and R. F. Ellen. Academic A.S.A. Monograph 18.

Jarman, Michael R.
    1972 European deer economies and the advent of the Neolithic. In *Papers in economic prehistory,* edited by E. S. Higgs. Cambridge University Press, New York.

Jochim, Michael A.
    1976 *Hunter–gatherer subsistence and settlement: a predictive model.* Academic Press, New York.

Johnson, Gregory A.
    1973 Local exchange and early state development. *University of Michigan Museum of Anthropology Papers 52,* Ann Arbor.
    1978 Information sources and the development of decision-making organizations. In *Social archaeology,* edited by C. L. Redman *et al.* Academic Press, New York.
    1982 Organizational structure and scalar stress. In *Theory and explanation in archaeology,* edited by C. Renfrew, M. J. Rowlands, B. A. Seagraves. Academic Press, New York.

Kant, Edgar
    1951 Omlandsforskning och sektoranalysis. In *Tatorter och Omland,* edited by G. Enequist. Lund, Sweden.

Leacock, Eleanor
    1954 The Montagnais "hunting territory" and the fur trade. *American Anthropological Association Memoir 78.*

Lee, Richard B.
    1979 *The !Kung San: men, women, and work in a foraging society.* Cambridge University Press, New York.

Levins, Richard
    1966 The strategy of model building in population biology. *American Scientist* 54:421–431.

Losch, A.
    1954 *The economics of location.* Yale University Press, New Haven.

MacArthur, Robert H., and Eric R. Pianka
    1966 On optimal use of a patchy environment. *American Naturalist* 100:603–609.

Madsen, Torsten
    1982 Settlement systems of early agricultural societies in East Jutland, Denmark: a regional study of change. *Journal of Anthropological Archaeology* 1:197–236.

Marshall, Lorna
    1976 *The !Kung of Nyae Nyae*. Harvard University Press, Cambridge.
Meggett, Mervin J.
    1962 *Desert people*. University of Chicago Press, Chicago.
Moore, James A.
    1977 *Hunter–gatherer settlement systems and information flow*. Paper presented at the Annual Meeting of the American Anthropological Association, Houston.
    1981 The effects of information networks in hunter–gatherer societies. In *Hunter–gatherer foraging strategies*, edited by B. Winterhalder and E. A. Smith. University of Chicago Press, Chicago.
    1983 The trouble with know-it-alls: information as a social and ecological resource. In *Archaeological hammers and theories*, edited by J. A. Moore and A. S. Keene. Academic Press, New York.
Orians, Gordon H., and Norlan E. Pearson
    1979 On the theory of central place foraging. In *Analysis of ecological systems*, edited by D. J. Horn. Ohio State University Press, Columbus.
Peterson, Jean Treloggen
    1978 Hunter–gatherer/farmer exchange. *American Anthropologist* 80:335–351.
Pred, Allan
    1967 *Behavior and location* (Vol. 1). Gleerup, Lund, Sweden.
Reynolds, Robert G.
    1978 On modeling the evolution of hunter–gatherer decision-making systems. *Geographical Analysis* 10:31–46.
Rogers, Edward S., and Jean H. Rogers
    1959 The yearly cycle of the Mistassini Indians. *Arctic* 12:130–138.
Salop, Steven
    1978 Parables of information transmission in markets. In *The effects of information on consumer and market behavior*, edited by A. A. Mitchell. American Marketing Association.
Schoener, Thomas W.
    1971 The theory of feeding strategies. *Annual Review of Ecology and Systematics* 2:369–404.
Sharp, Lawrence
    1952 Steel axes for stone-age Australians. *Human Organization* 11:17–22.
Silberbauer, George B.
    1981 *Hunter and Habitat in the Central Kalahari Desert*. Cambridge University Press, New York.
Smith, Bruce D.
    1974 Middle Mississippian exploitation of animal populations: a predictive model. *American Antiquity* 30:274–291.
Smith, Eric A., and Bruce Winterhalder
    1981 New perspectives on hunter–gatherer socioecology. In *Hunter–gatherer foraging strategies*, edited by B. Winterhalder and E. A. Smith. University of Chicago Press, Chicago.
Steward, Julian H.
    1938 Basin–plateau aboriginal socio-political groups. *Bureau of American Ethnological Bulletin* 120.
Turnbull, Colin
    1965 *Wayward Servants*. Natural History Press, Garden City, N.Y.

Welinder, Stig
    1975   Prehistoric agriculture in eastern middle Sweden. *Acta Archaeologica Lundensia Series in 9 Minore 4.*
Wiessner, Polly
    1982   Risk, reciprocity and social influences on !Kung San economics. In *Politics and history in band societies,* edited by E. Leacock and R. B. Lee. Cambridge University Press, New York.
Wiens, John A.
    1977   On competition and variable environments. *American Scientists* 65:590–597.
Williams, B. J.
    1975   A model of band society. *Memoirs of the Society for American Archaeology* 29.
Winterhalder, Bruce
    1977   *Foraging strategy alternatives of the boreal forest Cree: An evaluation of theories and models from evolutionary ecology.* Ph.D. dissertation, Cornell University.
    1981   Foraging strategies in the boreal forest: an analysis of Cree hunting and gathering. In *Hunter–gatherer foraging strategies,* edited by B. Winterhalder and E. A. Smith. University of Chicago Press, Chicago.
Wobst, H. Martin
    1978   The archaeo-ethnology of hunter–gatherers. *American Antiquity* 43:303–309.

CHAPTER 6

The Hunter–Gatherer/Agricultural Frontier in Prehistoric Temperate Europe

ROBIN W. DENNELL

Department of Prehistory and Archaeology
University of Sheffield
Sheffield, England

INTRODUCTION

Hunter–gatherers and agriculturalists coexisted in many parts of prehistoric Europe for several centuries, and in some areas, for millennia. In some cases, farming communities—particularly the earliest ones in temperate Europe—were scattered amongst predominantly hunter–gatherer populations; in other areas, and especially in later prehistory, the two were more clearly segregated, and a distinct frontier existed between them. The spread of agriculture was sometimes rapid, sometimes gradual (and occasionally it even retreated), while at other times little change occurred for long periods. There is a wealth of topics that could be explored concerning the relationships between hunter–gatherers and agriculturalists in prehistoric Europe. Two of the most fruitful that could be investigated are the ways in which they each influenced the behavior of the other; and the role that hunter–gatherer groups played in aiding or impeding the expansion and intensification of agriculture.

Unfortunately, however, the hunter–gatherer/agricultural frontier has received little of the attention that it deserves in studies of European prehistory. Instead, those who lived on either side of this frontier have been investigated in almost total isolation from the other. One obvious symptom of this "academic apartheid" is the way that prehistoric studies are structured in most European teaching and research institutions. In most cases a fundamental division is drawn between the study of the Paleolithic and Mesolithic on the one hand, and the Neolithic and later periods on the other; that is, between hunter–gatherer and supposedly agricultural societies. Only rarely are prehistorians trained to study both; in the majority of cases, the teaching of and research into the two are kept separate, thus attempts to investigate how these groups may have interacted in the past are seriously thwarted. As far as temperate Europe is concerned, local Mesolithic groups are assumed to have played no useful part in the expansion of agriculture across their territories, nor are later hunter–gatherer groups assumed to have had any significant relationships with agriculturalists in adjacent regions. As in the last century, the expansion of agriculture to areas such as central Europe and Britain is still explained as the result of agricultural colonization. Indeed, despite the realization over the last 15 years that the presence of Neolithic traits—notably pottery and polished stone—does not necessarily imply that agriculture was practiced, the Mesolithic–Neolithic interface is still treated as an appropriate point at which to demarcate the change from hunting–gathering to farming in Europe.

The reason why this frontier has been so neglected stems largely from the way that European prehistory has developed over the last two centuries. From the very onset of prehistoric studies in Europe, the frontier between hunter–gatherers and early farmers was drawn in *chronological* rather than *spatial* terms. This was partly a result of the influence of geologists, who were crucial in the early nineteenth century in establishing the antiquity of man and in providing a simple chronological framework for the Lower, Middle and Upper Paleolithic. Inevitably perhaps, their influence also encouraged the view that the prehistoric record was essentially similar to the geological one in consisting of a series of "epochs." It was not until the latter part of the last century that prehistorians recognized that some of these stages overlapped in different parts of Europe, so that, for example, the Neolithic of northern Europe was contemporaneous with the Bronze Age in the Aegean.

An important influence on nineteenth-century prehistorians was the evolutionary attitudes inherited from the eighteenth century about the general nature of human history. By the mid-nineteenth century most prehistorians accepted the view that man had passed through a series of distinct social, economic, and technological stages. Contemporary hunter–gatherers were thus "primitive" and at the bottom of the ladder of progress. Societies in western Europe were "advanced" and had climbed several rungs to the top of the ladder, while all other societies were somewhere in between. Consequently, modern hunter–gatherers in, for example, North America or Australia were simply living fossils—relics of the societies that had once inhabited Europe. This view originated in the mid-eighteenth century and was most forcefully advocated by economists and politicians in France and Scotland (see e.g., Pollard 1968). As Turgot, a noted French political economist, proclaimed in 1750: "a glance over the earth puts before our eyes . . . the whole history of the human race, showing us traces of all the stages through which it has passed, from the barbarism, still in existence, of the American peoples, to the civilisations of the most enlightened nations of Europe" (Meek 1973:89). Similarly, Condorcet—a slightly later French politician—maintained at the end of the eighteenth century that by using "tales that travellers bring back to us about the state of the human race among the less civilised peoples, and . . . theoretical observations about the development of our intellectual and moral facilities" (Condorcet 1955:8), it was possible to show that man has progressed from hunting through pastoralism to agriculture.

These stages were accepted by nineteenth- and many twentieth-century prehistorians as convenient pegs on which to hang their archaeological rags. In the early 1800s, the assumption that there had been a sequence of stone, bronze, and iron provided what proved to be an invaluable means of devising a coherent chronological framework, but it also reflected the belief that man had progressed through a series of stages. Thus Nilsson, in his *Primitive Inhabitants of Scandinavia* (1837; English translation, 1868: lxiii), began his highly influential work with the assertion that "the human race [is] constantly undergoing a gradual and progressive development," and therefore in Europe had progressed from hunter to pastoralist to farmer and ultimately to civilization. Archaeological stone tools from Europe could thus be legitimately compared with those used elsewhere by recent hunter–gatherers and safely attributed to similar groups, even without any biological evidence for their subsistence strategies. The same outlook can be seen in Westropp's (1872) *Prehistoric Phases*. Like Nilsson, Condorcet, and Turgot before him, he too maintained that there was "one uniform process of development for every race, each passing through successive stages before attaining its highest social development. . . . These successive phases are the rude and barbarous, the hunting, the pastoral and the agricultural." He then took the critical step of linking what was then a *proven* technological sequence with an *assumed* economic one; thus the Mesolithic became equivalent to hunting, the Neolithic to pastoralism, and the Bronze Age to agriculture. A half-century later, the same intellectual outlook enabled Sollas (1924) to compare Tasmanians with the Lower Paleolithic, Aborigines with the Mousterian, and the Eskimo with the Upper Paleolithic.

From the viewpoint of both recent hunter–gatherers and later European prehistorians, it was singularly unfortunate that the "primitive" societies of America, Australia, and Africa were observed by Europeans just at the time when the latter were annexing their lands and settling them with agricultural colonists. It was this contact experience that played so vital a role in determining the way that European prehistorians perceived the nature of the frontier between the last hunter–gatherers and the first farmers on their own continent. First, Europeans tended to have an exceedingly low opinion of hunter–gatherers: they were deemed to be savage, primitive, incapable of progress or of elevating themselves above their wretched state, and patently inferior to Europeans in every respect. In Nilsson's (1868:lxiv) opinion: "The earliest tribes, of which we find traces in every country, show that . . . they have belonged to a race of beings on the very lowest point of civilisation: mountain grottoes, subterranean caves, or stone caverns, their dwellings; rough-hewn stone flakes, their hunting and fishing implements; no domesticated animals except the dog. . . . The savage has few other than material wants, and these he endeavours to satisfy only for the moment. . . . He thinks and acts only for the day which *is,* not for the day which is *coming.*" The view that recent and prehistoric hunter–gatherers were incapable of learning how to practice agriculture is one that has persisted to recent times. Case (1969a), for example, maintained that one important reason why the Neolithic (and thus agriculture) of Britain must have originated from agricultural immigration was that "cereal cultivation with hand-tools demands not only knowledge but social effort and tradition: thus the possibilities are unlikely that it was . . . imitated by enterprising natives who had stolen or bartered for seed-corn overseas."

Second, because agriculture spread into hunter–gatherer territories during the eighteenth and nineteenth centuries in the Americas, Australia, and much of Africa by a process of ethnic replacement, so the same must have occurred in prehistoric Europe. A clear example of this supposition can be seen in an influential work by Boyd-Dawkins (1880:247) when he discussed "the arrival of the prehistoric farmer, and the herdsmen—the Neolithic civilisation" in Britain. He wrote "we have to chronicle in the Prehistoric period the changes wrought . . . by the invasions of new peoples, and the appearance of new civilisations—*changes similar to those which are now rapidly causing the hunters of the bison in the far west to disappear before the advance of the English colonist*" (italics mine).

Third, since indigenous hunter–gatherers played no useful part in promoting the spread of farming across their territories in recent times, then in temperate regions of Europe, aboriginal hunter–gatherers must have been equally inconsequential to the expansion of farming.

These attitudes were unfortunately reinforced by the lack of evidence (until well into the nineteenth century) that Europe was even occupied when supposedly first colonized by farming groups. According to those who supported the notion of the *ancien hiatus,* man had retreated to the far north with reindeer at the end of the last glaciation. The last of the Magdalenians thus became the first of the Eskimo or Lapps (depending upon one's preference), and Europe remained uninhabited until resettled by farmers several millennia later. Curiously and somewhat preversely, the abandonment of this view by the end of the last century made virtually no difference to explanations of how agriculture had spread into Europe. This was—as already noted—partly because of the low opinion prehistorians had of hunter–gatherers in general, but also because the evidence for the Mesolithic in particular was so derisory.

In contrast with the majestic cave paintings and naturalistic engravings of the late Paleolithic, there were only a few crudely daubed pebbles from sites such as Mas D'Azil. As Clark (1978:2) remarked, even the microlithic nature of Mesolithic technology seemed to emphasize the insignificance of their makers; and their main activity appeared to have been shell gathering, a humdrum activity with none of the glamour or skill of hunting reindeer or mammoth. Mesolithic societies were therefore (and still are in some quarters) described in terms of "decline" or "degeneration," and unfavorable analogies were often drawn between them and strandloopers of southern Africa and Australia. Not surprisingly, the Mesolithic became treated as the "scrag-end" of the Paleolithic and were regarded as an inconsequential and best-forgotten interlude between the rugged splendor of the late Paleolithic and the secure domesticity of the Neolithic. Its status was further diminished by the widely held view that the growth of dense tree cover in the early Holocene resulted in a catastrophic lowering of population during the Mesolithic to a level far below that of the late Glacial. The consequent combination of prejudices towards recent hunter–gatherers and the poverty of the evidence for the Mesolithic strongly reinforced the view that any contact between the last hunter–gatherers and first farmers in Europe must have been short, of no tangible benefit to agriculturalists, or to hunter–gatherers whose extinction was imminent, if not overdue.

At this juncture, a useful starting point is to consider some of the assumptions that have been consistently made about, first, the early farmers in Europe, and then their hunter–gatherer neighbors.

EARLY FARMERS AND COLONIZATION

We can note several crucial differences between the pattern of agricultural expansion in the eighteenth to nineteenth centuries, and that which probably characterized Europe several millennia earlier. First, recent agricultural colonists in Australia and Africa enjoyed a massive technological superiority over the aboriginal populations with whom they came into contact. In particular, they possessed the gun and the horse, which together allowed white settlers to defend themselves against, or to attack (or massacre) hunter–gatherer groups whose lands were being "appropriated." As one example out of a multitude that could be cited, we can note an incident at Myall's Creek in Australia in 1838, where 12 armed shepherds on horseback killed a group of 30 Aborigines; the only remarkable aspect of this encounter was that it resulted in the first execution of Europeans for killing Aborigines (Harrison 1978). In those parts of North America where Indians had already acquired guns and horses, the contest was less one-sided for a time, but the outcome still inevitable. Early European settlers also possessed metal axes, which were indispensable to the forest clearance that accompanied agricultural expansion into Canada, Australia, and much of Russia. The combination of the gun, horse, and metal axe had two catastrophic results on local hunter–gatherer groups. The first was that the gun and horse could be used to decimate their numbers: one of many sad examples that could be chosen is the decline in the aboriginal populations of Tasmania from approximately 20,000 in 1802 to only 320 in 1825 (Davies 1973:273). The second was that the gun and axe could eliminate much of their resources. Thus, the slaughter of perhaps 40–60 million bison in the Far West (Roe, 1951) and the clearance of vast areas of forest in New South Wales for sheep grazing made the position of aboriginal groups in those regions wholly untenable.

The situation in prehistoric Europe would have been very different. Early farming groups did not have the same technological superiority over indegenous hunter–gatherers, and would have been unable either to reduce their numbers or to deny them their food resources. Indeed, early farming settlements would have been highly vulnerable to hostile hunter–gatherers: their settlements could easily be attacked, standing crops damaged, and livestock stolen or killed. In view of such vulnerability, the lack of evidence for defended settlements or warfare during the initial phase of agricultural settlement in temperate Europe is particularly noteworthy; one has only to recall Childe's (1958) contrast of the peaceful nature of early farming in central Europe with the warlike tendencies of later societies.

It is unlikely that early farming communities would have been able to exert pressure on hunter–gatherer resources as in recent times. Colonial agriculture was encouraged to produce primary agricultural goods (grain, meat, wool) for export to the mother country (or, in the case of the United States, for the eastern seaboard), and thus produced far more than was needed for local consumption. By contrast, the first agriculture in temperate Europe was on a small scale and primarily concerned with subsistence.

Palynological data indicate that initial agricultural forest clearance was small-scale and it seems unlikely that the whole of temperate Europe was cleared of forest during the Neolithic. Clearance also would have been a slow process if polished stone axes were the main method, since these are at best only half as efficient and durable as metal ones (Coles 1979:103). Even if agriculturalists cleared forest by ring-barking and by the use of pigs and goats to prevent regeneration (see Rowley-Conwy 1981), it seems highly improbable that early farmers could have completely destroyed the hunter–gatherer resource base, even in those areas where there was only a slight overlap in time between the two.

This last point is strengthened if we consider the difference in scale between the agricultural colonization in recent times and that which occurred at the end of the Mesolithic in Europe. Nineteenth century colonization was on a massive scale, "inconceivable but for the economic and technological achievements of European civilisation in the nineteenth century" (Erikson 1976:10), and it resulted in the swamping of local hunter–gatherer populations. Although the total number of those who left Europe for the Americas, Africa, and Australia in the last century will never be known in detail, some 23 million are known to have departed between 1840 and 1900 (Erikson 1976:10). Not surprisingly, few hunter–gatherer societies entered the twentieth-century intact.

Although the difficulties of estimating late Mesolithic and early farming populations in Europe are daunting, the former are most unlikely to have been swamped by the latter. This problem has two components. The first is that the Near East is unlikely to have been a demographic cistern that overflowed its surplus population onto Europe; instead, early farming populations appear to have been very low. For example, in Iranian Kurdistan, settlements such as Tepe Asiab and Sarab had been founded by the seventh millennium b.c., yet in the neighboring Kangovar valley, there were no agricultural settlements for another 2000 years (McDonald 1979). In the Çumra basin of western Turkey, Can Hasan III is the only site known to have been occupied around 7000 b.c.; two millennia later, there were only three in this basin (French 1970). Another example are the islands of the eastern Mediterranean. At the beginning of the seventh millennium b.c., only 4 of the 80-odd islands were occupied; two millennia later, the number had scarcely doubled (Cherry 1981).

The second component is based on evidence from mainland Europe that suggests both low numbers of people in the initial phases of agricultural settlement, and very low growth rates for a long time thereafter. Large areas of southern Greece and Crete remained unoccupied by farming groups until the fourth or even third millennium b.c. (Halstead 1981); in the Nova Zagora region of southern Bulgaria, there were only 12 early Neolithic settlements, compared with about 30 by the late Neolithic (Dennell 1978). In the Middle Neckar region of Germany, the density of initial agricultural settlement was only $1/1000$ km^2 (Milisauskas 1978:99). If, as has been suggested (e.g., Hammond 1981), these settlements contained only 30–60 inhabitants, the first farming populations in temperate Europe may have been no larger than those of the local hunter–gatherers at the time of contact. For example, Clark (1972) suggested that preboreal population densities in Mesolithic Britain may have averaged $30-70/1000$ km^2; in the area of southwest Germany studied by Jochim (1976:135), the maximum density of Mesolithic population may have been $130/1000$ km^2.

Finally, we should consider the infrastructure available to recent settlers but not to prehistoric agricultural colonists. In addition to their superior numbers, recent colonists could rely upon large-scale transport, such as shipping (both across oceans and along major river systems), and later railways; rapid communication facilities (horse, and later telegraph); and a centralized authority that could provide military assistance if required. Because of these points, early agricultural communities in temperate Europe are unlikely to have been able to displace local hunter–gatherers, to appropriate their resources, or to combat them successfully if they proved hostile.

THE HUNTER–GATHERER POPULATIONS

A considerable amount of evidence from the last 15 years has shown that many of the prejudices towards hunter–gatherers in general, and those of the Mesolithic in particular, were unjustified. First, the distinction made between the food extraction of hunter–gatherers and the food production of agriculturalists has lost much of its former crispness. We note, for example, Australian data showing how food production—including the planting, protection, reaping, and storage of plant foods (Allen 1974); the construction of channels to breed eel (Lourandos 1980); and the burning of scrub to encourage the growth of plant foods (Gould 1971)—figured in aboriginal societies supposedly concerned only with food extraction. Secondly, Schrire's (1980) recent study of the San bushmen of the Kalahari indicates clearly that hunter–gatherers can adopt different subsistence strategies if they perceive that it is in their interests to do so. As she demonstrates, these people have alternated between hunting–gathering and herding their own or others' livestock in the last 300 years, and probably since they first came into contact with pastoralists a millennium or so ago.

Some mesolithic populations may have been practicing various forms of food production in temperate Europe by the time of agricultural contact.

For example, palynological data from Britain suggest that woodland was being managed systematically by burning (Mellars 1976), and game may have been provided with ivy as winter feed (Simmons and Dimbleby 1974). Evidence that red deer (Jarman 1972), cattle, or pigs (Bradley 1978:99) were being herded is inconclusive but intriguing. We can note also that there is no reason to suppose that population declined at the end of the last glaciation; on the contrary, the hunter–gatherer populations at the time of contact were probably the largest that had inhabited Europe to that time.

The balance of this study considers various types of frontiers that may have existed between hunter–gatherers and early agriculturalists in different parts of Europe. A more specific aim is to show that the spread of agriculture into this region need not be explained as the result of colonization by an incoming farming group at the expense of indigenous hunter–gatherers.

For the purposes of this study, we can follow Alexander's (1978) suggestion and distinguish between *mobile* and *static* frontiers.

MOBILE FRONTIERS

The expansion of agriculture across much of Europe after 6000 b.c. affords perhaps one of the clearest instances of a mobile frontier in European prehistory. Its main features have been calibrated by ^{14}C (Ammerman and Cavalli-Sforza 1971; Clark 1965) and can be presented as an isochronic map (see Figure 6.1). At present the resulting picture is of varying quality: as Barker (1975) pointed out, it is not always clear whether the spread of agriculture or pottery is being monitored. Nevertheless, the general pattern is reasonably secure: there was a rapid expansion of agriculture by pottery-using communities living in large, permanent settlements between 5300 and 4300 b.c. across much of southeast and central Europe; thereafter, agricultural expansion into northern and western Europe was more gradual and was seldom associated with large, year-round settlements until much later.

This type of isochronic map describes, but does not explain, what actually happened. In view of the diversity of the archaeological record for early agriculture in temperate Europe, it is quite possible that we are viewing the outcome of several processes. However, for reasons already explained, we are unlikely to be dealing with the same type of agricultural colonization as in recent times that resulted in the swamping of local hunter–gatherer populations.

Among the various types of mobile frontiers that could have resulted in the expansion of agriculture across prehistoric Europe, four can be considered. The first three are *porous*—they allowed for the transference of peo-

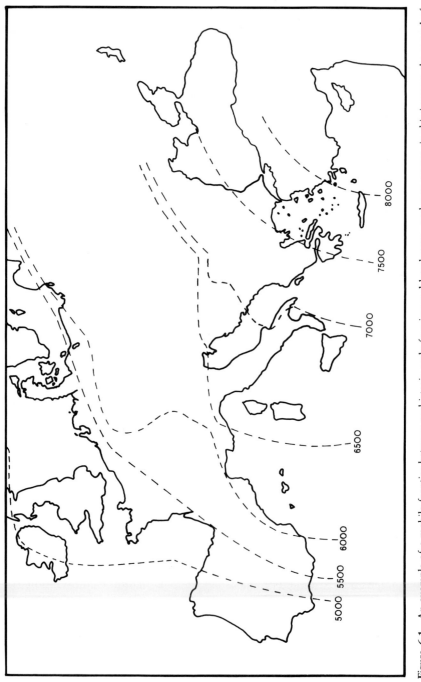

Figure 6.1 An example of a mobile frontier between prehistoric early farming and late hunter–gatherer groups, in this instance the spread of farming across Europe after 8000 b.p. As argued in the text, this type of frontier can be explained in several ways. (From Ammerman and Cavalli-Sforza 1971.)

ple, resources, and techniques across a frontier between early farming communities and hunter–gatherers in adjacent or even distant territories.)

Agricultural Expansion through Hunter–Gatherer Immigration

(This model assumes that an area was initially settled by a few small communities possessing new types of resources—notably domestic sheep-/goat, wheat, barley, and legumes—and novel techniques such as pottery making and stone polishing) Further assumptions are that they lived year-round in their settlements, exploited annual territories smaller than those of their hunter–gatherer neighbors, and had a higher net *per capita* productivity.) Because local hunter–gatherers used larger territories than the incoming group, and since the latter spent most of their time within their own area because of high labor requirements, contact between the two groups usually took place in the agricultural territory. This implies that hunter–gatherers spent more time in the vicinity of the agricultural settlement than vice versa.) If Baker (1978: 121–133) is correct (as seems reasonable) that most of the exploratory behavior leading to contact between the two groups would have been undertaken by subadult and young adult males, then this age group of the hunter–gatherers would also have been the most familiar with the agriculturalists. Let us consider first the likely responses of each group to the other, then the probable results of those responses.

The Viewpoint of the Agriculturalists

As a group the feelings of the agriculturalists were likely to have been mixed. On the one hand, suspicion and even fear of an alien group is both reasonable and probable. However, it is also reasonable to assume a general feeling that tensions and competition should be avoided as much as possible. First, they lacked the fire power and manpower to retaliate effectively, especially in what easily could have become guerrilla warfare in which they would have been seriously disadvantaged. Second, they would have had much to gain from amicable relations with their hunter–gatherer neighbors who possessed a considerable and potentially useful knowledge of the resources and terrain, and who also had useful resources such as furs, hides, game, and raw materials that could be obtained through exchange. Perhaps most important for newly founded communities in which children were economically useful at an early stage, and which might need to recruit people in its initial stages, hunter–gatherer populations were also potentially valuable as a source of mates and labor.)

The Viewpoint of the Hunter–Gatherers

As a group, the attitudes of the hunter–gatherers were also likely to have been mixed. Given the potential threat to their way of life, even if more imagined than real, some may well have felt hostility toward the incoming group. However, curiosity about the novel resources, techniques, and way of life of the immigrant population was likely to be equally appealing.

What would probably have been important were the attitudes of the subadults and young adults, particularly if, as suggested, they spent the most time in the vicinity of the agriculturalists. From their point of view, the life of the newcomers is likely to have held attractions. On this point we need to be wary: as ethnographic data indicate (e.g., Lee and DeVore 1968), hunter–gatherers can eat better and work less than their agricultural neighbors. The caloric and protein intake of the two groups need not have differed greatly when averaged over the year, but the agricultural community probably had to spend more time in obtaining and processing their food than the local hunter–gatherer groups. Agriculture had its advantages, however, in that much less time was wasted in searching for food, and the problems of procuring food in winter were mitigated by the storage of grain and pulses, and perhaps the stalling of livestock.

We can also suggest that an additional attraction of the agricultural lifestyle to subadult and young adult hunter–gatherers would have been its material culture—particularly more substantial houses, novel items such as pottery, polished stone, and so forth. To reinforce this point, we may draw an analogy with the spread of Western influence currently affecting many Third World countries, particularly since it is most often manifested among subadults and young adults. Here, the change in life-style engendered by moving from rural to urban areas may accrue no particular gain in terms of standard of living and economic autonomy; indeed, it may even be accompanied by a decline in the quality of life. However, the *perceived* change in status can be considerable since it provides access to the trappings of Western culture—the T-shirts, digital watches, television sets, and so forth—that carry with them considerable status value. The important point here is that social and economic change may be initiated for reasons that appear trivial or even ridiculous to outsiders (such as ourselves) but are nevertheless of great importance to their participants.

The Result of Contact: Hunter–Gatherer Assimilation

What is being proposed here is, in effect, fairly simple: (1) that both parties had a vested interest in maintaining amicable relationships with each other; (2) that the hunter–gatherer populations represented the most obvious and immediate source of recruitment for agriculturalists; and, (3) that they in turn provided a highly useful insurance policy for hunter–gatherer groups. Furthermore, it is also suggested that the symbols of the intrusive agricultural way of life could have been important devices for encouraging hunter–gatherers to transfer to agricultural groups. The net result would thus have been a gain of mates by the farming groups and a corresponding loss by the aboriginals. By this interaction, agricultural communities would have acquired the ability to found sibling settlements as well as the knowledge of where best to locate them. Within only two or three generations of agricultural incursion into a hunting–gathering territory (i.e., within the time resolution of ^{14}C), the indigenous communities would have lost most of their breeding potential and their long-term viability would thus have ceased. A rapid agricultural expansion thus could have occurred at the expense of hunting–gathering because, in effect, the agriculturalist group hijacked the mating and information network of the hunter–gatherers. (An alternative outcome to this sequence of events is discussed later in the context of static frontiers.)

This model can be examined against the data for early agricultural (Linearbandkeramik or LBK) settlement in central Europe. The main features of this evidence have been presented elsewhere (e.g., Hammond 1981; Milisauskas 1978; Tringham 1971), so only a few points need to be noted.

First, agricultural settlements were established rapidly across a large area of central Europe between 4500 and 4300 b.c. (see Figure 6.2). Initial expansion occurred in what have been called *Siedlungskämmern*, or settlement cells, located in river valleys and in areas where Mesolithic occupation appears to have been slight. Settlements seem to have been composed of 6 to 12 wooden longhouses in several small hamlets perhaps about 1 km apart rather than, as first thought, in large nucleated villages of up to 100 houses. Although present evidence is far from ideal, domestic wheat, barley, and legumes, as well as domestic cattle, sheep, and goat, provided the main sources of food. Contrary to earlier views, crop agriculture was not based upon shifting cultivation but upon some kind of short fallow or rotational system (see e.g., Willerding 1980). This point is highly relevant to explanations of how LBK expansion was accomplished so rapidly. A striking feature of the material culture is its homogeneity over a vast territory from Czechoslovakia to the Netherlands; another is the quality of its pottery and polished stonework. Finally, we can note that the LBK appears as a completely intrusive tradition into Mesolithic territory; that the overlap between the two seems to have been very brief (perhaps not more than a century), and that the appearance of the LBK was more or less synchronous with the demise of hunting and gathering in this region.

The prevailing explanation of LBK expansion is that it resulted from

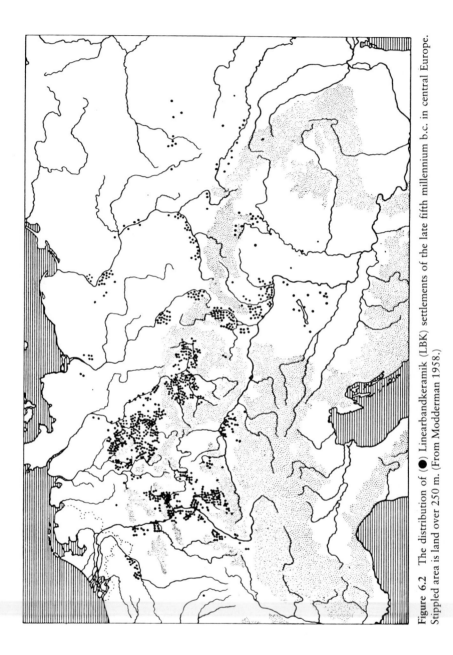

Figure 6.2 The distribution of (●) Linearbandkeramik (LBK) settlements of the late fifth millennium b.c. in central Europe. Stippled area is land over 250 m. (From Modderman 1958.)

agricultural colonization in which local populations played no part (see e.g., Hammond 1981; Tringham 1971). This view satisfactorily explains the complete break in material culture between the late Mesolithic and the LBK, and provides one explanation of how agricultural expansion was accomplished in a short period over a large area. It can, however, be criticized on two grounds.

First, it does not explain why hunting–gathering seems to have died out in the whole of this region as soon as agriculture appeared. As already stated, there is no evidence for warfare at the time of contact, and it is hard to imagine that local hunter–gatherers were so indifferent to their impending extinction as to take no retaliatory action. One explanation of this feature has been that agricultural expansion occurred in areas of marginal importance to local hunter–gatherers, thus competition was minimized. However, it remains to be demonstrated that these areas were marginal to Mesolithic occupation: given that many LBK sites in river valleys have been buried and found only through deep-ploughing, pipeline construction, and the like (see Hammond 1981:217), it would not be surprising if many smaller and less noticeable Mesolithic sites have escaped detection. Even if LBK settlement did occur in areas of unusually sparse Mesolithic population, it is also curious that there is as yet no evidence for the kind of *static* frontier that could have developed beyond these marginal areas between the two communities (see pp. 133–134) and been maintained for a long period.

Second, although very imperfect, skeletal data from LBK sites suggest that their inhabitants were similar to those of the late Paleolithic (Jelinek 1975); that is, there seems to have been no major degree of ethnic replacement.

In contrast, these difficulties are overcome if we assume that there was a *porous* frontier across which hunter–gatherers—especially those of reproductive age—migrated into agricultural groups, adopted their traditions, and provided much of the recruitment and knowledge needed for subsequent expansion. This model would account for the lack of evidence for any warfare; the rapid disappearance of hunting and gathering; the equally rapid expansion of agriculture; and the lack of evidence for substantial ethnic replacement.

Agricultural Expansion through Hunter–Gatherer Acquisition

This model shows how agriculture could have expanded into an area occupied by hunter–gatherers without any movement by a colonizing agricultural population. It rests on three assumptions:

1. That contact between hunter–gatherers and agriculturalists is more likely to occur in the vicinity of agricultural settlements than of hunter–

gatherers. As stated in the previous model, hunter–gatherer territories are usually larger than those of agriculturalists. Because of the amount of time that has to be expended within the confines of an agricultural territory, they are less likely to make long-distance trips than hunter–gatherers.

2. That hunter–gatherers will alter their subsistence strategy if they perceive it is advantageous to do so. Schrire's (1980) study of the San bushmen mentioned already provide one convenient instance; there is no reason why it should be unique. Mbuti shows they don't

3. That hunter–gatherers do not live in sealed cultural systems and would thus be aware of communities beyond their annual territories. As Wobst (1978) points out, ethnographic studies can all too easily—and wrongly—give the impression that recent hunter–gatherers were unaware of, and unaffected by, the world outside their own mating networks. This view is all the more likely to result when those aspects of their behavior that result from external contact are regarded as a distortion of their "real" behavior, are filtered out, and the rest treated as exemplifying their "traditional" way of life. So far as late Mesolithic Europe is concerned, its inhabitants are likely to have been aware of the fact that groups elsewhere used cereals, legumes, sheep, and pottery, just as early farming groups would have known of the existence of hunter–gatherer groups.

The starting point of this model is that some hunter–gatherer groups beyond the agricultural frontier were already trying to raise their food production before contact. In temperate Europe this could have been done by intensification; for example, by deliberate management of woodland to increase the amount of plant foods, or browse for game; perhaps by the herding of primary game animals such as red deer; or by more intensive usage of coastal and aquatic resources. It may also have been accomplished by more extensive foraging; in maritime areas, this could have been done by fishing further offshore for deep-sea fish.

In the course of more extensive food procurement trips, contact was made with agricultural groups. As in the previous model, initial contact was largely between subadult and young adult males; as before, it led to observation of new resources and techniques. Some skills, like potting, may have been learned by hunter–gatherers through imitation; others—such as cereal cultivation or sheep herding—required both observation and their acquisition. Initially, small-scale experimentation was practiced in the home hunter–gatherer territory as an insurance policy, or at most, as an adjunct to existing practices. Gradually, the introduced resources became more important and eventually supplanted those previously used. As a result, these populations achieved their own economic and social transformation and became agriculturalists without any colonization.

This model should have discrete archaeological correlates. The first is that there should be evidence in the hunter–gatherer territory of attempts to intensify food production immediately prior to contact. Second, as agricultural techniques and resources were initially incorporated into existing hunter–gatherer practices, there is unlikely to be a clear transition from one form of economy to the other. Indeed, there might be a period extending over several generations when these societies could be regarded as neither fully hunter–gatherer nor fully agricultural. Third, because hunter–gatherer contact with agricultural societies could take place along a wide front and with widely separated farming groups, developments in material culture in the hunter–gatherer territory are likely to show eclectic influences from several areas. In this respect, agricultural expansion through hunter–gatherer acquisition should be distinguishable from that brought about by colonization: in the latter case, newly founded agricultural settlements should be clearly attributable to a donor culture elsewhere. (We can also suggest that those hunter–gatherers who observed material items in agricultural communities may not necessarily have been those who made them later in the hunter–gatherer territory: pottery making, for example, may have been observed by young male hunter–gatherers, but made later by hunter–gatherer females. As a consequence, differences between the observed and the copied will be increased.) One further corollary of this model is that the *first* evidence for contact should be the presence of agricultural techniques and resources in the hunter–gatherer territories. This point emphasizes the need to be able to distinguish this type of agricultural introduction from that brought about by colonization.

One area where this model is applicable is Britain. First, late Mesolithic populations seem to have been attempting to intensify their food production in various ways: through forest clearance to increase the productivity and perhaps predictability of woodland resources (Mellars 1976); through providing animals with winter feed (Simmons and Dimbleby 1974); and perhaps through domesticating cattle and pig (Bradley 1978:99). These societies would thus not have been wholly unaware of the potential value of novel resources such as cereals, legumes, and sheep.

Second, seafaring was probably an integral part of Mesolithic life in coastal regions by the beginning of the fourth millennium b.c. At around 7000 b.c. Ireland was colonized, presumably by sea; in Scotland, the island of Jura was reached by 6000 b.c.; by the end of the fifth millennium b.c., the island of Oronsay was frequented throughout the year. Remains of deep-water fish have been retrieved from coastal middens at Oronsay and Morton, also in Scotland. The vessels used offshore are likely to have been more substantial than the simple dug-out canoes found in various lake and river deposits in northern Europe, and were probably like the composite skin-boats depicted in Norwegian rock engravings of the later Stone Age (Clark 1975:213–215).

Third, it is extremely hard in Britain to determine when the Mesolithic ended and the Neolithic began. This is because the same type of forest clearance that was associated with the Neolithic has been identified from palynological sources in contexts antedating the first evidence of pottery—one of the main Neolithic traits. In view of the fact that "the actual onset of Neolithic clearance is not easy to define" (Bradley 1978:99), and several workers (e.g., Pennington 1975; Spratt and Simmons 1976) have found it difficult to distinguish Mesolithic from Neolithic forest clearance, it is perhaps a moot point that Britain was ever occupied in the fourth millennium b.c. by two groups, one local and the other immigrant.

Fourth, the origins of the British Neolithic have always remained enigmatic. There is no single area in northern Europe that can be considered to contain the cultural traditions that were directly ancestral to those seen in Britain by the end of the fourth millennium b.c. Instead, the British Neolithic seems to be a hodge-podge of different traits that can be derived from a large expanse of the coastal hinterland from Jutland to Brittany. This feature has been explained in two ways. One is that the donor culture(s) may lie in areas now submerged (Case 1969b); the other is that colonizing groups from the continent faced such problems in learning seafaring and coping with an alien environment that their cultural traditions became warped in the process (see e.g., Bradley 1978:99). Both these explanations are untestable, and can be avoided if the expansion of agriculture to Britain is attributed to the contact by indigenous Mesolithic hunter–gatherer populations with a variety of agricultural groups along the north European coast and its hinterland.

Agricultural Expansion into Hunter–Gatherer Areas through Resource Migration

Another way in which agriculture could have extended its distribution into hunter–gatherer areas is through the movement of resources without human aid. Given the propensity of plant and animals to disperse of their own accord into new habitats, and their complete disregard for political frontiers (Elton 1972; see Figure 6.3), there seems little reason why resources such as sheep, goat, cereals, or legumes could not have migrated into hunter–gatherer territories in temperate Europe. Less likely, however, is that they were then adopted by hunter–gatherers as resources that could be developed for long-term use. Although there seems no reason to suppose that agriculture expanded into parts of temperate Europe in this manner, it

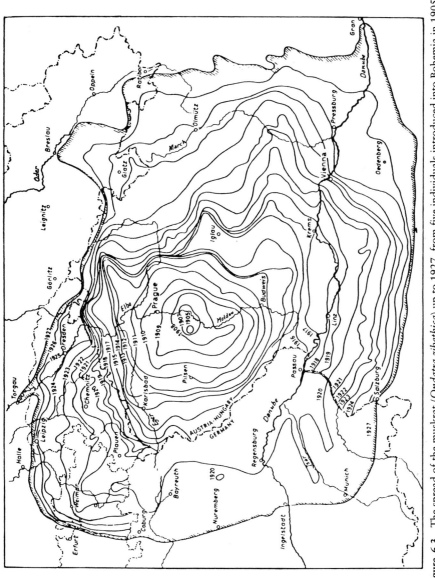

Figure 6.3 The spread of the muskrat (*Ondatra zibethica*) up to 1927, from five individuals introduced into Bohemia in 1905. This example shows the rapidity with which an animal species introduced into one area can colonize adjacent regions. Similar examples can be found for plant species. (From Elton 1972.)

may have occurred in southeast Europe in the early Holocene (Dennell 1983:158–168). This type of natural dispersal does, however, raise a problem that concerns studies of static open frontiers; that is, (the occasional presence of sheep bones in a hunter–gatherer site beyond the agricultural frontier could be attributed to an exchange network or could simply represent an animal that foolishly strayed onto the menu of a hunter–gatherer.)

Agricultural Expansion Through Colonization without Hunter–Gatherer Participation

For reasons already discussed, it is improbable that agriculture expanded in this way into the hunter–gatherer territories of temperate Europe; instead, this explanation tells us more about the ways that nineteenth-century prehistorians regarded modern hunter–gatherers and contemporary agriculture than about events several millennia ago. (There is, however, one variant of the colonial model that is at present untestable, but intriguing.)

(One possibility is that early agriculturalists (or their resources) brought with them diseases to which indigenous populations had little resistance. Any contact, therefore, brought with it disease and high hunter–gatherer mortality; agriculture thus advanced into freshly vacated areas.) Historical parallels are not hard to find; for example, the spread of cholera, influenza, the common cold, and tuberculosis wrought havoc among many aboriginal populations in areas affected by European contact. (What seems perhaps doubtful is whether European hunter–gatherers were as susceptible to the diseases of incoming agriculturalists as were the aboriginal populations of North America and Australia, which had been isolated from the rest of the world since the Pleistocene.)

STATIC FRONTIERS

(Static frontiers would have developed between hunter–gatherers and farmers in areas where hunter–gatherers felt no advantage in either acquiring and developing agricultural resources, or in becoming assimilated into agricultural groups (as perhaps in central Europe); or in regions that agriculturalists did not feel were worth colonizing. Two types of static frontier can be recognized: one open, the other closed.)

Open Static Frontiers

(From the viewpoint of agriculturalists, hunter–gatherers beyond the farming frontier could have provided a variety of useful commodities.)These might have included perishable items such as furs, skins, and game, or nonperishable goods such as amber, obsidian, greenstone, or flint. Conversely, farmers could have offered in exchange commodities such as pottery and polished stone, the contents of pots (e.g., alcohol), livestock (either dead or on the hoof), small amounts of grain, and perhaps milk products.

In principle, archaeological evidence of an open static frontier could be forthcoming from several sources. Trace element and other types of analysis should show whether agriculturalists imported raw materials from hunter–gatherers' areas or acquired them locally. On the hunter–gatherer side of the frontier, the presence of prestige items (such as imported pottery and polished axes) might be diagnostic, as well as fully processed grain that had been grown elsewhere. There might also be evidence in post-contact times of increased fur trapping or the emergence of local "big men" who enhanced their status by their ability to regulate exchange with agriculturalists.

The study of static open frontiers in European prehistory involves two main problems. The first problem is to locate the frontier between hunter–gatherers and agriculturalists. This cannot be done by simply assuming that the agricultural frontier lay at the boundary of the maximum distribution of items found in agricultural settlements. This is because these items—notably pottery, sheep/goat and cereals—may have been exchanged within this area with hunter–gatherer communities; consequently, the area in which agriculture was practiced may have been far smaller than that in which agricultural (and related) items were exchanged. This problem reinforces Barker's (1975) comment mentioned earlier about attempts to calibrate the spread of farming across temperate Europe: the first use of pottery, cereals and/or domestic livestock in an area may indicate only when these were acquired through exchange, not when farming was first practiced in that area. A pertinent example in this context is the Neolithic of western Russia where pottery, and occasionally domestic sheep, are found after 4000 b.c. in settlements whose inhabitants lived primarily by hunting and gathering (Dolukhanov 1979). In this instance, it is highly unlikely that agriculture was practiced in this region; rather, its inhabitants are better characterized as hunter–gatherers with limited access to agricultural commodities.

This point emphasizes the need to consider the overall context of the society in which agricultural items make their appearance. In more specific terms, it is necessary to see whether goods were produced in the same area that they were consumed. For example, the production of pottery may be evidenced by kilns, ovens, or clamps; of cereal crops by the presence of on-site crop processing activities; or of livestock by the frequencies of their anatomical elements and age profiles.

The second problem is in determining how a given static open frontier functioned; that is, in explaining how items produced on one side of the frontier came to be consumed, used, and discarded on the other. One possibility is that *symbiotic* relationships developed across the frontier so that each side benefited from the existence of the other. Alternatively, relationships could have been *parasitic* and dominated by raiding, abduction, and what Milisauskas (1978:85) euphemistically termed "negative reciprocity." The two might not be easily distinguishable. Suppose, for example, that items from agricultural settlements are found on the hunter–gatherer side of the frontier, but not vice versa: this evidence could indicate that agriculturalists exchanged goods that left archaeological traces (e.g., pottery, livestock, grain) for those that did not (such as fur and hides). On the other hand, this type of one-sided distribution could have resulted from hunter–gatherer theft rather than from some kind of Neolithic swap-shop. In this instance, clearer evidence of symbiotic relationships might come from the presence in agricultural settlements of items made from raw materials obtained in hunter–gatherer areas; or from materials obtainable only through the participation of hunter–gatherers in exchange networks between farming settlements. If relationships with hunter–gatherers had been parasitic and at the expense of agriculturalists, evidence of defended farming settlements and warfare might be obtained near the frontier. At present it is difficult to pursue these topics further in European prehistory because of the lack of attention given to the study of post-contact hunter–gatherer groups.

Closed Static Frontiers

One clear example of this type of frontier concerns the European Norse farming settlements on Greenland of the tenth to the fourteenth centuries (McGovern 1980). Here, relations with ther heathen Iniut neighbors were minimized, and contact between the two usually took place on the end of a projectile point. In the end, it was Norse society that collapsed and the Iniut who survived.

The closed static frontier should be marked archaeologically by a lack of evidence of exchange, and by evidence for warfare and defended farming sites. However, a less bellicose version of a closed static frontier might be one characterized by mutual indifference and indicated archaeologically by discrete spatial distributions of sites and artifacts, and by an absence of any indication of exchange. As yet, this type of study has been applied only to contemporaneous farming communities (e.g., Hodder 1977) and has not been undertaken in relation to prehistoric hunter–gatherer and agricultural societies in Europe.

DISCUSSION

The purpose of this essay has been to draw attention to the importance of the agricultural/hunter–gatherer frontier in European prehistory, and to show how it may have affected the spread of agriculture as well as the behavior of those on either side of this frontier. In doing so, I have suggested that the initial expansion of agriculture into temperate Europe is poorly explained in terms of an agricultural colonization in which local late Mesolithic hunter–gatherers played no part. This explanation is only one of many that could be used (see Figure 6.4), and probably reveals more about the attitudes of nineteenth-century prehistorians than about the ways agricultural expansion probably occurred. A more plausible explanation is that it owed much to the existence of indigenous hunter–gatherers, either by providing the necessary recruitment (as perhaps for the LBK), or in obtaining and subsequently developing agriculture in their own way (as suggested for Britain). Furthermore, the rate of agricultural expansion may have been overestimated by mistaking the acquisition of agricultural commodities by hunter–gatherers across open, static frontiers for actual agricultural colonization. In all these cases, our understanding of how farming spread into

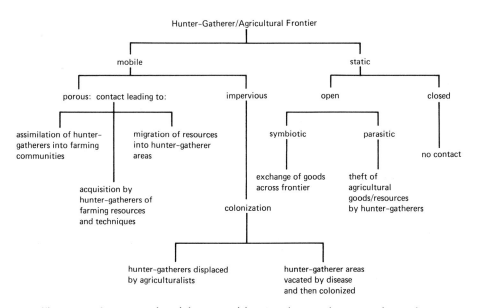

Figure 6.4 Some examples of the types of frontiers that may have existed in prehistoric temperate Europe between early agriculturalists and hunter–gatherer populations.

temperate Europe during and after the Neolithic will be seriously at fault unless the role of hunter–gatherers is integrated into explanations.

One important point to emerge in this essay is that contact between hunter–gatherers and agriculturalists is likely to have been initiated by hunter–gatherers in the territories of agriculturalists since the latter probably had smaller annual territories and higher labor requirements. Consequently, hunter–gatherers are more likely to have been better informed about agriculture than vice versa, and were probably in a better position to judge where agriculture could best be practiced in the future than were the farming communities. Because of this factor, the rate and pattern of agricultural expansion into hunter–gatherer territories was probably affected at least as much by the perception of hunter–gatherers as by that of agriculturalists. There is no reason why hunter–gatherers in temperate Europe should have returned from contact with early farming communities bearing the entire Neolithic package of pottery, polished stone, domestic plants and animals, and filled with an impulse to build villages and inhabit them year-round. Rather, they would probably have selected the techniques and/or resources that they thought would be useful and adapted them to their own ends. This point alone should argue for a much closer dialogue between those on either side of the Mesolithic–Neolithic frontier; it has perhaps been closed and static for too long.

ACKNOWLEDGMENT

I thank S. M. Stallibrass for useful comments on the final version of this chapter.

REFERENCES

Alexander, J.
    1978 Frontier studies and the earliest farmers in Europe. In *Social organisation and settlement, edited by D. Green, C. Haselgrove, and M. Spriggs. British Archaeological Reports International Series* 47.
Allen, H.
   ¬1974 The Bagundji of the Darling basin: cereal gatherers in an uncertain environment. *World Archaeology* 5(3):309–322.
Ammerman, A. J., and L. L. Cavalli-Sforza.
    1971 Measuring the rate of spread of early farming in Europe. *Man (N.S.)* 6:674–688.
Baker, R. R.
    1978 *The evolutionary ecology of animal migrations.* Hodder and Stoughton, London.
Barker, G.
    1975 Early neolithic land use in Yugoslavia, *Proceedings of the Prehistoric Society* 41:85–104.

Boyd-Dawkins, W.
1880 *Early man in Britain*. MacMillan, London.
Bradley, R.
1978 *The prehistoric settlement of Britain*. Routledge and Kegan Paul, London.
Case, H.
1969a Settlement-patterns in the north Irish Neolithic. *Ulster Journal of Archaeology* 32:3–27.
1969b Neolithic explanations. *Antiquity* 43:176–186.
Cherry, J. F.
1981 Pattern and process in the earliest colonisation of the Greek Islands. *Proceedings of the Prehistoric Society* 47:41–68.
Childe, V. G.
1958 *The prehistory of European society*. Penguin Ltd., London.
Clark, J. G. D.
1965 Radiocarbon dating and the expansion of farming culture from the Near East over Europe. *Proceedings of the Prehistoric Society* 31:58–73.
1972 Star Carr: a case study in bioarchaeology. *Addison-Wesley Modular Publications* 10:1–42.
1975 *The earlier stone age settlement of Scandinavia*. Cambridge University Press, Cambridge.
1978 Neothermal orientations. In *The early post-Glacial settlement of northern Europe*, edited by P. Mellars. Duckworth, London.
Coles, J.
1979 *Experimental archaeology*. Academic Press, London.
Condorcet, J. A. N. de C., Marquis de
1955 *Sketch for a historical picture of the progress of the human mind*. Translated by J. Barraclough. Weidenfeld and Nicholson, London.
Davies, D.
1973 *The Last of the Tasmanians*. Frederick Muller, London.
Dennell, R. W.
1978 Early farming in South Bulgaria from the VI to the IIIrd millennia B.C. *Brit. Archaeol. Rep. Internat. Ser.* 45:1–304.
Dennell, R. W.
1983 *European economic prehistory: a new approach*. Academic Press, London.
Dolukhanov, P.
1979 *Ecology and economy in Neolithic eastern Europe*. Duckworth, London.
Elton, C. R.
1972 *The ecology of invasions by animals and plants*. Chapman and Hall, London.
Erikson, C.
1976 *Emigration from Europe, 1815–1914*. Adam and Charles Black, London.
French, D. H.
1970 Notes on site distribution in the Çumra area. *Anatolian Studies* 20:139–148.
Gould, R. A.
1971 Uses and effects of fire among the western dessert Aborigines of Australia. *Mankind* 8:14–24.
Halstead, P. L. J.
1981 From determinism to uncertainty: social storage and the rise of the Minoan palace. In *Economic Archaeology, edited by A. Sheridan and G. Bailey*. Brit. Archaeol. Rep. Internat. Ser. 96.

Hammond, F.
  1981 The colonisation of Europe: the analysis of settlement process. In *Pattern of the past: studies in honour of David Clarke, edited by I. Hodder, G. Isaac, and N. Hammond.* Cambridge University Press, Cambridge.
Harrison, B.
  1978 The Myall Creek massacre. In *Records of times past,* edited by I. McBryde. Australian Institute of Aboriginal Studies, Canberra.
Hodder, I.
  1977 The distribution of material culture items in the Baringo district, western Kenya. *Man (N.S.)* 12:239–269.
Jarman, M. R.
  1972 European deer economies and the advent of the Neolithic. In *Papers in economic prehistory,* edited by E. S. Higgs. Cambridge University Press, Cambridge.
Jelinek, J.
  1975 Middle Neolithic antropological finds from Štúrovo, South Slovakia. *Anthropologie* (Czech) 13(3):183–192.
Jochim, M. A.
  1976 *Hunting–gathering subsistence and settlement: a predictive model.* Academic Press, New York.
Lee, R. B., and DeVore, I.
  1968 *Man the hunter.* Aldine, Chicago.
Lourandos, H.
  ⟶1980 Change or stability?: hydraulics, hunter-gatherers and population in temperate Australia. *World Archaeology* 11(3):245–264.
McDonald, M. M. A.
  1979 *An examination of mid-Holocene settlement patterns in the central Zagros region of western Iran.* Ph.D. dissertation, University of Toronto.
McGovern, T. H.
  1980 Cows, harp seals, and church bells: adaptation and extinction in Norse Greenland. *Human Ecology* 8(3):245–275.
Meek, R. L.
  1973 *Turgot on Progress, Sociology and Economics.* Cambridge: Cambridge University Press.
Mellars, P. A.
  1976 Fire ecology, animal populations and man: a study of some ecological relationships in prehistory. *Proceedings of the Prehistoric Society* 42:15–46.
Milisauskas, S.
  1978 *European prehistory.* Academic Press, London.
Modderman, P. J. R.
  1958 Die geographische Lage der bandkeramischen Siedlungen in der Niederlanden. *Palaeohistoria* 6:1–6.
Nilsson, S.
  1868 *The primitive inhabitants of Scandinavia,* edited by Sir J. Lubbock. Longmans, London.
Pennington, W.
  1975 The effect of Neolithic man on the environment in northwest England: the use of absolute pollen diagrams. *Council for British Archaeology Research Report* 11:74–86.
Pollard, S.
  1968 *The idea of progress.* Pelican Ltd., London.

Roe, F. G.
    1951   *The North American buffalo.* University of Toronto Press, Toronto.
Rowley-Conwy, P.
    1981   Slash and burn in the temperate European Neolithic. In *Farming Practice in British Prehistory,* edited by R. Mercer. Edinburgh University Press, Edinburgh.
Schrire, C.
    1980   An inquiry into the evolutionary status and apparent identity of San hunter–gatherers. *Human Ecology* 8(1):9–32.
Simmons, I. G., and Dimbleby, G. W.
    1974   The possible role of ivy (*Hedera helix* L.) in the mesolithic economy of western Europe, *Journal of Archaeological Science* 1:291–296.
Sollas, W. J.
    1924   *Ancient hunters and their modern representatives,* 3d ed. MacMillan, London.
Spratt, D. A., and Simmons, I. G.
    1976   Prehistoric activity and environment on the North York moors. *Journal of Archaeological Science* 3(3):193–210.
Tringham, R.
    1971   *Hunters, fishers and farmers of eastern Europe, 6000–3000* B.C. Hutchinson, London.
Westropp, H. M.
    1872   *Prehistoric phases.* Bell and Daldy, London.
Willerding, U.
    1980   Zum Ackerbau der Bandkeramiker. *Materialhefte Ur- & Frühgesch. Niedersachsens* 16:421–456.
Wobst, M.
    1978   The archaeoethnology of hunter–gatherers or the tyranny of the ethnographic record in archaeology. *American Antiquity* 43(2):303–309.

CHAPTER 7

Boundaries as Strategies:
An Ethnoarchaeological Study

IAN HODDER

Department of Archaeology
University of Cambridge
Cambridge, England

INTRODUCTION

This article explores the hypothesis that the degree of material culture distinctiveness at the borders between and within social units depends on the degree of negative reciprocity across those boundaries (Hodder 1979). In particular, I examine the reasons for negative reciprocity and the reasons for the symbolic involvement of material culture in such a strategy. In the example discussed, attention is focused on decorated calabash containers produced by women in the Baringo district of Kenya. It is shown that the existence and nature of the incised styles relate to the central position of women as reproducers in a society in which family, clan, and tribal expansion and competition depend on setting up multiple links between groups and on increased labor and access to that labor. The domestic context and women as both reproducers of laborers and as links to the productive resources of other clans are the focuses of the dominant tensions within society. Whether groups do or do not have decorated calabashes in the Baringo area depends both on internal social strategies and on the position of women and the domestic context, so it is insufficient to focus solely on between-group interaction and negative reciprocity.

The Archaeology of Frontiers and Boundaries **141**

There is a need to consider within-group organization since the fundamental structural differences identified by Woodburn (1980)—between hunter–gatherer systems in which there are immediate returns for labor, and hunter–gatherer and agriculturalist systems with delayed returns—are related by him to different types of social organization and material culture patterning. The interactions between these different societies, existing side by side, would themselves be expected to be structured by different internal strategies. Goody (1976) and Ingold (1980) have noted that in societies (such as hoe agriculturalists and milch pastoralists) where the amount of resources possessed by a productive unit are a direct function of the labor supply, there will be little attempt to restrict inheritance to particular lines of descent. But where there is a scarcity of productive resources rather than labor (as among plough agriculturalists), there will be a pressure to restrict the number of dependents in a household and to confine the range of potential heirs to direct descendents. Material implications of such differences might involve, for example, the presence or absence of communal tombs for the burial of the lineage ancestors. (Further material culture manifestations are discussed later.)

As a result of basic incompatibilities between types of social units (such as those with delayed versus immediate return for labor), change through time from one type of organization to another is often fairly abrupt; this has been noted in the change from Maasai pastoralist to Dorobo hunter–gatherer (Hodder 1982) and in the agricultural transformation of !Kung hunter–gatherers (Lee 1972). But one can rarely, if ever, isolate the incompatibility between contemporary and adjacent social units as the sole factor in maintaining material culture distinctions because the organizational differences are themselves part of, and involved in, between-group strategies. For example, there may be a demand for increased labor as social units compete at their peripheries, but the competition may itself be the result of internal social strategies leading to marked population increase.

The importance of considering material culture differences in relation to the internal properties of social and cultural units rather than simply in relation to their interactions, is emphasized by the fact that many, if not most, stable material culture and social boundaries cannot be equated with coherent and stable groupings of people. The historically attested movements across the Baringo boundaries have been massive. People "become" Dorobo because they have lost their cattle or because they want to hide there "real" identities (Hodder 1982). Regional material culture units often are not associated with a restriction of gene-flow, and many social and material boundaries may exist so that failure by individuals in one system can be compensated for by movement to another; the long interaction between !Kung and Herero has been documented (Wilmsen 1979, 1980).

Differences between cultural units are maintained in relation to organizational differences and sets of social interests, and the human populations may be transient, especially when looked at over the long term.

THE BARINGO DISTRICT

The mainly pastoralist Baringo tribes (Tugen, Njemps, Pokot) do maintain material culture distinctions, and they do prefer to marry within rather than across tribes (Hodder 1977). Despite this overall preference, there is marriage across borders and most individuals living in the boundary areas have in-laws and cattle-exchange friends in other neighboring tribes (Hodder 1982). Different types of artifacts show different distributions at the tribal borders; some show marked distinctions. Other styles and artifacts

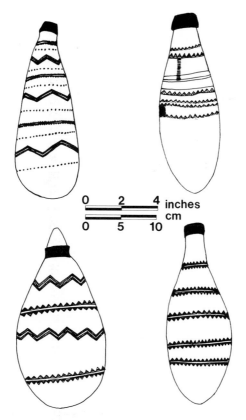

Figure 7.1   Examples of decorated calabashes from the Baringo district, Kenya.

move across the borders with ease. Each material culture category must be considered in its context of use before generalizations can be made about social processes. Before it is possible to explain why some artifacts form boundaries while others move across them, it is necessary to consider what the artifacts "mean" within their own cultural arena. The decorated calabash or gourd (Figure 7.1) is a good starting point in the Baringo area since it occurs frequently and its decoration, in contrast to many other utilitarian items, argues for some particular symbolic significance. In addition, while both the Tugen and Njemps—to whom this discussion is confined—use decorated calabashes, the degree and nature of use vary between and within

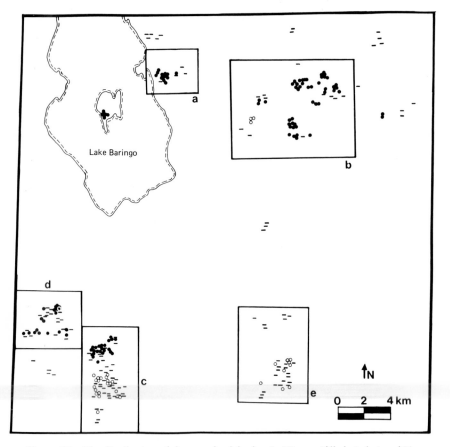

Figure 7.2 The distribution of decorated calabashes in Njemps (filled circles) and Tugen (open circles) compounds in the area around Lake Baringo. Compounds without decorated calabashes are shown as bars. Areas a–e are explained in the text.

the two tribes. It is possible, then, to begin the discussion of the nature of material culture boundaries by a consideration of this artifact.

The distribution of decorated calabashes in the border areas between the Tugen and Njemps is shown in Figure 7.2. While the decoration of calabashes by incising and burning the surface is particularly associated with Njemps women, calabashes with similar decoration occur in considerable quantities in neighboring Tugen compounds (Figure 7.2). Although in some cases the Tugen use a different, more free, design organization on calabashes, the majority of Tugen calabashes are similar to those made by the Njemps, and in some cases distinctive localized motifs are found distributed

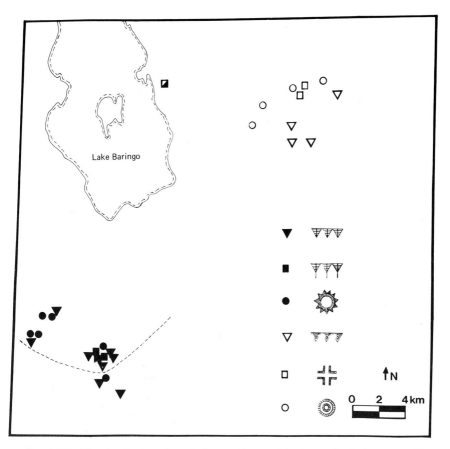

Figure 7.3 The distribution of particular motifs on calabashes in the Baringo area. The dashed line to the south of the lake indicates the boundary between the Njempa and Tugen tribes.

across the Njemps/Tugen boundary to the south of Lake Baringo (Figure 7.3).

There are a number of questions to be asked about these calabashes in relation to cultural boundary maintenance (see also Hodder 1982:68–73). Why are calabashes decorated at all? Why are calabashes decorated more by Njemps than by Tugen? Why are they decorated with zones of continuous motifs, usually including a zig-zag? Why do calabashes show localized styles (Figure 7.3) whereas items of female dress do not? It will be found that the answers to these different questions are closely linked, but it is necessary to begin by considering what calabashes are used for and what they are associated with in the Baringo context.

THE FUNCTIONS AND ASSOCIATIONS OF DECORATED CALABASHES

Many types of calabash containers are used in the Baringo area for a variety of purposes. In this essay, however, the discussion is limited to a bottle-shaped form with a closed leather top (Figure 7.1). Of the 140 decorated calabashes of this type drawn and studied in the Baringo area, all but one (to be discussed later) were made by and associated with women, and were frequently exchanged among women. Adults of both sexes use the calabashes, but they are predominantly used by women. In my sample, the decorated calabashes had been made by women of all ages from a time prior to marriage (in early teens) to around 50 years old. Most calabashes were recently made since the use-life is rarely longer than 2–3 years. As well as the association with women, calabashes are closely associated with milk. They are used as containers of milk (from cattle and goats). Milk is itself closely connected with fertility and strength and the calabashes are frequently used for providing milk for children up to their early teens. These associations have a long history in the Baringo area. In 1902 Johnston noted that, among Baringo and closely related tribes, during pregnancy women rarely touched meat but consumed large quantities of butter and milk. Richer men were said to drink blood mixed with milk. The associations between decorated calabashes, women, milk and fertility can be clarified by considering the Tugen and Njemps data separately.

In Tugen compounds an older woman without a family of young women and men rarely possesses any decorated calabashes since women use the calabashes to provide milk for their young children and their older circumcised but unmarried sons. The milk is drunk fresh, sour, or mixed with blood. There has been a long tradition among the Kalenjin (a grouping of tribes that includes the Tugen) that cattle and goat milk have a special significance. Huntingford (1953) noted that amongst the Kalenjin Nandi, milk was considered sacred. When the Tugen wish to swear at or show disdain for their Pokot neighbors, they talk about them having intercourse with a calabash.

Among the Njemps, calabashes have always been used as milk containers. Johnston (1902:814) noted that in both the pastoral Maasai and the then-settled agricultural Njemps, cows were milked by women in the village but by boys in the cattle camps. Milk was then kept in bottle-shaped gourds with leather covers. The milk was drunk fresh and the calabashes were carefully cleaned with burning grass and a special liquid. Today, among the now-pastoralist Njemps, the association between calabashes and women is perhaps emphasized by the one instance found in which a calabash was claimed to have been decorated by a man. This unmarried individual was also said to have made the *kerebé* (basket container) in the compound—again an artifact usually made by women in the Baringo area. In addition, the man was said to "sit like a woman" and had several effeminate or homosexual social characteristics.

Njemps children and old women are said to drink milk most frequently. The Samburu, from whom the Njemps are partly derived, are relevant in this regard. Spencer (1965:238) notes that milk mixed with water is poured over a woman outside the circumcision hut before her circumcision, and a similar mixture is used in male circumcision and in various male ceremonies (Spencer 1965:267–268). The Njemps association between decorated calabashes and circumcision is itself suggested by the similarity in the decoration of the calabashes and the female circumcision dress. Both use a running zig-zag motif as the main and most frequent design component.

THE SIGNIFICANCE AND INTERPRETATION OF CALABASH DECORATION

Several characteristics of the decoration of calabashes have been noted. These include the greater occurrence of such decoration amongst the Njemps; the localized motifs; the associations between calabashes, women, and milk; and the symbolic importance of milk in relationship to fertility and reproduction. Several of these relationships might be expected in all societies because of the association of women with child rearing. Thus the associations between women, milk, milk containers, fertility, and reproduction might be expected in most societies as biological and "natural." However, what is important in the Baringo context is that these relationships are isolated and emphasized by the use of decoration on milk containers but not on other types of calabashes, by the use of milk in ceremonies, and by the

feeding of milk to certain segements of society. It is these particular emphases that I wish to explore by placing them within their social context and by
applying general theories concerning the use of material culture within social strategies.

Calabashes and Reproduction:
A Bargaining Tool for Women

Within Baringo societies, and particularly among the Njemps, the real
power of women is apparently limited, and material culture is used by them
as part of the negotiation of social influence. In the Baringo area women are
primarily valued by older men because of their reproductive potential and as
objects of exchange. These two aspects of women are closely linked, but the
former component will be considered first. In many Kalenjin groups (including the Tugen), if a woman dies before bearing a child, the husband can
demand return of the stock (cattle and goats) given to the wife's father as
bridewealth. If she dies after bearing a child, but before the bridewealth
payment is completed, the husband must pay the balance. In the Maasai and
Njemps tribes (Huntingford 1953), payment of bridewealth establishes the
husband's rights over his wife's procreative faculties and over the children
she bears. A husband will not pay the bridewealth in full unless his wife
produces children and a Njemps man will remarry if his wife is thought to
be barren.

All groups living on the flat margins around Lake Baringo have recently
been concerned with rapidly increasing the number of live births. This is
particularly true of the Njemps who, at the beginning of this century, were
living in a few large, nucleated villages to the south of the lake. They had
little cattle and were heavily reliant on trade and irrigation agriculture.
Within the last generation they have abandoned the villages and split up
into individual family compounds in order to increase their cattle and tribal
area. If a man wants to increase the number of cattle he owns, he can raid
cattle from other tribes. This method is unreliable, however, especially since
the extension of colonial and postcolonial policing in the area. The main
methods open to him are to obtain cattle through the marrying of his
daughters to other men, and by borrowing cattle from his in-laws to be used
as the basis for his own herds. Thus the key to cattle wealth is the maintenance of a large family that can provide links to the other groups. "Cattle
friends" are also necessary in order to safeguard one's stocks against localized failures, disease, and scarcity. If many of one's cattle are "given out"
to widely dispersed allies, the security of one's stock is increased. Children
are also necessary as labor for the tending and milking of stock. Njemps

society is more polygamous than Tugen society largely because the Njemps have been successful in obtaining more cattle than the Tugen; they are thus more wealthy and able to obtain more wives. But the larger number of wives for the Njemps men is also part of the strategy to increase reproduction and cattle-exchange friends in order to increase cattle stocks. The Tugen, who have moved down from the hills to the west of Lake Baringo during this century to live in the flat area around the lake, have also been concerned with increasing cattle stocks in this lake-margin area with its extensive grazing pastures. These Tugen are more frequently polygamous than those who remain, with smaller stocks of cattle, in the more hilly regions.

The emphasis on women as reproductive units thus takes its place within the general strategy of Baringo males to increase cattle stocks and wealth. The symbolism of milk and fertility, and the decoration of milk containers could be seen as a straightforward manifestation of the strategy of wealth accumulation. The main concern is with reproduction, so everything immediately connected with it becomes important. But this is an inadequate explanation. How does a woman's concern to demonstrate her ability to produce children get transformed into her decoration of calabashes? What is the link between decorating calabashes and the social concern with reproduction? We still have not answered the questions, why decoration? and why this type of decoration?, although we have begun to see why the Njemps might be more concerned with calabashes and reproduction than many Tugen.

In reaching a more adequate understanding of the calabash decoration in relation to reproduction, the viewpoint of the older male and husband can be considered first since it is this viewpoint that would normally be described as providing the dominant ideology in Baringo societies. Men remain as *moran* (warriors) until their age-set matures, when many may be in their late twenties, and when they are allowed to marry. A man is rich who has many wives because this means that he has been able to amass considerable bridewealth and that he will be able to accumulate still more cattle through his children and the marriage of his daughters. His concern is with total rights over his wives and their offspring. We shall see that the wife's natal clan—her father and brothers—are able to exert from influence over the "sister's sons." But the husband is concerned with breaking these ties and with removing any ambiguity in his control over his wife and children and the stock that are allocated to them. A man may avoid his parents-in-law, so a young wife (usually in her mid-teens) must be prepared to accept isolation from her natal clan and complete absorption into her husband's family.

Hodder (1982) shows that the young wife uses aspects of dress and material culture to demonstrate a willingness to conform with her new role and the husband's control. That she decorates calabashes similar in detail to those in the new environment into which she moves on marriage is significant. The localized styles (Figure 7.3) and the copying of the decoration used by other wives of the same man, or by his mother and other relatives, can be interpreted by the husband as acquiescence and incorporation. That she decorates and, in her own words, "makes beautiful" the milk container (with all its symbolic associations) can be interpreted by him as showing a concern with fulfilling her task of reproduction and caring for children.

The decoration of calabashes and its localized styles could be taken as representing a male objective. The female point of view is masked or muted by the overriding dominance of the controlling husband. While this is certainly part of the answer—at least from the vantage of the male—there is a fuller and more complex interpretation: the possibility that women are not entirely muted, but that they negotiate influence and that they give meaning to their social position through the use of calabashes decorated with associated symbolism.

The calabashes—made by women and used largely by women—are to a certain extent outside male control. While a man can, in the Baringo area, beat his wife if he disapproves of her actions, the reliance on reproduction in order to accumulate cattle wealth gives a certain influence to women. This influence is extended by cooperation between women as well as between women and their sons. Women cooperate with each other in keeping their adultery secret and, particularly amongst the Njemps, co-wives have strong ties. Once a woman has circumcised and married sons, she achieves social status. She cooperates with her sons in building up their herds so that they can marry, and there is constant tension and antagonism between, on the one hand, women and their sons and, on the other hand, older males. This relationship between women and sons is reinforced in songs and in various items of dress. To a certain extent, then, women are able to negotiate their social position. One avenue in which inroads are made is in the manipulation of the male view of calabash decoration, milk, and fertility. Calabashes are frequently given by women to daughters, mothers-in-law, co-wives. Women in local areas copy each other's designs and borrow each other's tools to execute them. This action in material culture thus helps to form the solidarity between women who have come from different and often widely separated origins, and who have been brought together into one male-centered family, lineage, and clan. The localized calabash decoration sets up ties and mutual support. It is only by presenting this common front that actions such as adultery are possible, and that absolute control by the husband can be threatened. The support from and control over young sons is emphasized in the giving of milk, and sometimes of calabashes, to them.

That the calabash should be a focus for the negotiation of female influence is appropriate since this artifact is a symbol of the reproduction on which older men depend for their own social status. The calabash decoration, carried out by women, emphasizes the control by women of the reproductive forces on which older men depend. The decoration and the associated symbolism establish female control and threaten male dominance.

The relevance of the contradictory male and female views of the calabash decoration to the social strategies of men and women can be clarified by comparing the Tugen and the Njemps and by considering other types of evidence, particularly the internal organization of settlements.

The Njemps stress agnatic descent and resources are inherited within male-centered lines. Sons are allotted cattle, but a girl is allotted nothing for she has no inheritance rights to her father's herds. Rather, a woman is allotted rights in her husband's herds on marriage and this reinforces the separation noted above between a woman and her natal clan. However, the husband can manipulate these rights for himself and it is against his efforts to do this that the wife and son cooperate in order to build up the son's herds. The concern of older Njemps men, is therefore, to control the activities of women and to diminish the cooperation between wives and sons. One result is that Njemps compounds are frequently extremely large containing co-wives and sons (sometimes with their wives) within the same fenced area. This arrangement allows closer observance and control by the husband and father, but it also allows greater cooperation between women, and between mothers and sons. Each wife has her own hut which is to some extent avoided by her classificatory fathers and brothers. The hut is thus controlled by the husband and it emphasizes the separation between a woman and her natal family. Yet the grouping of the huts of women allows closer cooperation against the male-centered line that has brought them together.

Among the Tugen, on the other hand, each wife usually has a separate compound that commonly contains only two buildings—her hut and her own millett and maize store. In my sample, I came across frequent cases in which a woman had left her husband to live with her son and his wife in their compound (although this also happens amongst the Njemps). The Tugen older men often say they allow physical separation of the compounds of their co-wives in order to minimize jealousy and quarreling, yet this strategy implies less concern with absolute control by older men over women and sons in the domestic context. It is among the Tugen, especially those living away from the lake margins, that calabash decoration is less frequent. Here there is less social concern, less potential for increasing cattle wealth (because of the heavily eroded and depleted environment); therefore, from the male point of view there is less need to control female reproductive abilities, and from the female point of view, less ability to negotiate in this arena.

In the upland Tugen areas, one often finds a triangular relationship in which a man deals with the competing claims of his two wives. But among the Njemps there is a two-way dichotomy between husband and wives. As with the Samburu, a husband "must resign himself to being an outsider to the bond that tends to unite all women and accept it as an inevitable consequence of the enormous social barrier that separates him as an elder from them" (Spencer 1965:226). In fact, it is the woman who is an outsider, brought into her husband's patriclan. Yet, by using strategies such as the decoration of calabashes, a woman makes the husband an outsider in his own house.

If my hypothesis concerning the meaning and function of calabash decoration is correct, a relationship should occur in the Baringo area between the numbers of huts in a compound and the number of decorated calabashes. Areas where there are many large compounds containing several co-wives should also be areas in which milk-container calabashes are frequently decorated since it is in these areas that the tension between men and women in relation to their reproductive potential is greatest and where control over women is emphasized. These should also be areas where the accumulation of cattle wealth is most marked. We have already seen that the expected relationships do occur in that the Njemps have more cattle, more huts per compound, and more calabash decoration than the Tugen. But there is much variation between localities in the Baringo area, and the Tugen who have recently moved down to the margins of Lake Baringo where rich grazing lands occur have increased their cattle, have adopted the Njemps compound organization and have decorated more of their calabashes.

In Figure 7.2 five main settlement clusters have been isolated and labeled a through e. In each cluster the number of compounds with more than one living hut can be expressed as a percentage of the total number of compounds. It is also possible to calculate the frequency of occurrence of decorated calabashes in each settlement cluster. The number of decorated calabashes in a settlement cluster is divided by the total number of compounds visited in that cluster. The resulting ratio can only provide a rough guide to the frequency of calabashes since certain difficulties were encountered in collecting the data. For example, calabashes are exchanged, are taken out for the day, may be in the hut of someone who is not available, and so on. However, the variation in the ratio is sufficient to allow gross trends to be identified despite the sampling problems. The results are expressed in Table 7.1.

The data thus support the argument concerning the meaning and role of

Table 7.1

The Distribution of Calabashes and Large Compounds in Baringo
Settlement Clusters[a]

	Settlement clusters				
	a	b	c	d	e
Percentage of compounds with	73	67	36	28	25
more than one living hut	(11)	(24)	(58)	(21)	(24)
Ratio of number of calabashes	.75	.83	.52	.45	.25
to number of compounds	(16)	(60)	(81)	(42)	(32)

[a]Sample sizes in parentheses.

the calabash decoration. The decoration occurs most frequently when, from the husband's point of view, female reproduction is to be increased but controlled as an essential part of the strategy of accumulating cattle wealth, and when, from the woman's point of view, her importance in reproduction and her consequent cooperation with other women and sons in her husband's family, allow her to negotiate social status. The calabash containing milk, as a symbol of reproduction, fertility, and family care is at the center of the resulting tension. To decorate it with motifs elsewhere associated with circumcision emphasizes the women's central role and confronts the patriclan.

Calabashes and Women in the Exchange Network

The matter is still more complex. Up to this point the study has centered on calabashes within the patriclan. I have tried to show that the decoration and its localized styles set up links between women associated together after marriage. Yet, despite the localized distribution of certain motifs (Figure 7.3), the calabashes are everywhere much the same. The decoration is nearly always zoned, usually incorporating zig-zag lines, dots, and triangles. The cap is made of leather and is often decorated with colored beads. This widespread similarity corresponds to the widespread tribal motifs of all types of female decoration—the necklaces, earrings, hair, clothes, and so on. Why are these widespread motifs maintained despite the concern identified above to separate women from their natal clans?

Part of the answer is that the conformity in dress within a tribe means that a man can assess the degree of acquiescence of a prospective marriage partner. After marriage, her overt acceptance of the rules of the tribe and her submission to her husband's control are shown in how she acts, dresses, and decorates the objects she uses. But the regional similarities have additional significance which, once again, can be considered from both the male and the female viewpoints.

Although the husband's attempts to isolate wives from their natal clans have been emphasized, it is also the case that such links are to be maintained. A man has certain rights over his sister's children, especially boys, who must, for example, get his permission for circumcision. Daughters are important to a man because they allow links to the resources of other clans through the exchange of daughters for bridewealth, and provide "sister's sons" that he can exploit. But these ties across clans depend on the performance of women. The prestige of a clan and the demand for its women depend on the success (in reproduction, for example) of previous women married from that clan. Thus the accumulation of wealth through cattle and cattle friends in other clans depends on the exchange of women and on ties created through women. The widespread uniformity in women's dress and material culture, from the male point of view, relates to their widespread common exchange value, and to the need to keep links between patriclans open. The accumulation of wealth within social units (the patriclans) depends on the manipulation of links between those units set up by the exchange of women. These links contradict the separation and closure of the agnatic descent groups but are necessary to the accumulation of its wealth.

From the elders' point of view, women should be displayed as objects of exchange. The main way in which this is achieved is through dress. By extensive decoration of the female body with beads, bangles, and baubles, symbolic reference is made to prestige value. This is represented verbally by saying that young women need to be beautiful while older women frequently say that they do not decorate themselves because they do not need to be beautiful anymore. While these symbolic associations are particularly relevant to female attire, similar statements are made about the decoration of calabashes because it heightens the attractiveness and value of the owner.

Again, Baringo women should not be represented as being duped by the dominant male ideology into thinking of themselves as objects of exchange, although it is largely this viewpoint that is expressed verbally by women to men. The widely similar styles of dress and calabash decoration are negotiated between men and women and have clear advantages for women. In particular, within the exchange network women are at the point of tension between the closed patriclan and the links that must be maintained between patriclans. These links depend to some degree on female decorative competence. The women's ties to brothers and fathers can be directed against the husband and mother–brother/sister–son relationships can be exploited. Sons cooperate with mothers and they have many common aspects of dress. For example, both Njemps women and unmarried Njemps men wear similar small earrings in the upper parts of their ears. Whereas calabashes are commonly exchanged between married women within a patriclan, items of dress are more frequently exchanged between mothers and married daughters in order to maintain links to the natal clan. The widespread styles of items of female and young male dress and decoration are an ever-present threat within male-centered descent groups, referring to the internal weakness of ideology of the patriclan.

Calabash Decoration: Conclusion

It has been suggested that the decoration of calabashes has different significance for different groups within Baringo societies, and that the calabash decoration and its meaning are negotiated as part of the strategies of individuals with differing and often contradictory interests. At the risk of oversimplification, the points of view of women and older men can be represented diagrammatically, although these viewpoints vary enormously according to age and a wide range of other variables (Figure 7.4).

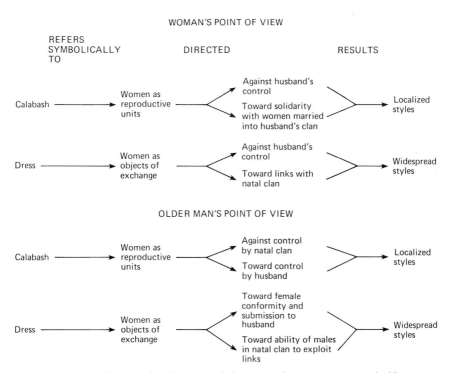

Figure 7.4 Significance of calabashes and dress according to women's and older men's points of view.

The spatial localization of the detailed calabash designs separates a woman from her natal clan but sets up ties of solidarity with other women who have married into a male-centered group. This new solidarity is best presented through references to female fertility and reproduction. The connotations of the calabash decoration itself (associated with circumcision) and of the calabashes (as milk containers) provide the most appropriate and highly emotive threat to the male agnatic group since the accumulation of cattle wealth depends on the female reproduction of laborers and on daughters for exchange. The widespread similarities in dress and certain aspects of calabash decoration, on the other hand, threaten the agnatic group by reference to and maintenance of necessary affinal links through women.

BOUNDARIES BETWEEN REGIONAL
SOCIAL UNITS

The differences between the Tugen and Njemps in the use of decorated calabashes occur partly because of differences between the social strategies of individuals within the two groups. Tugen women sometimes decorate calabashes with wholly novel designs. These are done "by myself, I did not copy anyone." As seen in the different types of compound organization, Tugen women are less closely controlled by adult males. In the Tugen hilly areas there is less concern with rapid reproduction and less opportunity for accumulating cattle wealth. As a result, women have less potential to negotiate social position through reference to reproduction and fertility, there is less polygamy and less solidarity between women, less cooperation between mothers and sons, and less concern with women as objects of exchange. In reference to the latter point, young Tugen women generally have less bodily decoration during day-to-day activities, they have stopped wearing the full range of types of ear decoration and wear fewer necklaces and bracelets.

Since the abandonment of the Njemps villages on the flatlands, on the other hand, there has been a growing concern to increase cattle wealth rapidly. Male interests have centered on increasing labor power and on exchanging women for cattle in order to establish cattle friends. In this context women negotiate their position by reference to the central role of reproduction.

The differences between the Tugen and Njemps in the use of calabashes can thus ultimately be linked to differing social strategies. However, the distinctions noted are not simply between tribal groups since those Tugen who have recently moved down into the area around Lake Baringo have also been concerned to increase numbers and accumulate cattle wealth. Their use of calabashes and the organization of their compounds attests to the use of strategies similar to the Njemps. Thus a link appears to be evident between a type of social strategy and a type of cultural organization. It is possible to generalize and to suggest that in small-scale lineage-based so-cieties in which the major concern is to increase labor power, the control of women by men and the negotiation of position by women will become the dominant feature of social relations and will often involve cultural elabora-tion of the domestic sphere as the focus of male—female tensions. However, in small-scale societies where the limited resource is not labor but land, women will be important in the negotiation between men for land, but will be undervalued as reproducers; there will be less opportunity for the domes-tic sphere to be the focus for symbolic manipulation.

The preceding approximation to a generalization, which clearly needs to be examined in other social contexts, provides possible reasons for cultural differences between ethnic groups that follow different social strategies. However, the Tugen bordering the Njemps at the lake margin are following similar strategies and yet retain many cultural differences from the Njemps. While Njemps and neighboring Tugen have similar compound plans and calabash decorations, a range of other artifacts (such as female dress) shows clear differences between the Tugen and Njemps (Hodder 1982).

The borders between the Tugen and Njemps are maintained as part of a between-group interaction which is itself linked to the same social strategies and tensions within these groups. These tribes consist of loose groups of patriclans, and we have seen that older males exploit the links between agnatic groups in order to accumulate cattle wealth for their own group and to safeguard their cattle stocks in a harsh and unpredictable environment. It has been shown (Hodder 1982) that cattle-exchange friends and affinal links do occur across the Tugen and Njemps borders, but it has also been shown (Hodder 1977) that there is a clear preference for marriage within the tribal group. The existence of the social and cultural border between Tugen and Njemps thus appears to have many disadvantages. It limits the range of affinal links that can be used by the elders to increase cattle wealth (Hodder 1977). On the other hand, the borders are important for young men—we have seen how young men are prevented from marrying by the older men and how their access to cattle wealth is restricted. In the system of generalized reciprocity within the tribe, the young man's ability to build up cattle resources is limited. But the existence of the borders allows negative reciprocity—raiding cattle in order to achieve something for nothing. For the young man, the raiding and the treating of "them" differently from "us" is part of their antagonistic relationship with the elders. For the young man also, success in raiding prepares him for adulthood and marriage. For the older men, on the other hand, the involvement of young men in raiding and long preparation for adulthood prevents them from competing for wives and cattle resources through the system of generalized reciprocity within the tribe. For the older men also, raiding for cattle is a means of accumulating wealth within the patriclan. Thus, despite the disadvantage that the borders limit (to some degree) access to the resources of other clans by marriage ties, the cultural borders and the negative reciprocity that is possible across them are part of the conflicts between older and younger men for women and reproductive and productive resources.

This discussion should not be construed to imply that the formal social categories, tribes, and patriclans have any constancy of personnel. As already noted, the amount of migration between tribes has been great, but newcomers have taken their positions within the ideology of categories and groupings. Immigrants "become" Njemps and Tugen with great ease without disturbing the total structure of social relations.

Another general distinction between the Tugen and Njemps is that the Njemps' borders are more closed than the Tugens. Many artifact types diffuse from the Njemps to the Tugen, but movement in the other direction is less common (Hodder 1977). Although the Njemps as a group have been concerned to increase their size, wealth, and areal extent, the concern has been to accumulate wealth within closed but related patriclans within tribal borders. The tensions between old and young, men and women that have been identified in this paper are correspondingly stronger and the borders are maintained as part of these tensions. For example, when non-Njemps women marry into an Njemps family, the male pressures on them to conform are strong and the female desire to manipulate their solidarity is high. As a result, women are "invisible" in material culture as they move from one group to the other. In addition, the Njemps have higher rates of polygamy, so competition between older and younger men for women and cattle is considerable, and the distinct Njemps border is maintained as a part of these strategies. While the Tugen bordering the Njemps on the lake margins have followed similar paths—and this explains the maintenance of a Tugen border—internal tensions within many parts of the Tugen are of a different nature and so the use of individual styles of calabashes and dress and the adoption of outside traits are more appropriate.

All social boundaries are to some extent open. Indeed, they only exist because of the need to regulate and control interaction. However, there is variation both in the degree of openness and closure of different regional boundaries and in the degree of openness and closure of different types of interchange at the same boundary. The degree to which social boundaries are open or closed depends on the extent to which they are involved in different types of internal social conflict. In this essay it has been shown that the internal organizational differences between social units which lead to differences in material culture patterning are not sufficient to explain the existence of social and material culture boundaries. These boundaries—

formed as part of internal social strategies—are maintained as components in certain types of between-group interaction (in this case negative reciprocity). To explain the negative reciprocity, it is necessary to look at internal social strategies. Similarly, to explain why some artifacts are used to emphasize social boundaries while others are not, we need to look at internal strategies (in this case those involving relationships between old men, young men, and women) and at the particular meanings that have come to be associated historically with particular material attributes (containers, milk, decorations of a particular type). These meanings are created through associations with functions and they are emphasized in ways that are archaeologically identifiable (as in the decoration of milk containers). Our understanding of the maintenance of social boundaries through the use of material symbols must not only concern general models for internal and between-group social strategies, but must also concern general models for the construction of meaning within historical contexts.

REFERENCES

Goody, J.
    1976   *Production and reproduction.* Cambridge University Press, Cambridge.
Hodder, I.
    1977   The distribution of material culture items in the Baringo district, Kenya. *Man* 12:239–269.
    1979   Social and economic stress and material culture patterning. *American Antiquity* 44:446–454.
    1982   *Symbols in action.* Cambridge University Press, Cambridge.
Huntingford, G. W. P.
    1953   *The southern Nilo-Hamites.* Ethnographic Survey of Africa, International African Institute, London.
Ingold, T.
    1980   *Hunters, pastoralists and ranchers.* Cambridge University Press, Cambridge.
Johnston, H.
    1902   The Uganda protectorate. Hutchinson, London.
Lee, R. B.
    1972   *The !Kung San: men, women and work in a foraging society.* Cambridge University Press, Cambridge.
Spencer, P.
    1965   *The Samburu.* Routledge and Kegan Paul, London.
Wilmsen, E.N.
    1979   *Prehistoric and historic antecedants of a contemporary Ngamiland community.* Working Paper 12, Boston University African Studies Centre.
    1980   *Exchange, interaction and settlement in North Western Botswana: past and present perspective.* Working Paper 39. Boston University African Studies Centre.
Woodburn J.
    1980   Hunters and gatherers today and reconstruction of the past. In *Soviet and Western anthropology,* edited by E. Cellner. Duckworth, London.

PART III

Complex Society

CHAPTER 8

Surplus Flow between Frontiers and Homelands

ROBERT PAYNTER

Department of Anthropology
University of Massachusetts
Amherst, Massachusetts

INTRODUCTION

This essay models frontier–homeland relations in stratified societies. Descriptive and analytic models are presented along with a case study demonstrating the usefulness of these perspectives. The models are designed to elucidate three characteristics of frontiers in stratified societies, namely, their large spatial scale, the systemic quality of interactions, and the role of the production and distribution of social surplus. The case study is drawn from historical-period New England.

In addition to adaptations to local ecological situations, cultural variability is also a function of interactions over large areas (e.g., Adams 1975). Though diffusion is almost synonymous with large-scale interactions in the anthropological literature, recent work makes it clear that a number of other relations have significant spatial dimensions. For instance, working with the insights of Barth (1969), a number of archaeologists have investigated the subdivision of areas along ethnic lines (e.g., Hodder 1979; Plog 1980; Wobst 1977). The spatial dimensions of ethnic processes have been joined to the study of political–economic relations by Cole and Wolf (1974). Finally, the large, spatial scale of production and distribution has been studied for the modern world (Amin 1980; Frank 1978; Wallerstein 1974, 1980; Wolf 1982), the Islamic World (Boone and Redman 1980;

Thorbahn 1979), Mesopotamian civilization (Kohl 1978; Lamberg-Kar-lovsky 1975; Schneider 1977; Tosi 1977), and Mesoamerica (Blanton *et al.* 1981; McGuire 1980), among other areas (Friedman and Rowlands 1978).

Considering spatial processes of surplus production and distribution, or ethnicity, significantly alters the role of space in theories of cultural variability. Under the diffusionist paradigm, similarities are due to diffusion, and by implication, direct or indirect culture contact; differences are in part the result of a lack of contact. Concern with the spatial processes of surplus production and distribution, or ethnicity, indicates something different; namely, that culture contact regularly creates differences. When contact creates differences, standard measures of interaction are inappropriate. For instance, the volume of similar material in two areas may be a poor indicator of the degree of contact (preservation issues aside), and the lack of similar assemblages and architecture cannot be taken, on its own, to indicate isolation. Thus, many culture histories based on presumed isolation require reinterpretation in light of these new approaches to large-scale spatial process.

Reinterpretation is not hampered by a lack of methodology. Considerable advancement has been made in analyzing artifact assemblages for indications of long distance exchange (e.g., Hodder and Orton 1976; Pires-Ferreira 1975; Renfrew 1969, 1975, 1977). Analyses of regional settlement patterns provide clues to the scale and nature of political–economic interactions (e.g., Blanton 1976; Johnson 1977; Paynter 1982). However, these methods, with some notable exceptions (Pires-Ferreira and Flannery 1976; Johnson 1980), are open to Johnson's criticism of sterile formalism (1977:500–501). Coming to grips with long distance processes is, therefore, less a problem in method and more a problem in theory.

A place to begin such theory building is with frontier studies. Frontiers obviously involve large-scale spatial relations and the behavior on frontiers has been addressed from different theoretical positions. A frontier implies at least three cultural forms: the frontier, the homeland, and the aboriginal culture impacted by the expanding homeland culture. Different approaches to spatial process account for these differences in a number of ways. For instance, under the *diffusionist approach,* the variability is due to differential diffusion of homeland traits to the frontier and virtually no diffusion to the aboriginal area. With time comes increasing similarity. The *surplus production and distribution approach* accounts for the frontier and many aspects of the aboriginal culture as responses to the movement of surpluses toward the homeland. Time alone is not likely to alter the distribution of traits and, in fact, is as likely to intensify the differences. Finally, an *ethnicity approach* identifies the frontier zone as an area of competition and differentiation, again relations that do not necessarily tend toward cultural homogeneity.

This study contributes to understanding frontier–homeland relations with a political–economic approach, and focuses on models involving the production and distribution of surplus. The first section presents descriptive models of supraregional change, distinguishing between clinal and modular landscapes, and between clinal and clonal developmental trajectories. The problem of accounting for these landscapes and trajectories is initially taken up in the second section where an analytic framework of the key structural positions in frontier development is introduced. The third section introduces notions of domination and resistance as principles integrating the various actors found in frontiers—principles that allow a different understanding of why specific frontiers follow specific developmental trajectories. The utility of these frameworks for studying an empirical situation is the subject of the fourth section, where some problems in the development of historical-period New England are considered. Refining the frameworks presented and using them to analyze other situations of frontier development would give a political–economic appreciation of frontiers and such ethnological questions as, what kinds of societies regularly create frontiers?; under what conditions do frontiers rise up and come to dominate the homeland?; and, under what conditions does a frontier status persist? These are clearly key issues in the development of contemporary stratified societies, and they represent poorly understood aspects of societies of the past. Elucidating them is worth our attention.

DESCRIPTIVE MODELS OF FRONTIER DEVELOPMENT

Hudson (1977:12) points out that a *frontier* "in spatial terms . . . [is] a fringe or an outer boundary." An edge must have a center; thus, a descriptive model of a frontier implies the existence of a homeland (a center). Abstractly it is possible to consider the frontier and the homeland as two distinct subregions within a culture area. However, empirically, on the ground, there is no line in space where the homeland ends and the frontier begins. Describing these interregional relations, then, involves supraregional models of continuous distributions over the larger culture area. This section considers the nature of some descriptive models of these large-scale distributions.

Frontier–homeland supraregional models are a special case of models involving all sorts of interregional interactions. Other models might invoke long distance trade, political domination by indirect rule, or the diffusion of esoteric information from one culture to another. Frontier–homeland relations however, suggest the total displacement of one way of life by a part of a different way of life. Thus, frontier–homeland relations have a distinctive synchronic character—the frontier as part of a larger more complex cultural whole; and, a distinctive diachronic character—the frontier as an experiment that will either fail or develop into a full culture.

A number of variables have been used to compare the frontier and the homeland. For instance, some approaches characterize the frontier as being somewhat less than the homeland. Variables for this comparison include population density (Hudson 1969), surplus accumulation (Frank 1978; Wallerstein 1974, 1980), richness and complexity of culture (Hartz 1964), and, for lack of a better word, cultural inertia (Service 1960). Alternatively, other descriptive comparisons stress that the frontier is somewhat more than the homeland. For some, frontiers are seen as being more innovative (Service 1960; Giddens 1973), more resource abundant (Green 1979), or more culturally diverse (Miller and Savage 1977).

Supraregional descriptive models can be made by mapping the distribution of these variables over space. For instance, imagine standing in the homeland of a landscape defined by population density. As one travels outward, toward the frontier, population density declines. This landscape, physically, resembles an inverted bowl, and this is a general description of landscapes on which frontiers are considered somewhat less than the homelands. Alternatively, if the variable describing the landscape is more frequent on frontiers, then the supraregional landscape resembles a bowl set right side up. In the following, these synchronic supraregional landscapes are referred to as *clinal landscapes.*

Clinal landscapes, as a general model, can be contrasted to *modular landscapes,* a class of large-scale landscapes that do not incorporate frontier–homeland relations. On a modular landscape the distribution of the variable moves through peaks and troughs. A three-dimensional physical model of this landscape is a table of bowls rather than a single bowl. Each bowl represents a relatively autonomous culture area with the centers of equal value, although possibly of differing quality.

Both clinal and modular landscapes have been studied, empirically and theoretically. Most notably, the supraregional clinal distribution of trade items (such as obsidian) has received the attention of Renfrew (1975, 1977), Hodder and Orton (1976), and Pires-Ferreira (1975). Different behavioral conditions, such as simple distance effects, directional trade, central-place trade, random-walk models, and so on, effect the shape of the curve describing the distribution (see also Earle and Ericson 1977). On the other hand, size and areal characteristics of modular landscapes have been investigated by Renfrew (1975) particularly in his study of early state modules.

Frontier–homeland landscapes are clinal landscapes on which the differences are due to the frontier being only a recently created part of a larger culture. This suggests a developmental question: how might these relations between frontiers and homelands change over time? Given synchronic models of clinal and modular landscapes, three diachronic trajectories come to mind: clonal trajectories and two versions of clinal trajectories.

1. The first is one in which a clinal landscape develops into a modular landscape. Given that the initial clinal landscape is a frontier–homeland situation, the development of the modular landscape represents a process of cloning of the homeland culture, a developmental trajectory referred to as *clonal*. Numerous examples of clonal developmental trajectories can be found in the archaeological literature (e.g., Binford 1968; Wobst 1974). Deetz's (1977) discussion of historical New England exemplifies clonal trajectories in stratified societies. He posits three stages of historical New England culture change: a yeoman English culture stage (1620–1660), a folk culture stage (1660–1760), and a period of reintegration into European culture and development of a North American mass culture (from 1760 to the nineteenth century). Changes in the form and composition of New England material culture—including architecture, mortuary art, and ceramic assemblages—coincide with and are due to this sequence of cultural phases.

The initial period consists of the partial culture of the English yeoman farmer exhibiting English architectural styles, Puritan mortuary themes, and a dairy ceramic assemblage. With relative isolation from Britain, independent variations on this English culture develop into the regional folk cultures of the second period. Through time, as population grows, New England develops an elite, and the elite reestablishes contact with Britain, principally through the education of its children. Symmetrical architectural styles, secular mortuary art, and individualized table services diffuse into the colonies associated with the Renaissance based Georgian mind-set.

If the data were systematically collected and mapped, supraregional maps of the New England–England landscape for each of these stages would disclose a clonal developmental trajectory. Imagine the maps describing population density and an index of cultural complexity. During the first stage the cline from the homeland to the New England frontier would follow a precipitous drop for both these variables. A map of the second stage would disclose less of a difference between the two areas. By the third stage New England would begin to take on values similar to those of England. Similar maps would result on landscapes defined by density of elite architecture, assemblages of table services, or mortuary art distributions. (These maps, of course, take the North Atlantic into consideration.)

2. An alternative developmental trajectory maintains a clinal landscape over time, with clinal landscapes developing into clinal landscapes. Two logical versions are (1) the case of no spatial movement of the cline, and (2) the case in which the cline relocates itself in space. The former is an instance

in which the synchronic clinal relations perpetuate themselves in their same locations within the supraregional area. In the latter, the relations break down and often reverse their effect, resulting in a movement of the cline in space.

Examples of relatively stationary clinal landscapes include relations between the Mesopotamian heartland and the Iranian plateau, the valley of Mexico and Kaminaljuya, and between Europe and Africa during much of the modern period. Discovering such landscapes raises the issue of why they persist—an issue often forgotten in attempts to account for the rise and fall of cultures.

3. In the other version of the clinal developmental trajectory, the cline moves through space. Examples of this are found in Wallerstein's (1974, 1980) descriptions of modern world system development. For instance, Wallerstein sees the core of the European world system shifting in space from the Iberian Peninsula to northwest Europe and then to North America. With the shift of the core from one area to another, there is a concomitant decline of the old core into semiperipheral status. During the fifteenth and sixteenth centuries, the core was located in Spain and Portugal. During the seventeenth century the Netherlands became, for a time, the new core. Britain attained this status at the expense of both the Netherlands and France by the middle of the eighteenth century. The core moved again to the United States, at the expense of Europe, after World War II (Wallerstein 1974, 1980).

The New England–Europe landscape takes on a different character when placed in this world systems perspective. Wallerstein's landscapes are described in terms of the density of social surplus accumulation, strength of state apparatus, mode of labor mobilization, and source of ideology and finance. Over time, the distribution of these variables changes, with New England rising from the position of a semiperiphery (Wallerstein 1980:236–237) to that of a core, while England declines from core status to that of a semipheriphery. The clinal relation remains, though it changes in space. This contrasts with Deetz's clonal trajectory, describing very different landscapes.

Considering frontier change with models of supraregional development raises a number of points. For one, these trajectories raise interesting problems in ethnology. For instance, are different kinds of supraregional landscapes characteristic of different types of stratified societies? Similarly, do different types of stratified societies develop along specific trajectories? Paying attention to the nature of synchronic landscapes and their diachronic developments should provide insight into underlying cultural process.

A drawback to using these large-scale models is operationalizing them. The collection of data to construct, for instance, New England–England landscapes presents many practical problems. There are obvious problems involving data collection at reasonable levels of resolution for variables such as mortuary style distribution, or cultural complexity, or surplus accumulation. Even if this could be mapped, resolving the issue of a Deetzian clonal trajectory versus a Wallersteinian clinal trajectory may lie in methodological choices of a temporal scale and these methodological problems of studying large systems are not well understood. Methods developed by geographers (Muller 1973; Peet 1969, 1972) for analyzing documentary data are instructive for the analysis of archaeological data. However, the problem of compiling enough information from the material record alone limits the analytic use of these models.

A role for these models as explicit hypotheses does not exhaust the use of these large-scale models. They can also serve as metaphors guiding future research. Kuhn (1972:184) includes the notion of metaphor in his discussion of a disciplinary matrix. The ideas of a discipline include testable hypotheses, and notions that define essential categories of the world, thereby providing the primitive concepts structuring research. Using systems analysis to model culture is one familiar example of the latter from anthropology. Thinking about the effects of external connections by placing regions on supraregional landscapes is another. Supraregional landscape models, even if difficult to test (Lewis 1977; Paynter 1982), have a use in directing our attention to external processes shaping cultural adaptations.

Finally, one needs to keep in mind that while there is a need to describe relations in supraregional terms, and to be as precise as possible about how to measure these relations, descriptive models (such as clinal and modular landscapes) and diachronic models (such as clonal and clinal trajectories) are only descriptive. Causality requires considering underlying social relations. One framework for investigating political–economic relations is suggested in the following sections.

BEHAVIORAL RELATIONS IN FRONTIERS

Surplus Flow and Supraregional Models

Any attempt at explanation exists within an intellectual setting (e.g., Harvey 1973; Kuhn 1972). The following is developed from a materialist position within anthropology (M. Harris 1968:634–687; 1979; Kohl 1981; Price 1982; Wolf 1982), and it presumes that an understanding of cultural similarities and differences arises from a consideration of the material conditions of people's lives. Cultural materialist approaches, of course, cover an enormous range of theory and a few key concepts help fix my position under this rubric.

Two specific notions underpin the following. The first is that when studying human societies, the social relations as well as the ecological relations must be analyzed to understand material conditions (e.g., Friedman and Rowlands 1978; Sahlins 1976). Archaeologists have effectively analyzed ecological relations, only recently turning their attention to the variety of social relations used to appropriate natural resources.

Second, the notion of surplus usefully describes the nature of these material conditions (Wolf 1982). All societies produce surpluses; the issue is how this is done and what happens to these surpluses (M. Harris 1959; Wolf 1966:4).

What are the social and ecological relations conditioning surplus production in frontier–homeland situations? And, how do they affect the developmental trajectory of this supraregion? The following review is restricted to considering these issues for stratified societies (Fried 1967:186), although ranked and egalitarian societies also deserve attention. Addressing the issues of material relations and effects involves delineating the strategic social and ecological relations involved in surplus production that are likely to have an impact on frontier developmental trajectories.

Samir Amin (1980:131–149) provides a beginning point for answers. He suggests that one initially consider the class relations of both the homeland and frontier area when trying to elucidate developmental trajectories. Homelands and frontiers, or cores and peripheries, in his terminology, would appear as clinal supraregions. By emphasizing class relations Amin calls attention to *social actors* who are the primary producers of surplus but who have unequal access to this surplus and elites who control the surplus. In the peripheral area, such as a frontier, the elites may be divided into two factions: those interested in supporting the flow of surplus out of the periphery, and those attempting to capture and keep these surpluses within the periphery (Amin 1980:136–141; Schneider *et al.* 1972). More is said about these elites later. For now, following Amin, a behavioral model seeking to account for clinal distributions of surplus needs to consider primary producers and elites.

A problem with models that stress social conditions, such as Amin's, is that they overlook the very real conditions imposed upon production due to the relations with the frontier's environment, both natural and cultural. Recent research in ethnohistory and anthropology (e.g., Ceci 1977, 1980; Jennings 1975; Moore 1981; Salisbury 1982; Wolf 1982) calls attention to the fact that frontiers are rarely open habitats. Even if the aboriginal population does not inhabit the same niche as the expanding culture, expansion leads to interaction. Interaction with the aboriginal population is instrumental in early stages of surplus extraction. Furthermore, these surpluses are not abstract items, but are real resources extracted from real ecosystems. As cultural ecological studies abundantly point out (e.g., D. Harris 1972; Rappaport 1968), resource extraction from specific ecosystems often involves disturbing the ecosystem. This is especially likely to be the case on a frontier where a culture is exploiting an unfamiliar habitat. Thus, an important component in models of frontiers should include the actors of the aboriginal cultures as well as the nature of the regional ecosystem.

These considerations suggest that behavioral models aiming at accounting for synchronic surplus flows between frontiers and homelands, and diachronic changes following clinal or clonal trajectories, need to consider a number of relations. On the frontier there are the relations between elites and primary producers, between members of the colonizing culture and the aboriginal culture, and between both of these cultures and the frontier's ecosystem. Furthermore, these frontier relations are conditioned by relations in the homeland, relations between elites and primary producers, homeland ecological relations, and importantly, relations between homeland elites and populations in the frontier as well as between homeland primary producers and frontier populations. A full global model of surplus flow—theoretical or descriptive—is thus a rather complex affair. The following considers some of these strategic relations, principally from the point of view of elucidating surplus flow in the frontier.

Frontier Surplus Flows

At least four key levels are involved in modeling frontier surplus production and distribution:

1. The local environment—with the local ecology as the ultimate source of material.
2. Frontier primary producers responsible for surplus production.
3. Regional elites who channel in greater or lesser amounts the flows from the frontier.
4. The core elites with an interest in homeland frontier relations.

Other positions are involved in a full model of frontier social organization; however, these four strategic levels need to be considered when modeling the specific problem of how surplus is produced and distributed. To facilitate the use of this model, some examples are presented of the interests each of these key levels has in surplus flow, and some of their effects on frontier development are suggested.

Local Environment Relations

There is little that needs to be said about the importance of understanding the processes of the local ecology since this is given in much contemporary archaeological research. It is obviously important if we are interested in the production and export of surplus because we have to know something about the natural world from which the products are extracted. Note, this last point is not to say that the environment either determines or is the major factor of change regarding the production of surplus; rather it is to point out that the opportunities for surplus production are constrained in important ways by ecological relations.

Modeling the local ecology is not a descriptive task exclusively. It is important to grasp the ecosystemic relations of the natural environment. This requires interpreting the empirical data in light of general ecosystem theory. For instance, May's (1973) work on community matrices, J. Maynard Smith's (1974) models of predator prey systems, and Horn's (1974) theories of succession all offer largely untapped perspectives on how ecosystems respond to changing production strategies (see also Cody and Diamond 1975; May 1976). By knowing ecosystem structure and process, we are in a better position to evaluate ecosystem constraints on human production. Examples of the use of such approaches in archaeology include D. Harris's (1972) analyses of early agricultural systems, Green's (1979, 1980) studies of frontier agriculture, Perlman's (1976) analyses of settlement-subsistence systems, and Keene's (1982) analyses of diet.

A second important component of the local environment is the aboriginal population. All too often this social aspect of the environment is not included in models of general frontier process. For instance, Hudson's (1969) important models stress the pressures for land competition emanating from the core without taking into consideration the resistance to expansion offered by aboriginal populations. Similarly Wallerstein (1974) emphasizes the dynamics of capitalist expansion without paying enough attention to aboriginal response (e.g., Ceci 1977; Moore 1981; Wolf 1982). Even when aboriginal populations are considered, they are frequently misunderstood. Two recurring problems are the overemphasis on the limited spatial extent of these societies (Paynter and Cole 1980), or an emphasis on the stability of aboriginal society (e.g., Martin 1973). Fried (1975), Wolf (1982), and Leacock (1981) all criticize simplistic models and suggest more realistic alternatives.

Some ethnohistorians have been incorporating these critiques and are making more valid studies of frontiers (Jennings 1975; Salisbury 1982). In these, the cross-cultural contact experience is seen as a zone of interaction (Cooter 1977; Miller and Savage 1977) within which the social relations of the aboriginal population condition and change the colonizing population to significant extents. Since aboriginal labor is often responsible for surplus production at some stage in frontier development, a clear understanding of how ranked, egalitarian, and noncapitalist stratified societies mobilize labor and produce surpluses is crucial for elucidating the relations driving surplus production on frontiers.

In sum, since the surplus is extracted from frontier ecosystems and is often produced by aboriginal labor, these relations require attention to understand surplus flow and frontier change. The local ecology certainly conditions the amount of energy necessary to gain various forms of production. Minor adjustments in homeland subsistence strategies will be necessary in the new environment. Furthermore, inappropriate homeland production procedures might trigger unforeseen ecological catastrophes, thus drastically altering the developmental trajectory of the frontier. Similarly, resistance by aboriginal populations can affect the developmental trajectory from frontier status while easy domination can provide the impetus for fast change.

Primary Producers

A variety of social relations surround frontier production. For instance, production can take place in households (Hopkins and Wallerstein 1977:135); under arrangements of sharecropping or tenancy (Wallerstein 1974:106–107); under the wage relation; on plantations through slave labor (Wallerstein 1974:87–96; Williams 1944); and so on. Of this inexhaustive list two things are clear: first, any frontier is likely to consist of a number of these forms of surplus production; second, elucidating surplus flows requires linking these institutions backward to the local ecology and forward to the frontier and homeland elite.

Wolf's (1966:4–17) models of household production exemplify how the dynamics internal to primary-producer production can be articulated with other social and ecological positions. The key notion in his model is that of a fund. Model householders place production into various funds earmarked for different purposes. Wolf (1966:6–9) specifically considers four funds. Payments into a *caloric fund* are used to meet the biological demands of the household. Production sent to other funds is properly considered as surplus production. For instance, some production in agricultural households is contributed to a *replacement fund* for seed stock or feed for animals, or to replace worn-out tools and buildings through exchange with local craftspeople. Other production goes to the *ceremonial fund*. This surplus is used for local community ceremonies, such as celebrations of life-cycle events involving interhousehold exchanges (Saitta 1982) including births, first haircuts, adolescent rites of passage, weddings, funerals, and so on, as well as participation in local political and religious rituals (e.g., a town meeting and feast days). Payments into the ceremonial fund take many forms including the producing or obtaining of costumes, food, and gifts. Finally, some householders pay into a *rent fund*. They find themselves under obligations to the elites—those who control strategic resources, especially land and armed forces. Gaining access to these resources, such as using land for production or keeping the militia away from the door, is based on channeling surplus to the elites as taxes, tributes, tithes, rents, and so on.

The perpetuation of frontier status—that is, a clinal developmental trajectory—results when there is no change in the institutional basis for surplus production. In other words, as long as primary producers continue to meet fund payments, then frontier status will be recreated. Change in this institutional form or production results when fund payments change.

One instance of change results from a failure to make payments. Failure to make payments into any of these funds is likely to put the household in jeopardy. Thus, the primary producers are pulled in a number of directions simultaneously. Either a large demand for payment into one fund, such as into the replacement fund after a bad harvest, or into the rent fund after increased demands from core elites, or the cumulative effects from all of these can lead to household failure.

Wolf (1966:6–9) presents an example of a household in jeopardy. A German peasant household had a 40-acre farm producing 10,200 pounds of grain crops a year. Of this production, 3400 pounds went into seed stock, 2800 pounds went to feed the four horses, and 2700 pounds went in rents. This left 1300 pounds for the caloric fund (on the assumption that none went to ceremonial fund payments). The result was a daily caloric budget of 1600 calories per person, a value below that usually needed by adults (e.g., FAO/WHO 1973). This is clearly a household in jeopardy. Participation in community affairs is minimal, caloric intake is precariously low, and alleviation of these problems by cutting into rent payments is likely to incur the wrath of the elite. This household is not likely to reproduce its biology, its internal social relations, its ties to other households, or the relations of stratification. If other households face similar problems, general culture change is expectable. One change involves restructuring the payments, such as by changing the technology of production or altering payments to the elite. Alternatively, no change in the structure of payments will also lead to a change, most likely the abandonment of the area. The point is that underpayment is symptomatic of systemic problems and is likely to trigger large-scale change.

The trajectory taken is dependent upon a number of factors, including the nature of the subsistence system, the relations among primary producers, and the relative political strength of primary producers and elites. The utility of Wolf's model of payments is that it identifies these connections and thereby suggests some of the factors conditioning frontier development.

Wolf's models are especially useful on frontiers where households are an important unit of production, consumption, and social reproduction. Where production involves slave labor or migratory wage labor, or any other labor forms, production needs to be conceptualized with different funds. Although the funds for these different forms of labor organization will be different from those under household production, they too need to be set in a large relational context. This context, suggested in Wolf's model, traces surplus flows from the local environment into and between primary producers and ultimately to regional and core elites.

Regional Elites

Regional elites represent a third set of interests found on the frontiers of stratified societies. By definition, *regional elites* are those who control some of the surpluses produced by the primary producers. In terms of modeling their relation to surplus production and disposition, it is fair to assume that they will follow strategies that perpetuate their access to their social position as elites. This can be accomplished in a number of ways. Schneider *et al.* (1972) have discussed some of these strategies at great length, and their argument provides useful insight into the relations of elites. They distinguish between regional elites following a dependency strategy and elites following a development strategy. *Dependency elites* perpetuate their elite position by channeling surplus from the periphery towards the homeland. Not all surplus will move in this direction, as the dependency elites use some to solidify their position, such as by maintaining a local militia or administrative bureaucracy, or by monumental construction projects, and so forth. Because they do channel surpluses to the homeland, they have the support of the homeland if the frontier primary producers try to oust them. The *development elite* strategy entails maintaining their position by isolating the periphery from the demands of the homeland. Success rests, in part, on developing alliances with frontier primary producers, alliances based on keeping surplus production within the frontier area and lessening the primary producer's burden of surplus payments.

These strategies are obviously not completely exclusive. Elites are likely to mix core dependency with developing an independent base in their attempts to perpetuate their social position. Any frontier will exhibit some mix of both strategies. Furthermore, interpreting these strategies in prehistoric settings raises considerable methodological problems. Clues might lie in data from elite residences disclosing symbolic alignment with or opposition to homeland symbolic systems (Schneider 1979). Our attention to backward links to primary producers also might disclose these strategies. For instance, since a successful developmental strategy relies on mobilizing frontier populations against the homeland, studying the conditions giving rise to successful mobilization may provide essential clues. These can be found in investigations of primary producers rather than elite residences. One body of literature that might be tapped for models of these conditions concerns rebellions and revolutions (Moore 1966; Wolf 1969) about which more is said later. Even though the methodological problems of distinguishing dependency and development strategies are real, they do deserve attention. The success of these strategies greatly conditions surplus flows as well as the diachronic direction of frontier change. For example, a frontier characterized by dependency elites is an area likely to follow a clinal trajectory with little shift in the location of the cline. Alternatively, development elite strategies can lead to frontier developmental trajectories along clonal paths. This role of the elites in surplus flow is crucial for understanding frontier development.

Homeland Elites

A fourth component constraining surplus flow in frontiers are the homeland elites. *Homeland elites* reside in the homeland, or core area, coordinating and benefiting from the extraction of surplus from frontier and homeland primary producers. When frontier colonization leads to surplus accumulation controlled by elites, then the logic behind homeland elite interests condition the developmental trajectories of the frontier. If the frontier is key to homeland elites maintaining their positions, then clinal trajectories are likely results. Alternatively, if homeland elites do not depend heavily on surplus flows from the frontier, or if frontiers can subvert homeland demands, clonal trajectories and even possibly clinal trajectories moving in space may result. The theoretical problem is to better understand the role that long distance exploitation plays in elite strategies and the methodological problems involved in interpreting the success and failure of varying strategies.

Precious little guidance on the theoretical problem exists in the literature on homeland or core elites (e.g., Amin 1980:133–149; Finley 1973; Friedman and Rowlands 1978; Wallerstein 1974, 1980). Probably the best understood political economy that regularly produces frontier–homeland relations is capitalism. Though the theoretical position of frontiers is a point to debate (Brenner 1977), the following general sketch of elite interests describes some of the basic functions of frontiers.

European homeland elites used a number of strategies to extract surpluses from European primary producers. By the fifteenth century feudal extraction was supplemented by capitalist wage relations (Sweezy 1942:61–62). For a number of reasons, capitalist elites extracted surpluses from frontiers to support their accumulation strategies at home. Frontiers, for instance, provided sources of exotic raw materials used in monopoly exchanges as well as the raw materials for industrialization. Frontiers also provided areas where labor, unfamiliar with capitalist production, was brought into the production system. As a result, labor on the frontiers was drawn into capitalist production through slavery, tenancy, or various other arrangements (Williams 1944). Finally, frontiers provided markets for capitalist production. Thus, an understanding of the capitalist frontier has to take the interests of core elites—especially the search for raw materials, labor, and marketing—into consideration.

Precapitalist elites' use of the frontiers is not based on similarly strong theory. Theoretically, not all precapitalist stratified societies need to have systemically produced frontiers, though empirical evidence from the Southwest (McGuire 1980), the Iranian plateau (Lamberg-Karlovsky 1975; Kohl 1978), and the Yucatan (Sabloff and Rathje 1975), among other areas, suggests that some kind of large-scale process operated. One important interest attributed to precapitalist elites is the obtaining of slaves for homeland production (Finley 1973). Obviously, drawing slaves from frontiers has certain advantages since the slaves are unfamiliar with the culture of the homeland, and possibly have distinctive physical and behavioral traits. The frontier aimed at capturing slaves should look distinctive from those under capitalism, in part because homeland settlement of the slavery frontier would not likely be by whole families.

Another proposition for precapitalist societies suggests elite interests in obtaining exotic, luxury items (Friedman and Rowlands 1978:219). These are used as prestige items demonstrating the elevated position of the holder, and necessary for others to similarly exercise power. Imported exotic items support these few positions of prestige because they are scarce. However, models emphasizing this dimension of long distance process do not explain why distance, rather than a local monopoly or control of skilled labor, was used to create scarcity. Frontiers associated with this process should disclose mining operations and partial finishing sites as potential archaeological clues (Lamberg-Karlovsky 1975; Tosi 1977).

In a brief exposition, I (Paynter 1981:128–129) drew on the work of Wolf (1966) and Finley (1973) to suggest a precapitalist process to stimulate settler frontiers. In some precapitalist formations elites draw their base of power from participating in a bureaucracy. This participation gains them access to tributes from serfs. Given the instability of political fortunes, some elites might try to hedge against political disaster by building up a surplus of tribute. This could be done in preindustrial societies only by increasing the number of serfs under their domain. One way to accomplish this would be to colonize frontiers and open more land. These settler frontiers would exhibit agricultural settlements with more complete domestic units, as well as a displacement of aboriginal cultures, thus producing archaeologically distinctive traits.

The diversity of ideas concerning precapitalist elite interests in frontiers in part reflects a lack of theory. It also reflects the reality that a diversity of these processes existed and have yet to be fully elucidated. Building this kind of theory is certainly crucial for understanding supraregional change, however, since homeland elites have the potential to wield the most amount of power of any of the actors participating in frontier–homeland relations. Their interest in doing so, as well as their success or failure, will condition the type of trajectory observed.

Strategies of Domination and Resistance

One of the reasons for distinguishing these four levels of interaction is to point out that all the pieces do not necessarily (and in fact are unlikely to) neatly feedback and support one another. For instance, the extractive procedures followed by the primary producers are not necessarily going to lead to ecosystem regeneration. Or for that matter, the demands for surplus placed on the primary producers by elites may themselves be the cause of ecological degradation. All demands for surplus are not going to be met; primary producers losing their ability to reproduce their households might resist demands for more production. In some situations, the primary producers find allies among the regional development elites in the resistance of core elite demands. In other situations, core elite–regional dependency alliances might subvert these resistance efforts.

The point is this: in any specific situation there will be a specific mix of strategies of resistance as well as strategies of domination being exercised by members of these various levels. The total systemic trajectory is emergent from these interlevel interactions. The total system of surplus flows is not solely in the interest of the core elite, nor is it solely in the interest of the primary producers. Delineating these levels within a frontier is just the starting point for further elucidating the developmental trajectory of the frontier. How surplus is produced and distributed is a result of the tensions and struggles—understood as the strategies of domination and resistance—practiced by the individuals in these different roles (Amin 1980).

Domination and resistance can be exercised in all domains of culture. For instance, resistance can be exercised in the economic domain by witholding surpluses, or monopoly cornering of markets can be a tactic of domination used by elites. Domination can be exercised in the political domain by stationing troops just as riots, rebellions, and revolutions represent resistance. The symbolic domain can be manipulated in either case through such acts as wearing distinctive clothing (Schneider 1979; Tryon 1917:54–55) or adhering to specific beliefs. In a given setting any and all of these elements of a cultural system may be part of the tactics used in the strategies of domination and resistance.

Two brief examples illustrate the tensions between levels and their potential effects on the developmental trajectory of frontiers. The examples emphasize tactics using the political and economic domains. Fuller analyses of a situation would also investigate symbolic manipulations.

What conditions might underlie a frontier's population backing a development elite and attempting, as a region, to redefine its ties to both the regional elites, and through them with the core? The literature found on peasant revolts is ripe with suggestions, including those in Wolf (1969) and Friedrich (1977). One condition, found in many of these works, is the notion of an ecological crisis among the peasantry. When peasants are no longer able to meet their fund payments because of increasing peasant household sizes, or a degrading environment, or escalating rent demands from the core elites, the peasants will be in an energetic bind. Physical resistance to further surplus extraction is a likely result. As Wolf (1969:293) points out, peasant rebellion is rarely enough to generate success in eluding core demands. Successful resistance also involves being a sufficient distance from the core to be insulated from retaliation, and mobilizing a regional development elite as leadership for the peasant uprising. Only when the peasantry has been moved by a crisis in the material relations and led at a safe distance from the core by a new elite can the frontier redefine its obligations with the core. Such a successful rebellion is one behavioral scenario behind a clonal trajectory.

Another example of primary-producer resistance and elite response is found in postrevolutionary New England (Szatmary 1980). In this case, it is an international economic crisis rather than an ecological crisis that stimulates resistance. After the Revolution, British colonial policies officially restricted United States direct trade with the British West Indies. Even though illegal trade was conducted, the economic position of New England merchants, and particularly those of the Connecticut River valley, became precarious. Prior to the Revolution these merchants had exported foodstuffs and other staples to the West Indies in return for bills of exchange which were used to obtain manufactured items from Britain. The manufactured items were then traded to the interior farmers for the staples sent to the West Indies. Because of time delays, credit was the basis for the exchanges.

When it became clear that the Connecticut River valley merchants were no longer able to pay for manufactured items with goods or credit from the West Indies, British manufacturers stopped granting the New England merchants credit on manufactured items and called in past loans made to the merchants. Payment of these loans was, in turn, required from more remote merchants, and finally from the staple-producing farm households in the interior. By the mid-1780s almost 3000 debt cases were heard in the interior county of Hampshire involving roughly 30 percent of the males over 16 (Szatmary 1980:29). Fear of losing property and being jailed conditioned a revolt known as Shays' Rebellion, but the revolt was swiftly put down by forces allied with the merchants. Not the least of the farmers' problems stemmed from their difficulty in developing a group of leaders—development elites—to organize their legal efforts and their military campaign. The defeat of the farmers perpetuated the clinal relations between the backcountry and the urban merchants.

These examples point out the utility of approaching clinal and clonal trajectories within the framework of dominance and resistance. First, this does seem to be an approach by which the determinism involved in simplistic developmental models or world system models can be avoided. Any particular trajectory reflects the differential success of social actors at the various levels in realizing their goals, and is not a foregone conclusion.

Second, the conditions that surrounded these outcomes pose interesting problems for further research. For instance, the broad issue of the conditions of clinal versus clonal trajectories is refined by this framework. Clinal trajectories with no spatial change are associable with the success of core elite domination strategies. Evidence of such poses questions about the cooptation of regional elites, about how ecological crises were averted, and, if not averted, how primary-producer mobilization was subverted. Alternatively, clinal trajectories moving in space reflect the subversion of homeland elite strategies, not only with regards to the frontier, but also with regards to exploiting the homeland primary producers. Clonal trajectories suggest the successful alliance of regional development elites and frontier primary producers. The conditions surrounding this resistance of homeland extraction would be worth further investigation. Identifying patterns in these conditions is the basis of useful ethnological generalization.

In sum, clinal and modular landscapes and clinal and clonal trajectories representing the distribution of social surplus on supraregional landscapes require behavioral models. These models should address ecological relations as well as the interests of primary producers, regional elites, and homeland elites in the production and distribution of social surplus. No single set of interests or ecological constraints stimulate a particular trajectory. The clinal or clonal trajectory emerges from the differential success of strategies of domination and resistance. Full elaboration of these for a specific area is a very large undertaking, however, even asking about frontier change with this framework brings a new perspective—one that avoids the localism of narrow ecology and the misconceptions about space in diffusionist interpretations. The next section makes these points by addressing some problems in the developmental trajectory of historical New England.

FRONTIER CHANGE IN
HISTORICAL NEW ENGLAND

A preliminary analysis suggests the utility of the model of frontier surplus flow and strategies of domination and resistance when investigating homeland–frontier relations. It involves a problem for a part of historical New England, the abandonment of the hill towns in western Massachusetts. The abandonment of these towns is associated with the moving of the frontier through New England and the subsequent development of New England into an industrial core area. Although it is not a complete analysis, it does suggest ways to synthesize the historical archaeology of the rural north. A major reason for presenting this analysis is to raise new questions and suggest further research using the frontier surplus flow model and domination–resistance strategies.

New England Farm Abandonment

During the nineteenth century a part of New England was abandoned in association with the development of industrial workforces and westward expansion (Matthews 1962). The uplands of western and northern New England were the principal areas of net population loss. The following analyses concern Hampshire County in western Massachusetts (Figure 8.1). Within this region a number of towns experienced depopulation and others saw considerable demographic growth. Comparing these different towns provides some insight on the processes responsible for abandonment and growth. Understanding why people left the hill towns and why the valley towns grew is one step towards understanding how the frontier passed through this area and, ultimately, why New England followed a clinal developmental trajectory eventually rivaling the English homeland for political, economic, and ideological hegemony.

Three models accounting for abandonment are considered. Each emphasizes different levels in the model of frontier surplus flow. The first stresses local ecological relations as the conditions of depopulation. The second

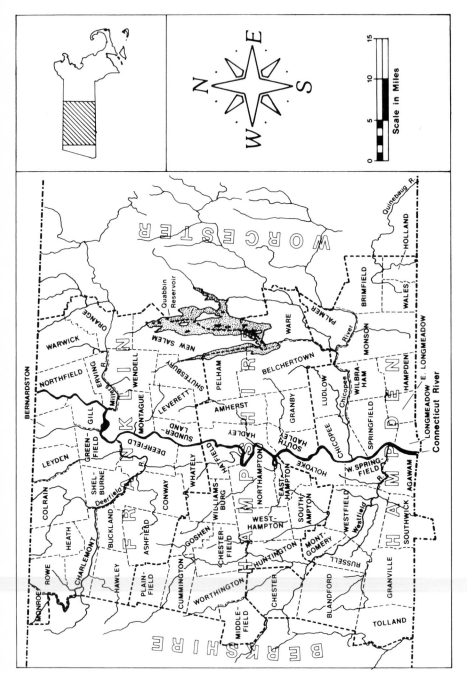

Figure 8.1   The Connecticut Valley of western Massachusetts.

suggests that the social relations of primary producers were responsible for westward migration and, by implication, upland New England's depopulation. The third suggests that the interests of regional and homeland elites need to be taken into account, along with ecological and primary producer relations, when considering the depopulation of this area.

The Depopulation of the
Connecticut Valley Hill Towns

Hampshire County lies within the Connecticut River watershed of western Massachusetts. Major geomorphological features of the Connecticut River watershed include the north-south tending valley of the Connecticut River and the east-west tending valleys of the Miller's, Deerfield, Westfield, and Chicopee Rivers. These five valleys were major transport arteries in the nineteenth century. The uplands to the east and west (the Worcester plateau and the Berkshires, respectively) differ from the Connecticut River valley lowland in the center, along a number of ecological variables. Generally, the soil, terrain, and climate of the lowlands was more conducive for labor and capital-intensive production than that of the uplands (Klimm 1933; Pabst 1941; Paynter 1982).

Subregions within the valley had different demographic and settlement patterns. Until the close of the Seven Year's War (1763), settlement was concentrated in the lowlands of the valley. After the decline in frontier hostilities, however, the uplands were rapidly settled. This initial period of expansion was followed in the first half of the nineteenth century by uneven demographic change. Generally, the valley lowland towns tended to gain population, while the hill towns, after a period of growth in the beginning of the nineteenth century, lost population (Klimm 1933; Pabst 1941; Paynter 1982).

A number of studies have been made of these contrasting demographic trends. Of particular interest is the work of geographer L. E. Klimm (1933). Klimm identifies five town types based on differing demographic trends. Four of these are found in Hampshire County (Figure 8.2). Rapid population gainers are Northampton-type towns. Hadley-type towns grew, slowed, and then grew again. Unclassified towns grew and then reached a stable size. Finally, towns that displayed growth and then decline (the decline beginning between 1810 and 1830) are Ashfield-type towns. Of these four town types, the Ashfield towns are the only ones with most of their land above 500 feet. The Ashfield towns are located within the New England uplands that more generally lost population in the nineteenth century.

Population density figures for Hampshire County also disclose these tendencies. County density in 1800 was 40.04 people per mile^2. This increased

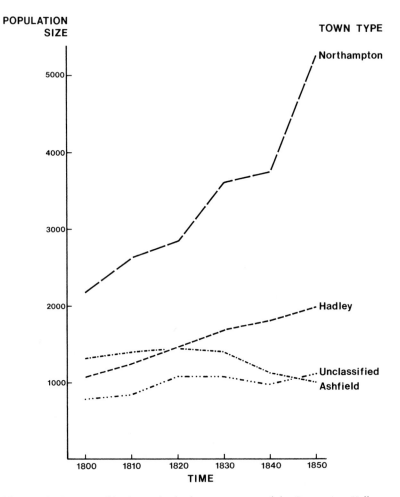

Figure 8.2 Demographic change in the four town types of the Connecticut Valley.

to 60.49 people per mile^2 by 1850. The Northampton-type towns grew dramatically from 44.03 people per mile^2 in 1800 to 106.64 people per mile^2 in 1850. All other town types similarly exhibited growth in population density *except* for the Ashfield-type towns, the average of which fell from 39.05 people per mile^2 in 1800 to 36.32 people per mile^2 in 1850.

Accounting for these different trends entails modeling underlying behavioral relations. There are a number of suggestive notions of eighteenth- and early nineteenth-century rural life that lead to implications for demographic change. For instance, some archaeologists and geographers (e.g., Klimm

1933; Thorbahn and Mrozowski 1979) account for depopulation by emphasizing the relations between primary agricultural producers and the natural environment. Some social historians, such as Henretta (1978) emphasize the social relations within the families of primary producers. Alternatively, Lemon (1980) calls attention to the interests of homeland elites by placing farmsteads within the context of changes in a world-scale capitalist social formation.

The implications for depopulation are most easily seen with the ecological approach. For instance, Klimm (1933:44) accounts for the abandonment of hill towns as follows: "The topography is so rough and the soil so poor in the Uplands that a living could be made in agriculture only with the greatest difficulty. The thin soil "wore out" in a very short time." Soil exhaustion provided the push out of the region and the more fertile soils of the west provided the pull. As a result, the hill towns were depopulated. Thorbahn and Mrozowski (1979) argue that deforestation associated with agricultural production created the potential for flooding within the hill towns. This flooding covered good agricultural land with boulders and alluvium, and stripped topsoil from other productive lands. The result was a very strong push out of the uplands.

For Henretta (1978) the source of difficulty for rural farmers lies not in the environment but within the social relations of the primary producers. One of the problems faced by lineal families was "the continual pressure of population on the existing capital stock; the rate of natural increase constantly threatened to outstrip the creation of new productive resources; cleared land, machinery, housing and livestock" (Henretta 1978:24). When a population put pressure on the capital stock a solution was to move part or all of the family to the West (Henretta 1978:27). As Henretta notes (1978:9), "Massive westward migration enabled a rapidly growing Euro-American population to preserve an agricultural society composed primarily of yeoman freeholding families in many eastern areas." In this case, hill-town farm depopulation is not as much abandonment of degraded habitat as it is a release of surplus population to pursue their life elsewhere.

The model emphasizing the place of western Massachusetts within the capitalist world system also has implications for depopulation. From this point of view, any local unit's production is related to the production and accumulation of surplus over the scale of the society. The family farm is part of "an interlocked landscape like a jigsaw puzzle . . . an instrument of empire building" (Lemon 1980:131). Much of this production, from the sugar plantations of the West Indies to the farms of the rural north, was based on tilling the soil. Total depopulation of an area amounted to withdrawing some soil from agricultural production. Partial depopulation of an area, such as encountered in the hill towns, suggests a change in land use from a labor-intensive form to a less labor-intensive form. Unlike the lineal family model, this source of demographic change does imply changes in production. Thus, in the model of elite interests, demographic change is due to changing land use rather than the abandonment of a degraded environment or a response to primary producers.

Which processes drove the frontier through western Massachusetts? If the dominant processes concern either primary producer–natural environment relations or lineal family demography, then the forces shaping frontier development are largely found within the frontier itself. This frontier change would be unrelated to processes of world-scale surplus flow or class struggles over surplus production. Alternatively, evidence for shifting land use patterns suggests that class relations, including regional and homeland elite interests, were conditioning frontier development. In this case, depopulation reflects class struggle over the use of land in the form of the unsuccessful resistance by some primary producers to the demands by elites for new forms of surplus. A closer consideration of these towns sheds some light on the relevant processes.

Model Evaluations

Ecological Relations

I begin by considering the ecological model for abandonment. The degradation proposition is that the hill-town environments were marginal for mixed agricultural production. The climatic conditions, soils, and terrain made hill towns susceptible to erosion and soil infertility, especially with the primitive agricultural practices of the late eighteenth- and early nineteenth-century farmers. Once biodegradation began, the lands of New York and the Old Northwest attracted Massachusetts hill-town populations.

Documentary material—Massachusetts tax valuations for 1771, 1831, and 1841—allow for some initial assessments of this ecological scenario. A basic expectation is that evidence for biodegradation should be more prevalent in hill towns than in the other towns.

Two measures were used, an index of biodegradation and a measure of productivity. The index of biodegradation was constructed from the valuations from 1831 and 1841. These delineate the number of unproductive acres—unimproved and unimprovable acres—and the number of productive acres—acres in woodlots, pastures, fresh meadows, mowing, and tillage. If biodegradation were solely responsible for hill-town abandonment, then the hill towns should have relatively large numbers of unproductive acres and relatively small numbers of productive acres. Dividing the unproductive acres by the productive acres provides an index of bio-

Table 8.1

Biodegradation Index: Unproductive Acres/Productive Acres[a]

A. TOWN-TYPE STATISTICS (1831 and 1841)

		County	Northampton type	Hadley type	Hill-town type	Unclassified type
$\bar{X}$	31	.67	.63	.39	.69	.83
	41	.48	.44	.09	.45	.72
SD	31	.49	.37	.08	.63	.27
	41	.32	.35	.04	.26	.28
MD	31	.60	.67	.39	.46	.89
	41	.49	.40	.09	.41	.75
N	31	23	6	2	10	5
	41	23	6	2	10	5

B. HILL-TOWN COMPARISONS TO COUNTY MEAN AND MEDIAN VALUES

	Year (1831)	Year (1841)
$\bar{X}$	Hill Town > County	Hill Town < County
MD	Hill Town < County	Hill Town < County

C. RANK ORDERS OF VARIOUS TOWN TYPES

	$\bar{X}$		MD	
	Year (1831)	Year (1841)	Year (1831)	Year (1841)
1.	Hadley	Hadley	Hadley	Hadley
2.	Northampton	Northampton	Hill town	Northampton
3.	Hill town	Hill town	Northampton	Hill town
4.	Unclassified	Unclassified	Unclassified	Unclassified

[a]From Massachusetts tax valuations. 1 = least degraded.

degradation. Under the biodegradation proposal, the hill towns should have the most degraded land and, thus, the largest indexes of degradation.

The tax data only weakly support this suggestion (Table 8.1). Ideally, the hill-town index should be greater than the aggregate county index and greater than the index for other towns. However, only when using the mean index of degradation in 1831 is the hill-town index greater than the county index. Importantly, the hill towns never have the largest index; in fact, the hill towns are quite close to being the second *least* degraded town type.

A second evaluation of the biodegradation scenario can be made with productivity figures from the 1771 and 1831 tax valuations. Each reports information on acres in tillage and bushels of grain produced. If biodegradation were a primary factor in abandonment, then the hill towns should

Table 8.2

Productivity Index: Bushels of Grain/Acres of Tillage[a]

A. TOWN-TYPE STATISTICS (1771 and 1831)

		County	Northampton type	Hadley type	Hill-town type	Unclassified type
$\bar{X}$	71	6.86	6.17	8.21	8.01	6.31
	31	12.26	11.10	6.92	15.12	10.06
SD	71	1.73	.62	na	2.56	1.13
	31	5.06	4.73	2.97	5.08	1.18
MD	71	6.30	6.32	8.21	8.15	5.48
	31	13.03	11.08	6.92	13.55	9.86
N	71	12	4	1	3	4
	31	22	6	2	10	4

B. HILL-TOWN COMPARISONS TO COUNTY MEAN AND MEDIAN VALUES

	Year (1771)	Year (1831)
$\bar{X}$	Hill Town > County	Hill Town > County
MD	Hill Town > County	Hill Town > County

C. RANK ORDERS OF VARIOUS TOWN TYPES

	$\bar{X}$		MD	
	Year (1831)	Year (1841)	Year (1831)	Year (1841)
1.	Hadley	Hill town	Hadley	Hill town
2.	Hill town	Northampton	Hill town	Northampton
3.	Unclassified	Unclassified	Northampton	Unclassified
4.	Northampton	Hadley	Unclassified	Hadley

[a]From Massachusetts tax valuations. 1 = most productive.

display relatively low productivity after the period 1810–1830. Table 8.2 has these productivity values. The hill-town values do *not* support the bio-degradation scenario. The mean and median productivity values for the hill towns is greater than the county mean and median values in 1771 and 1831. Furthermore, rank orderings of the town types based on the mean and median values disclose that the hill towns were the second *most* productive towns in 1771 and the *most* productive in 1831.

These two indexes by no means demonstrate that biodegradation played no role. Larger samples (including the towns of Franklin and Hampden counties), shorter time intervals (creating a continuous sequence), and field surveys analyzing hill-town soil conditions (Thorbahn and Mrozowski 1979) all would be useful to fully elucidate the role of biodegradation.

However, these assessments do not strongly support the biodegradation model and do suggest that, minimally, more than biodegradation was at work.

Primary Producer Interests

An alternative hypothesis for depopulation is based on the lineal family model of rural northern social relations. Most of the hill towns were incorporated in the second half of the eighteenth century and reached their population peaks between 1810 and 1830. This demographic peak may be due to the demographic dynamics of lineal family reproduction in a relatively young colonizing population, and not the operation of class processes. The following is one model of these dynamics.

Assume that a town is colonized by a young population with high fertility, relatively low mortality, and a balanced sex ratio—not an altogether unreasonable assumption for the Connecticut River valley in the late eighteenth century (Swedlund *et al.* 1976). Furthermore, assume that the population is composed of young adults intent upon improving the material conditions of their and their children's lives. Consistent with the lineal family model (Henretta 1978), the principal adult concern is to amass enough surplus to leave their children the wherewithal to reproduce a lineal family. This surplus may take the form of a nearby farmstead, the capital to make a farmstead in a new area, or the parent's farm.

A town following this strategy could have the following growth pattern. Assume that the initial wave of colonization fills all the available farmland. No new households could be moved in without a household moving out. However, since these are young couples, this economic limit is not the demographic limit. The population of the area could still grow and support larger families, as long as these larger families did not constitute new households. An economic crisis occurs when the children come of an age to start new households. The solution that reproduces the lineal family lies in outmigration. As the older children move elsewhere to find available land, the town's population declines. Thus, a boom—bust cycle characterizes the demography of the town based on the economic limit set by the reproduction of the lineal family. The observed demographic pattern of hill-town population growth and decline would be due to the passing of this wave of dependent children through the area.

Studies of the demography of the Connecticut River valley in the eighteenth and early nineteenth centuries suggest equal parity in sex ratio, birth spacing of about 30 months, and dependency periods of 27 years for males and 22–24 years for females (Temkin-Greener and Swedlund 1977). If the entire stock of available farmsteads was occupied in the first colonization,

Table 8.3
Model Lineal Family Demographic Pattern

Year	Males	Females	Total
0	1	1	2
5	2	2	4
10	3	3	6
15	4	4	8
20	5	5	10
25	6	6	12
30	5	5	10
35	4	4	8
40	3	3	6
45	2	2	4

then after 22 to 27 years the area would begin to see demographic decline as the oldest children move to other areas to establish their families.

The result, for instance, might look like the model values in Table 8.3, in which the pattern of population growth and decline is simply in response to the problem of reproducing lineal families. For ease in modeling, assume that the town has room for only one farm. (Calculating figures for larger, more realistic towns involves multiplying by the constant of the number of farms per town.) The year of colonization sees this farm occupied by a childless couple. With birth spacing of 30 months and relatively equal sex ratio, a census of the area after 5 years reveals a two-child, four-member household. Population growth continues until some time between the twenty-fifth and thirtieth years when the first children move elsewhere to find the land to start their own lineal families. This begins a period of population decline—a decline that continues until one of the ultimate children gains access to the farm, then the boom–bust cycle would begin again.

How then do we evaluate if the empirical pattern of hill-town depopulation is due to the underlying processes of lineal family reproduction (modeled in Table 8.3)? One method is to examine the population structure of the model and the towns. Population structure is studied by analyzing the population by age–sex categories. A familiar representation of this information is a population pyramid (e.g., Pressat 1972; Wilson and Bossert 1971) in which the proportion of individuals in equal age intervals are plotted by sex as bar graphs. The proportions appear on the x axis and age groups on the y axis, males are plotted to the left and females to the right.

Figure 8.3 is a description of the changing population structure modeled in Table 8.3. The graph of year 0 is of the very young, high-fertility, low-mortality, initial colonizing population. The bulge in the younger years

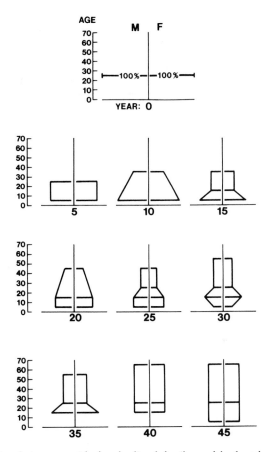

Figure 8.3 Population pyramids for the lineal family model of settlement growth and abandonment.

(e.g., year 10) is due to births to the first generation couple. As these children age, the bulge shifts up through the age categories (e.g., year 35). As any but the ultimate children (male and female) reach the category of 25–30, they out-migrate. Thus, the bulge does not continue up the age categories as in unconstrained models of aging populations; nor do third generation children appear in the younger age categories until the ultimate second generation males and females, those inheriting the family farm, bear them. In sum, this sequence of age structure graphs is expectable if the lineal model is responsible for the increase and then decrease in hill-town populations. The sequence is what can be compared against empirical plots of age structures.

TOWN TYPE

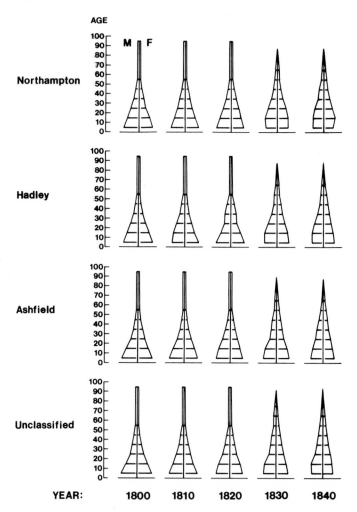

Figure 8.4 Population pyramids for the Connecticut Valley town types: 1800–1840.

Figure 8.4 contains the empirical plots for the years 1800 through 1840. Three points should be noted about the construction of these graphs. First, all four town types are graphed on separate lines. Second, the data for the graphs is from federal census data. It was not until 1830 that the federal census reported demographic information in 10-year intervals, thus, 10-year intervals had to be constructed for the first 3 years. The procedure was to calculate the average population per year per category (total population per age–sex category/number of years per age–sex category) and assign this to each year within each age–sex category. With estimated numbers of people per year, it is possible to regroup the age–sex categories into 10-year intervals and create the very smooth graphs for the years 1800–1820. This assumes an even distribution of people within each age–sex category. Other routines for estimating the number of people per year could have been used (e.g., linear interpolation or exponential functions), however, their use would not change the overall appearance of the graphs. It is this overall form rather than any particular value that is important for comparison to graphs of the lineal family model. Third, the empirical graphs are quite similar in form to other graphs from the area. For instance, Swedlund *et al.* (1976) report population pyramids for towns in Franklin County that have quite wide bases and then decline through the older (upper) age categories. Thus, the techniques for constructing these graphs do not appear to have grossly distorted them.

Analysis of the empirical graphs does not support the proposition that the lineal family model was responsible for depopulation. First, the empirical plots do not exhibit the transformation sequence characteristic of the lineal family model. Rather, the empirical plots stay remarkably the same over the 40-year period. The only notable trend in the empirical plots is the decrease in the relative proportion of people in the youngest age category. This undoubtedly reflects the secular decline in fertility characteristic of the area, the New England region, and the United States generally during the first half of the nineteenth century (Swedlund *et al.* 1976; Temkin-Greener and Swedlund 1977). The out-migration of the hill towns would not appear to be solely due to a crisis driven by the logic of lineal family reproduction.

Second, the population structures for the various town types do not vary. Similar internal demographic relations are associated with towns losing population, gaining population, and staying relatively stable. This suggests that out-migration and in-migration, as well as local fertility and mortality, are responsible for town demographic growth patterns. Thus, understanding these growth patterns, such as hill-town depopulation, requires considering factors operating beyond the scale of the Connecticut River valley (Knights 1971; Swedlund *et al.* 1976; A. Swedlund, personal communication, 1983).

The discrepancy between the population structures for the empirical towns and the population structures for the lineal family model, and the similarity of population structures for all towns, indicates that the lineal family crisis is not responsible for the depopulation phenomenon. Note, I am neither concluding that lineal family processes were not operating in the area, nor that lineal family processes are never associated with stable, young population structures, such as those in the empirical graphs. The sole point is that the lineal family model producing a boom–bust pattern also produces a population structure pattern that is not found in the empirical record. This together with the similarity of structures for all the towns suggests that the depopulation of the hill towns needs to be understood in light of additional factors. The frontier surplus flow model suggests that interests of regional and homeland elites need to be taken into consideration.

Elite Interests

Elite interests, whether regional or homeland, dictate that land be put to use to contribute to their accumulation of surplus. This general interest can have any number of implications on specific frontiers ranging from occupying a frontier to fend off other elites, to using a frontier as a safety valve for resisting primary producers at home, to extracting surpluses from frontier production. Generally, from the elite's point of view, frontier land should be used to, minimally, not interfere with and, maximally, contribute to their accumulation of surplus. Thus, elite interests involve a concern over land use.

The following suggests how elite interests in land use changed during the period of hill-town depopulation. The opening decades of the nineteenth century saw the Connecticut River valley operating in the changing British world system. The Connecticut River valley supplied rural products, such as pot ash, pearl ash, staves, hoops, shingles, and foodstuffs (such as grains and packed meat) to the cities of North America and the plantations of the West Indies. Regional elites—the merchants in the valley (Martin 1939) located in the entrepôts of Springfield, Northampton, and Hartford, Connecticut,—mediated and benefited from the flow of surplus rural production. The network was one in which rural producers received British manufactures from merchants in exchange for rural products. Merchants obtained the manufactures with bills of exchange they received when trading rural products to West Indian planters and urban merchants (Martin 1939). The hill-town primary producers were one ultimate source of this surplus by their following of a mixed agricultural strategy, meeting their own needs, and sending a variety of rural products to the merchants.

A number of factors came together toward the end of the eighteenth century and the beginning of the nineteenth century to alter this surplus flow. Among these factors were struggles over political autonomy and economic control between the regional elite of North America and the British homeland elite. Manifestations of this struggle were the American Revolution, the trade embargoes, and the War of 1812. Furthermore, British homeland elite accumulation strategies shifted from using mercantile strategies based on reexporting tropical groceries (such as sugar) to strategies based on industrialization (e.g., Davis 1973; Martin 1939; Szatmary 1980; Wallerstein 1980; Williams 1944). The sum effect was to reduce the connection between the West Indies and the Connecticut River valley, with the ultimate effect of disrupting the flow of bills of exchange against British manufactures (Martin 1939; Szatmary 1980).

With these changes in world-scale surplus flow, some regional elites in the Connecticut River valley also changed their accumulation strategies. The new strategies involved industrializing the valley and resulted in the location of substantial textile and small-arms manufacturing mills in the lowland towns of, for instance, Chicopee, Holyoke, and Northampton (Deyrup 1948; Shlakman 1935). This change in elite accumulation strategies altered their demands for primary production. For instance, wood for construction of factories, workers' housing, and heating would be in demand. Similarly, food would be required for the growing industrial workforce, and hay for the horses providing lowland transportation. Finally, wool from sheep would be in demand for the textile mills. The change in regional elite accumulation strategies would thus demand new forms of rural production.

What might be the spatial pattern of response to these changes? Thünen models (Chisholm 1962) suggest that more labor-intensive production (such as market gardening) is located near the growing centers while less-intensive production (such as dairy, lumber, or pastoralism) occurs at greater distances. These different land-use zones appear as a series of roughly concentric rings centered on emerging centers. Empirical studies of upstate New York (Conkling and Yeates 1976:49) and of the Connecticut River valley (Paynter 1982) identify the development of these intensification patterns in association with North American development. Thus, a change in the spatial division of labor is expectable with a shift in the nature of elite demands for surplus.

It is clear that elites realized their interests and redirected the production patterns of the valley towards industry during the first half of the nineteenth century. Water-powered factories arose at major power sites (LeBlanc 1969) and industrial centers experienced large population gains (Klimm 1933). What has usually not been considered is the effect of these changing elite demands for surplus on demographic change in towns that did not adopt industry. However, there are good theoretical and empirical reasons for suspecting that changes in elite tactics toward industrialization would also have affected agricultural practices as well. It is here that the link can be made between changing elite interests and the depopulation of the hill towns.

Changing agricultural practices, from mixed agriculture to greater specialization, have the following demographic implications. Assuming that rural producers lived near their fields, a switch to less labor-intensive production, such as pastoralism or wood or hay production, would create a depopulation of the area, while a switch to more labor-intensive production, such as market gardening or other labor intensive cash crops, would create a population increase. For the hill towns this switch might have been from a mixed agricultural productive base in which surplus rural products were sent to merchants for regional export, to a more specialized, less labor-intensive production base, such as using the land to produce timber and/or animal products. This change in land use, to less-intensive land use, might be responsible for hill-town depopulation. If this is the case, then a shift in productive practices should be associated with the depopulation of the early

Table 8.4

Value of Tobacco per Unit Area (in Dollars)[a]

A. TOWN-TYPE STATISTICS (1845 and 1855)

		County	Northampton type	Hadley type	Hill-town type	Unclassified type
$\bar{X}$	45	4.82	17.73	.69	.20	.23
	55	47.58	31.31	446.76	.00	2.60
SD	45	13.33	21.33	.69	.61	.46
	55	126.17	33.55	55.72	.00	5.21
MD	45	0	9.78	.69	0	0
	55	0	18.06	446.76	0	0
N	45	23	6	2	10	5
	55	23	6	2	10	5

B. HILL-TOWN COMPARISONS TO COUNTY MEAN AND MEDIAN VALUES

	Year (1845)	Year (1855)
$\bar{X}$	Hill Town < County	Hill Town < County
MD	Hill Town = County	Hill Town = County

C. RANK ORDERS OF VARIOUS TOWN TYPES

	$\bar{X}$			MD	
	Year (1845)	Year (1855)		Year (1845)	Year (1855)
1.	Northampton	Hadley		Northampton	Hadley
2.	Hadley	Northampton		Hadley	Northampton
3.	Unclassified	Unclassified		Hill town	Hill town
4.	Hill town	Hill town		Unclassified	Unclassified

[a]From Massachusetts state census. 1 = greatest value of tobacco.

nineteenth century. A number of indexes provide some insight on the nine-teenth-century land use.

One labor-intensive cash crop that became important in the Connecticut River valley in the nineteenth century was tobacco (Ramsey 1930). Table 8.4 reports data from the Massachusetts census in 1845 and 1855 on this relatively labor-intensive crop (Ramsey 1930). It is clear from Table 8.4 that the hill towns did not adopt tobacco production. Hill-town mean value of tobacco per unit area is less than the county mean in both 1845 and 1855. While the median equals the county median, this is at a value of zero for both years. Of the four town types, the hill towns have the lowest mean and median values of tobacco per unit area produced in both years. On the other hand, the relative importance of tobacco for the Hadley-type towns, just

Table 8.5
Feet of Lumber per Unit Area (Times 10^3)[a]

			A. TOWN-TYPE STATISTICS (1845 and 1855)			
		County	Northampton type	Hadley type	Hill-town type	Unclassified type
$\bar{X}$	45	11.74	9.34	27.75	10.42	10.85
	55	20.82	18.17	48.44	20.95	12.70
SD	45	11.23	7.55	19.81	8.86	9.15
	55	15.35	9.98	.62	14.80	12.10
MD	45	10.15	9.99	27.75	9.33	14.58
	55	17.99	17.06	48.44	18.46	4.88
N	45	23	6	2	10	5
	55	23	6	2	10	5

B. HILL-TOWN COMPARISONS TO COUNTY MEAN AND MEDIAN VALUES

	Year (1845)	Year (1855)
$\bar{X}$	Hill Town < County	Hill Town > County
MD	Hill Town < County	Hill Town > County

C. RANK ORDERS OF VARIOUS TOWN TYPES

	$\bar{X}$		MD	
	Year (1845)	Year (1855)	Year (1845)	Year (1855)
1.	Hadley	Hadley	Hadley	Hadley
2.	Unclassified	Hill town	Unclassified	Hill town
3.	Hill town	Northampton	Northampton	Northampton
4.	Northampton	Unclassified	Hill town	Unclassified

[a]From Massachusetts state census. 1 = greatest amount of lumber produced.

Table 8.6
Cords of Firewood Produced for Market per Unit Area

A. TOWN-TYPE STATISTICS (1845 and 1855)

		County	Northampton type	Hadley type	Hill-town type	Unclassified type
$\bar{X}$	45	31.82	42.21	52.01	9.56	55.81
	55	66.90	98.15	87.20	30.17	94.75
SD	45	39.70	57.90	2.01	9.92	34.21
	55	47.38	54.11	7.34	25.13	26.76
MD	45	23.60	24.34	52.01	3.8	45.53
	55	65.73	84.64	87.20	20.78	97.50
N	45	23	6	2	10	5
	55	23	6	2	10	5

B. HILL-TOWN COMPARISONS TO COUNTY MEAN AND MEDIAN VALUES

	Year (1845)	Year (1855)
$\bar{X}$	Hill Town < County	Hill Town < County
MD	Hill Town < County	Hill Town < County

C. RANK ORDERS OF VARIOUS TOWN TYPES

	$\bar{X}$		MD	
	Year (1845)	Year (1855)	Year (1845)	Year (1855)
1.	Unclassified	Northampton	Hadley	Unclassified
2.	Hadley	Unclassified	Unclassified	Hadley
3.	Northampton	Hadley	Northampton	Northampton
4.	Hill town	Hill town	Hill town	Hill town

[a]From Massachusetts state census. 1 = greatest number of cords of firewood.

when their populations began their second growth spurt, suggests that adoption of tobacco or lack of its adoption significantly affected the demographic trends of agricultural towns.

It is easier to characterize what the hill towns were not producing than to generalize about what was produced. However, there is some evidence suggesting that the hill towns were engaged in less labor-intensive production. Table 8.5 reports the mean and median values for feet of lumber prepared for market in 1845 and 1855. Though the county mean and median values are greater than those for the hill towns in both years, by 1855 the hill towns were the second most important lumber producers in the county. Although lumber figures are consistent with the hypothesis that hill-town depopulation coincided with a shift to less labor-intensive land use, Table

Table 8.7

Animal Density (Excluding Humans)

		A. TOWN-TYPE STATISTICS (1831)				
		County	Type	Type	Type	Type
$\bar{X}$	31	141.68	151.23	136.05	146.13	123.60
SD	31	47.48	44.72	44.00	54.75	26.71
MD	31	130.69	147.60	136.05	140.65	127.53
N		23	6	2	10	5

B. HILL-TOWN COMPARISONS TO COUNTY MEAN AND
MEDIAN VALUES

Year (1831)

$\bar{X}$	Hill Town > County
MD	Hill Town > County

C. RANK ORDERS OF VARIOUS TOWN TYPES

$\bar{X}$	MD
Year (1831)	Year (1831)
1. Northampton	Northampton
2. Hill town	Hill town
3. Hadley	Hadley
4. Unclassified	Unclassified

[a]From Massachusetts tax valuations. 1 = greatest number of animals per unit area.

8.6 indicates that they were clearly not engaged in producing firewood. So, if the shift to less-intensive woodlots is in part responsible for depopulation, it was not brought about by a switch to directly providing firewood for the lowland towns.

Another less-intensive land use is pastoralism. The mean and median animal density is reported in Table 8.7 for 1831. The hill towns have denser animal populations than the county, and are the second most dense towns in the valley. This measure also supports the notion that hill towns were shifting to less labor-intensive land use in the early nineteenth century.

Conclusions

Although precise characterization of hill-town production awaits further study, it is clear that (1) the area was engaged in some form of production during the period of depopulation, (2) the new production practices were less labor-intensive than those followed in other agricultural towns, and (3) these changes were consistent with the changing elite interests of this period. It appears that the hill towns were not so much being abandoned as being used differently. This difference was consistent with the change in the area's place within the world system of surplus flows, namely its change from being a semiperiphery producing agricultural staples to support accumulation in urban areas and the West Indies, to becoming an industrial center with a new set of production demands.

This change in world surplus flows means that change in the Connecticut River valley has to be understood as, in part, an attempt by North American elites to preempt British homeland elite's access to surplus. Taking elite interests into consideration by no means suggests that this is the only point of view needed to understand demographic change and frontier development. The social relations of the primary producers, those people responsible for the change in population, and their relations with the local ecosystem also need consideration. There is much more that needs to be done to fully understand the processes of each of the levels and the nature of their interactions. What the above analysis points out is that the entire range of processes found in the frontier model of surplus flow needs to be taken into account; attempts to explain late eighteenth- and early nineteenth-century culture change that focus on only one set of these processes will be insufficient.

CONCLUSIONS

One of the reasons for explicitly laying out the model of frontier surplus flow and the strategies of domination and resistance is to stimulate further research on frontier development. Analyzing frontier change in a number of different settings should provide insight into the mechanisms of large-scale culture change as well as into the theory needed to understand this diversity. Although conducting analyses outside of capitalist settings seems warranted, the New England problem is by no means solved. The analysis of depopulation suggests that the model of frontier surplus flows might provide some insights into broader issues of New England culture change, some of which are discussed in the following.

Conditions of New England Development

The analyses of the depopulation of western Massachusetts point out the necessity of setting this particular frontier in its larger systemic context. This larger perspective is being used by South (1977, 1978) and Lewis (1976, 1977) in their studies of South Carolina's place in the British world system. However, the dominant interpretive tradition in New England historical archaeology pays primary attention to the larger context of the ideological domain of northern culture (Deetz 1977). A fruitful direction for problem solving in New England would be to consider the larger context for other domains of culture as well. One way to do this would be to use the frontier surplus flow model to analyze the competing interests and alliances responsible for the area's developmental trajectory. Completing such a task is well beyond my present scope. However, some preliminary research suggests that further work is warranted.

A brief perusal of the massive literature on European economic history presents some remarkable correlations between European development and Deetz's three stages for New England. Briefly, Deetz's analysis of the material record uses an early yeoman stage (1620–1660), a folk period (1660–1760), and a period shaped by the introduction of the Renaissance-derived, Georgian mind-set (1760 to early 1800s). The principal explanatory processes are diffusion and cultural drift, with diffusion being responsible for the first and third stages, and drift shaping the development of regional folk cultures in the second. Noting some changes in Europe that coincide with these changes suggests that the political–economic processes of domination and resistance—expressed in the actions of homeland elites, regional elites, and primary producers in New England—also played a part.

Broad European political–economic trends identify the "long fifteenth century" and the "long seventeenth century" (Cippola 1976:231–233; de Vries 1976:2–29; Wallerstein 1974:67–70, 1980:3–34). The long fifteenth century was a period of expansion and economic growth. European colonization of the world began in this period, an expansion based on an economic upswing. Rising grain prices, increasing populations, increasing trans-Atlantic trade volumes and values, and increasing capital accumulation all attest to this growth. The hegemonic powers in the fifteenth century were Portugal and then Spain. The long fifteenth century ends with the spread of an economic downturn throughout Europe. This started in the Mediterranean polities as early as the late 1500s and reached northwestern Europe, and particularly England, by the mid-seventeenth century (Wallerstein 1980:18–25).

The following period, the long seventeenth century, was characterized by economic stagnation (Wallerstein 1980:13–34) or possibly crisis (de Vries 1976:1–29). Northwest European polities, particularly the Dutch and English, did well only in comparison to the rest of Europe. Grain prices, populations, trade volumes, and capital accumulation either leveled off or declined. Economic hegemony was exercised by the Dutch in the mid-seventeenth century (Wallerstein 1980:37–71) primarily due to their successful wresting of trade from the Iberian polities. However, the Dutch were unable to establish political hegemony as well, thus the period saw numerous struggles between core states (particularly the Dutch, English, and French) for political supremacy. Political hegemony in the core was established only with the English defeat of the French in the Seven Years War (1763). The rise of Britain to economic, ideological, and political supremacy in the European world stimulated a new stage of world system growth (Wallerstein 1980:75–125, 245–289).

This developmental trajectory for the core, even sketched this generally, has a number of interesting implications for studying the northern colonies. For one, the dates in this scenario nicely coincide with the periods identified by Deetz. Separatist and Puritan colonization occurred while England was still experiencing economic growth. By the second period (1660), England's growth had slowed, and stagnation lasted during Deetz's stage of isolated folk development (until 1760). The ascension of England to core hegemony neatly coincides with the introduction of the Georgian mind-set and associated material culture into the northern colonies.

The coincidence of these periods certainly suggests that the cause of New England development is related to the changes in the European political–economic scene. Exactly how these two trajectories are linked needs further attention. The frontier surplus flow model and strategies of domination and resistance suggest some lines of research that would illuminate these connections. Three issues in particular come to mind.

First, recalling the importance of considering relations between homeland and aboriginal populations leads to characterizing colonization as the successful domination of Anglo land-use patterns over aboriginal patterns. While this ultimately entailed the virtual extinction of Native Americans from New England, during the initial period it involved the substantial articulation of Native American and Anglo interests (Jennings 1975; Salisbury 1982), particularly with regard to the fur trade (Ceci 1977; Thomas 1979). Thus, the primary producers initially included both yeoman farmers and Native Americans interacting with each other and with regional and core elites. Understanding the initial period requires broadening this definition of primary producer and unraveling the flows across these ethnic boundaries. I suspect that the Anglos will look less like yeoman, and the Native Americans less like an aboriginal culture once this is completed.

A second point of potential research concerns the folk period. This period is considered as one in which the northern colonies develop in relative isolation from core interests, an isolation brought on by benign neglect. Some characteristics of the second period suggest that more than relative isolation, or benign neglect, were at work. For instance, evidence in the material record for continuous flows of items across the Atlantic, and evidence that New England elites accumulated surplus by moving New England products throughout the Atlantic economy, attests to the continued importance of homeland–frontier relations (Bailyn 1955; Innes 1978). One way to accommodate the evidence for cultural divergence with evidence for continuous contact is to consider this as a period of successful regional resistance of core surplus extraction. Development elites and primary producers forged alliances that succeeded in redirecting surplus flows for the improvement of their material conditions. These improvements are seen, for instance, in the improvement of housing in the area (Carson *et al.* 1981), the development of interregional marketing networks (Friedmann 1973), and the development of social stratification (e.g., Innes 1978; Main 1965). Specifying the material conditions of this successful resistance requires more attention.

Third, considering the second period as one of successful regional resistance, rather than as isolation, helps set the stage for the third period, the reintegration of New England into broader European cultural tradition. A paradox in present conceptions of this period is that just as ideological hegemony, in the form of the Georgian mind-set, was reestablished over the area, the region vehemently rejected attempts to reestablish political, economic, and symbolic hegemony. Regional rejection was a realization of the interests that dominated the past century—those of development elites and their allied primary producers. The Georgian mass culture represented the fact that British elites, having favorably resolved problems in the core, could reassert some form of control over the nature of surplus flows in New England. Due to resistance the nature of this control took on a new form. Rather than following a colonial strategy in which political and ideological control established the basis for surplus extraction, the third period might better be understood as the realization of a neocolonial strategy in which economic control was the basis for political and ideological hegemony (Amin 1980:138–139).

These are but a few of the possible research avenues suggested by contemplating the correlation of Deetz's temporal stages and broader trends in European economic history. The depopulation example clearly points out that successful interpretations of New England's development requires setting the ecological context as well as addressing the interests of a broad range of actors. Whether the preceding suggestions prove tenable awaits further research. That the issues are worth addressing is clear. One payoff is understanding why and how one colony escaped the trap of underdevelopment and rose to hegemony in our present world. Understanding this would contribute to Deetz's (1977:158) goal of discovering the origins of the modern world, a truly anthropological issue.

Summary

Frontiers are best understood as sets of relations. This study has reviewed the relations between frontiers and homelands. Depending on the nature of these relations, frontier and homeland trajectories can lead to the development of clonal and clinal supraregional landscapes. In the former, the frontier develops into a variation of the homeland culture. In the latter, either the homeland effectively underdevelops the frontier, or the frontier turns the tables on the homeland and becomes the cultural core. Techniques are certainly available to archaeologists to identify when an area stands in a frontier–homeland relationship to another area. The problem we face is primarily one of developing theory to account for these supraregional relations.

One framework for addressing why frontiers develop as they do is the model of frontier surplus flow. Taking into consideration ecological relations as well as the interests of the primary producers, regional elites, and homeland elites allows one to describe how surpluses flow in the area. Understanding surplus flow, by assessing the relative success of each level's strategies of domination and resistance, provides an important insight into why development follows a specific trajectory. The example of change in population size of the hill towns of western Massachusetts points out the utility of considering these various levels as well as noting the correlations between Deetz's stages and general patterns of European economic change. Not the least indication of the usefulness of this approach is the variety of different research problems and perspectives that it suggests.

Finally, archaeology should be concerned with understanding the social relations underlying the different development trajectories of frontier areas. We have a battery of techniques to pursue these issues. Furthermore, it is increasingly apparent that all forms of cultural systems are influenced by factors emanating from outside the regional system. Understanding frontier–homeland relations provides an understanding of one form of these large-scale interactions, and thus insight into one of the major factors conditioning cultural similarity and difference. Moreover, the variety of homeland–frontier relations is greatest in the archaeological record. Ethnographic and ethnohistoric records principally reveal the workings of capitalist core–periphery relations. Historical archaeology of European societies can contribute to an understanding of the variety of relations found within the capitalist world system. These will become even clearer when set in the comparative context generated by studies by prehistorians of long distance relations in noncapitalist societies. With this information, frontiers will be understood in a truly ethnological, broadly theoretical perspective.

REFERENCES

Adams, R. McC.
    1975 The emerging place of trade in civilizational studies. In *Ancient civilization and trade,* edited by J. A. Sabloff and C. C. Lamberg-Karlovsky, pp. 451–465. University of New Mexico Press, Albuquerque.
Amin, S.
    1980 *Class and nation, historically and in the current crisis.* Monthly Review, New York.
Bailyn, B.
    1955 *The New England merchants in the seventeenth century.* Harper & Row, New York.
Barth, F. (editor)
    1969 *Ethnic groups and boundaries.* Little-Brown, Boston.
Binford, L. R.
    1968 Post-pleistocene adaptations. In *New perspectives in archaeology,* edited by S. R. Binford and L. R. Binford, pp. 313–341. Aldine, Chicago.
Blanton, R. E.
    1976 The role of symbiosis in adaptation and sociocultural change in the Valley of Mexico. In *The valley of Mexico,* edited by E. Wolf, pp. 181–201. University of New Mexico Press, Albuquerque.
Blanton, R. E., S. A. Kowalewski, G. Feinman, and J. Appel
    1981 *Ancient Mesoamerica.* Cambridge, New York.
Boone, J. L. and C. L. Redman
    1980 *Alternate pathways for the growth of cities.* Paper presented in the symposium on the Evolution and Organization of Urban Systems at the 79th Annual Meeting of the American Anthropological Association, Washington, D.C.
Brenner, R.
    1977 The origin of capitalist development. *New Left Review* 104:25–92.
Carson, C. N., N. F. Barka, W. M. Kelso, G. W. Stone, and D. Upton
    1981 Impermanent architecture in the southern American colonies. *Winterthur Portfolio* 16:135–196.
Ceci, L.
    1977 *The effect of European contact and trade on the settlement pattern of Indians in Coastal New York, 1524–1665: The archaeological and documentary evidence.* Ph.D. dissertation, City University of New York. University Microfilms, Ann Arbor. Order No. 77–13,655.
    1980 Locational analysis of historic Algonquin sites in Coastal New York: a preliminary study. In Proceedings of the Conference on Northeastern Archaeology, edited by J. A. Moore. *Research Reports, Department of Anthropology, University of Massachusetts* No. 19:71–92. Amherst, Mass.
Chisholm, M.
    1962 *Rural settlement and landuse.* Aldine, Chicago.
Cipolla, C.
    1976 *Before the industrial revolution.* Norton, New York.
Cody, M. L., and J. Diamond (editors)
    1975 *Ecology and evolution of communities.* Harvard University Press, Cambridge, Mass.

Cole, J. W., and E. R. Wolf
   1974   *The hidden frontier.* Academic, New York.
Conkling, E. C., and M. Yeates
   1976   *Man's economic environment.* McGraw-Hill, New York.
Cooter, W. S.
   1977   Preindustrial frontiers and interaction spheres: prolegomenon to a study of Roman
          frontier regions. In *The frontier,* edited by D. H. Miller and J. O. Steffen, pp. 81–
          107. University of Oklahoma Press, Norman.
Davis, R.
   1973   *The rise of the Atlantic economies.* Cornell University, Ithaca, New York.
Deetz, J. F.
   1977   *In small things forgotten.* Anchor, New York.
de Vries, J.
   1976   *The economy of Europe in an age of crisis, 1600–1750.* Cambridge, New York.
Deyrup, F. J.
   1948   Arms makers in the Connecticut Valley: a regional study of the economic develop-
          ment of the small arms industry, 1798–1870. *Smith College Studies in History*
          (Vol. 33). Smith College, Northampton, Mass.
Earle, T. K. and J. E. Ericson
   1977   *Exchange systems in prehistory.* Academic, New York.
FAO/WHO
   1973   *Energy and protein requirements.* Food and Agriculture Organization/World
          Health Organization, United Nations, Rome.
Finley, M. I.
   1973   *The ancient economy.* University of California Press, Berkeley.
Frank, A. G.
   1978   *World accumulation, 1492–1789.* Monthly Review, New York.
Fried, M.
   1967   *The evolution of political society.* Random House, New York.
   1975   *The notion of tribe.* Cummings, Menlo Park, Calif.
Friedman, J., and M. J. Rowlands
   1978   Notes towards an epigenetic model of the evolution of "civilization." In *The*
          evolution of social systems, edited by J. Friedman and M. J. Rowlands, pp. 201–
          276. University of Pittsburgh Press, Pittsburgh.
Friedmann, K. J.
   1973   Victualing Boston. *Agricultural History* 47:189–205.
Friedrich, P.
   1977   *Agrarian revolt in a Mexican village.* University of Chicago, Chicago.
Giddens, A.
   1973   *The class structure of advanced societies.* Harper & Row, New York.
Green, S.
   1979   The agricultural colonization of temperate forest habitats. In *The frontier: com-*
          parative studies (Vol. II), pp. 69–103. University of Oklahoma Press, Norman.
   1980   Toward a general model of agricultural systems. *Advances in Archaeological Meth-*
          od and Theory 3:311–355.
Harris, D.
   1972   The origins of agriculture in the tropics. *American Scientist* 60:180–193.
Harris, M.
   1959   The economy has no surplus? *American Anthropologist* 61:189–199.

1968 *The rise of anthropological theory.* Crowell, New York.
1979 *Cultural materialism.* Random House, New York.
Hartz, L. (editor)
1964 *The founding of new societies.* Harcourt, Brace, New York.
Harvey, D.
1973 Revolutionary and counter-revolutionary theory in geography and the problem of ghetto formation. In *Social justice and the city,* edited by D. Harvey, pp. 120–152. Johns Hopkins University Press, Baltimore.
Henretta, J. A.
1978 Families and farms: mentalité in pre-industrial America. *William and Mary Quarterly* 35:3–32.
Hodder, I.
1979 Economic and social stress and material culture patterning. *American Antiquity* 44:446–454.
Hodder, I., and C. Orton
1976 *Spatial analysis in archaeology.* Cambridge, New York.
Hopkins, J., and I. Wallerstein
1977 Patterns of development of the modern world-system. *Review* 1:111–145.
Horn, H.
1974 The ecology of secondary succession. *Annual Review of Ecology and Systematics* 5:25–37.
Hudson, J. C.
1969 A location theory for rural settlement. *Annals of the American Association of Geographers* 59:365–381.
1977 Theory and methodology in comparative frontier studies. In *The frontier,* edited by D. H. Miller and J. O. Steffen, pp. 11–31. University of Oklahoma Press, Norman.
Innes, S.
1978 Land tenancy and social order in Springfield, Massachusetts, 1652–1702. *William and Mary Quarterly* 35:33–66.
Jennings, F.
1975 *The invasion of America.* Norton, New York.
Johnson, G.
1977 Aspects of regional analysis in archaeology. *Annual Review of Anthropology* 6:479–508.
1980 Spatial organization of Early Uruk settlement systems. In *L'archéologie de l'Iran du début de l'epogue Néolithique à 333 avant notre ère—perspectives et limites de l'interpretation anthropologique des documents,* edited by M. T. Barrelet. *Centre Nationale Researche Scientifique Collogue International* No. 580:223–263.
Keene, A.
1982 *Prehistoric foraging in a temperate forest.* Academic, New York.
Klimm, L. E.
1933 *The relation between certain population changes and the physical environment in Hampden, Hampshire, and Franklin Counties, Massachusetts, 1790–1925.* Unpublished Ph.D. dissertation, University of Pennsylvania. Philadelphia.
Knights, P.
1971 *Plain people of Boston.* Oxford University Press, New York.
Kohl, P. L.
1978 The balance of trade in southwestern Asia in the mid-third millennium B.C. *Current Anthropology* 19:463–492.

1981   Materialist approaches in prehistory. *Annual Review of Anthropology* 10:89–118.
Kuhn, T.
1972   *The structure of scientific revolutions* (second ed.). University of Chicago Press, Chicago.
Lamberg-Karlovsky, C. C.
1975   Third millennium modes of exchange and modes of production. In *Ancient civilization and trade,* edited by J. A. Sabloff and C. C. Lamberg-Karlovsky, pp. 341–356. University of New Mexico Press, Albuquerque.
Leacock, E. (editor)
1981   *Myths of male dominance.* Monthly Review, New York.
LeBlanc, R. G.
1969   Location of manufacturing in New England in the nineteenth century. *Geographic Publications at Dartmouth* (No. 7). Dartmouth College Press, Hanover, New Hampshire.
Lemon, J. T.
1980   Early Americans and their social environment. *Journal of Historical Geography* 6:115–131.
Lewis, K.
1976   Camden: frontier town. *Occasional Papers of the Institute of Archaeology and Anthropology, University of South Carolina, Anthropological Studies* (No. 2). University of South Carolina, Columbia.
1977   Sampling the archaeological frontier. In *Research strategies in historical archaeology,* edited by S. South, pp. 151–201. Academic, New York.
McGuire, R. H.
1980   The Mesoamerican connection in the Southwest. *The Kiva* 46:3–38.
Main, J. T.
1965   *The social structure of revolutionary America.* Princeton University Press, Princeton, N.J.
Martin, C.
1973   The European impact on the culture of a northeastern Algonquin tribe. *William and Mary Quarterly* 31:3–26.
Martin, M. E.
1939   Merchants and trade of the Connecticut River Valley, 1750–1820. *Smith College Studies in History* (Vol. 24). Smith College, Northampton, Mass.
Matthews, L. K.
1962   *The expansion of New England.* Russell and Russell, New York.
May, R. M.
1973   *Stability and complexity in model ecosystems.* Princeton University Press, Princeton, N.J.
May, R. M. (editor)
1976   *Theoretical ecology.* Saunders, Philadelphia.
Maynard Smith, J.
1974   *Models in ecology.* Cambridge University, New York.
Miller, D. H., and W. W. Savage, Jr.
1977   Ethnic stereotypes and the frontier. In *The frontier,* edited by D. H. Miller and J. O. Steffen, pp. 109–137. University of Oklahoma Press, Norman.
Moore, Barrington
1966   *Social origins of dictatorship and democracy.* Beacon, Boston.
Moore, J. A.
1981   The effects of information networks in hunter-gatherer societies. In *Hunter–*

gatherer foraging strategies, edited by B. Winterhalder and E. A. Smith, pp. 194–217. University of Chicago Press, Chicago.

Muller, P. O.
  1973   Trend surfaces of American agricultural patterns: a macro-Thünen analysis. *Economic Geography* 49:228–242.

Pabst, M. R.
  1941   Agricultural trends in the Connecticut Valley region of Massachusetts, 1800–1900. *Smith College Studies in History* (Vol. 26). Smith College, Northampton, Mass.

Paynter, R.
  1981   Social complexity in peripheries. In *Archaeological approaches to complexity,* edited by S. E. van der Leeuw, pp. 118–141. Universiteit van Amsterdam, Amsterdam, The Netherlands.
  1982   *Models of spatial inequality.* Academic, New York.

Paynter, R., and J. W. Cole
  1980   Ethnographic overproduction, tribal political economy and the Kapauku of Irian Jaya. In *Beyond the myths of culture,* edited by E. Ross, pp. 61–99. Academic, New York.

Peet, R.
  1969   The spatial expansion of commercial agriculture in the nineteenth century. *Economic Geography* 45:203–301.
  1972   Influences of the British market on agriculture and related economic development in Europe before 1860. *Institute of British Geographers, Transactions* 56:1–20.

Perlman, S. M.
  1976   *Optimal diet models and hunter–gatherers: a test on Martha's Vineyard.* Ph.D. dissertation, Department of Anthropology, University of Massachusetts. University Microfilms, Ann Arbor. Order No. 77–15, 110.

Pires-Ferreira, J. W.
  1975   Formative Mesoamerican exchange networks with special reference to the Valley Of Oaxaca. *Memoirs of the Museum of Anthropology 7.* Ann Arbor, Michigan.

Pires-Ferreira, J. W., and K. V. Flannery
  1976   Ethnographic models for formative exchange. In *The early Mesoamerican village,* edited by K. V. Flannery, pp. 286–291. Academic Press, New York.

Plog, S.
  1980   *Stylistic variation in prehistoric ceramics.* Cambridge University Press, New York.

Pressat, R.
  1972   *Demographic analysis.* Aldine, Chicago.

Price, B.
  1982   Cultural materialism: a theoretical review. *American Antiquity* 47:709–741.

Ramsey, E.
  1930   The history of tobacco production in the Connecticut Valley. *Smith College Studies in History* (Vol. 15, nos. 3–4). Smith College, Northampton, Mass.

Rappaport, R. A.
  1968   *Pigs for the ancestors.* Yale University Press, New Haven.

Renfrew, C.
  1969   Trade and culture process in European prehistory. *Current Anthropology* 10:151–169.
  1975   Trade as action at a distance: questions of integration and communication. In *Ancient civilization and trade,* edited by J. A. Sabloff and C. C. Lamberg-Karlovsky, pp. 3–59. University of New Mexico Press, Albuquerque.

1977   Alternative models for exchange and spatial distribution. In *Exchange systems in prehistory*, edited by T. K. Earle and J. Ericson, pp. 71–90. Academic, New York.

Sabloff, J. A. and W. L. Rathje
1975   A study of changing pre-Columbian commercial systems. *Monographs of the Peabody Museum, Harvard University* No. 3. Cambridge, Mass.

Sahlins, M.
1976   *Culture and practical reason.* University of Chicago Press, Chicago.

Saitta, D.
1982   The archaeology of households. *Conference on New England Archaeology Newsletter* 2:1–12.

Salisbury, N.
1982   *Manitou and Providence.* Oxford University Press, New York.

Schneider, J.
1977   Was there a pre-capitalist world-system? *Peasant Studies* 6:20–29.
1979   Peacocks and penguins: the political economy of European cloth and colors. *American Ethnologist* 5:413–447.

Schneider, P., J. Schneider, and E. Hansen
1972   Modernization and development: the role of regional elites and noncorporate groups in the European Mediterranean. *Comparative Studies in Society and History* 14:328–350.

Service, E.
1960   The law of evolutionary potential. In *Evolution and culture*, edited by M. Sahlins and E. Service, pp. 93–127. University of Michigan Press, Ann Arbor.

Shlakman, V.
1935   Economic history of a factory town: a study of Chicopee, Massachusetts. *Smith College Studies in History* (Vol. 20). Smith College, Northampton, Mass.

South, S.
1977   *Method and theory in historical archaeology.* Academic, New York.
1978   Historic site content, structure, and function. *American Antiquity* 44:213–237.

Swedlund, A., H. Temkin-Greener, and R. Meindl
1976   Population studies in the Connecticut Valley. *Journal of Human Evolution* 5:75–93.

Sweezy, P.
1942   *The theory of capitalist development.* Monthly Review, New York.

Szatmary, D. P.
1980   *Shays' Rebellion.* University of Massachusetts Press, Amherst.

Temkin-Greener, H., and A. Swedlund
1977   Secular trends in mortality in the Connecticut Valley: 1750–1850. *Population Studies* 32:27–41.

Thomas, P.
1979   *In the malestrom of change.* Ph.D. dissertation, Department of Anthropology, University of Massachusetts.

Thorbahn, P.
1979   *The precolonial ivory trade of East Africa.* Unpublished Ph.D. dissertation, Department of Anthropology, University of Massachusetts.

Thorbahn, P., and S. Mrozowski
1979   Ecological dynamics and rural New England historical sites. In Ecological anthropology of the Middle Connecticut River Valley, edited by R. Paynter. *Department of Anthropology, University of Massachusetts, Amherst. Research Reports* 18:129–140. Amherst, Mass.

Tryon, R. M.
    1917   *Household manufactures in the United States.* Johnson Reprint, New York.
Tosi, M.
    1977   The proto-urban cultures of Eastern Iran and the Indus civilization. In South Asian
            Archaeology, edited by M. Tosi. *Instituto Universitario Orientale Seminario D.
            Studi Asiatici, Series Minor* 7:149–171. Naples, Italy.
Wallerstein, I.
    1974   *The modern world-system* (Vol. 1). Academic, New York.
    1980   *The modern world-system* (Vol. II). Academic, New York.
Williams, E.
    1944   *Capitalism and slavery.* Putnam's, New York.
Wilson, E. O., and W. H. Bossert
    1971   *A primer of population biology.* Sinauer Associates, Stamford, Conn.
Wobst, H. M.
    1974   Boundary conditions for paleolithic social systems. *American Antiquity* 39:147–
            178.
    1977   Stylistic behavior and information exchange. In For the director, edited by C.
            Cleland. *Anthropological Papers, Museum of Anthropology, University of Michi-
            gan, No. 61:317–342.*
Wolf, E.
    1966   *Peasants.* Prentice-Hall, Englewood Cliffs, N.J.
    1969   *Peasant revolutions of the twentieth century.* Harper & Row, New York.
    1982   *Europe and the people without history.* University of California Press, Berkeley,
            Calif.

CHAPTER 9

Evolution on the Industrial Frontier

DONALD L. HARDESTY

Department of Anthropology
University of Nevada
Reno, Nevada

INTRODUCTION

The study of cultural change on the frontier demands some kind of general theory from which a set of explanatory principles can be derived. Elsewhere, I have argued that the synthetic theory of biological evolution is appropriate for this purpose (Hardesty 1980–1981), a position that others have taken for the general study of cultural change (Dunnell 1980; Kirch 1980). In this essay the frontiers of complex industrial societies are examined within such an evolutionary framework. Industrial frontiers are similar to other kinds of frontiers in being "high-risk" boundaries, but have effective environments and ecological relationships that are quite distinctive. Thus, the historian Jerome Steffen makes a typological distinction between insular and cosmopolitan frontiers of American civilization, the latter including the industrial frontier (Steffen 1979, 1980). *Insular,* or *isolated, frontiers,* to Steffen, were what Frederick Jackson Turner had in mind when he proposed the now-famous frontier thesis of the development of American civilization. Insular frontiers were diverse, often economically self-sufficient, and, above all, isolated (Steffen 1980:xii–xiii). The *cosmopolitan frontier,* in contrast, was ignored by Turner's thesis but was much more widespread geographically, including fur trading, ranching, and industrial frontiers such as mining throughout the Americas. Unlike agrarian or insular frontiers, the cosmopolitan frontier was

> short term and economically specialized. National and international affairs determined success there. As a result there was a lack of insulation from national developments and no commitment to indigenous development. Thus no fundamental alteration in economic, political, and social institutions and behavior patterns followed. When change did occur on these frontiers, factors extrinsic to their environments were the cause. (Steffen 1980:xvii)

When interpreted in the context of evolutionary theory, Steffen's typology of frontiers may provide significant insight into the dynamics of human behavior in boundary regions. The key difference between agrarian and industrial frontiers is the extent to which local groups or settlements are isolated. Isolation in evolutionary theory is an important ingredient in the processes of *differentiation*—whether involving the formation of new species or new ethnic groups (see Abruzzi 1982). With increasing isolation comes more group differences from historically unique events. And with increasing isolation there is less likelihood that the differences among groups will be "swamped" by the same process or historical event. Agrarian frontiers are made up of groups that are more isolated and participate less at national and regional levels of sociocultural integration than are groups on industrial frontiers. Accordingly, agrarian frontiers are expected to be, culturally, the most diversified. Furthermore, patterns of cultural change on agrarian frontiers are expected to be *mosaiclike,* most similar to the kind of change taking place in networks of islands (see, for example, MacArthur and Wilson 1967). Industrial frontiers, however, have quite different patterns of cultural change and diversity. The differences among groups are expected to be less than on agrarian frontiers because of greater integration into a common national system. Perhaps the greatest impact of that integration upon the frontier is the reduction of differences among groups through the *standardization* of environments and cultures. In effect every effort was made to *create* an urban industrial culture and environment for each frontier settlement. The construction of railroads and telegraph lines made possible not only a continuous flow of materials (such as canned foods, clothing, and kerosene lamps) from the industrial heartland to the frontier but also a continuous exchange of information, which made possible the importation of the same attitudinal and value environments (see Hardesty 1980a, 1981; Ostrogorsky 1980; Teague 1980; Teague and Shenk 1977). Of particular importance in this regard is the establishment of an urban middle class Victorian culture throughout the nineteenth-century industrial frontier (see, for example, Baker 1978). Standardization of frontier environments was an underlying current.

Even when the natural environments of the industrial frontier were quite variable, every attempt was made to use the same adaptive solutions. The mining industry is a good example. Ore bodies differ from place to place in geological and mineralogical characteristics, yet a standardized industrial technology was used by mining and milling operations. Mining and milling equipment was manufactured by a relatively few companies in a few large industrial centers in America or Europe and shipped to all frontier industrial colonies. Thus Robert Randall (1972:153–154) describes the silver mining venture of the Real del Monte Company, a British corporation, in Hidalgo, Mexico, as follows:

> The concern in Mexico depended on the home country for much of its equipment and for nearly all of its vital machinery. Indeed, the invoices and other records of stores shipments found among company papers list almost everything imaginable, from the gigantic boiler for a seventy-five-inch steam engine to pen holders, quills, and ink powders used in writing.

Cultural change on the industrial frontier is marked by *correlated episodes* rather than by mosaics. The integration of frontier settlements into a common national/regional system creates a context within which environmental fluctuations and local sequences of change are autocorrelated. Innovations spread rapidly throughout the frontier and replace older forms. Industrial technologies are particularly good examples. Thus, the cyanide leaching process of milling silver ores completely replaced pan amalgamation and older leaching technologies on the mining frontiers of the American West during the first decade of the twentieth century (Dorr 1936:4). And pan amalgamation milling had spread in much the same way during the 1860s. The pattern of change over time is steplike or discontinuous but more or less simultaneous throughout the frontier. How to best explain such a pattern is at this point questionable. One possibility is the "punctuated equilibrium" model presently being developed in paleobiology (Gould and Eldredge 1977; Stanley 1979), which already has been suggested as an appropriate model for the prehistory of the southwestern United States (Berry 1982). Here, change is portrayed as a series of random jumps in an otherwise stable, unchanging world. Such "punctuations" are the result of rare innovations that are exceptionally successful and that rapidly expand, replacing older forms. Although the model is intended to explain long-term patterns of biological evolution, the possibility that behavioral change on the industrial frontier can be explained in a similar way should be investigated. To do so, however, requires that competing explanations of abrupt change such as "catastrophe theory" (Renfrew 1978) also be evaluated and rejected.

THE DEVELOPMENT OF ECOSYSTEMS ON THE
INDUSTRIAL FRONTIER

In another study I argued that the frontier can be usefully treated as an *ecosystem* (Hardesty 1980–1981). Determining how ecosystems develop on the frontier is a critical part of such a research strategy. What is presently known about the development of frontier ecosystems suggests that it is less controlled by equilibrium-maintaining mechanisms operating at the level of the ecosystem than it is by the "evolutionary ecology" of the constituent individuals and populations (see Smith and Winterhalder 1981). Here, the evolutionary ecology approach to ecosystem development is used to model spatial patterns of industrial frontier ecosystems. Charnov's marginal value theorem (1976) from optimal foraging theory is used (Krebs and Davies 1978; Pulliam 1976). The theorem stipulates that "the optimal predator should stay in each patch until its rate of intake (the marginal value) drops to a level equal to the average of intake for the habitat" (Krebs and Davies 1978:43). And "average" intake is net, which implies that the cost of moving among patches and of acquiring resources in the patch must be subtracted from whatever is taken. The industrial frontier is a web or archipelago of patches (R. M. Morse, *The Bandeirantes*, p. 30, as cited in Hennessy 1978:17) in the form of ore bodies, tree tracts, salt deposits, and the like. Some, such as tree tracts, are renewable; others are nonrenewable. Miners, loggers, and other industrial colonists move into each patch and, according to the marginal value theorem, are expected to stay there until its net yield drops below that likely to be obtained from an "average" patch elsewhere on the frontier. How long they stay, and therefore their rate of movement among patches, is dependent upon the rate of patch renewal, variability of patch, size of the patch, technological efficiency of exploitation ("capture" cost), transportation cost, and market price. Minimizing transportation cost and maximizing each of the other variables for each patch type maximizes the amount of time expected to be spent in the patch and, therefore, minimizes the rate of movement among patches. All but size and variability of the patch are environmental variables that change stochastically. Changes in technological efficiency, for example, may follow the sudden invention of a new milling procedure (such as cyanide leaching) and make patches that had fallen below the average once again profitable to colonize. The prediction of the innovation itself is impossible, as is the prediction of a sudden jump in market prices that would also send the profitability of the patch to above the average. On the other hand, it is important to note that since market prices and technological innovations are rapidly disseminated throughout the frontier, the profitability relationship among the patches may remain the same even though the average-intake line has been raised. In this case, one would expect the patches to be "recolonized" in *the same order* as the pioneering colonization.

This model suggests ways of predicting rates of patch abandonment and recolonization. High patch-renewal rates, such as with many species of trees, bring relatively rapid rates of recolonization. Thus, although the Carson Range of the Sierra Nevada was quickly logged over in the 1860s and 1870s to provide the Comstock Lode mines with timber for underground workings and steam boilers, it was reoccupied by the lumber industry in the 1920s and is again today (Hardesty 1974). The archaeological record of these patches is thus expected to show regularly spaced recolonizations over time. Temporal spacing is entirely dependent upon the rate of renewal. In dramatic contrast are nonrenewable resources such as ore bodies and salt deposits. For these there are two patterns of abandonment and recolonization. If the patch is relatively small and resources easily accessible (such as marsh salt deposits), it is occupied only once and abandoned permanently when the resource is exhausted. The salt industry in the Great Basin, for example, is expected to follow this kind of frontier colonization pattern. Such settlements have a relatively short life-span, and contemporaneous settlements are expected to have few differences in behavior. The reason is that most colonies carry a relatively short "time slice" of a standardized technology and a common imported environment.

In contrast is the abandonment and recolonization pattern expected for frontier patches with nonrenewable resources that vary randomly, are not easily "captured" with available technology, are of a large size, or all three. The best example is the ore bodies of some precious metals, such as silver. Silver ore is difficult to mine because the ore body cannot be easily located underground, and it is difficult to recover silver from the ore because it is chemically bound into a variety of complex compounds. In such cases, the cycles of abandonment and recolonization of the patch are more likely to be irregularly spaced in time and to reflect fluctuations in market prices, the rate of technological innovation, and other variables of the national/international environment from which the colonies originate. The Bullfrog claim in Death Valley National Monument is a good example of such a patch (Greene and Latschar 1980:897ff.; Hardesty 1980a, 1981). In August of 1904 a mining claim was filed for a quartz outcrop on Bullfrog Mountain, not far from Rhyolite, Nevada. The original Bullfrog Mine was developed at the site over the next 3 years, and the Bullfrog West Extension Mine was started in 1906 on the same outcrop but just west of the original mine. Neither mine was very productive. The original Bullfrog, for example, yielded about $10,000 in gold bullion before it was closed in 1907. Closely following suit was the West Extension Mine which closed in 1913. After abandonment the claim lay dormant until 1929, after which time the mines

were reopened and worked off and on until the late 1950s. Then the claim
was again abandoned. In 1981, and continuing to the present, new work on
the claim was begun, initially to rework the waste rock dumps of the original Bullfrog and West Extension mines with new, more efficient milling
technology but ultimately likely to once again mine the claim, this time with
an open pit. How long this latest effort continues depends upon the market
price of gold, which can fluctuate sharply during the course of a few
months. The pattern of abandonment and reworking of the Bullfrog claim is
best explained by a combination of specific characteristics related to the ore
body (the ore environment), the rise and fall in the market price of gold, and
technological innovations. Initially, the industrial colony worked the claim
continuously until the limits of the ore body were better known and until
new, more profitable patches were discovered at nearby Rhyolite. The claim
was then recolonized repeatedly from the 1930s through the 1950s and
again in the 1980s as rising market prices increased gold values and as
enhanced gold milling technology allowed more gold to be recovered from
low-grade ores that previously had been tossed aside and from old mill
tailings.

What about the expected behavior of industrial settlements in such
patches with nonrenewable, randomly encountered resources? Differences
in behavior should be relatively great among these patches in comparison to
the "salt" pattern. Patches are being occupied repeatedly at different times
according to the sequence predicted by the Charnov (1976) model. Sudden
fluctuations in market prices can truncate the sequence at any time, somewhat later starting again either at the beginning or close to the beginning of
the sequence if the price rises again. Since each recolonization at a new time
period is likely to bring with it a new imported environment—or a new
"time slice" of behavior from rapidly changing industrial centers—the environments in each patch are, in effect, constantly undergoing random
fluctuations.

PROCESSES OF ECOSYSTEM DIFFERENTIATION
ON THE INDUSTRIAL FRONTIER

In addition to colonization processes, ecosystems on the industrial frontier also develop or evolve a niche structure through the operation of several
processes that differentiate group behaviors. Two are especially effective
and both originate in historically unique events: the development of "appropriate" technology and the coping behavior of immigrants carrying an
exotic culture into the frontier.

Appropriate Technology and Group Differentiation

The idiosyncracies of local environments sometimes make *unique* technologies more cost effective than a standardized industrial technology. Such "appropriate technology" introduces a considerable amount of variability among the groups occupying industrial frontiers. An example is the technological difference between the Cortez and Reese river mining districts in central Nevada (Hardesty and Edaburn 1982). The two districts are only about 60 miles apart, have quite similar ore bodies, and both were formed in the early 1860s. Miners colonizing both districts carried with them the same general knowledge of mining and milling processes—knowledge mostly acquired on the Comstock Lode in western Nevada and in California. Initial attempts to mine and extract silver from the ore bodies were more or less identical. The *Washoe process* of milling the ore was used, in which the ore is crushed and then finely ground in pans to which mercury, salt, water, and copper sulfate have been added to form an amalgam of mercury and silver; the heavier amalgam is settled out in large tubs, and the mercury is driven off in retort furnaces to form the bullion (Egleston 1887; Eissler 1898; Oberbillig 1967). That process had been developed for the predominantly silver chloride ores of the Comstock Lode and worked well for the oxidized surface ores of the Reese River district. Washoe pan amalgamation, however, simply did not work for the Cortez district ores, which were mostly made up of the sulfides of antimony and arsenic. Nor did the process work for the deeper ores (those deeper than 60 feet below the surface) of the Reese River district. The problem was solved by development of the *Reese River process* of milling. Here the ores were roasted in a furnace in the presence of salt prior to pan amalgamation. The chloride in the salt replaced the sulfide in the ore, creating silver chloride, which could be milled using the traditional Washoe process. Throughout the 1860s and 1870s both the Cortez and Reese river districts used the Reese River process of milling. At this point, the two districts had diverged technologically from the Comstock and other mining districts but were not significantly different from each other.

Divergence between the two districts, however, started in the 1870s. Differences in mining methods are especially obvious. In the Reese River district, the ore body is widely dispersed, nearly invisible on the surface, and almost randomly encountered. Accordingly, the risk of mining ventures was high. The Manhattan Company, which did most of the mining and milling in the district, responded to this problem by instigating the "contract and tribute" system (Vanderburg 1938:77). Rather than doing its own underground work, the company leased all of its claims. In return the lessee paid the company as little as 7% of the value of the ore recovered or a set price for each foot of underground workings if no ore was found. The lessee was also obligated to have the ore custom milled at the company-owned Manhattan Mill in Austin, Nevada. An entirely different mining system was used in the Cortez district. Here, the ore body was much more concentrated, more visible, and larger than the Reese River district. The "Nevada Giant," as the lode was called, was most effectively mined with large groups controlled by a single company. Toward this end, and to save labor costs, the Tenabo Mill and Mines Company employed immigrant Chinese miners. The company maintained a close relationship with the Chinese community, drawing upon a pool of paternalistic "goodwill" when the mines were not producing to keep the miners working for no more than subsistence wages (Bancroft 1889).

By the 1880s technological divergence between the two districts was also apparent in the milling process. The mills in the Reese River district continued to use the Reese River variant of pan amalgamation throughout the nineteenth and into the first decade of the twentieth century. But in 1886 the Tenabo Company in the Cortez district built a new mill and installed *Russell leaching process* equipment (Bancroft 1889). In this process, the crushed ore was leached with sodium hyposulfite and cupreous hyposulfite to bring the silver into solution as sodium silver hyposulfite; sodium or calcium sulfide was then added to precipitate the silver as silver sulfide, after which the sulfur was driven off in retort furnaces to form silver bullion (Stetefeldt 1895). The new mill combined the roasting furnaces of the Reese River process with the Russell leaching process to create a silver milling technology with high efficiency for the Cortez ore body (Bancroft 1889). Cost reduction at the mill was achieved by taking advantage of specific environmental features of the district. For example, calcium sulfide was used in the leaching process instead of the more common sodium sulfide. Egleston (1887:531) observed that sodium sulfide is a more effective precipitator of silver but that calcium sulfide is cheaper if "lime is counted as next to nothing." The Tenabo Company quarried the abundant limestone next to the mill and built a kiln to make the large quantities of lime needed.

The use of appropriate technology introduced several differences between the two districts that can be explained as adaptive solutions to unique local environments. But the processes of *episodic evolution* acting at the national/regional level swamped the differences in the first decade of the twentieth century. *Cyanide leaching* technology was developed and applied to silver milling. In this process first potassium cyanide and later sodium cyanide are used to bring silver into solution, after which zinc dust or shavings and lead acetate are added to precipitate the silver compound (Dorr 1936). In 1908 the mill in the Cortez district was converted to cyanide leaching technology; in 1911 the first cyanide mill in the Reese River district was constructed. Henceforth, both districts have used only cyanide processing with very similar technology. The technological differences between these two industrial frontier settlements was greatly reduced by the introduction of a new highly standardized and efficient industrial technology.

Ethnicity and Group Differentiation

Behavioral differentiation on the industrial frontier also originated in immigrants carrying non-Western cultures. For them, the industrial frontier was anything but a standardized, imported environment requiring little adaptive change. Both social and physical environments posed a complex set of new problems with which the immigrants had to cope. For the most part, industrial environments in the nineteenth century were created by people carrying a Victorian cultural tradition, in which social relations, work patterns, cosmology, and consumption habits were defined by an urban middle class society in Europe and America (Howe 1975). Ethnic groups from any other than a Victorian cultural tradition entered an historically unique social setting. New roles had to be established within the social fabric of the industrial colony—a fabric that was woven by Victorianism; consequently the roles emerged out of a complex pattern of racial prejudice, ethnocentrism, ethnicity, and acculturation (see, for example, Despres 1975; Forbes 1968; Lyman 1970; Weiss 1974). Both economic and technological behavior had to be modified to cope with the Victorian environment. Tools and work habits, for example, were often changed drastically among immigrant workers in such situations, both because of the cost of importing traditional tools and because of engagements in activities for which there were no traditional counterparts (Spier 1958). In contrast to such rapid and abrupt adaptations to the industrial frontier environment, however, are instances in which traditional foods were made available to the non-Victorian ethnic group so that little or no adaptive change took place. Immigrant Chinese laborers, for example, were usually provided with traditional Chinese food, either directly through a company store or indirectly through Chinese merchants living in the settlement who imported the necessary foods (Teague and Shenk 1977). In general, however, adaptive change is expected to be a much more significant source of variability among industrial settlements having large non-Victorian populations than it is among those having mostly Victorian populations.

Recent historical and archaeological research on an immigrant Chinese community in the Truckee Basin of eastern California provides a good example (Elston *et al.* 1980, 1982). The Truckee Basin was an important laboring center on the western edge of the nineteenth-century American frontier. Growth of the lumbering industry in the basin can be traced to the demand for wood products created by the beginning of work on the Central Pacific Railroad in 1863 (Angel 1880:73; Knowles 1942; Meschery 1978). The Central Pacific imported Chinese laborers to work on the railroad, making up a relatively large percentage of the Truckee Basin population until the completion of the railroad through the area. After completion of the railroad, the Truckee lumber industry found a market in the mines and mills of Nevada and Utah where support timbers and charcoal were shipped, and in the California population centers where boxes, shingles, door and window frames, and the like were shipped. Part of the industry, such as Sisson, Wallace, and Company, employed the immigrant Chinese originally working in railroad construction as woodcutters and charcoal makers (Angel 1880). The Truckee Basin was a classic industrial frontier settlement, geographically isolated from the major western centers of American civilization in San Francisco and on the edge of the eastward expanding frontier but closely linked to national and international markets and patterns of behavior through the railroad.

Some of the adaptive changes expected in the immigrant Chinese settlement in the Truckee Basin emerge from the concept of "sojourner" (Sui 1952). Most of the immigrants had no plans to make their new home permanent; rather, they expected to stay only long enough to make a fortune and then return to China. For that reason, traditional values and lifestyles were retained as much as possible; no attempt was made to learn the foreign language; "chinatowns" and other geographically localized racial/cultural settlements were formed to duplicate traditional ways and to minimize social interaction with Westerners as much as possible; and strong ethnocentric sentiments about the superiority of the homeland were expressed (Lee 1960; Sui 1952:35–37; Sung 1967). The concept of sojourner, therefore, suggests that any change in functional behavior within the immigrant community arose absolutely out of necessity and in areas that were relatively unimportant to the maintenance of traditional Chinese culture. Two aspects of behavior appear to have undergone the greatest amount of change: the organization of the household and technology. Because the sojourner viewed immigration as a temporary employment opportunity, no effort was made to bring families. This, in combination with restrictive immigration legislation that greatly restricted the flow of women into the United States, created the "separated family" (Lee 1960:203) or the "mutilated family" (Sung 1967:155) in which wives and children remained in China. For that reason, the immigrant household was made up almost exclusively of adult males in various numbers. Spier (1958) has studied the conditions under which the sojourners adopted Western tools in nineteenth-century California and concludes that traditional tools were used whenever possible but that Western tools were readily adopted under two sets of circumstances: (1) "the work of the Chinese was closely controlled by American employers, who often furnished the tools"; and (2) "the occupation of the Chinese was one for which there probably was no precedent in their experience" (Spier 1958:111). Such activities as logging, railroad construction, and mining fit into the latter category. Thus, LaLande (1981) finds that the immigrant Chinese placer mining technology in the Applegate Valley of southwestern Oregon was almost exclusively Western in origin. Store records show that shovels, picks, galvanized steel buckets, axes and hatchets, quicksilver, lumber, nails, and blasting powder were purchased by the Chinese miners in the Applegate. In addition one miner, Gin Lin, installed a hydraulic giant (a high-pressure water nozzle) and diversion ditches, using professional surveyors.

Both the household and technological expectations of the sojourner model are met by the Truckee Basin data. The 1870 federal population census of Truckee, for example, lists only a single household in the Chinese community that may be a nuclear family. By far the largest number were single male (15) or multimale households (77). The latter ranged from 2 to 21 in size, with the greatest number (58) in the 2 to 5 category. In addition, the community included a few single female (7) and multifemale (3) households, nearly all of which, according to the census taker, were composed of "prostitutes." That same pattern of household composition is reported for the Chinese settlement at Lovelock, Nevada, which, in 1870, consisted of a single household of 19 adult male railroad laborers and one cook (Rusco 1981). What is presently unknown are the organizational rules controlling variability in the size of the sojourner households.

Archaeological research on a group of ruined log cabins occupied by Chinese woodcutters and charcoal burners some time during the period from 1860 to the early 1880s provides information about technological change (Elston *et al.* 1980, 1982). Most domestic and logging activities used Western technology and commodities. Thus, the cabins were heated with cast iron stoves and lighted by kerosene lamps with glass chimneys and fueled by kerosene originating in Boston. In addition, *canned* vegetables, fruits, fish, beef, and lard originating in a variety of American cities were used for food, along with pepper sauce, pickles, and a wide variety of wine, liquors, and patent medicines. Mill files, cut nails, and shovels of Western origin were also used. The greatest retention of traditional Chinese behavior is found in tableware, some aspects of subsistence, and in the use of opium and its associated paraphernalia. Imported *swatow* and celadon bowls dominate the tableware assemblage, and the absence of Western utensils suggests the continued use of chopsticks. *Jian you* earthenware food jars and soy sauce pots made up a large proportion of the food containers recovered from the sites (Langenwalter 1980). And, finally, opium pipe-bowl and opium tin fragments in the assemblages suggest retention of opium use.

Charcoal-making technology is another specific area where adaptive change in sojourner behavior can be observed. If Spier's model is correct, the technology was adopted totally from the Western repertoire because it was unlikely that rural farmers in Kwangtung Province, Manchuria, where most of the immigrants originated, were familiar with the activity. Charcoal ovens in the western United States occurred in two forms: earthen pit ovens and the stone or brick oven (Murbarger 1965; Young and Budy 1979:116–119). The latter were mostly restricted to juniper and mountain mahogany habitats because of the higher burning temperatures required (Young and Budy 1979:117). Throughout the western United States the simple and cheap earthen pit oven was most common. Documentary and archaeological evidence suggest that this technology was almost certainly used in the nineteenth-century charcoal industry in the Truckee Basin; furthermore, the basin was dominated by pine, which does not demand high-burning temperatures to make charcoal. Archaeological expectations for earthen pit ovens are derived from documentary and oral descriptions of their construction (U.S. Forest Service 1943; Wigginton 1979). According to these descriptions, cordwood was stacked upon a level or leveled ground surface and then covered with earth. An oven "chimney" was left inside. The chimney was then filled and the stack covered with combustible material such as grass and dry twigs. Finally, a layer of clay was placed over the stack and holes punched in this outer "skin" for draft. The stack was then lit through one of the holes, and the wood allowed to burn for several days up to a month to make charcoal. Someone was required to watch the burning constantly, so the stack was almost always located near a residential structure. From this description several material correlates for the archaeological record can be identified including a leveled ground surface, circular to oval-shaped charcoal/ash concentrations, clay deposits, nearby house ruins, and the like. Excavation of several charcoal/ash scatters in the vicinity of the log cabin sites yielded the archaeological data expected of an earthen pit oven (Elston et al. 1982) and thus supports the hypothesis that immigrant Chinese charcoal makers adopted prevailing Western technology.

SUMMARY AND CONCLUSIONS

Several issues about the process of social and technological change on the industrial frontier have been raised in this study. Perhaps the most important is that an explanatory framework grounded in the principles of evolution and ecology may provide insight into the border dynamics of even complex, industrial societies. If so, the opportunity is presented for developing a general theory of boundaries and frontiers out of the framework, which has applicability to both simple and complex societies and which can be derived from scientific evolutionary theory. To be sufficiently general, such a theory must be capable of comprehending both the relatively slow, gradual, and expansive change of agrarian frontiers, and the episodic change of industrial frontiers.

Another issue raised in this essay is the extent to which environment affects group differences on the frontier. The most common scenario of the frontier has colonists moving into a radically new environment for which their traditional behavior is poorly suited. Geographical differences in local frontier environments suggest that the adaptive behavior of colonists should vary greatly from place to place, but the industrial frontier environment is often quite different. Industrial centers sending out the colonists attempt to control frontier environments as much as possible by establishing transportation and communication ties to national and international networks. Such "imported" environments are expected to greatly reduce differences among industrial colonies. Not only are such things as food and other supplies imported to the settlements, but also many randomly changing dimensions of the environment, such as technological innovations, change *simultaneously* throughout the frontier. Environmental homogeneity and, therefore, few adaptive differences in behavior are expected.

Controlled environments and national/international integration on the industrial frontier are, however, incomplete. The more this is true, the more behavioral differences are expected among industrial settlements. Group differentiation occurs more frequently in technological behavior and in the behavior of ethnic groups carrying cultural traditions significantly different from the industrial society. Industrialized technology is standardized; however, differences in the resources being exploited by industrial settlements, such as ore bodies, often demand specific local adaptations. Such "appropriate technology" may introduce considerable variation among settlements within an otherwise standardized industrial frontier. Social environments are also standardized by the simultaneous introduction of the urban middle class behavior of Victorianism, but, as with technology, adaptive variability is sometimes introduced when non-Victorian ethnic groups are employed as workers in industrial settlements. For such groups the social environment on the frontier is quite different and demands locally specific adaptations in patterns of behavior. Exactly what social changes take place is probably best conceptualized as a random process within a general model—specific, complex, and historically unique causes are usually involved, such as ethnic relations, institutionalized racial prejudice, ethnocentrism, and the like, which can be identified in each case but which are not repeated. For example, the nineteenth-century immigrant Chinese working in such industrial occupations as mining and lumbering appear to have changed in quite similar ways on the western American industrial frontier. Household composition, technology, and other aspects of behavior changed as if adapting to a radically new environment. Food habits, ritual patterns, and some aspects of settlement and community patterns changed hardly at all, reflecting a perceived "sojourner" status.

There is one final conclusion: The process of change in human behavior on the frontiers of complex industrial societies can be understood within the arena of scientific evolutionary theory. At the same time, it is clear that we presently lack a set of explanatory principles capable of dealing with the *creative* behavior of organisms toward their environment, such as the "imported" environments of industrial societies (Hardesty 1980b).

ACKNOWLEDGMENTS

I thank Robert Dunnell, Kenneth Lewis, Gary Palmer, John Swetnam, and George Teague for comments on a draft of this chapter. None is, of course, responsible for the shortcomings of this version.

REFERENCES

Abruzzi, W.
  1982 Ecological theory and ethnic differentiation among human populations. *Current Anthropology* 23 (1):13–35.
Angel, M. (editor)
  1880 *A history of Nevada County, California.* Thompson and West, San Francisco.
Baker, S.
  1978 Historical archaeology for Colorado and the Victorian mining frontier: review, discussion, and suggestions. *Southwestern Lore* 44(4):11–31.
Bancroft, H. H.
  1889 *History of the life of Simeon Wenban* (from *Chronicles of the kings*). The History Company, San Francisco.
Berry, M.
  1982 *Time, space, and transition in Anasazi prehistory.* University of Utah Press, Salt Lake City.
Charnov, E. L.
  1976 Optimal foraging: the marginal value theorem. *Theoretical Population Biology* 9:129–136.
Despres, L.
  1975 Ethnicity and resource competition in Guyanese society. In *Ethnicity and resource competition in plural societies,* edited by Leo Despres, pp. 87–117. Mouton, The Hague.

Dorr, J. V. N.
   1936   *Cyanidation and concentration of gold and silver ores.* McGraw-Hill, New York.
Dunnell, R.
   1980   Archaeology and evolutionary theory. In *Advances in archaeological method and theory* (Vol. 3), edited by Michael Schiffer. Academic Press, New York.
Egleston, T.
   1887   *Metallurgy of silver, gold and mercury in the United States.* (Vol. 1). Wiley, New York.
Eissler, M.
   1898   *The metallurgy of silver* (fourth ed.). Crosby, Lockwood, London.
Elston, R., D. L. Hardesty, and S. Clerico
   1980   *Archaeological investigation on the Hopkins land exchange.* Intermountain Research, Silver City, Nevada.
Elston, R., D. L. Hardesty, and C. Zeier
   1982   *Archaeological investigations on the Hopkins land exchange* (Part II). Intermountain Research, Silver City, Nevada.
Forbes, J.
   1968   Frontiers in American history and the role of the frontier historian. *Ethnohistory* 15:203–235.
Gould, S., and N. Eldredge
   1977   Punctuated equilibria: the tempo and mode of evolution reconsidered. *Paleobiology* 3:115–151.
Greene, L. W., and J. A. Latschar
   1980   *Historic resource study, a history of mining in Death Valley National Monument.* Historic Preservation Branch, National Park Service, Denver.
Hardesty, D. L.
   1974   *The archaeology of logging in Little Valley, Nevada.* Paper presented at the 1974 Annual Meeting of the Society for Historical Archaeology, Oakland, Calif.
   1980a *Evaluation of historical archaeological resources in Bullfrog claim and mining sites: Nye County, Nevada, Death Valley National Monument.* University of Nevada, Reno.
   1980b The use of general ecological principles in archaeology. In *Advances in archaeological method and theory* (Vol. 3), edited by Michael Schiffer, pp. 157–187. Academic, New York.
   1980–1981 Historic sites archaeology on the western American frontier: theoretical perspectives and research problems. *North American Archaeologist* 2(1):67–82.
   1981   *Recovery of historical archaeological data in Bullfrog claim and mining sites: Nye County, Nevada, Death Valley National Monument.* University of Nevada, Reno.
Hardesty, D. L., and S. L. Edaburn
   1982   *Technological systems on the Nevada mining frontier.* Paper presented at the 1982 Annual Meeting of the Society for Historical Archaeology, Philadelphia.
Hennessy, A.
   1978   *The frontier in Latin American history.* University of New Mexico Press, Albuquerque.
Howe, D.
   1975   American Victorianism as a culture. *American Quarterly* 27:507–532.
Kirch, P.
   1980   The archaeological study of adaptation: theoretical and methodological issues. In *Advances in archaeological method and theory* (Vol. 3), edited by Michael Schiffer, pp. 101–156. Academic, New York.

Knowles, C.
  1942   *A history of lumbering in the Truckee Basin from 1856 to 1936*. Office Report
         from the bibliographical research conducted under WPA Official Project No.
         9512373 for the Forest Survey Division, California Forest and Range Experiment
         Station. Nevada Historical Society, Reno.
Krebs, J. R., and N. B. Davies
  1978   *Behavioral ecology*. Blackwell Scientific Publications, London.
LaLande, J.
  1981   *Sojourners in the Oregon Siskiyous: adaptation and acculturation of the Chinese
         miners in the Applegate Valley ca. 1855–1900*. Master's thesis, Oregon State
         University, Corvallis.
Langenwalter, P. E.
  1980   The archaeology of 19th century Chinese subsistence at the Lower China Store,
         Madera County, California. In *Archaeological perspectives on ethnicity in Amer-
         ica*, edited by Robert Schuyler, pp. 102–112. Baywood, Farmingdale, N.Y.
Lee, R. H.
  1960   *The Chinese in the United States of America*. Hong Kong University Press, Hong
         Kong.
Lyman, S.
  1970   *The Asian in the west*. Desert Research Institute Publications in the Social Sciences,
         Reno, Nevada.
Meschery, J.
  1978   *Truckee*. Rocking Stone Press, Truckee, Calif.
Murbarger, N.
  1965   Forgotten industry of the frontier. *Frontier Times* 39(3):26–27, 58–60.
Oberbillig, E.
  1967   Development of Washoe and Reese River silver processes. *Nevada Historical Soci-
         ety Quarterly* 10(2):20ff.
Ostrogorsky, M.
  1980   *Idaho model of frontier settlement*. Idaho State Historical Society, Boise.
Pulliam, H. R.
  1976   On the theory of optimal diets. *American Naturalist* 108:59–75.
Randall, R. W.
  1972   *Real del Monte*. University of Texas Press, Austin.
Renfrew, C.
  1978   Trajectory, discontinuity and morphogenesis: the implication of catastrophe theo-
         ry for archaeology. *American Antiquity* 43:203–244.
Rusco, M.
  1981   Counting the Lovelock Chinese. *Nevada Historical Society Quarterly* 24(4):319–
         328.
Spier, R.
  1958   Tool acculturation among 19th century California Chinese. *Ethnohistory* 5(2):97–
         117.
Stanley, S.
  1979   *Macroevolution: Pattern and Process*, W. H. Freeman, San Francisco.
Steffen, J.
  1979   Insular versus cosmopolitan frontiers: a proposal for comparative American fron-
         tier studies. In *American west, new perspectives, new dimensions*, edited by Jerome
         Steffen, pp. 94–123. University of Oklahoma Press, Norman.
  1980   *Comparative frontiers*. University of Oklahoma Press, Norman.

Stetefeldt, C. A.
  1895 *The lixiviation of silver-ores with hyposulphite solutions with special reference to the Russell process.* Privately printed by Tuttle Morehouse and Taylor Press, New Haven, Conn.
Sui, P. C.
  1952 The sojourner. *American Journal of Sociology* 58:34–44.
Sung, B. L.
  1967 *Mountain of gold.* Macmillan, New York.
Teague, G.
  1980 *The Reward mine and associated sites.* Western Archeological Center Publications in Anthropology, No. 11. National Park Service, Tucson.
Teague, G., and L. Shenk
  1977 *The Harmony borax works.* Western Archeological Center Publications in Anthropology, No. 6. National Park Service, Tucson.
U.S. Forest Service
  1943 *How to make charcoal on the farm.* U.S. Forest Service, Washington, D.C.
Vanderberg, W. O.
  1938 *Reconnaissance of mining districts in Eureka County, Nevada,* Information Circular No. 7022. U.S. Bureau of Mines, Department of Commerce, Washington, D.C.
Weiss, M. S.
  1974 *Valley City: a Chinese community in America.* Schenkman, Cambridge, Mass.
Wigginton, E. (editor)
  1979 *Foxfire 5.* Anchor/Doubleday Press, Garden City, N.Y.
Winterhalder B., and E. Smith (editors)
  1981 *Hunter–gatherer foraging strategies.* University of Chicago Press, Chicago.
Young, J. A., and J. D. Budy
  1979 Historical use of Nevada's pinyon-juniper woodlands. *Journal of Forest History* 23(3):112–121.

CHAPTER 10

Urban Hinterlands as Frontiers of Colonization

PATRICIA E. RUBERTONE
Department of Anthropology
Brown University
Providence, Rhode Island

PETER F. THORBAHN
Public Archaeology Laboratory, Inc.
Providence, Rhode Island

INTRODUCTION

Recent perspectives on the nature of cities are marked by a conceptual shift away from a perception of cities as bounded, internally autonomous units (Adams 1977). Instead of depicting cities as unique *places* exhibiting distinctive demographic, economic, social, and cultural features as has been the trend in anthropology and other disciplines (e.g., Adams 1966; Berry 1967; Blanton 1976; Redfield and Singer 1954; Sjoberg 1960; Weber 1958), cities are being viewed *within networks* of wider ecological and social relationships. This change in emphasis directs attention away from the city—or central place—as a context for social action (Rollwagen 1975) toward a more dynamic landscape in which city, hinterland, and the frontier of settlement are not static units, but are more complex, interconnected groupings subject to change through time. The logical implication of this new direction in complex societies research is that "rural" and "urban" have come to be recognized as closely interrelated rather than polarized abstractions (Adams 1977:267–268).

The Archaeology of Frontiers and Boundaries   **231**

While this picture is readily apparent in contemporary American society in which the metropolis has been replaced in many areas by some amoebalike megalopolis, this blending of rural and urban is not simply a phenomenon of twentieth-century urbanization. Studies of city and countryside in ancient and historical times hint of the dynamic aspects of this connection. Archaeological studies have yielded evidence linking both hinterland and peripheral areas to urban centers (Adams 1974; Lamberg-Karlovsky 1975; Rathje 1971; Wright 1969). Cities, in fact, may take active roles in organizing their hinterlands and in facilitating the integration of rural economies in the wider urban network. This may involve the coordination of rural production, the organization of the movement of produced items, and even the management of labor associated with these activities.

In this study we are concerned with the spatial patterning that reflects the organization of the urban–hinterland system through time. Given the notions presented previously, we are making three fairly straightforward assumptions:

1. the frontier of the urban–hinterland system may change in response to economic, demographic, and environmental processes;
2. there may be internal spatial zonation within the urban–hinterland system; and also
3. the boundaries of spatial zones within the urban hinterland system may change in the process of settlement evolution.

Most settlement models appropriate to the study of urban–hinterland systems, however, depict locational patterning among *places* across the landscape. In *central place models,* the spacing of settlements reflects some underlying behavioral process from which implications may be drawn regarding the *range* of a hinterland for any order of place in the settlement hierarchy. *Dendritic patterns,* on the other hand, provide descriptive models of regional integration emphasizing the nature of the connection between peripheral areas and a center. In both models, the emphasis is on the nature of links between places and the places themselves. These concerns represent one aspect of the regional system—what geographers have referred to as the "skeleton" of a regional system (Haggett 1966:153). Models of land use provide another dimension of the regional landscape. They allow us to examine *surfaces.* From this viewpoint, it is possible to investigate areal zonation within the broader geography and thus explore any spatial patterning that may be associated with the evolution of the urban–hinterland landscape.

Much of the research on land-use modeling has been derived from the work of Johann Heinrich von Thünen (Hall 1966) in the nineteenth century. In his land-use model, areal distribution of types of agricultural activities is depicted in concentric land-use zones around a single, centrally located city. Underlying the relative placement of land-use zones in the model is the notion of competition between crops and farming practices for the use of any particular plot of land (Chisholm 1962:20). The crop yielding the highest economic rent—that is, the surplus that a given volume of inputs of capital and labor can produce on a unit area of land—is the one that is planted on that particular plot. In this model, it is distance that influences the location of different activities in space (i.e., land-use types).

In the archaeological literature, the effect of distance on regional land use is most apparent in catchment analyses (Flannery 1976; Rossman 1976; Vita-Finzi and Higgs 1970; Zarky 1976). Here distance determines the economic range of a site, that is, a subsistence territory in which resources are available to and utilized by the site's inhabitants. In many of these studies the catchment boundary or economic range is set at a fixed distance from a site, usually a 5-km radius for sedentary economies and a 10-km radius for mobile ones (Chisholm 1962). The inference is that beyond this radius, transport and other costs far exceed benefits gained from the exploitation of the area's resources.

The point to be made is that the notion of distance is treated differently in each of these approaches to the study of land-use surfaces (Paynter 1980:150). In catchment analyses, distance (from a settlement) determines whether or not a plot of land will be used. As a result, the potential variability in the spatial distribution of activities such as land-use among different societies is virtually ignored. According to the von Thünen principles of land-use modeling, distance has a continuous effect (Paynter 1980:150). Plots of land that may be ecologically similar but located at different distances from the settlement will be used differently. Consequently, this approach to land-use modeling is more appropriate to the study of patterning in the urban–hinterland landscape that we are attempting here. We are not simply interested in identifying the boundary demarcating the extent of the urban–hinterland system, but in identifying zonation within it.

While these boundaries or zones within the urban–hinterland system may be viewed as a series of distinct land-use types (e.g., intensive agriculture, woodland, extensive agriculture) as represented in the von Thünen ring model, the alternative is to consider spatial zonation in terms of more general locational principles derived from this model. This approach avoids the limitations presented in attempting to reconstruct the specific patterns of land use in the von Thünen ring model since its high empirical content makes it difficult to evaluate using either archaeological data or documentary evidence. It is unreasonable to assume that the detailed information needed to define distinctive rings of land-use types across a region would be available in the archaeological record, and even if it were, the sampling problem alone would be mind-boggling. While documentary sources do offer detailed information on some specific land-use practices, these data often lack the comparability needed for diachronic and regional analyses. Consequently, it is questionable whether reconstruction of the form and content of land-use zones is even a desirable goal for research seeking to explore variability in the urban-hinterland landscape through time.

Our aim in this essay is to use the theoretical models of density surfaces developed by locational geographers to examine data on historic settlement and land use in western Rhode Island. By using these models we hope to identify and explain spatial patterning within the urban–hinterland system that is defined by this study area in relation to a single urban center—the city of Providence. The details and results of this study are presented in the following sections.

THE STUDY AREA

The study area has been defined as the communities of Rhode Island extending from Narragansett Bay west toward the Connecticut border (Figure 10.1). While it is recognized that adjacent areas within Rhode Island (e.g., the area to the east of Narragansett Bay) and in neighboring Massachusetts and Connecticut could have participated in this same urban–hinterland system, these areas were excluded from our study for several reasons. First, the territory to the east of Narragansett Bay includes the immediate hinterland of Newport which was one of Rhode Island's major coastal urban centers during previous centuries. Second, the extension of our study area beyond Rhode Island's political borders into the state of Connecticut to the west and into the Commonwealth of Massachusetts to the north and east would have introduced serious difficulties in terms of data comparability. Massachusetts and Rhode Island records at any point in time differ in terms of their organization and specific content.

Finally, the decision to limit the study area to Providence and its western hinterland reflected a need to provide a specific regional context for an archaeological study of eighteenth- and nineteenth-century rural domestic sites and land-use practices being conducted in Coventry and Foster, Rhode Island by one of the authors (Rubertone 1984). These investigations are focused on the physical remains of a farm complex, limited activity sites (e.g., charcoal-processing areas, mill sites), and ecological traces of landscape alteration that provide behavioral evidence of the decisions made in the past regarding settlement and land use. By placing this archaeological study area in a wider regional context, we hope to distinguish between those

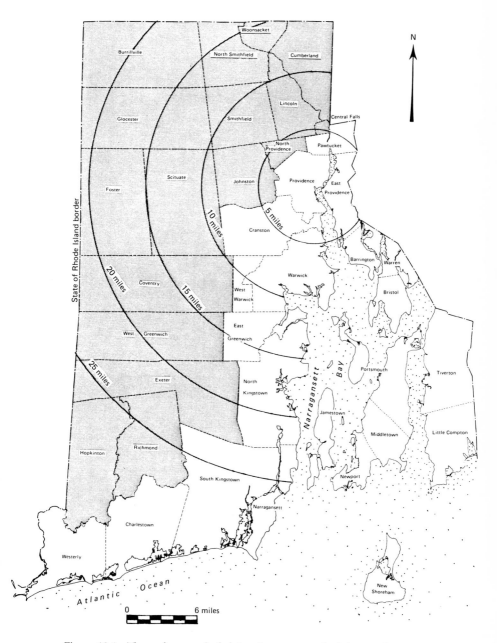

Figure 10.1 The study area: shaded, interior sector; unshaded, coastal sector.

processes specifically related to the immediate environment and those attributed to broader social and economic trends.

The significance of the study area, however, also may be gauged from historical interpretations of New England urbanism. Many of these studies attempt to fit New England's cities and towns into some regional pattern of societal and economic development. According to these generalizations, Providence's role in the region could have followed one of several alternative schemes. Each has direct implications for understanding its relation to the surrounding hinterland.

In a *geographic model* which depicts distinctive internally homogeneous bands of social and economic development for preindustrial New England (Main 1965), our study area falls into a commercial coastal zone composed of large and small cities. Successive bands of occupation reaching into the countryside differ from the coastal zone and from each other not only in terms of settlement form, but culturally, socially, and economically as well. This model implies that areas defined as urban and rural are quite different, representing distinctive and immutable categories. The empirical evidence, however, indicates that the system of homogeneous bands is not an adequate representation of the region. There was a high degree of heterogeneity among towns within each geographic band as well as between the bands themselves.

Another possible scenario correlates patterns of regional development with transportation and communication routes. According to this *transport model*, a relationship is proposed between location on a through highway, a settlement's ability to establish effective communication networks, and patterns of town growth. From the eighteenth century, roads of primary and lesser importance passed through Providence linking it to other towns. While the model suggests that transport infrastructure and, consequently, costs were distributed differently between cities and communities in the hinterland, the pattern is not that clear-cut—at least not in this case.

In general, road conditions were poor and overland transport was expensive until well into the nineteenth century. Water transport provided a cheaper alternative, but most of New England's rivers were navigable only for short distances and therefore posed certain limitations as effective channels of communication. Attempts to improve the situation through the construction of canals began in the early nineteenth century. The Blackstone Canal, for example, begun in 1825 and completed three years later, was an attempt to open up the Blackstone River valley and thus link Providence to Worcester (Rubertone and Gallagher 1981). The canal, which was maintained for about 10 years, was not a complete success as droughts in the summer months and ice during the winter often made sections of the canal impassable. Coastal waterways as communication routes were not beset with the difficulties presented by the roads and river valleys and were important transportation corridors. There were, however, considerable disparities in the harbor capabilities along the coast which resulted in differences among coastal towns and, of course, between the coast and interior sections of New England. In sum, the difficulties presented by roads and river valleys as communication routes suggest that the transport model fails to adequately account for regional development in the preindustrial period; it also does not effectively explain in all cases the relation of cities to their hinterlands.

A final pattern of regional development that has been suggested is a *central place model* which attempts to show relationships between large cities of the period, their satellite towns, and to some extent their hinterland areas. In a central place model where hierarchical relationships are the basis for regional organization, Providence would be classified as a secondary urban center if judged on the basis of population estimates (e.g., Bridenbaugh 1971). Regional central place hierarchies based on population estimates for preindustrial New England, however, must be approached cautiously. The use of population estimates for establishing a hierarchy of towns may be misleading since towns were territorial units of varying areal size.

When this variable is taken into consideration and densities calculated for the population estimates mentioned previously, no clear nested pattern exists among New England's important towns. Boston is by far the first-ranking city indicating that preindustrial New England may be characterized as a primate urban system (Table 10.1). This assessment also may be inferred from historical interpretations in which colonial Boston surpasses other towns in the region and is a focal point for commerce, politics, and religion (McManis 1975). According to this interpretation, Boston, as a primate center, may have played an important role concerning the integration and boundary maintenance of a broad regional system (Kowalewski 1982).

When alternative measures are used to assess town size and importance, different patterns emerge. Cook (1976), for example, developed an index based on each town's assessed value corrected for variations in territorial size. The assumption underlying this index is that property values would be highest for urban areas and proportional to the marketing potential of the rural areas. The distribution of towns with similar values according to this index has some important implications for understanding New England urbanism. While towns with high values cross-cut broad geographic areas, there is considerable variation among towns at a local level. These results suggest that no one model can adequately explain New England urbanism.

According to Cook's index (1976:79), towns along the shores of Nar-

Table 10.1

Population Densities for Major New England Towns at End of
Colonial Era

Town	Acres[a]	Population[b]	Population density
Boston	1000	16,000	16.0
Providence	3500	4,361	1.2
Newport	3500	11,000	2.2
New Haven	8900	8,295	.9
Norwich	6700	7,032	1.1
New London	6200	5,366	.9
Salem	5200	5,337	1.0
Hartford	5400	4,881	.9
Middletown	8500	4,680	.6
Portsmouth	11000	4,590	.4
Marblehead	2800	4,386	1.6

[a]From Cook 1976.
[b]From Bridenbaugh 1971.

ragansett Bay exhibited fairly high values compared to interior towns. Among those towns, however, both Providence and Newport stood out as notable centers (Cook 1976:79). Yet, each had a very different type of hinterland and perhaps a different kind of relationship with its surrounding area. Thus, it would seem that urban–hinterland relations exhibited considerable diversity. In some situations (e.g., Providence) it appears that urban–hinterland links were of primary importance. Alternatively, there were cases (e.g., Newport, Boston) in which broader concerns, especially commercial ties and even political hegemony were the dominant factors affecting regional patterns.

In summary, when various schemes of regional development for preindustrial New England are examined, it is clear that no one set of variables is sufficient to explain the observed diversity among *all* urban forms and the countryside. The approach taken in this essay is to focus on *one* urban–hinterland locale—Providence and western Rhode Island—in order to begin to identify what the relationships were and what regularities existed in the past. For this reason, we have selected to examine patterns of settlement and land use associated with the historical development of this urban–hinterland area.

METHODS OF ANALYSIS

Our main objective is to investigate the relationship between historic settlement and land-use patterns and models of density surfaces developed by locational geographers in order to identify and explain internal zonation within the urban–hinterland study region. One way of looking at the relationship of density to distance over a surface is that the density of a variable decreases with increasing distance from the center of the surface, that is, density decays with distance.

The simplest *distance decay model* in locational geography was proposed by Clark (1951) in which the density of a variable (in his study, population) decreases at an exponential rate with distance from an urban center:

$$y = ae^{-bd}$$

Where y is the density of the variable, e is the base of natural logarithms (2.71828), b is the rate of decay, and d is the distance. The exponential decay of density with distance is founded on theories of movement or transport-cost minimization in regional systems (Johnston 1973).

We selected two key variables from the historic data—population density and percentage of cleared land—in order to examine processes of settlement and land-use patterns, respectively. By looking at population density, we avoid the problem presented by using uncorrected population estimates for the towns (see Table 10.1). The percentage of cleared land has been selected as a measure of historical land use since it may reflect a number of processes associated with economic development and frontier expansion (e.g., farming, timbering, settlement).

Three dates (1689, 1774, and 1865) covering a 177-year range were examined. This period covers the latter part of the initial European colonization of Rhode Island and extends to a point in time near the beginning of the cotton textile industry in Providence, ca. 1790. The period ends at the close of the Civil War. The exact dates examined, however, were dictated by availability of comparable data. The sources of information were Whitney's (1961) study of the historical demography of the Narragansett Bay region, Dyer's (1871) compilation of early valuation and census records, and Snow's (1867) report on the 1865 Rhode Island census.

The basic analytic procedure was to construct gradients of population density and percentage of cleared land from Providence out to the limit of the study area. This involved two cross-cutting units of analysis. Density decay surfaces around an urban center have two components: a concentric one, as in the von Thünen land-use model, and a sectoral component due to major transport routes or linear patterns of specific resources along these routes (Haggett *et al.* 1977:191).

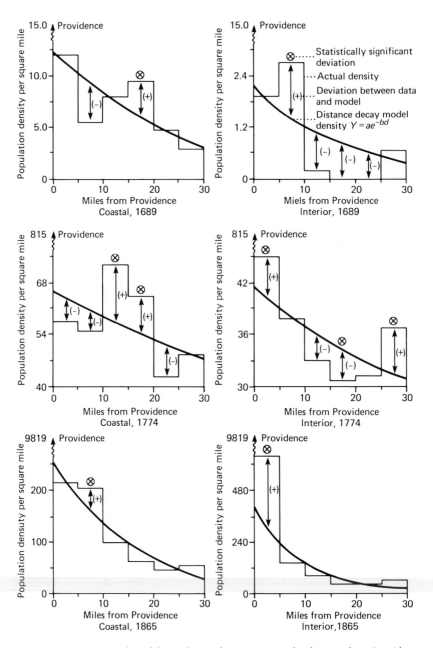

Figure 10.2 Actual and model population densities versus the distance from Providence, 1689–1865.

The *concentric component* was constructed by drawing rings at 5-mile increments around Providence and calculating the area of each town that fell within a ring (Figure 10.1). The historic data were recorded by town, so after computing the population density and percentage of cleared land, an average for each 5-mile ring was obtained by weighting the town statistics for their proportion of area in the ring.

The *sectoral component* was represented by dividing the study area into two sectors (Figure 10.1). Those towns along the coast of Narragansett Bay and Block Island Sound were in the coastal sector. The other sector consisted of towns in the interior of the state. Before the development of turnpikes in the middle of the eighteenth century and railroads in the nineteenth century, Narragansett Bay was certainly a major transport route. In addition, access to marine resources in estuaries and along the coast clearly produced a nonuniform distribution of natural resources between the coastal and interior sectors of the study region. The division of the region into rings around Providence crossing interior and coastal sectors was designed to account for uniform trends of distance from Providence and distortions in the distance decay surfaces due to an unequal ease of transport and accessibility to natural resources in the historic period.

Once the concentric gradients had been constructed for the coastal and interior sectors of the Providence–hinterland region, least square regression lines of Clark's distance decay function were estimated. The values for Providence were not included in the regression in order to avoid skewing the least squares solution toward the origin. The differences between the actual population densities and percentages of cleared land were then examined for statistically significant (90% confidence level) deviations between the actual and model gradients (see Wonnacott and Wonnacott 1977:348–349 for methods). These significant deviations are used to estimate the internal boundaries of zones where settlement processes and land-use patterns changed markedly from the distance decay model (Figure 10.2).

In summary, the historic data on population densities and percentages of cleared land were organized into spatial units that would account for patterning among concentric rings around Providence and between coastal and interior sectors of the urban–hinterland region. Wherever there were significant deviations (either positive or negative) from the distance decay model, these were interpreted to be internal boundaries of population or land-clearing zones within the region.

POPULATION AND SETTLEMENT PROCESSES

Figure 10.2 contains the actual population densities for 1689, 1774, and 1865 along with the model distance decay curves. The pattern of the zone boundaries, as estimated by the deviations, in both the coast and the interior sectors is striking. Beginning in 1689 there was a marked tendency for an increase of population between 10 and 20 miles from Providence along the coast. This pattern was especially clear by 1774. In contrast, there were very low population densities between 10 and 25 miles in the interior until after 1774. Yet by 1865 both the coastal and interior sectors closely fit the distance decay model. In other words, the population densities of the coastal sector and interior were nearly mirror images up to 1774. The population density curve for the coast is convex with an excess of population centered around 15 miles from Providence. The interior population densities represent a concave curve with a deficiency of population from 10 to 25 miles from Providence. By 1865 patterns of population had shifted to high densities near Providence in both the coastal and interior sectors.

There are other aspects of the patterns to be considered. The coastal sector had continuous population growth throughout the 1689-to-1865 period. Yet in 1774 and 1865, the only area of the interior to gain appreciable population was near Providence. There was scarcely any change in population densities beyond 15 miles from the city.

These patterns of settlement have few correlates in the literature on distance–population density models. Other studies of historic trends in population distribution suggest that the rate of distance decay *decreased* during the nineteenth and twentieth centuries for cities such as London, New York, and Chicago (Haggett *et al.* 1977:221–224).

In Table 10.2, R^2 shows the degree of correspondence between the distance decay model and the data. The value of b is the rate of distance decay in the model. In the seventeenth and eighteenth centuries the distance decay model does not correspond very well to the actual population densities. The R^2 values for both the coast and interior sectors are lower for 1689 and 1774 than for 1865. In terms of the rates of distance decay, b, there is a decrease from 1689 to 1774 but from 1774 to 1865 there is a substantial increase. The sequence of changes in b applies to both the coast and the interior.

These results imply that the settlement processes in Providence and its hinterland did not operate uniformly either through time or in space. In particular, the distance decay model fails to account for how the region was colonized. As early as 1689, for example, there was a concentration of population along the coast at a distance of 10–20 miles from Providence in the area of East Greenwich and North Kingstown whereas at the same distance from Providence the interior was always underpopulated.

Throughout this period Providence dominated the population distribution of the region. This concentration of population in the cities of preindustrial America (Bridenbaugh 1938; Whitney 1961), and their centrality in

Table 10.2

Regression Statistics for Population Densities

	Coast		Interior	
Year	R^2	b	R^2	b
1689	.670	.045	.417	.064
1774	.245	.010	.413	.010
1865	.877	.062	.734	.105

the postindustrial era (Clark 1951) has been emphasized by historical demographers. In terms of absolute numbers, however, Providence contained 7.2% of the total Rhode Island population in 1779, and still only 29.5% in 1865. To account for the vast majority of the population at any point in time—especially the processes of regional settlement through time—we must look to the rural areas.

Our results also show that there was a strong sectoral bias to the way in which the area around Providence was settled by Anglo-Americans. A secondary population center along the coast existed as early as the seventeenth century. We know that one of the first trading posts beyond Providence was established on the coast at Wickford in North Kingstown in the 1640s. This area of the coast from 10 to 20 miles from Providence continued to grow in population through the eighteenth and nineteenth centuries.

Yet, there was a deficit of population in the 10–20 mile zone of the interior, along with the slow rate of population growth in this zone from 1774 to 1865. This suggests that the influence of Providence and the secondary center around North Kingstown dropped off precipitously in the interior. To account for settlement patterns in the interior, it may be suggested that distance may have served as a limiting factor that could have operated in at least two ways. First, difficulties of transportation and communication could have minimized the control of rural areas by urban elites. Second, the absence of any secondary centers emerging in the interior suggests that the rural area served as a frontier of settlement.

LAND-USE PATTERNS AND FOREST CLEARANCE

The clearing of forests served two distinct purposes in preindustrial Rhode Island. On the one hand, forest products were the primary source of building materials, fuel, and other products until the beginning of the twentieth century. On the other hand, forests represented the major obstacle to the creation of farming and grazing lands. The von Thünen land-use model, however, predicts that when forests were used to produce valuable products such as lumber, potash, charcoal, or firewood, they would have been exploited on a sustained-yield basis and conserved as a key resource (Haggett *et al.* 1977:205–207).

Where intensive and extensive farming provided the maximum economic return, wood from forests would have been a waste, or at best, a by-product of land clearing. According to von Thünen land-use principles, the sequence of land use around a city should be a pattern of intensive agriculture closest to the city, followed by zones of sustained-yield forestry, extensive farming and grazing. For the analysis of land-use patterns in the Providence–hinterland region, this would mean that there should be more cleared land near Providence, followed by a drop-off, and finally an increase in the amount of cleared land.

Figure 10.3 shows the percentages of cleared land for the coastal and interior sectors of the study area for 1774 and 1865; there are no comparable data before the late eighteenth century. Nonetheless, the interior patterns for 1774 might hint at how earlier land-use patterns developed. In the interior, there is a consistent decrease in the percent of cleared land with distance from Providence. By comparison, the coastal pattern for 1774 shows some indication of organization of land-use according to von Thünen principles. There is more cleared land close to Providence and significantly less cleared land between 5 and 15 miles from the city.

By 1865 the patterns are as predicted by the von Thünen model. Significantly more land was cleared in the 5–10 mile zone of the coastal sector. This may indicate that more land was being used for intensive agriculture. In the interior, significantly more land was cleared between 25 and 30 miles from Providence, which might suggest the existence of extensive farming and grazing areas.

As further evidence of intensive and extensive land-use practices, the coastal towns of Cranston and Warwick, located 5–10 miles from Providence, had 46.1% of the total area in farmland, either plowed, mowed, or in pasturage. Hopkinton and Richmond, located beyond the 25-mile zone, had only 36.9% of their area farmed. In Cranston and Warwick 10.1% of this farmland was plowed, but the far interior towns of Hopkinton and Richmond had only plowed farmland. These figures confirm the sequence of intensive and extensive agricultural land-use predicted by von Thünen principles. From 10 to 20 miles along the coast and from 10 to 25 miles in the interior, there was a significantly less cleared land (Figure 10.3). This could have been a zone of sustained-yield forestry.

To see if there is any significance to the pattern of land clearance, Figure 10.4 shows the distribution of cattle per square mile for the whole region in

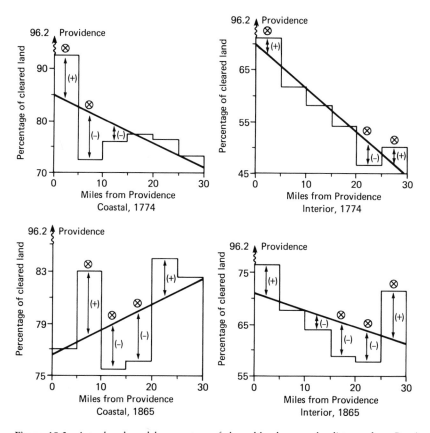

Figure 10.3 Actual and model percentage of cleared land versus the distance from Providence, 1774–1865.

1780 and 1865. The lowest densities of cattle occur in exactly those zones where there is less cleared land—10 to 25 miles from Providence. Transport costs of livestock cannot explain this pattern because in 1780 the density of cattle at 20 to 25 miles from Providence was approximately the same for the 0–10 mile zone. Therefore, the key to the pattern of land clearance appears to be in the intensive and extensive agricultural land-use practices.

The ratio of sheep to cattle in the coastal communities of Cranston and Warwick in 1865 was .4 sheep for every head of cattle. In the interior towns of Richmond and Hopkinton there were 2.7 sheep for every head of cattle. Distance from Providence seems to be related to intensive pasturing with higher proportions of milch cows near the city and extensive grazing indicated by a higher proportion of sheep in the far interior.

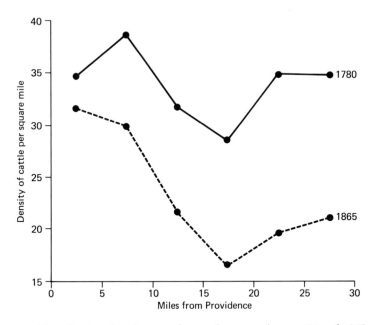

Figure 10.4 Density of cattle versus distance from Providence, 1780 and 1865.

Unfortunately, there are no complete records of forest production for any year in the study period, so the existence of a sustained-yield forestry zone must be stated as an untested hypothesis. Nonetheless, the zonation of land use in concentric rings around Providence can be confirmed for intensive and extensive agriculture for 1865.

SUMMARY AND CONCLUSIONS

We have attempted to examine spatial patterning in the urban–hinterland landscape through time. Through the analysis of settlement pattern data (specifically population densities) and patterns of land clearance, we have shown that no simple distance–decay relationship exists between city, hinterland, and the frontier of settlement.

Using historic data from western Rhode Island and Providence during the preindustrial period, the distance-decay model provides a good framework for the settlement of both coastal and interior towns only toward the end of the period. Prior to that time, the settlement and population processes affecting coastal and interior towns were quite different. While the appearance of population centers along the coast may be a phenomenon that was related to Providence's growth as a center and its need to ensure control of the hinterland's resources, the fact that such centers do not also appear in the interior weakens this argument; the emergence of population centers along the coast may have been an independent process. Beyond the immediate environs of the city, populations of the interior towns were maintained at densities lower than predicted by the model.

The analysis of land-clearance patterns also has indicated zoning across the urban–hinterland landscape. The distance-decay model best describes the variability among the towns for the interior and coast for the early data on land use (i.e., 1774). By the end of the preindustrial period, patterns of land use show considerable deviation from this model. From patterns of land clearance, it may be inferred that zonation and the sequence of land use around Providence followed locational principles predicted from the von Thünen land-use model.

By focusing our analysis on Providence and the towns of western Rhode Island, we have attempted to explore the relationship between city and hinterland in a single, local setting. The empirical evidence presented here indicates that the relationship is a complex one subject to variation across space and change through time. It is clear that neither a single set of variables nor a single model can account for preindustrial urbanism. While this is true for this North American case, it also is valid for other areas that have been the scene of secondary urban development during the historical period such as Morocco (Boone and Redman 1982).

For Providence and its western hinterland, the articulation between city and countryside seems to have been an important one. Judging from the patterns of land use, articulation between city and countryside appears to have intensified in the process of regional development for this study area. It is suggested that future research concerning North American historic urbanism be addressed to examining the nature of urban–hinterland relations and their implications for archaeological studies. We suspect that differences in the ways that cities articulate with their hinterland may lead to formulation of more interesting models of urbanization relevant not only to historical, but also to prehistoric studies.

REFERENCES

Adams, Robert McC.
   1966   *The evolution of urban society*. Aldine, Chicago.
   1974   Anthropological perspectives on ancient trade. *Current Anthropology* 15:239–258.
   1977   World picture, anthropological frame. *American Anthropologist* 79:265–279.

Berry, Brian
  1967   *The geography of market centers and retail distribution.* Prentice-Hall, Englewood
         Cliffs, N.J.
Blanton, Richard E.
  1976   Anthropological studies of cities. *Annual Review of Anthropology* 5:249–264.
Boone, James L., and Charles L. Redman
  1982   Alternate pathways to urbanism in the medieval Maghreb. *Comparative Urban
         Research* 9(1):28–38.
Bridenbaugh, Carl
  1938   *Cities in the wilderness.* Ronald Press, New York.
  1971   *Cities in revolt.* Oxford University Press, New York.
Chisholm, Michael
  1962   *Rural settlement and land use.* Aldine, Chicago.
Clark, C.
  1951   Urban population densities. *Journal of the Royal Statistical Society* 114:490–496.
Cook, Edward M.
  1976   *The fathers of the towns.* John Hopkins University Press, Baltimore.
Dyer, Elisha
  1871   *Valuation of the cities and towns in the state of Rhode Island.* State Printers,
         Providence.
Flannery, Kent
  1976   Empirical determination of site catchments in Oaxaco and Tehuacan. In *The early
         Mesoamerican village,* edited by Kent Flannery, pp. 103–117. Academic, New
         York
Haggett, Peter
  1966   *Locational analysis in human geography.* St. Martin's, New York.
Haggett, Peter, A. D. Cliff, and A. Frey
  1977   *Locational analysis in human geography* (second ed.). Wiley, New York.
Hall, P. (ed.)
  1966   *Von Thünen's isolated state.* Pergamon, New York.
Johnston, R. J.
  1973   *Spatial structures.* St. Martin's, New York.
Kowalewski, Stephen A.
  1982   The evolution of primate regional systems. *Comparative Urban Research* 9:60–78.
Lamberg-Karlovsky, C. C.
  1975   Third millenium modes of exchange and modes of production. In *Ancient civiliza-
         tion and trade,* edited by Jeremy Sabloff and C. C. Lamberg-Karlovsky, pp. 369–
         408. University of New Mexico Press, Albuquerque.
Main, Jackson T.
  1965   *The social structure of revolutionary America.* Princeton University Press, Prince-
         ton, New Jersey.
McManis, Douglas
  1975   *Colonial New England: a historical geography.* Oxford University Press, New
         York.
Paynter, Robert
  1980   *Long distance processes, stratification and settlement pattern: an archaeological
         perspective.* Unpublished Ph.D. dissertation, Department of Anthropology, Univer-
         sity of Massachusetts, Amherst.
Rathje, William
         1971   Praise the gods and pass the metates: a hypothesis of the development of lowland

rainforest civilizations in Mesoamerica. In *Contemporary archaeology,* edited by Mark Leone, pp. 365–392. Southern Illinois University Press, Carbondale, Ill.

Redfield, Robert, and Milton Singer
    1954   The cultural role of cities. *Economic Development and Cultural Change* 3:53–73.

Rollwagen, Jack
    1975   Introduction: the city as context: a symposium. *Urban Anthropology* 4(1):1–4.

Rossman, David
    1976   A site catchment analysis of San Lorenzo, Veracruz. In *The early Mesoamerican village,* edited by Kent Flannery, pp. 95–103. Academic, New York.

Rubertone, Patricia E.
    1984   Historical landscapes: archaeology of place and space. *Man in the Northeast,* in press.

Rubertone, Patricia E., and Joan Gallagher
    1981   Archaeological site examination: A case study in urban archaeology. Roger Williams National Memorial. *U.S. Department of the Interior National Park Service, North Atlantic Regional Office, Cultural Resource Management Study 4.*

Snow, Edwin M.
    1867   *Report upon the census of Rhode Island, 1865.* State Printers, Providence.

Sjoberg, Gideon
    1960   *The preindustrial city: past and present.* Free Press, New York.

Vita-Finzi, Claudio, and Eric Higgs
    1970   Prehistoric economy in the Mt. Carmel area of Palestine: site catchment analysis. *Proceedings of the Prehistoric Society* 36:1–37.

Weber, Max
    1958   *The city.* Free Press, New York.

Whitney, H. A.
    1961   *The Narragansett region, concentration of population 1635–1885.* University Microfilms, Ann Arbor.

Wonnacott, T. H., and R. J. Wonnacott
    1977   *Introductory statistics for business and economics* (second ed.). Wiley, New York.

Wright, Henry
    1969   The administration of rural production in an early Mesopotamian town. *University of Michigan Museum of Anthropology Anthropological Paper 38.*

Zarky, Allen
    1976   Statistical analysis of site catchments at Ocos, Guatemala. In *The early Mesoamerican village,* edited by Kent Flannery, pp. 117–128. Academic, New York.

CHAPTER 11

Functional Variation among Settlements on the South Carolina Frontier: An Archaeological Perspective

KENNETH E. LEWIS

Department of Anthropology
Michigan State University
East Lansing, Michigan

INTRODUCTION

The expansion of British settlement in eighteenth-century South Carolina involved a series of events and changes that reflect the operation of a developmental process common to areas undergoing agricultural colonization. Because human behavior is revealed in the material record of the society in which it took place, evidence of this process of colonization is likely to be discernible in the archaeological remains of frontier settlements. This study demonstrates how archaeological methodology may be employed in observing aspects of frontier change on the basis of material data obtained from the sites of settlements in a former colonial area.

The recognition of frontier change requires an understanding of this phenomenon as a larger process as well as the manner in which this process affects various aspects of a society. Frontier change, like other behavioral processes, may be analyzed through the use of models designed to organize observations of change into a series of explanatory hypotheses. These hypotheses, in turn, establish a predictive framework within which to investigate new observations. The characteristics of a model, distilled from a comparative study of colonial societies, describe the nature of frontier change and form the basis on which additional cases of colonization may be analyzed. If analogies are employed linking the characteristics of the model to basic economic activities within the past society, it should be possible to predict the form that evidence of this process will take in the archaeological record that society left behind.

In this essay I describe briefly a comparative model of agricultural colonization and explore certain aspects of this process in terms of the historical development of South Carolina. The occurrence of frontier change should be observable in the documentary record as well as its archaeological counterpart. Both will be examined independently not only to illustrate the utility of the model but also to demonstrate the ability of either methodology to provide data capable of revealing processes of change.

THE INSULAR FRONTIER MODEL

The colonization of South Carolina in the seventeenth and eighteenth centuries took place as part of the expansion of Europe, a largely economic process that began in the fifteenth century. A result of this expansion was the development of a "world economy" characterized by a geographical division of labor associated with production. At the center of the system lay the *core states,* from which colonization was directed. *Peripheral areas,* in newly colonized regions, occupied the outer limits of settlement (Wallerstein 1980:21). Production in peripheral areas was strictly controlled by the core states. It was confined to lower-ranking goods that were integral to daily life in the economy's core, but which were produced by less well-rewarded labor (Wallerstein 1974:302). Such goods usually consisted of raw materials to be exchanged for manufactures and services from the core states (Gould 1972:235–236).

Successful colonization required control over production in colonial areas. This was achieved through the migration of factors (or commercial agents) from the core state and the establishment of political and military authority in the peripheral regions. In general, two types of factor migration occurred, each of which was linked to a different form of settlement. The first was associated with the production of noncompetitive commercial commodities, often in an environment different from that of the homeland. It involved the development of enclave settlements whose residents remained socially and economically tied to the homeland as temporary residents rather than pioneers. The second type of factor migration centered around the production of competitive agricultural commodities and required the extensive migration of labor from the homeland. The desire of migrants to settle permanently in the colony created a pattern of development characterized by local reinvestment, a reduction of transfer flows to the mother country, and the spread of settlement throughout the area of colonization (Gray 1976:129–130).

Colonization associated with these two types of factor migration reflects the development of separate forms of production, each of which required a distinct settlement system and a different form of interaction with the core state. The extent and nature of the interacting links, or "insularity," of the colony is indicated by the degree of change a colonial society has undergone. Colonies with few or tenuous links have greater insularity and are likely to have witnessed more extensive adaptation than those that maintained closer ties. Steffen (1980:xvii–xviii) defined two categories of frontier settlement on the basis of their insularity. *Cosmopolitan frontiers* involve short-term, economically specialized activities closely tied to the national economy of the homeland. These factors mitigate the occurrence of social, economic, and political change in general. Such change is more pervasive on *insular frontiers,* where a commitment to long-term indigenous development tends overall to decrease the area's ties to the national economy and allow fundamental change to occur. Cosmopolitan frontiers include those devoted to trapping and trading, mining and other industrial activities, establishing a military presence, and certain types of exploitative plantation agriculture. Insular frontiers, on the other hand, are characterized by permanent agricultural settlement on small farms or plantations (Leyburn 1935; Steffen 1980:xvii–xviii; Thompson 1973:11).

This essay is concerned with change in insular frontier regions and concentrates on modeling certain aspects of this process. In particular, the development of settlement patterning is explored because this facet of colonization is basic to the organization of the region as a socioeconomic entity. The development of an insular frontier may be seen as an example of agricultural expansion in which the types of production activities carried out are related to their distance to market. The efficiency of transport, and hence its cost, increases with distance, so that the greatest competition for land and its most intensive use are closest to the central market (Thünen 1966), in this case an entrepot linking the colony to the homeland. The pattern of land use is not static, but rather it changes in response to greater demand and to changes in the technology of supply. Increases in demand and advances in technology permit an enlargement of the agricultural supply area, extending the distance at which various types of production can take place profitably (Peet 1970–1971:188–189). The resulting spatial organization of production and its change through time conditions the nature of settlement in insular frontier regions, helping to produce the distinct patterns observed by geographers, anthropologists, and historians.

Hudson (1969) developed a model—based on analogies drawn from ecological spatial distribution theory—that describes several stages of development through which colonial settlement patterns are likely to pass. The first is a stage of *colonization,* characterized by a random distribution and associated with an area's initial occupation. With additional population growth, settlement begins to *spread* out from older centers, producing a clustered distribution in the second phase of the region's development. Finally, as vacant land is occupied at the close of the frontier period, *competition* for remaining resources occurs and a readjustment in the pattern of growth takes place. This results in a state of relative equilibrium characterized by an even distribution of settlement.

Because a frontier area is in the process of being inhabited by an intrusive society, its population density is markedly lower than that in the homeland. This lower density is reflected in the pattern of settlement growth, which reveals an initial spread as population pressure increases, followed by a subsequent filling-in of areas originally avoided by settlement. The population density of a frontier region affects the form of the transport network and the hierarchy of settlements that support the region's trade with the outside world. As a producer of raw agricultural commodities, a colony should exhibit a settlement and transportation organization adequate to handle the movement of goods out of the region.

Earle and Hoffman (1976:11) suggested that the form of a frontier settlement network is shaped, in part, by the transport requirements of the crops exported. Perishable, bulky crops needing processing prior to marketing require a relatively complex system of support involving storage facilities, in-transit processing and packaging industries, and shipping services usually contained in settlements arranged in a linear network. Conversely, commodities that are nonperishable and require no processing can be shipped via a much simpler system supported by fewer, less complex settlements.

The nature of the settlement hierarchy is also related to population density. Berry (1967:33–34) observed that in a settled area a hierarchy of settlements is present, each of which performs certain functions. As the population density of the area declines, an upward shift in these functions occurs so that the services performed by a community at a lower level in the hierarchy must now be carried out by one at a higher level. As the population density increases, the opposite effect occurs.

In a frontier region the population density is low, yet the collection, processing, and transport of agricultural commodities still require a settlement system of at least minimal complexity. Most insular frontier areas share a basic hierarchy of settlements that reflects both of these conditions. Because the population density is initially too low to support an elaborate hierarchy, most economic, social, and political functions are concentrated in key settlements strategically placed along the colonial network of trade and communications. The most important of these is the *entrepot,* which is situated at the edge of the area of colonization. It constitutes the major collection and redistribution point in the area and is the primary link with the homeland. Within the region itself, *frontier towns* are the key settlements. They serve as centers of trade and communications, as points of processing, collection, and distribution, and through their direct link with the entrepot, connect the frontier with the national culture of the parent state. *Nucleated settlements* appear as subsidiary loci of activity in the area of colonization. More numerous than frontier towns, they possess a lesser number of specialized activity functions and are linked to the entrepot through these larger settlements (Casagrande *et al.* 1964:312–314).

The hierarchy of settlements arising in the frontier period is, of course, transitory, serving to integrate the region during its period of rapid growth and development. The rise in population density accompanying the competition for resources in the last phase of colonization places increased demands on the economic, social, and political institutions of the colony. This results in a restructuring of the trade and communications network and a shift in the pattern of central place settlements. The increased level of socioeconomic integration that accompanies the "maturing" of an area of colonization affects the function of settlements established earlier and can bring about their growth or decline in response to the changing cultural landscape (Casagrande *et al.* 1964:311).

In short, settlement patterning on the frontier represents a functional adaptation to economic conditions created by economic expansion and the need to collect and transport export commodities out of a region of dispersed settlement and low population density. The form and content of insular frontier settlement should be discernible in existing historical and archaeological evidence pertaining to an area where this type of frontier colonization occured. Two elements crucial in recognizing the occurrence of this process are overall settlement distribution and the presence of specific frontier settlement types. In the following discussion, questions relating to these subjects are posed of data from our study area, a region of insular frontier settlement.

SOUTH CAROLINA'S DEVELOPMENT IN HISTORICAL PERSPECTIVE

The expansion of the frontier in South Carolina was largely a two-phase process. Initially colonized in 1670, the Atlantic coastal region of the province around the entrepot of Charleston was settled first. By the beginning

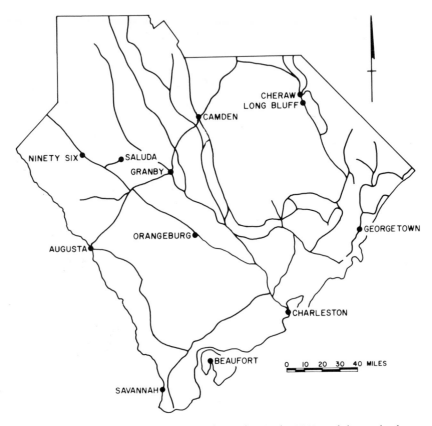

Figure 11.1 Principal settlements in South Carolina in the 1760s and the overland transportation network of the frontier. (From Faden 1780; Mouzon 1775.)

of the eighteenth century, settlement extended northeastward from
Charleston to Georgetown and southwestward to Beaufort (Figure 11.1).
The coastal region developed a plantation economy based on the commercial
production of rice and later indigo as major crops; although, naval stores and
cattle were also important early commodities (Clowse 1971:130–134; Gray
1933:55). Transport was via navigable coastal rivers which permitted the
collection of commodities at the two subsidiary ports and their direct shipment to the entrepot (Petty 1943:20).

   Although Charleston also served as the focal point of a far-flung Indian
trading network stretching throughout the Southeast by 1700 (Crane
1929:131–136), colonization of the South Carolina interior did not com-
mence until the second quarter of the eighteenth century. Following the

establishment of nine townships on major inland rivers in 1731, immigration into the backcountry began (Meriwether 1940:19–20; Brown 1963:2). Actual settlement, however, did not follow the anticipated pattern (Petty 1943:42). Instead, it occurred only in those townships whose locations were intersected by the road system set up to accommodate the Charleston-centered Indian trade. This differential development reflects the importance of access to the trade and communications network in the development of settlements in a frontier region. The overland transport network became the framework for the settlement of the interior, with the earliest and most intensive occupations taking place adjacent to these transport routes.

During the frontier period central settlements developed along major interior routes, and their distribution was influenced by the transport and processing requirements of the area's principal commercial crop, grain. As a perishable, bulky commodity that had to be ground into flour prior to distant shipment, grain production required a relatively complex system of transport. Consequently, the settlement pattern of the interior assumed a linear form, with the principal inland processing centers situated on routes leading to the entrepot of Charleston and the subsidiary settlements located on routes leading to these centers.

Figure 11.1 shows the distribution of inland settlements in the third quarter of the eighteenth century, by which time the development of this region was well under way. Interior settlements all appear to lie on routes linked directly to Charleston. One settlement, however, dominated the trade of the region. Camden arose as a frontier town in the 1750s. It was the site of numerous stores and mills erected to process and store grain from the interior prior to its shipment to the entrepot. In the following decade Camden became the major inland center of break-in-bulk and small-scale industrial activities, surpassing all other frontier settlements (Schulz 1972:33). If one analyzes data relating to the extent of Camden's trade, the structure of the commercial network of the frontier is discernible. From the graphic display of such data in Figure 11.2, we can observe that Camden lay at the center of a vast economic hinterland that stretched over central and eastern South Carolina and spilled over into neighboring North Carolina as well (Schulz 1976). Similarly, Augusta, on the Georgia border, exercised a commercial influence in Georgia that extended into western South Carolina (Drayton 1802:213).

Camden's hinterland encompassed the nucleated settlements of Cheraw and Granby, lying respectively on the Pee Dee and Congaree rivers (Fig. 11.1). Agents of Camden's major mercantile firm, Joseph Kershaw and Company, established subsidiary stores at these locations to serve the surrounding dispersed settlements (Drayton 1802:210–212; Mills 1826:614; Sellers 1934:89). Long Bluff, another nucleated settlement on the Pee Dee

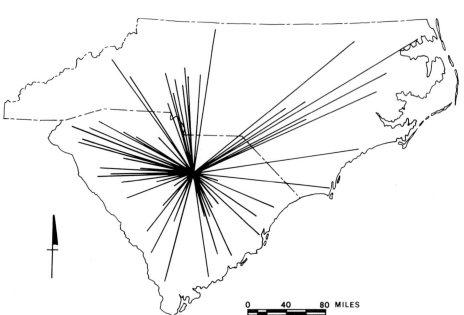

Figure 11.2 Camden's economic hinterland in the late 1770s, as reflected by the distribution of customers of Joseph Kershaw and Company in Camden. (From Schulz 1976:94.)

River (Fig. 11.1), also fell within Camden's economic hinterland, but unlike Cheraw and Granby, was primarily an administrative settlement with only a minor role as a trading center (Gregg 1867:186–187). Ninety Six, the only other inland nucleated settlement, was tied economically to Augusta, whose location on the Savannah River provided it with a direct link to the entrepot of Savannah, Georgia (Fig. 11.1) (Coleman 1976:215).

In addition to its role as a focus of economic activity, Camden gained a political function with the establishment of frontier judicial districts in 1769 (Brown 1963:111). Ninety Six and Long Bluff also became district seats. These three settlements were chosen as administrative centers because of their central locations within the areas they served. The political division of the backcountry did not alter the economic system that served as the area's principal means of integration, and the settlements' additional administrative roles failed to alter their relative status in the frontier settlement hierarchy.

The overall settlement pattern of the frontier appears to have emerged from a random arrangement associated with the initial occupation of the townships to a more evenly spaced distribution as settlement spread out from these areas. This process can be observed by comparing Figure 11.1, showing the distribution of the principal frontier settlements in the 1760s, with Figure 11.3, illustrating the distribution of district seats at the close of the frontier period in 1800. By the end of the eighteenth century increased settlement density and the expansion of cotton agriculture resulted in an increased competition for land and brought about a shift in the transportation network that combined to reshape the settlement pattern of the frontier period (Mills 1826:699). The changing economic structure was accompanied by the rise of new centers of activity within the area of colonization as well as a reorganization of the structure that governed it.

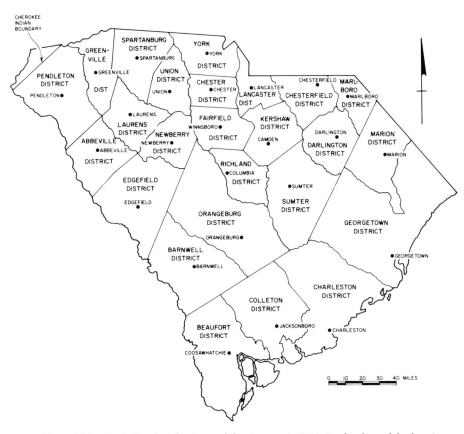

Figure 11.3 South Carolina districts and district seats in 1800. By the close of the frontier period, increasing population density and competition for resources had resulted in an evenly dispersed pattern of settlement as reflected in the distribution of these administrative centers. (From South Carolina Archives n. d.)

Table 11.1

Nearest-Neighbor Values for Principal
Settlements in South Carolina:
1760 and 1800

Date of settlement distribution	Nearest-neighbor value
1760	1.4019
1800	1.7491

The trend toward even spacing of settlement may be determined statistically by calculating and comparing nearest-neighbor values for the distributions shown in Figures 11.1 and 11.3. *Nearest-neighbor analysis* is a technique that measures the deviation of the distribution of a population in space from a random toward an anticlustered or clustered pattern. A value of zero indicates maximum aggregation, while 1 signifies a random distribution, and 2.1491 denotes an even spacing of individuals (Clark and Evans 1954). Nearest-neighbor values for settlement in South Carolina are shown in Table 11.1. These values indicate a steady progression toward even spacing throughout South Carolina as a whole. Although we lack information about total settlement, these incomplete data are expected to reflect the general distribution of settlement. The overall patterns shown appear to support the trend predicted in the insular frontier model.

Documentary evidence pertaining to the early development of South Carolina indicates the change in overall settlement patterning and the appearance of the specific settlement types associated with insular frontier areas. These two aspects of colonization reflect the process of change described in the insular frontier model and imply the occurrence of that process in South Carolina. Just as we have been able to observe settlement type and patterning through the use of documentary sources, it should also be possible to recognize these phenomena in the archaeological record. Material data of various kinds is examined in the following discussion in order to explore the nature of colonial settlement.

AN ARCHAEOLOGICAL VIEW OF SETTLEMENT

The investigation of settlement distribution and composition involves two aspects of settlement patterning and must be carried out using two different types of material data. Because the study of form involves the settlement system as a whole and its changes through time, it must be examined on a regional basis at various points in its development. The study of settlement composition, on the other hand, focuses attention on specific loci of activity as they existed at the peak of their development during the colonial period. This study of frontier settlement in South Carolina is divided into two sections, dealing respectively with the regional and specific aspects of colonial settlement in this area.

The archaeological resources of South Carolina, like those of most other states, have been explored only partially at present. While some portions of the state have been investigated thoroughly, others have received only minimal scrutiny. An archaeological examination of frontier development will yield the best results in areas where material evidence is most complete. Consequently, our study focuses on a portion of the area of colonization for which adequate data are presently available and upon those early settlements whose sites have been examined archaeologically.

Regional Settlement Patterns

An insular frontier region is assumed to have experienced settlement-pattern change resulting in a more evenly spaced distribution of settlements. In order to observe this trend on the basis of material evidence, it is necessary to observe and plot the locations of settlement sites over time. This can be accomplished for certain regions of South Carolina where adequate settlement data are available in the form of archaeological sites, standing structures, or cemeteries with marked stones.

Archaeological sites can be dated on the basis of certain classes of temporally sensitive artifacts. Ceramics, for example, are particularly useful in that the relative frequency of occurrence of various types can provide a median date for an archaeological occupation as well as an estimate of its range (see South 1972, 1977:214–218). Similarly, the study of white clay pipestems has also been helpful in determining the median dates of an occupation based on a statistical analysis of pipe-stem hole diameters (Heighton and Deagan 1972; Walker 1967). Numerous other artifacts also possess date ranges useful in bracketing the occupational range of seventeenth- and eighteenth-century sites (see Noël Hume 1970). The dating of standing structures must rely on an analysis of their architectural style as well as of the artifacts contained in the framework of the buildings themselves. The latter might include nails, locks, hardware, and other artifacts that are likely to have changed in form or style through time (see Mercer 1923; Nelson 1968). Finally, cemeteries may be dated by the earliest burial recorded on a tombstone.

Archaeological, architectural, and cemetery surveys provide extensive coverage of certain portions of South Carolina. By observing the distribution of sites in one such region at regular intervals, it is possible to measure their tendency toward an evenly spaced distribution through time. The patterning revealed by the sequential distributions should provide more detailed information regarding settlement growth than is available from existing written sources because only the larger settlements within the region are usually documented. The picture of settlement distribution provided by material data should substantiate the hypothesized pattern for insular frontier regions.

A comparison of site distributions over a portion of north-central South Carolina, encompassing the upper Broad and Catawba river drainages, may be used to illustrate settlement spread in the interior of the colony. This region has been the subject of numerous archaeological, architectural, and cemetery surveys.[1] These have provided data from which it has been possible to extrapolate the expansion of settlement during the second half of the eighteenth century. The distributions show that initial settlement was widely-separated in this frontier region (Figure 11.4A). Twenty years later it had

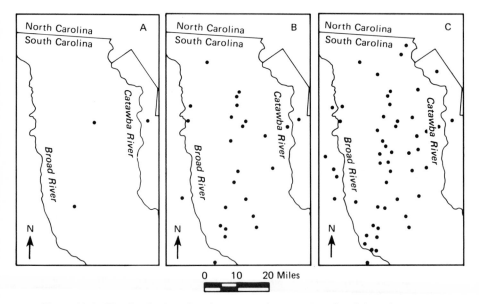

Figure 11.4 The distribution of settlements on the upper Broad and Catawba (Wateree) rivers in (A) 1760, (B) 1780, and (C) 1800. A trend through time toward even spacing is evident in the settlement patterns revealed by the distribution of archaeological sites, standing structures, and cemeteries. (From Site Inventory Record; Cemetery Records; Central Midlands Planning Council [1974]; Santee–Wateree Planning Council [1972]; Central Piedmont Planning Commission [1971]; and Catawba Regional Planning Council [1976].)

Table 11.2

Nearest-Neighbor Values for Settlement
Sites in North-Central South Carolina:
1760, 1780, and 1800

Date of settlement distribution	Nearest-neighbor value
1760	1.1256
1780	1.1307
1800	1.1610

spread out in linear fashion in the interriverine area as well as along the two rivers (Figure 11.4B). By the close of the century, settlement in these three areas had grown together (Figure 11.4C), filling in most of the remaining unoccupied territory. A trend toward even spacing is apparent in these maps as settlements spread outward from points of initial occupation to cover most of the region. If this trend is measured statistically by comparing nearest-neighbor values for each of the settlement distributions (Table 11.2), the anticipated change from a random distribution on the earliest map (Figure 11.4A) to an evenly spaced layout on the map of 1800 (Figure 11.4C) is clearly evident. Patterned change in the distribution of settlement sites is similar overall to that implied by documentary sources and supports the expectations derived from the model of insular frontier change.

Settlement Composition on the Frontier

The identification of specific settlement types is crucial to delineating the structure and organization of a frontier region. Apart from the entrepot, the two principal settlement types within the area of colonization are frontier towns and nucleated settlements. Each plays a specific role in the regional socioeconomic system and is characterized by certain physical attributes that reflect its function. A frontier town occupies a central position in the settlement hierarchy, therefore it should be the site of the greatest concentration of economic activity as well as one of the largest settlements in the area of colonization, second only to the entrepot. Nucleated settlements are smaller and are likely to have contained fewer of such specialized activities. Evidence of the relative size and content of these settlements should be discernible in the archaeological record.

Of the frontier settlements illustrated in Figure 11.1, few have been examined archaeologically. For this reason, the sample of sites is restricted to a limited number of examples. These include the frontier town of Camden and the nucleated settlements of Long Bluff and Ninety Six. Documentary sources reveal that Camden was the principal commercial settlement in the interior of South Carolina from the 1750s to the end of the century (Meriwether 1940:170). Ninety Six and Long Bluff, on the other hand, were primarily administrative centers that played much less significant roles in the economic system of the frontier (Gregg 1867:466; Watson 1970).

In order to determine the size, form, and content of these settlements, it is necessary to analyze archaeological evidence pertaining to each of these aspects of composition. Size and form may be ascertained from data relating to structure and activity distributions on the sites of each settlement. The function of the settlements, on the other hand, must be determined on the basis of their contents. Because the sites of all three settlements have been examined extensively, it is possible to determine size and form in all of them. The nature of their investigation, however, permits the contents of only two to be examined in some detail. The entire site of Camden (38KE1) was sampled and several areas were explored intensively (Lewis 1976). Ninety Six (38GN4) was examined by means of sampling and other exploratory techniques to reveal features that were subsequently excavated (Holschlag and Rodeffer 1977; South 1970). Long Bluff (38DA5) was investigated through the use of an extensive sampling methodology designed primarily to determine its basic layout and boundaries (Lewis 1978), but the data obtained from this work are insufficient to determine the nature of past activities at Long Bluff. On the basis of information obtained from the archaeological record at each of these sites, several statements may be made concerning the nature of the past settlements there.

With regard to absolute size, it has been estimated that the frontier towns of South Carolina would have been smaller than their contemporary counterparts in Europe because these colonial settlements would have lacked the large supporting populations associated with market towns. This condition should have resulted from the lower population density of the frontier region occasioned by the rapid spread and wide dispersal of settlement accompanying the occupation of an area of colonization (Potter 1965:661). Rather than following the traditional European process of settlement evolution—in which a settlement's relative status as a center of socioeconomic activity develops in response to increased population density and economic complexity (Blouet 1972:4; Grove 1972:560)—the frontier town arises in its central role without first passing through intermediate stages of growth. Nucleated settlements, lacking the concentration of various specialized activities associated with the frontier town, are likely to have fallen below the size limit of the latter. If established for a specialized purpose, such as the site of a court, these settlements might have contained a relatively small population similar to that found in the case of imposed political centers in contemporary Europe (Flatres 1971:176–179).

A comparison of the number of structures found at Camden, Ninety Six, and Long Bluff (Figures 11.5–11.7) reveals that these settlements contained an estimated 28, 12, and 10 structures respectively (Holschlag and Rodeffer 1977; Holschlag et al. 1978; Lewis 1978, 1980, 1981; South 1971). The three settlements appear to fall into two groups in terms of size, reflecting the predicted difference between frontier towns and nucleated settlements. Camden's size also compares favorably with that of contemporary frontier towns in neighboring North Carolina (Lewis 1980:186) but falls well below the size of English market towns of the eighteenth century (Lewis 1977:178–179).

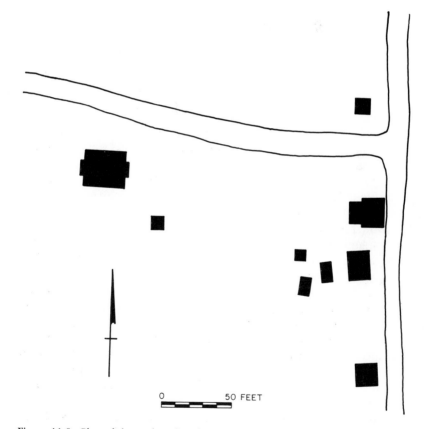

Figure 11.5 Plan of the nucleated settlement of Ninety Six in the 1770s as revealed by archaeological investigations. Military features associated with its Revolutionary War occupation have been omitted. (From Holschlag and Rodeffer 1977; South 1970.)

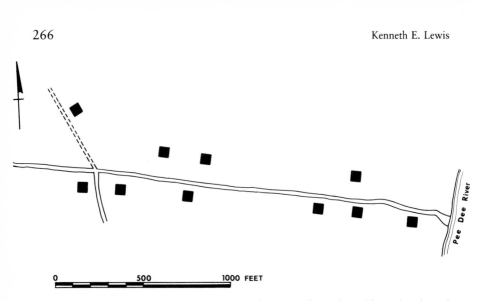

Figure 11.6   Plan of the nucleated settlement of Long Bluff as indicated by archaeological investigations. (From Lewis 1978.)

An examination of settlement layout reveals that the disparity in size is also reflected in the layout of the three settlements. All three of the settlements were situated at crossroads along principal overland transport routes. Ninety Six and Long Bluff developed as row settlements (Figures 11.5 and 11.6), a European form usually associated with small trading settlements (Page 1927:448). Its linear form was adaptive for small settlements in that it permitted equal access of all of its parts to the road (Beresford and St. Joseph 1958:126–127).

Camden, however, exhibits a more complex pattern of settlement (Figure 11.7). In addition to lying along either side of a main road, Camden's structures were also arranged perpendicular to it, creating a grid layout. The appearance of a grid reflects the settlement's greater size as well as its more complex organization. Designed to consolidate space as well as to provide easy access to all parts of the settlement, the grid plan was employed extensively in European colonial town planning (Reps 1965:176). Camden's original survey, completed in the early 1770s (South Carolina, Records of the General Assembly, Act #1702 [1798]), indicates that such a layout was envisioned by its planners, however, the form of actual settlement appears to have been varied slightly from their original intent.

The recognition of activity patterning in the three frontier settlements has been more difficult to ascertain. Only at Camden and Ninety Six were archaeological data adequate to measure activity variation, and even here we were able to discern only the most basic patterning. Because the function

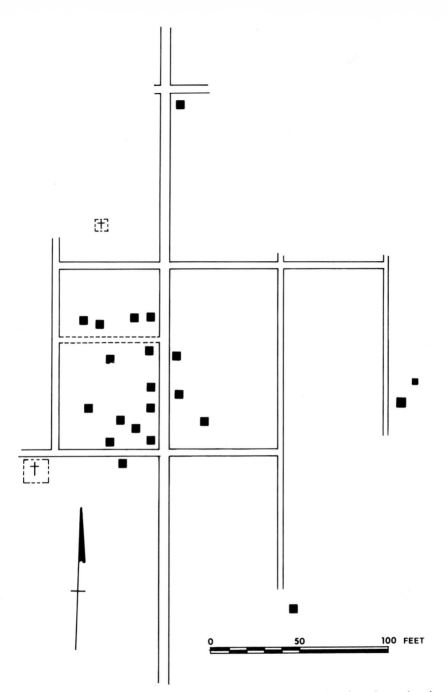

Figure 11.7 Plan of the frontier town of Camden in the 1770s based on the results of archaeological investigations. Military features built during its Revolutionary War occupation are not shown. (From Lewis 1976.)

of the frontier town makes it the focus of economic and other integrating institutions within an area of colonization, these settlements are likely to exhibit a relatively higher occurrence of structures and activity areas devoted to economic and other specialized activities than would be the case in other frontier settlements. In order to examine this assumption, a comparison of the class of artifacts associated with domestic activities may be made in each distinguishable structure-based activity area at both sites. Ten such areas were defined at Camden and two have been distinguished by data obtained from the site of Ninety Six. A comparison of the percentage frequencies of occurrence of the two artifact classes reveals that in the town area of Ninety Six as a whole and in three areas at Camden, domestic activity artifacts comprise from 79 to 84% of the total. This group of areas contains the highest frequency of these artifacts and is most likely to represent the archaeological output of domestic occupations. A second group of areas at Camden exhibits a slightly lower percentage frequency range of domestic artifacts (71–74%) and may represent the remains of mixed activity occupations, perhaps residences combined with businesses. A third group, composed of two groups at Camden and one at Ninety Six, contains the lowest frequencies of domestic artifact occurrence (60–67%) and is likely to represent specialized activity sites. Two of these areas—the Ninety Six jail and Joseph Kershaw's brewery in Camden (Holschlag et al. 1978; Lewis 1976:59)—are known to have been nondomestic in nature. This documentary information supports the archaeological conclusions regarding the function of these and other areas at the two sites.

The numerical dominance of domestic activity artifacts at Ninety Six suggests that this settlement was not a focus of specialized activity on the frontier. With the exception of the jail, it appears to have been largely a domestic settlement similar to the nucleated settlements described in the model. In contrast, Camden possessed a relatively smaller domestic component. Here the greater part of the settlement seems to have consisted of a combination of business–residences and specialized activity areas. In addition to the areas identified on the basis of artifact content, two additional specialized activity structures at Camden were identified on the basis of their architecture—a powder magazine and a jail similar in form to that at Ninety Six (Calmes 1968; Lewis 1981). The concentration of specialized activities at Camden reflects its role as a frontier town and sets it apart from other colonial settlements because of its content as well as its size.

Material evidence from South Carolina permitted us to discern several important aspects of insular frontier colonization. By observing the changing distribution of settlement over time, it was possible to demonstrate a trend toward an evenly spaced pattern of settlement within the area of colonization. The hierarchy of settlement associated with regions of insular frontier colonization has also been observed archaeologically in South Carolina. An examination of the form and content of three excavated sites provided evidence of a frontier town and two nucleated settlements, the two principal site types found in the interior of an insular frontier region. Their presence, and that of the dispersed settlements illustrated in the regional maps (Figure 11.4A–C), indicate that the composition and organization of this area compared favorably with those predicted in the model and demonstrate that these aspects of the colonization process are discernible archaeologically.

CONCLUSIONS

A process of insular frontier colonization appears to have dominated the historical development of areas occupied as a result of the agricultural expansion of complex states. English colonization in eighteenth-century South Carolina has provided a case study in which aspects of this process were examined through documentary sources as well as the material record. Each of these data sets was assumed to be capable of providing evidence of insular frontier change when examined in terms of a model of this process. In order to explore insular frontier change in South Carolina, a model capable of predicting the form, content, and evolution of a colonial region was developed. The model's characteristics were then examined in light of data obtained from the documentary and material records. Both sources provided information regarding settlement location, patterning, and composition. The results showed that in the study area the overall distribution of settlements, their nature, and their change through time are discernible. It is particularly important to note that material evidence by itself permitted the recognition of the crucial characteristics of insular frontier change.

This study was intended as a general exploration of insular frontier development in South Carolina. Because it was a preliminary investigation, it has focused only on certain aspects of this process. These involved settlement and activity patterning and reflect, to a large extent, the nature of the available archaeological data for this region. These data were obtained, for the most part, from archaeological surveys and initial exploratory excavations at specific sites. This work was designed to produce only basic site information and not data sufficiently detailed to measure all aspects of settlement form and composition. Material evidence capable of addressing such questions at these sites must await the completion of large-scale, intensive investigations aimed at producing this information. Intensive archaeological excavations will permit gathering of data capable of addressing problems of inter- and intrasite varibility useful in discerning patterning related to settlement organization and function. The recognition of such functionally related patterning has been a major component of archaeological research design and this approach should yield profitable results in the analysis of colonial settlement.

Although this essay concentrates only on particular aspects of insular frontier colonization, it is likely that other important elements of this process will also be recognizable through studies of material evidence. Archaeological data can provide a detailed account of past processes of sociocultural change and, in many cases, may supply the most complete record of the past. Even in the context of historic sites, material evidence should be seen as much more than a footnote to the written record. The formation of the archaeological record is clearly linked to the form, organization, and content of the cultural processes that produced it. The identification and exploration of these processes can permit the description and explanation of historical developments in regions where the processes are found to have occurred. When employed together with explanatory models, archaeology may be used to investigate a variety of processes that underlie past continuity and change.

Insular frontier colonization is associated with agricultural expansion by complex societies. Because of the large role these societies have played in the development of the modern world, this form of colonization often appears to dominate and divert attention from all others. It must be seen instead as only one of several processes of frontier change, each of which represents an adaptation to the social, economic, and political conditions faced by societies in movement. Cosmopolitan frontiers of several types have also characterized the expansion of nation-states (see Hardesty, Chapter 9, this volume) and a diversity of frontiers have been identified in present and past societies discussed in this volume and elsewhere (for example, see Miller and Steffen 1977; Savage and Thompson 1979). The occurrence of many frontier types indicates that the systematic outward movement of peoples into new lands has assumed many forms. Because the greater part of these frontier movements are likely to have taken place in the distant past where written documentation was poor or nonexistant, the importance of employing archaeology in their investigation cannot be overestimated. The study of frontiers appears to hold the key to explaining a significant part of the past, and archaeology can play a potentially large role in obtaining the data necessary to turn that key.

NOTE

1. Data used in these surveys have come from a variety of sources. The most comprehensive include: Site Inventory Record; Cemetery Records; Central Midlands Planning Council (1974);

Santee-Wateree Planning Council (1972); Central Piedmont Planning Commission (1971); and Catawba Regional Planning Council (1976).

REFERENCES

Beresford, M. W., and J. K. S. St. Joseph
    1958 *Medieval England, an aerial survey.* Cambridge University Press, Cambridge.
Berry, Brian J. L.
    1967 *Geography of market centers and retail distribution.* Prentice-Hall, Englewood Cliffs, N.J.
Blouet, Brian W.
    1972 Factors influencing the evolution of settlement patterns. In *Man, settlement, and urbanism,* edited by Ruth Tringham and G. W. Dimbleby, pp. 3–15. Duckworth, London.
Brown, Richard Maxwell
    1963 *The South Carolina Regulators.* Harvard University Press, Cambridge, Mass.
Calmes, Alan
    1968 The British Revolutionary War fortifications of Camden, South Carolina. *Conference on Historic Site Archaeology Papers* 2:50–60.
Casagrande, Joseph B., Stephen I. Thompson, and Philip D. Young
    1964 Colonization as a research frontier. In *Process and pattern in culture, essays in honor of Julian H. Steward,* edited by Robert A. Manners, pp. 281–325. Aldine, Chicago.
Catawba Regional Planning Council
    1976 *Historic sites surveys, Chester, Lancaster, Union, and York Counties.* Catawba Regional Planning Council, Rock Hill, S.C.
Cemetery Records
    South Caroliniana Library, University of South Carolina. Columbia, S.C.
Central Midlands Planning Council
    1974 *An inventory and plan for the preservation of historical properties in the Central Midlands region.* Central Midlands Planning Council, Columbia, S.C.
Central Piedmont Planning Commission
    1971 *Survey of historic sites, Chester County.* Central Piedmont Planning Commission, Rock Hill, S.C.
Clark, Philip J., and Francis C. Evans
    1954 Distance to nearest neighbor as a measure of spatial relationships in populations. *Ecology* 35(4):445–453.
Clowse, Converse D.
    1971 *Economic beginnings in colonial South Carolina.* University of South Carolina Press, Columbia, S.C.
Coleman, Kenneth
    1976 *Colonial Georgia, a history.* Scribner's, New York.
Crane, Verner W.
    1929 *The southern frontier, 1670–1732.* University of Michigan Press, Ann Arbor; reprint ed. Ann Arbor Paperbacks, 1956.
Drayton, John
    1802 *A view of South Carolina.* W. P. Young, Charleston; reprint ed. The Reprint Co., Spartanburg, S.C., 1972.

Earle, Carville, and Ronald Hoffman
   1976   Staple crops and urban development in the eighteenth-century South. *Perspectives in American History* 10:7–80.
Faden, William
   1780   A map of South Carolina and a part of Georgia. Color map on 4 sheets, 146 × 123 cm, scale ca. 1:320,000. London.
Flatres, P.
   1971   Hamlet and village. In *Man and his habitat, essays presented to Emyr Estyn Evans,* edited by R. H. Buchanan, Emrys Jones, and Desmond McCourt, pp. 165–185. Barnes & Noble, New York.
Gould, J. D.
   1972   *Economic growth in history, survey and analysis.* Methuen & Co, London.
Gray, H. Peter
   1976   *A generalized history of international trade.* Holmes & Meier, New York.
Gray, Lewis Cecil
   1933   *History of agriculture in the southern United States to 1860,* 2 vols. Carnegie Institute of Washington; reprint ed. Peter Smith, Glouster, Mass., 1958.
Gregg, Alexander
   1867   *History of the old Cheraws.* Richardson, New York; reprint ed. The Reprint Co., Spartanburg, S.C., 1965.
Grove, David
   1972   The function and future of urban centres. In *Man, settlement, and urbanism,* edited by Ruth Tringham and G. W. Dimbleby, pp. 559–565. Duckworth, London.
Heighton, Robert F., and Kathleen A. Deagan
   1972   A new formula for dating kaolin clay pipestems. *Conference on Historic Site Archaeology Papers* 6:220–229.
Holschlag, Stephanie L., and Michael J. Rodeffer
   1977   *Ninety Six: exploratory excavations in the village.* Star Fort Historical Commission, Ninety Six, S.C.
Holschlag, Stephanie L., Michael J. Rodeffer, and Marvin L. Cann
   1978   *Ninety Six: the jail.* Star Fort Historical Commission, Ninety Six, S.C.
Hudson, John C.
   1969   A locational theory for rural settlement. *Annals of the Association of American Geographers* 59:365–381.
Lewis, Kenneth E.
   1976   Camden, a frontier town in eighteenth century South Carolina. *University of South Carolina, Institute of Archeology and Anthropology, Anthropological Studies* 2.
   1977   Sampling the archeological frontier: regional models and component analysis. In *Research strategies in historical archeology,* edited by Stanley South, pp. 151–201. Academic Press, New York.
   1978   An archeological survey of Long Bluff State Park, Darlington County, South Carolina. *University of South Carolina, Institute of Archeology and Anthropology, Research Manuscript Series* 129.
   1980   Pattern and layout on the South Carolina frontier: an archaeological investigation of settlement function. *North American Archaeologist* 1(2):177–200.
   1981   The Camden jail and market site: a report on preliminary investigations. *University of South Carolina, Institute of Archeology and Anthropology, Research Manuscript Series* 171.
Leyburn, James G.
   1935   *Frontier folkways.* Yale University Press, New Haven, Conn.

Mercer, Henry C.
  1923 The dating of old houses. *Bucks County Historical Society Papers 5*. reprint ed.
        Bucks County Historical Society, New Hope, Penn., 1976.
Meriwether, Robert L.
  1940 *The expansion of South Carolina, 1729–1765*. Southern Publishers, Kingsport,
        Tenn.
Miller, David Harry, and Jerome O. Steffen (editors)
  1977 *The frontier, comparative studies*. University of Oklahoma Press, Norman.
Mills, Robert
  1826 *Statistics of South Carolina*. Hurlbut and Lloyd, Charleston; reprint ed. The Re-
        print Co., Spartanburg, S.C., 1972.
Mouzon, Henry
  1775 An accurate map of North and South Carolina. Col. map on 2 sheets, each 50 ×
        142 cm., scale ca. 1:530,000. Robert Sayer and J. Bennett, London.
Nelson, Lee H.
  1968 Nail chronology as an aid to dating old buildings. *American Association of State
        and Local History, Technical Leaflet 48*.
Noël Hume, Ivor
  1970 *A guide to artifacts of colonial America*. Knopf, New York.
Page, William
  1927 Notes on the types of English villages and their distribution. *Antiquity* 1(4):447–
        468.
Peet, Richard
  1970–ﾠVon Thünen theory and the dynamics of agricultural expansion. *Explorations in
  1971 Economic History* 8:181–201.
Petty, Julian J.
  1943 The growth and distribution of population in South Carolina. *South Carolina State
        Planning Board, Bulletin* 11: reprint ed. The Reprint Co., Spartanburg, S.C.,
        1975.
Potter, J.
  1965 The growth of population in America, 1700–1860. In *Population in history: essays
        in historical demography*, edited by D. V. Glass and D. E. C. Eversley, pp. 631–
        679. Aldine, Chicago.
Reps, John W.
  1965 *The making of urban America, a history of city planning in the United States*.
        Princeton University Press, Princeton, N.J.
Santee-Wateree Planning Council
  1972 *Historic preservation plan and inventory*, Santee-Wateree Planning Council.
        Sumter, S.C.
Savage, William W., Jr., and Stephen I. Thompson (editors)
  1979 *The frontier, comparative studies*, Vol. 2. University of Oklahoma Press, Norman.
Schulz, Judith J.
  1972 *The rise and decline of Camden as South Carolina's major inland trading center,
        1751–1829: a historical geographic study*. Unpublished master's thesis, Depart-
        ment of Geography, University of South Carolina.
  1976 The hinterland of Revolutionary Camden, South Carolina. *Southeastern Geog-
        rapher* 16(2):91–97.
Sellers, Leila
  1934 *Charleston business on the eve of the American Revolution*. University of North
        Carolina Press, Chapel Hill.

Site Inventory Record
    Institute of Archeology and Anthropology, University of South Carolina, Columbia, S.C.
South, Stanley
    1970 Exploratory archeology at Ninety Six. *University of South Carolina, Institute of Archeology and Anthropology, Research Manuscript Series 6.*
    1971 Exploratory archeology at Holmes' fort, the blockhouse, and jail redoubt at Ninety Six. *Conference on Historic Site Archaeology Papers 5:35–50.*
    1972 Evolution and horizon as revealed in ceramic analysis in historical archaeology. *Conference on Historic Site Archaeology Papers 6:71–116.*
    1977 *Method and theory in historical archeology.* Academic Press, New York.
South Carolina, Records of the General Assembly
    Acts, Bills and Joint Resolutions, 1691–1972. South Carolina Archives, Columbia, S.C.
South Carolina Archives
    n.d. Guide maps to development of South Carolina parishes, districts, and counties, from maps in South Carolina county inventories made by the W.P.A. Historical Records Survey, Columbia, S.C.
Steffen, Jerome O.
    1980 *Comparative frontiers: a proposal for studying the American West.* University of Oklahoma Press, Norman.
Thompson, Stephen I.
    1973 Pioneer colonization, a cross-cultural view. *Addison-Wesley Modules in Anthropology 33.*
Thünen, Johann Heinrich von
    1966 *Isolated state; an English translation of* Der Isolierte Staat, translated by Carla M. Wartenberg, edited with an introduction by Peter Hall. Pergamon Press, Oxford.
Walker, Iain C.
    1967 Statistical methods for dating clay pipe fragments. *Post Medieval Archaeology 1:90–101.*
Wallerstein, Immanuel
    1974 *The modern world system, capitalist agriculture and the origins of the European world economy in the sixteenth century.* Academic Press, New York.
    1980 *The modern world system II, merchantilism and the consolidation of the European world economy, 1600–1750.* Academic Press, New York.
Watson, Margaret J.
    1970 *Greenwood County sketches.* Attic Press, Greenwood, S.C.

CHAPTER 12

The Arctic Frontier of Norse Greenland

THOMAS H. McGOVERN

Department of Anthropology
Hunter College, City University of New York
New York, New York

> *The answer to your query as to what people go to seek in that country (Greenland) and why they fare thither through such great perils is to be sought in man's three-fold nature. . . . The third (motive) is a desire for gain; for men seek wealth wherever they have heard that gain is to be gotten, though on the other hand there may be great dangers too. But in Greenland . . . whatever comes from other lands is high in price, for the land is so distant from other lands that men seldom visit it. And everything that is needed to improve the land must be purchased abroad, both iron and all the timber.*
>
> (*King's Mirror*, ca. 1217–1260, Larsen 1917:142)

INTRODUCTION

Recent research into the calculation of optimal foraging strategies and the investigation of observed deviations from optimal balances of efficiency, uncertainty, and hazard (Jochim 1976; Perlman 1980; Winterhalder and Smith 1981) has tended to concentrate upon hunter–gatherers only loosely tied to larger world systems. It may prove useful to also investigate archaeologically the extent to which asymmetric political and economic relationships may induce noticeably suboptimal balances of cost and benefit in the subsistence of peripheral populations. As the quotation above suggests,

275

the medieval Norse colony in West Greenland occupied a distant periphery of the European market system, and an investigation of its relationship to the continent may provide a valuable case study.

In complex societies local subsistence strategies are often as strongly conditioned by proximity to market centers as by the constraints of local ecology. This fundamental observation of the locational geographers (Chisolm 1962; Cristaller 1933; Haggett 1965; Thünen 1875) has influenced cultural anthropologists (Barlett 1980) and archaeologists (Clarke 1977; Hodder and Orton 1976; Johnson 1975; Vita-Finzi and Higgs 1970) for some time, and has had an equally important impact on economic history (Wallerstein 1974, 1979). Movement costs tend to determine both the intensity of interaction between market center and peripheral producer and the types of goods exchanged.

The sixteenth- to nineteenth-century expansion of the European world system (and the eventual development of competing cores in former peripheries) was closely linked to the reduction of the costs and hazards of long distance voyages (Davis 1973; Mendlessohn 1976). These changing core–periphery relationships are increasingly providing a central focus for North American historical archaeology (Paynter 1982). However, this sixteenth- to seventeenth-century transatlantic expansion was not the first extension of European settlement and economy into the western hemisphere. The asymmetric economic relationships that so enraged the Boston merchants of the 1770s had Medieval counterparts in the Scandinavian North Atlantic.

The island groups of the North Atlantic had been settled over a period of about 300 years during the Viking age by Scandinavians sailing from Norway and the British Isles. The nearer island groups (Shetlands, Orkneys, Northern Hebrides) were settled in the eighth century A.D. while the larger and more distant islands of Iceland and Greenland were initially colonized around A.D. 870 and A.D. 985 (Jones 1964). The short-lived Vinland colony seems to have failed in the early eleventh century (A. Ingstad 1977; B. Wallace, personal communication, 1982), and for the next 500 years Greenland remained the westernmost (and most marginal) of the medieval Scandinavian North Atlantic communities.

The causes of the initial migrations are still debated, but rapidly improving maritime technology, expanding population, warm and relatively stable ninth- to twelfth-century climate, and the desire for political independence (so strongly expressed in the Icelandic sagas) all probably played a role (McGovern 1980/1981). The political independence of the island communities from the developing Norwegian state was to prove short-lived. The nearer islands were incorporated into the Norwegian kingdom in the twelfth century, while Iceland and Greenland held out until 1262–1264 (Sveinsson 1953).

A growing body of archaeological (Bigelow 1984; Buckland *et al.* 1982; Donaldson *et al.* 1981; McGovern and Bigelow n.d.; Mathiesen *et al.* 1981; Morris 1981) and documentary (Gelsinger 1981; Gunnarson 1980) data suggest that the subsequent development of interregional trade in the Scandinavian North Atlantic closely approximates von Thünen's market proximity model. Late Norse Shetland (Bigelow 1984) and some of the Arctic islands of northern Norway (Bertelsen 1979; Mathiesen *et al.* 1981) seem to have been drawn into a growing bulk trade with the mainland—exchanging dried fish for grain and manufactured goods. Iceland originally made high-quality woolen cloth its staple export, but also gradually shifted to dried fish as the demand in Hanseatic, English, and south European markets expanded dramatically (Gelsinger 1981). While the nearby Shetlands and Orkneys seem to have been closely bound to the Norwegian homeland in the later Middle Ages, contact with Iceland was less regular and the medieval sources are full of Icelandic complaints about the infrequency of sailings (Gunnarson 1980; Ogilvie 1981).

Greenland was still more remote, and climatic changes in the later Middle Ages (Gribben and Lamb 1978) were to significantly raise the hazards of the Greenland voyage. This position on the medieval "world's rim" tended to restrict the Greenland trade to low-bulk, high-value items (like metal in exchange for walrus ivory and bear hide). The Greenlanders also did not seem to have shared in the expansion of the dried fish trade. As argued later, fishing seems to have played a minor role in the distinctive subsistence strategy of the Norse Greenlanders. Instead of intensifying a component of local subsistence systems, the Norse Greenlanders carried out a remarkable long-range "cash hunt" for ivory and hide—a hunt they called the *Nordrsetur* voyage. Before we turn to a model for the Nordrsetur hunt and a discussion of the impact of transatlantic trade on Norse Greenland's ultimately unsuccessful struggle to survive climatic change and culture contact, it may be helpful to briefly outline local Greenlandic settlement, subsistence, and political organization (McGovern 1981).

LOCAL GREENLANDIC SETTLEMENT AND SUBSISTENCE

While the eventual extinction of the Norse colony in Greenland also destroyed most of the documentary evidence for the settlement, the hard work of several generations of predominately Danish archaeological researchers has created a rich body of data that supplement remaining documentary fragments and modern biological data (Andreasen 1980, 1981, 1982; Bruun 1896, 1916; Krogh 1967, 1982; McGovern 1979a *et seq.*;

Meldgaard 1977; Nørlund 1924; Nørlund and Stenberger 1934; Roussell 1936, 1941; Vebaek 1943 *et seq.*). This combined data base reveals that the Norse settled two areas on the low Arctic southwest coast of Greenland (Figure 12.1). The more southerly Eastern Settlement in the modern Narssaq and Julianehaab districts was the larger, with a maximum population around 4000–5000. The smaller Western Settlement, with a maximum population of about 1000–1500) lay some 400 km to the north in modern

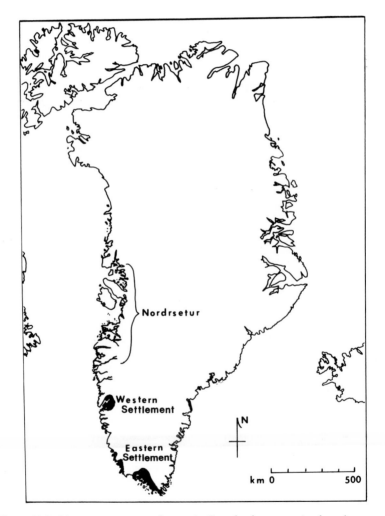

Figure 12.1 Norse permanent settlement in Greenland was restricted to the two areas providing pasture vegetation for the Norse domestic animals.

Godthaab district. As a number of researchers have noted (McGovern 1980b; McGovern and Jordan 1982; Roussell 1936), the location of these settlements seems to have been largely determined by the distribution of plant communities suitable for pasture. The scattered pastures of the southwest coast were critical to the survival of imported domestic animals (mainly cattle, sheep, and goats) whose wool, milk, and meat formed a mainstay of the Norse economy in Greenland. While limited use may have been made of local and imported wild plants (McGovern *et al.* 1983; Kristjansson 1980), Greenland seems to have always been beyond the limits of economically viable grain agriculture (Fredskild 1973; Larsen 1917; McGovern and Bigelow n.d.).

While the pasture requirements of their domestic animals seem to have effectively tied the permanent Norse settlements to the inner portions of a few of the southwestern fjords, the Norse also hunted wild animals inhabiting other resource spaces. Caribou were taken in some numbers, especially in the western settlement (cf. McGovern 1979a; McGovern and Jordan 1982), and seals (especially the migratory harp seal) seem to have been a particularly vital resource to smaller farmers with fewer cattle (McGovern 1982). Seabirds, ptarmigan, and small whales filled out the Norse diet in Greenland. While larger whales were probably eagerly consumed whenever they became beached (Kristjansson 1980), there is no evidence that the Norse Greenlanders practiced active hunting of the baleen whales.

As noted, there is also no evidence that they made extensive use of the fisheries that made such a contribution to interregional trade and local subsistence in the eastern portion of the Scandinavian North Atlantic. Despite fine-mesh wet sieving (1-mm mesh) and extensive whole-soil column sampling (McGovern *et al.* 1983) carried out in the major midden excavations in the western settlement from 1976 to 1977 (Andreasen 1980; McGovern and Bigelow 1977; Meldgaard 1977), and the smaller test pits of the 1981 survey (McGovern and Jordan 1982), only a handful of fishbone was recovered (as in the older unsieved excavations (Degerbøl 1929 *et seq.*). Conditions of organic preservation in the Norse middens are generally superb so fish remains would have been preserved—hair, wool, insects, feathers, and baleen are commonly recovered, as are large quantities of mammal and bird bone in good condition. While some fish may have been fed to cattle or otherwise eliminated from the archaeological record, the excavations of contemporary Norse sites in Shetland and northern Norway produced collections that are 60–75% fishbone (Bigelow 1984; Mathiesen *et al.* 1981), making total attrition of fish remains an unlikely argument.

Fishing technology is also conspicuously absent in the extensive excavated artifact collections reported from Norse Greenland. While pierced steatite or pecked-pebble linesinkers are common finds in late Norse contexts in Shetland (Bigelow 1984) and Iceland (Thordur Tomasson, personal communication, 1980), less than a half-dozen possible linesinkers have been recovered from the over 50 excavations of Norse farms in Greenland. While more research is clearly needed to clarify this problem, it seems certain that the later medieval Norse Greenlanders did not expand their fishing in response to the growing continental demand for dried fish.

LOCAL GREENLANDIC POLITICAL ORGANIZATION

Like contemporary Iceland, Norse Greenland seems to have undergone a transition from chiefly oligarchy to provincial status in an increasingly stratified medieval state in the period 1000–1264. The initial settlement was made by aristocratic *Landnamsmen* (first or pioneer settlers) like Eirik the Red, who took the best pastureland for themselves and parceled out lesser farm sites among followers and later arrivals. Many of the surviving place names (e.g., Einarsfjord, Eiriksfjord, Hrafnsfjord, Eiriksey) reflect this initially broad division of land and resources. Archaeologically the chiefly manors can be distinguished easily from smaller farms by the size of their associated farm buildings and the richness of the pastures within the 5-km radius "site territories" (Higgs 1972, 1975; McGovern 1980a, b, 1981). As in Iceland, it is likely that this initial division promoted future intensification of differences in rank, as small landholders' dependence upon the larger farms increased due to periodic hunting failure and stock loss (McGovern 1981; Sveinsson 1953).

Christianity arrived soon after the new settlement, but may have initially had little impact on the chieftains' power (which had always been partly religious in nature) as small local churches seem to have been run as the family property of the landowner (Krogh 1967). A more important change came in 1127 when the Greenlanders traded a live polar bear to the Norwegian king for their own bishop (*Einar Sokkason's Story*, trans. Jones 1964). The new bishop was presented with a large manor and some of the colony's best grazing land at Gardar (modern Igaliko) in the eastern settlement. Under a succession of foreign-born bishops, the power and holdings of the Greenlandic church grew rapidly, and the single surviving episcopal steward's report (mid-fourteenth century) indicates that the church in Greenland then controlled two-thirds of the best grazing land in the eastern settlement. The disproportionately large size of the Greenlandic churches has long been noted (McGovern 1981; Nørlund 1936), and they were well furnished with imported bells and stained glass. As argued elsewhere, late Norse Greenland seems to have become a sharply stratified community;

with a few large farmers, the king's representative, and especially the bishop at Gardar exercising considerable control over Greenlandic economy and society (McGovern 1980a, 1981).

THE IMPORTANCE OF TRANSATLANTIC TRADE

Norse Greenland was thus a small, increasingly hierarchical community whose subsistence economy was based upon both pasture-dependent caribou and domestic animals and seasonally aggregated migratory seals. Despite the apparent lack of grain or large amounts of fish, the Greenlandic subsistence economy seems to have allowed both survival and modest prosperity for nearly 500 years. The degree to which this small community was influenced by external market forces has been a matter of some debate. Some scholars (Nørlund 1936) have suggested that the decline of contact between Greenland and Europe in the fourteenth and fifteenth centuries was a major cause of the decline and extinction of the colony. More recently, the Danish historian Finn Gad (1970) argued that overseas trade must have played a minor role in the Greenlandic economy, and that its reduction could not have been fatal to the colony. To evaluate these contrasting positions, it is necessary to estimate the volume of trade (as measured by possible cargo size), the frequency of voyages, and the value of the imported items to the Greenlanders. Gad (1970:125) argues convincingly that the cargo capacity of the clinker-built *knarrer* used in the transatlantic trade was small—much lower than that of the Hanseatic *cogs* that were to replace Scandinavian-style shipping in the North Sea and North Atlantic (Crumlin-Pedersen 1972; McGrail 1980). Gad also totals the number of recorded sailings to Greenland and concludes that the average household in Norse Greenland could have consumed no more than 27–67 kg of imports yearly. While there may have been unrecorded voyages not included in Gad's totals, it is certain that contact was always irregular and subject to considerable delay. In 1279 Pope Nicholas wrote that the see of Gardar in Greenland was "visited only infrequently on account of the [unpredictably] cruel ocean" (Gad 1970:122). In 1308 Bishop Arni of Bergen sent Bishop Thord of Greenland a letter that provided news of the previous eight years. Normally seafarers would set out in early summer, winter in Greenland, and return the next summer, but delays and disasters were not uncommon.

There is some artifactual and linguistic evidence that supports Gad's thesis of limited contact. While the Norse Greenlanders seem to have participated in some of the changes in artifact form and frequency that characterize the late Norse transition in the eastern Atlantic Islands (e.g., transition to double-sided combs and foliate decorative motifs), they were not affected by a host of other changes such as the reintroduction of home-made pottery, rectangular steatite vessels, and a distinctive marrow-extraction technique (Bigelow 1984). The Greenlanders' written and spoken language seems to have diverged from the common Scandinavian of the later Middle Ages. Conservative grammatic forms and a local variant of the runic alphabet distinguished the later Greenlanders from the other North Atlantic communities (Moltke 1936) and may likewise hint at greater isolation.

It would thus seem that part of Gad's thesis is undeniably correct: contact was irregular and the cargo capacity of available transatlantic shipping was too small to allow the regular exchange of bulk cargos of low unit value (especially perishable ones like fish and grain that would not survive long-term storage in bulking centers at either end of the trade link). Gad is thus also correct in his assertion that the Greenlandic subsistence economy had to succeed or fail on its own—no reliance could be placed on continental grain supplies in times of scarcity. In the short term, the Greenlandic economy seems to have been the most tightly bounded of all the North Atlantic settlements.

However, the short-term self-sufficiency of the Norse Greenlanders does not seem to have discouraged them from expending limited time and resources on acquiring just the sort of high-unit-value, low-bulk, imperishable trade goods that could tempt Europeans' "desire for gain." Despite the low volume of the imports and their irregular delivery, the Norse Greenlanders seemed to have been dependent upon them in the long term. One import critical to the long-term maintenance of Norse technology in Greenland was metal—bronze and iron. Bronze was used for decorative purposes, furniture fittings, and especially for the common, round tripodal cooking pots. Iron was even more vital, being used for boat and house construction as well as for axes, knives, scissors, and many other items.

Greenland has extensive deposits of bog iron, and some ore extraction seems to have taken place on a few of the larger farms (Ø29, Ø 47,V 51: Nørlund 1930, Nørlund and Stenberger 1934; Roussell 1936, 1941). However, large-scale iron smelting was dependent upon massive quantities of charcoal (Clarke 1979). Local dwarf willow and birch thickets were probably rapidly cleared at first settlement (Fredskild 1973; McGovern and Jordan 1982) and driftwood supplies would have been needed for wooden artifacts (Roussell 1941, Figs. 169, 172–176), construction timber, and raw material for boat building (Kristjansson 1980).

There is pervasive archaeological evidence of a chronic metal shortage in Norse Greenland. Ingenious bone substitutes for Norse artifacts normally made of metal are common. These include a number of whalebone belt buckles (Roussell 1941, Fig. 161, no. 101, Fig. 164), a whalebone battle-axe head (Roussell 1936, Fig. 74), and even a working padlock of bone

(Vebaek 1956b). Metal cooking pots were sometimes repaired with locally abundant steatite (Roussell 1941:256, no. 94). This impression of "metal poverty" is reinforced by comparison with other contemporary rural communities. While sampling and excavation problems (and variation in conditions of preservation) make a rigorously quantified comparison of iron artifact frequencies somewhat problematical, it is very clear that much more iron and bronze was available to be lost by Norse farmers at Sandwick in the Shetlands (Bigelow 1984) and at the English villages of Wharram Percy (Hurst 1979:108–121), Barton Blount, and Goltho (Beresford 1975:79–98). Metal finds at these peasant settlements closer to centers of marketing and manufacture are many times the size of collections from the bishop's palace at Gardar or the manor at Brattahlid (Nørlund 1930; Nørlund and Stenberger 1934). It thus seems that the Greenlandic demand for metal could only be met through participation in overseas trade, and that that demand was not being completely satisfied. It would thus seem that in the long term, the acquisition of trade goods and contact with the European homeland *was* important to the maintenence of Norse technology in Greenland.

The maintenence of a metal-based technology, however, may not have been the only incentive to active Greenlandic participation in transatlantic trade. The social (or "ideotechnic") component of the European connection should not be overlooked either. The increasingly powerful Greenlandic churchmen, like the resident royal officer, drew their legal authority and its material trappings from Europe. They were also clearly less isolated than the common farmer. Greenlandic royal agents engaged in illegal land speculation in Norway while brother bishops in Iceland and Norway sent their colleague in Gardar rich ecclesiastical vestments, receipts for crowberry communion wine, and patterns for the latest fashions in secular dress (Gad 1970). Episcopal signet rings in gold (Nørlund 1930) as well as church bells probably cast in England (Meldgaard 1977) crossed the North Atlantic along with timber and iron.

A European-derived elite taste in clothing (as well as church doctrine and royal orders) seems to have affected Greenlandic commoners. A number of nearly complete sets of fifteenth-century clothing preserved by permafrost in the Eastern Settlement cemetery at Herjolfsnes indicate that even the everyday dress of lower-ranking Greenlanders imitated contemporary European styles. Long woolen gowns, hoods with trailing liripipe streamers, tall cylindrical "Burgundian" caps, and button-fronted jackets all suggest temperate Europe rather than Arctic Greenland (Nørlund 1924). Wear marks and patches on the grave clothing and the carvings of Thule Inuit, who saw the living Norsemen (Gulløv 1982), strongly suggest that these were not simply ceremonial dress.

As is argued later, there is considerable evidence that the Eurocentric Greenlandic elite was able to affect a good deal more than clothing fashions in this ultimate periphery of the Scandinavian North Atlantic, and that they may have acted as better agents of European commerce than stewards of their own community. However, it may be useful to first attempt to model the remarkable Nordrsetur hunt that produced goods that could maintain this irregular but important link to Europe. Our evidence for the hunt is documentary, place name, biogeographical, locational, artifactual, and zoo-archaeological, and these diverse data sources are discussed in turn before the model is presented.

DOCUMENTARY EVIDENCE FOR THE NORDRSETUR

Our earliest written record of the northern hunting ground dates to the approximately 1170 source *Historia Norvegiae* (see Jansen 1972) which mentions Norse hunters operating far to the North of the settlements, and their contact with the *Skraeling* (who were probably Thule Inuit). A colorful character in *Erik's Saga,* probably composed in the thirteenth century (Magnusson and Palsson 1963), was Thorhall the hunter, a rough and partly pagan man who was supposed to have spent much of his life hunting in the waste places of the north. The saga of King Hakon Hakonsson (set in 1264) records that when the Greenlanders submitted to his royal authority, they agreed to pay him manslaughter fines for killings in the Nordrsetur as well as in the settlement areas (GHM II:779; Nansen 1911: 299). Scaldic lays and heroic poems also mentioned the Nordrsetur, and one long poem entitled *"Nordrsetudrapa"* was known in the Middle Ages, though it is now preserved only in a few fragments. These fragments refer to storms and drifting snow and hard sea spray (GHM III:235; Nansen 1911:298). The better-preserved *"Skald-Helga Rimur"* mentions the dangers of the voyage north, and that the Nordrsetur was the refuge of outlaws (GHM II:492–525; Nansen 1911:299).

The most complete descriptions of trips to the Nordrsetur are found in the collection *Annals of Greenland* made in the seventeenth century by the Icelander Bjorn Jonsson (GHM 1839–1845, I:88ff.). Jonsson had access to many manuscript sources that are now lost, and his *Annals* contain stories found nowhere else. Unfortunately, Jonsson often fails to identify his sources, and he seems to be quite willing to extensively "improve and correct" sources that were fragmentary or seemed contradictory to him (Gad 1970; Nansen 1911). Jonsson is thus a dangerous source himself, and it is often impossible to judge the accuracy of any of his stories.

Uneven as they are, the documentary sources serve to establish several points:

1. The Nordrsetur hunt's objectives were walrus, polar bear, seals, and driftwood.
2. The hunt provided major portions of the goods needed for transatlantic trade, as well as making some contribution to subsistence.
3. The hunting grounds lay well to the north of the western settlement.
4. The journey to the Nordrsetur was considered dangerous and the Nordrsetur itself a fit home for outlaws and heathen Skraeling.
5. "Six-oared boats" were used in coastal hunting voyages frequently enough to provide a common measure of distance.
6. Church officials and wealthy secular farmers seem to have played an important role in the Nordrsetur hunting and in northward voyages of exploration.

LOCATING NORDRSETUR PLACE NAMES

A number of these sources give specific place names within the Nordrsetur region. The best sources for Nordrsetur place names are, unfortunately, some of our least reliable: The uncertainly attributed passages in Bjørn Jonsson's *Annals* (in GHM 1839, III:228–229, 242–243), and some of the scaldic verse fragments. Not surprisingly, these obscure sources are capable of multiple interpretation and there has been considerable debate about the placement of Norse names on modern maps of the Nordrsetur region (cf. Gad 1970:85–89, 136–140; H. Ingstad 1966:81–84; Nansen 1911:300–311). The most important and most often repeated place names in the Nordrsetur are *Eysunes* ("fire point"), *Bjarney* ("bear island") *Kroksfjord* ("crooked fjord"), *Kroksfjartharheithr* ("heaths by Kroksfjord"), *Greipar* (something like "cruel ones" in the feminine gender), and *Karlsbuthir* ("Karl's booths"). Translations follow Gad (1970) and Nansen (1911). Both Kroksfjartharheithr and Karlsbuthir are repeatedly mentioned as sites of seasonal hunting camps, and Kroksfjord is given as a common reference point.

Some of these place names may be readily localized today. Bjarney took 12 days to row around, and thus can only be the great island of Disko itself. Eysunes does not appear to refer to volcanic activity, it is absent in the region; instead, it probably refers to fires in the soft coal and schist caused by landslides. Rosenkrantz (1932) documented a natural fire of this sort on the north coast of the Nugssuaq Peninsula, and also recorded traces of earlier fires along the peninsula's south shores. Rosenkrantz argues that this only area where the Norse could have seen such a burning point; thus Nugssuaq would seem to be the Norse Eysunes. Kroksfjord is a bit harder to pinpoint because there are a great many crooked fjords in west Greenland. H. Ingstad (1966:84) argues for Diskofjord on Disko Island. Gad (1970) suggests several possibilities in the Disko Bay region, while Nansen (1911) suggests that the channel of the Vaigat and the north end of Disko Bay itself may have made up this well-known feature. Kroksfjartharheithr is clearly nearby, and both Gad (1970) and Nansen (1911) identify this place name

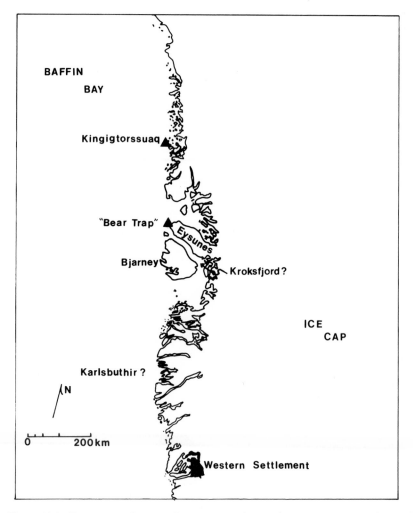

Figure 12.2 Reconstructed Norse place names in the Nordrsetur region. Triangles mark the location of the only known Norse sites in the Nordrsetur.

with the shores of Disko Island and the Nugssuaq Peninsula. While the first four place names can be located in the Disko Bay region with fair certainty, the location of Karlsbuthir is less sure. It is definitely south of the Disko region, but its precise placement depends on various authors' assessments of what was meant by a day's row in a six-oared boat. At present, we are probably correct in placing Karl's booths somewhere in the broad area of Holsteinsborg and Sukkertoppen districts (Figure 12.2), but Greipar is still more difficult to place upon modern maps. Gad (1970) suggested that the name itself may be poetic fiction, while H. Ingstad (1966:83) tentatively locates it in the modern Kangatsiak–Egedesminde area. Other place names are still more mysterious, and there seems little hope of tying any to actual topographic features. While we lack the detail and precision provided by the place name evidence for the other North Atlantic settlements, several generations of documentary and topographic research have at least provided us with a few points of reference within the Norse northern hunting grounds.

LOCATING NORDRSETUR RESOURCES:
BIOGEOGRAPHICAL EVIDENCE

We are told that the Norse hunters sought a range of resources in the Nordrsetur, including driftwood, seals, bear, and walrus. In our attempt to understand the structure of the Nordrsetur hunt, it may be useful to locate concentrations of these resources in western Greenland. Most of the driftwood that comes ashore in Greenland is carried over the pole from Siberia (Koch 1945), and moves down the east coast on the east Greenland current. Most of the driftwood that accumulates on the west coast is carried from east Greenland by the north-flowing Irminger current. The greatest concentrations of driftwood in all periods are thus in the islands and outer fjords of the southwest coast in or near the Norse settlement areas. These regions may have been rapidly stripped of ancient driftwood collections during the early years of the settlement, and it is likely that any Norse Greenlander on any kind of voyage would have been on the lookout for stranded timber, as are modern Icelanders and Shetlanders (Kristjansson 1980). However, it seems unlikely that driftwood collection was the central purpose of the northern trips, or that driftwood resources were ever disproportionately rich in the Nordrsetur area.

Evidence for the distribution of game species in west Greenland is relatively rich. Sources include the annual *Summary of Catch Statistics* (Ministry of Greenland, 1954–present), less detailed Royal Greenland Co. purchase records (to the early nineteenth century in some localities; see Vibe 1967), modern biological survey results (Loughry 1959; Mansfield 1966;

Table 12.1

Relative Proportions of Seal Species Identified in Quantifiable Norse Animal-Bone
Collections[a]

Site	Harp	Hooded	Common	Ringed	Bearded
Eastern Settlement					
Ø17a upper	72.22	16.67	9.26	0	1.85
Ø17a lower[b]	29.69	6.25	57.81	1.56	4.69
Ø29 North Farm	79.17	9.38	1.04	5.21	5.21
Ø71 N	63.46	19.23	9.62	0	7.69
Ø71 S	66.32	27.49	3.44	.34	2.41
Ø149	39.53	40.70	11.63	2.33	5.81
Ø167	64,20	27.16	4.94	2.47	1.23
mean	64.15	23.44	6.66	1.73	4.03
n (late phase)	6	6	6	6	6
Standard deviation	13.43	10.86	4.13	2.05	2.58
Coeff. var. (%)	20.94	46.33	62.01	118.50	64.02
Western Settlement					
V34	65.52	0	25.86	1.72	6.90
V48 III	55.33	0	38.67	0	6.00
V48 II[b]	58.29	0	39.20	0	2.51
V48 I[b]	58.01	0	40.88	.55	.55
V51 Sandnes	68.73	0	25.06	1.99	4.22
V52a	65.22	0	26.34	1.79	6.65
V53c	61.11	0	25.93	1.85	11.11
V53d	70.79	0	16.85	0	12.36
V54	64.29	0	26.19	0	9.52
V59	39.00	.71	54.61	3.55	2.13
mean	61.25	.09	29.94	1.36	7.36
n (late phase)	8	8	8	8	8
Standard deviation	10.14	.25	11.59	1.27	3.45
Coeff. var. (%)	16.56	277.78	38.71	93.38	46.88

[a]Based on total number of bone fragments. Note the importance of migratory harp seals to
both settlements, and the greater exploitation of hooded seals in the eastern settlement. Note
also the rarity of ringed-seal bones in the Norse middens.
[b]Excluded from summary statistics of later phase collections.

Rosendahl 1961; Vibe 1950, 1956, 1967), and scattered anecdotal reports
by trained observers (Jensen 1928; Rink 1877; Ross and MacIver 1982;
Scoresby 1820).

Seal hunting and the processing of seals for storage as blubber-filled skins
is mentioned in the Nordrsetur accounts (Table 12.1). As noted, the migratory harp and hooded seals formed the main targets of Norse sealing.
Some hooded seals do move up the west coast in summer, however, the harp
seals would be far more numerous in the central west coast, and would keep

closer in-shore (Vibe 1967). The harp seal migration passes up the west coast in a wave that peaks in the south-central districts (Julianehaab, Narssaq, Frederikshaab, Godthaab, Sukkertoppen, Holsteinsborg, Egedesminde, Christianshavn) in May to June. The harp migration peaks in late summer (July to September) in the northern Disko Bay region (Jakobshavn and Vaigat) and in the Umanak and Upernavik districts further north (Rosendahl 1961). The northern end of Disko Bay, especially the Vaigat region (Figure 12.3), would be a particularly rich sealing grounds in late summer in periods when the harp migration followed the general pattern of

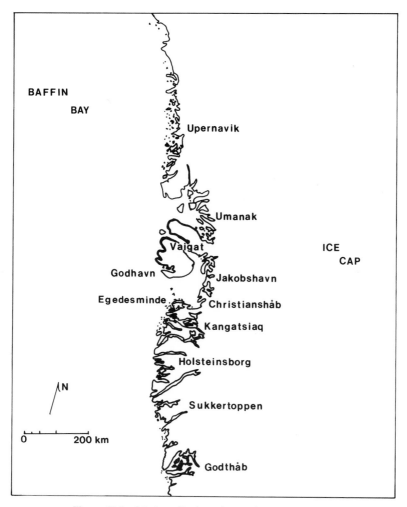

Figure 12.3   Modern districts of central-west Greenland.

the past 100 years. Norse hunters sailing north from the settlements in Julianehaab and Godthaab districts in early summer would thus be following the peak of the harp migration, and might have been able to supplement the spring seal catch in the outer fjords of the settlement areas. However, seal blubber or even sealskins would make relatively unattractive trade items, and a crude econometric analysis (see below) suggests that seals may have been a second- or third-choice cargo for hunters returning from the Nordrsetur.

Polar bears are repeatedly mentioned as a Greenlandic specialty. In *Einar Sokkason's Story* (Jones 1964) two live polar bears are brought to Norway as royal bribes. In *Audun's Saga* (Magnusson and Palsson 1962), the Icelander hero spends all his money on a live bear in Greenland, and then manages to make his fortune by presenting it to King Svein of Denmark. Polar bear skins were probably a more common export, and there are many examples of their use by both clerical and secular elites in Europe as spectacular status symbols (Ingstad 1966).

Individual polar bears (*Ursus* or *Thalarctos maritimus*) have been recorded in all parts of Greenland, but they are most common on the east coast and in the northern districts of the west coast from Umanak to Thule. Vibe (1967) demonstrates the close correlation between bear sightings, heavy drift (or landfast ice), and concentrations of the ringed seals who are the bears main prey. Fluctuations in past sea ice conditions may have brought such optimal bear habitats closer or further from the Norse settlements, with the most significant changes affecting the east coast (Vibe 1967:62). However, the optimal polar-bear habitat most accessible to the Norse for most of the Middle Ages would have been the northwest coast area from Umanak northwards into glacier-lined Melville Bay.

Even in optimal habitats polar bears are normally solitary unless mating or rearing cubs. Their position at the apex of a complex marine food chain keeps their density low, except when an unusual concentration of carrion (like a beached whale) may draw a number of bears together.

Although driftwood, seals, and polar bears are mentioned in the documentary sources, it seems likely that walrus (*Odobenus rosmarus*) were a primary target of the Nordrsetur hunters. Walrus provided valuable sea ivory for European book covers, reliquaries, staffs, scepters, and croziers. Walrus ivory seems to have been an important part of the Greenland bishopric's tax and tithe payments to Norway. In 1327 the Greenlanders paid about 668 kg of walrus ivory in a special crusade tithe and Peter's Pence (Gad 1970:136–137). This amount represented the tusks of about 191 animals, and suggests the importance of walrus in the Nordrsetur hunt and overseas trade. Walrus also provided first-quality ships line, as the *King's Mirror* reports: "Its hide is thick and good to make ropes of: it can be cut into leather strips of such strength that 60 or more men may pull at one rope without breaking it" (Larsen 1917:140). Since the zooarchaeological evidence also indicates that walrus were a mainstay of the hunt, it may be useful to attempt to model walrus population distribution in more detail.

While isolated walrus again may be found virtually anywhere in Greenland, their major concentrations are on the west coast, from the Godthaab district north to Thule. Modern catch data from the period 1954–1974 indicate that modern Greenlandic walrus hunters are most successful in Holsteinsborg district in the south-central zone and in Godhavn district on Disko Island (Figure 12.4). Many walrus are also taken at Thule in the extreme northwest (over 332 animals from 1939 to 1940), but catch returns from Thule are too sporadic for comparison with the more southerly districts. In the south-central districts catch data is usually available for smaller settlements within the district boundaries. Figure 12.5 shows the modern settlements whose hunters reported taking more than 10 and more than 50 walrus in any year of the 1954–1974 period. This detailed and generally accurately recorded modern catch data (Petersen 1973) clearly has great potential for modeling faunal resources on the local level. However, the catch returns must be used with an awareness of some limiting factors that may be especially relevant to an attempt to locate walrus concentrations.

1. The catch statistics are only a *proxy* measure of faunal resources; they are not a census or a probabalistically selected sample of any prey population.

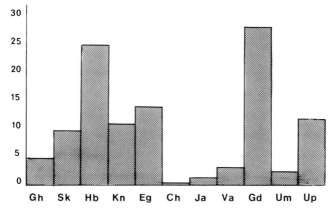

Figure 12.4   Reported mean walrus catches in central-west Greenland 1954–1974 (with a few omissions). Gh, Godthåb; Sk, Sukkertoppen; Hb, Holsteinborg; Kn, Kangatsiaq; Eg, Egedesminde; Ch, Chrsitianshåb; Ja, Jakobshavn; Va, Vaigat; Gd, Godhavn; Um, Umanak; Up, Upernavik. (Data from Danish Ministry for Greenland's *Annual Summary of Catch Statistics,* Copenhagen.)

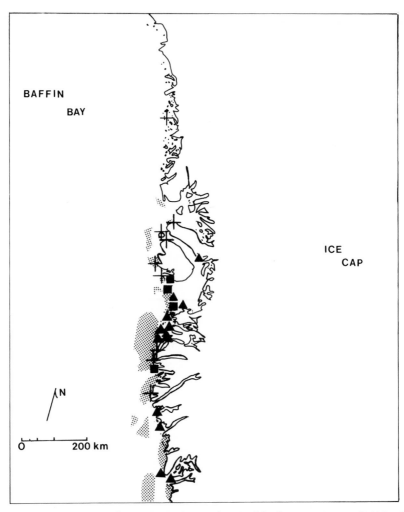

Figure 12.5 Recent walrus concentrations and optimal feeding areas (textured). Triangles (▲) mark location of communities reporting 10 or more walrus killed in any year 1954–1974. Squares (■) mark communities reporting 50 or more walrus kills. Crosses (+) mark reported concentrations of 100 or more walrus sighted by biological surveys. (Data from *Summary of Catch Statistics;* Jensen, 1928; Mansfield 1966; Rink 1877; Vibe 1967.)

2. Figure 12.5 shows the location at which the catch was *reported* not the location of the kill.
3. Many walrus killed are probably not recovered or reported. The ratio of kill to recovery varies widely and may sometimes be as high as 5 to 1 (Freeman 1969/1970, 1974/75; Perry 1967; Mansfield 1966).

4. Changing sea-ice conditions may have significantly altered the distribution and behavior of marine game animals (Vibe 1967).
5. Changes in hunting technology (larger fiberglass boats with more powerful engines) and in settlement patterns (increasing nucleation) have also affected hunting strategies in the past three decades.
6. Most importantly, the walrus of west Greenland are today a *remnant* of a much larger premodern population. Intensive predation by seventeenth- to nineteenth-century whalers greatly reduced populations in the Davis Strait area, particularly affecting the walrus of west Greenland, southern Labrador, Newfoundland, and St. Lawrence. Shuldham (1775) reports the slaughter of over 1200 walrus in one day in the Magdalen Islands. Otto Fabricius (1780) reported significant declines in walrus populations in west Greenland as a result of European overhunting. In the nineteenth and early twentieth centuries, whalers regularly killed hundreds of walrus in a single voyage (Scoresby 1820), and between 1905 and 1909 whalers out of Dundee alone took nearly 3000 walrus from the shores of Davis Strait (Perry 1967:123).

It is probable that despite the addition of outboard motors and modern rifles, the twentieth-century catch records represent a "worst case" scenario, and that medieval walrus populations were much larger. But was the distribution of these larger herds similar to the reduced modern ones?

Fortunately, the biological requirements of walrus are reasonably well known and these restrict the possible distribution of walrus populations both ancient and modern. Walrus feed on a range of marine bivalves of the sea bottom, including *Cerripes groenl.*, *Mya truncata*, *Astarte borealis*, and *Saxiclava arctica* (Vibe 1950, 1967). The cockles (*C. ciliata* and *C. groenl.*) seem to be particularly favored, and together with the clams (*S. artica* and *M. truncata*) normally form the bulk of the walrus diet. These bivalves are found in their greatest concentrations in relatively shallow waters between 38 and 83 m deep, and prefer a bottom of gravelly mud flats or submerged morainal deposit (Perry 1967:97–98). This sort of bottom at these depths is not uncommon along the central west-coast area. As Figure 12.5 indicates, modern catch reports and suitable feeding areas do seem to overlap well (note that Figure 12.5 is a considerable simplification due to its reduction from a much larger scale; compilation from USDMA 1968).

Walrus are definitely capable of feeding at depths of over 120 m, although a practical limit is probably closer to 85–90 m (Perry 1967:98), which matches the lower depth range of their main prey species. Walrus alternate periods of intensive feeding (often resting on ice floes between dives) and long periods of rest on land or large ice floes. During their resting periods, the walrus often congregate in great numbers, piling together in large heaps (Bruemmer 1974:93). Even today, these resting concentrations may contain up to several hundred individuals (Mansfield 1966). In late summer, or when ice floes are otherwise unavailable, walrus "haul out" to rest on land. These hauling out places (or *uglit*) are returned to regularly and may be used for many generations. Favored uglit locations are on exposed islands or headlands that are within range of suitable feeding areas (walrus may actually use heavy surf as an aid to hauling out). Terraced beaches 80–100-m broad at the shoreline, backed by cliffs or steep bluffs on the landward side, and with a rapid offshore drop-off that minimizes tidal shoreline changes seem to be most favored. Estuaries with a heavy discharge of fresh water and extensive tidal mud flats are avoided (Perry 1967:57–58).

According to available charts, topographic maps, and air photos, locations having favorable uglit characteristics (as defined by Perry's Canadian and Alaskan data) are fairly numerous in the central west coast of Greenland (especially in the Holsteinsborg–Egedesminde region), but are somewhat more limited in the northern Disko Bay area. In combination with the modern catch data and Mansfield's (1966) biological survey data, the placement of topographically suitable uglit and offshore feeding grounds can give us a working model for likely walrus distributions in the past. These various (and largely independent) sources of data do produce a mutually reinforcing and consistant pattern (Figure 12.5) that suggests a degree of temporal stability. While more biological, archival, and archaeological research is clearly needed to test and refine this distributional model, it does seem reasonable to use this nineteenth- to twentieth-century data as a proxy for medieval walrus population distribution. Note, however, that larger medieval walrus populations may have occupied more localities and medieval uglit would almost certainly have held many more individuals. While climatically induced changes in walrus behavior may have occurred during the Norse period (Vibe 1967), the nineteenth-century "Little Ice Age" data suggest that location of feeding grounds and suitable uglit may condition walrus distribution as strongly as moderate fluctuations in sea-ice conditions.

LOCATIONAL EVIDENCE FOR THE NORDRSETUR HUNT

The uniformitarian assumptions of our biogeographical walrus distribution model are also bolstered by the location of Norse Nordrsetur place names (Figure 12.2) and by the location of the Norse sites currently known in the Nordrsetur area. The northernmost of the sites is on an island north of Upernavik called Kingigtorssuaq (Figure 12.2). Three small cairns were located on the rocky spine of the island and one contained a 10-cm long rune stone (Gad 1970:137). The inscription stated that Erling Sigvatsson, Bjarni Thordarsson, and Eindridi Oddsson built the cairns "on the Saturday before Rogation Day," and ends with what seems to be a magical formula. The runes are a type in use between 1250 and 1300, and the date has been taken to be April 25 in the modern calendar (Gad 1970). While there is some dispute over this calendrical conversion (Gad 1970:138), it does seem that at least three Norsemen were in the Upernavik area in the early spring, probably before the breakup of the sea ice, thus these rune carvers may have wintered in the Nordrsetur (H. Ingstad 1966).

The second Norse Nordrsetur site is located at the tip of the Nugssuaq Peninsula (probably the Norse Eysunes) at the northern end of Disko Bay (Figures 12.2 and 12.6). This is a rectangular stone structure with well-laid foundation courses of large stone blocks and carefully squared and lapped corners. Its drystone walls still stand some 2-m high and enclose an area of 20–24 m² (H. Ingstad 1966:82). The site has long been known as the "bear trap" (Rink 1877:349), but is definitely a building rather than a trap and is certainly of European origin. Excavations by Jørgen Meldgaard in 1953 (Vebaek 1956b:736) indicated that the structure is Norse and not the product of seventeenth- to nineteenth-century whalers. Unconfirmed stories of a rune stone supposedly removed from the structure in the nineteenth century (Rink 1877) would seem to support Meldgaard's assessment. The structure's function has been variously interpreted. Meldgaard initially identified the ruin as a chapel (Gad 1970:137), but has since retracted this preliminary interpretation (J. Meldgaard, personal communication, 1976). In form and construction the Nugssuaq structure most resembles a Norse skemma or storage building. While much larger than most farm skemma and with roughly three times the floor area of the Angissunguaq skemma in the outer fjord sealing grounds of the western settlement (Berglund 1973), the Nugssuaq structure is the size and shape of the skemma buildings of larger farms like V7 Anavik (Roussell 1941).

A site catchment analysis of the surroundings of the Nugssuaq structure may aid in its interpretation. As argued elsewhere (McGovern 1980b), site territory analysis can be applied to maritime economies if we have some idea of the normal operating range of ancient watercraft and of their limiting features. Fortunately, the documentary sources inform us that the six-oared boat was the usual Nordrsetur vessel, and give us the basis for estimating the average "day's row."

While authors have variously calculated the distance covered in a day's row by six rowers in a six-oared boat (H. Ingstad 1966), it seems likely that this distance fell somewhere in the 30–40-km range. Figure 12.6 indicates the 30–40-km radius marine site territory of the Nugssuaq structure relative

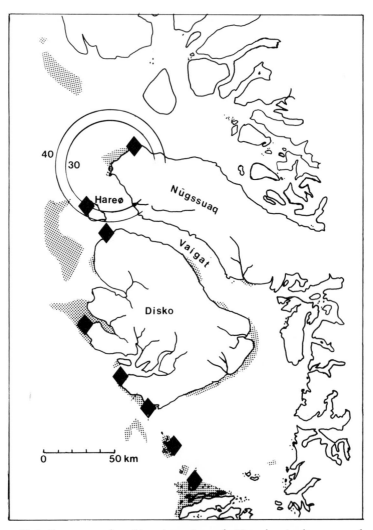

Figure 12.6 Reconstructed maritime site territory of a Norse hunting base centered on the Nugssuaq structure, with 30- and 40-km radius catchment areas indicated. Diamonds (♦) indicate modern walrus uglit; textured areas represent probable walrus feeding areas.

to suitable walrus feeding areas and recently occupied uglit. Note that hunters based near the bear trap would have been able to reach uglit on Hare Ø and northern Nugssuaq Peninsula within a day or less. A few more days' row would put Norse hunters in range of the uglit along the west coast of Disko Island (probably the Norse Bjarney). Larger medieval walrus populations may have occupied additional potential uglit on Hare Ø, northern Disko Island, and the tip of Nugssuaq itself.

Hunters based on the Nugssuaq site would also be well placed to exploit other game resources. The vallies of Nugssuaq Peninsula hold the only sizable caribou populations in the north Disko–Umanak area (Vibe 1967). In addition, the modern hunting communities of the Vaigat regularly report the highest catch of harp seals per hunter of all the communities in the Disko Bay–Upernavik area (Rosendahl 1961:18). The Vaigat harp seal catch peaks in August, suggesting that this resource would also have been accessible to late summer hunters based upon the bear-trap site.

As several authors have noted (Jochim 1981; McGovern 1980a; Osborne 1977; Perlman 1980), maritime economic strategies must balance optimization of resource exploitation with the minimization of the considerable hazards of marine hunting and fishing. The Nugssuaq site is particularly well situated to minimize such hazard as well as to allow easy access to a range of marine and terrestrial resources. The islands at the tip of the peninsula provide a protected harbor under most weather conditions. The tip of Nugssuaq was called "Three Islands Point" by nineteenth-century English-speaking sailors (Rink 1877:349) and was well known as a safe anchorage. Modern charts (Geodetisk Institut 1972; USDMA 1968, Chart 38440) still mark the point as one of the only all-weather anchorages in a 75-km radius. If the sheltered waters of Three Islands Point could protect nineteenth-century whalers, they would have provided an even better refuge to Norse craft (which could be hauled ashore). The tip of Nugssuaq Peninsula would also remain free of land-fast ice longer than the inlets and fjords of the inner parts of Disko Bay and the Umanak district, allowing for a longer navigation season and providing some protection from an unseasonably early freeze. It thus seems likely that the Nugssuaq structure was the center of a major Nordrsetur hunting station—very probably one of those seasonal camps along Kroksfjord mentioned by the documentary sources.

Stories of another rectangular stone structure in the Holsteinsborg district (perhaps the Norse Karlsbuthir area?) have been in circulation for over a century (H. Ingstad 1966; Nansen 1911; Rink 1877). However, the structure has never been professionally documented and a recent survey failed to locate it (C. Andreasen, personal communication, 1981). While it seems certain that the Nugssuaq station was not unique, other Nordrsetur hunting stations have thus far eluded documentation.

ZOOARCHAEOLOGICAL EVIDENCE

Thanks to the foresight of early excavators like Bruun (1896, 1916) and Roussell (1936, 1941), collections of unmodified animal bones were made

Table 12.2

Walrus and Polar-Bear Bones in Norse Animal-Bone Collections[a]

Site	Walrus	Polar bear
Eastern Settlement		
Ø47 (Gardar)	X	X
Ø29 (Brattahlid)	X	X
Ø149 (nunnery)	X	X
Ø71 N	X	
Ø71 S	X	
Ø167	X	X
Ø68		
Ø66	X	
Ø64a	X	
Ø64c	X	X
Ø2		
Ø20		
Ø17a (late)	X	
Ø17a (early)	X	X
Middle Settlement		
M15	X	
M21		
Western Settlement		
V51 (Sandnes)	X	X
V35	X	X
V52a	X	X
V53d	X	
V53c	X	
V63	X	
V53a		
V59	X	X
V54	X	X
V45	X	X
V29	X	
V50a	X	
V44	X	
V36		
V16	X	
V48 III	X	X
V48 II	X	X
V48 I	X	X

[a]Presence versus absence. Despite a low relative frequency in all collections, at least a few walrus bones are present at most sites with zooarchaeological samples.

from many of the Norse sites excavated in the first half of this century. These collections significantly augment later bone samples (Degerbøl 1929, 1934, 1936, 1941, 1943; McGovern 1979a, 1982; McGovern and Bigelow n.d.). While many of the Norse collections are too small to reasonably quantify, a surprising number of these samples contain at least a few walrus and polar bear bones. Table 12.2 presents the presence or absence of walrus and bear bones in all the existing Norse bone collections. Note that the majority of site collections have some walrus bone and that many have at least a few fragments of polar bear as well. Walrus and bear bones are found on large farms with churches (Ø 47, Ø 29, Ø 149), smaller coastal farms (Ø 17a V48, V 16, V 50a), and on inland farms several hours walk from the fjordside (Ø 167, Ø 64a, Ø 64c, Ø 71N, Ø 71S V53d, V53c, V54, V35). While walrus bones are more common than bear bones, walrus remains normally make up only a small proportion of the zooarchaeological collections large enough to quantify (eastern settlement mean = .43%; western settlement mean = 1.78%). Table 12.3 presents this walrus bone data. Note the greater amounts of walrus bone in the northernmost western settlement, and the rather uneven distribution of walrus bone in the western settlement collections. The church farm V51 Sandnes is one of the largest farms in the western settlement (McGovern and Jordan 1982), V52a is one of the church farm's largest neighbors (McGovern 1982), while V48 is one of the smallest farms in the area.

The two deeply stratified bone collections (Ø 17a and V 48) appear to present a common pattern of declining frequency of walrus bone from their early phases (eleventh to early twelfth century) into their later phases (twelfth to fourteenth century). However, "trace" species (like the walrus in the Norse collections) are particularly subject to haphazard depositional effects, and additional well-stratified collections are needed to test this apparent pattern.

The parts of the walrus and bear skeleta present in the Norse farm sites suggest a specialized butchery pattern. Polar bear bone fragments are mostly phalanges, patellae, metapodials, and other elements likely to be left in a hide by a quick and rough field skinning. Many of the phalanges show fine slice marks at an angle suggesting their removal during the final finishing of a hide. Most of the walrus fragments are from the maxilla, especially from around the deeply rooted tusks (Figure 12.7). These fragments seem to be the result of careful removal of the thick and valuable tusk root; a chisel-like tool being used to break through the thick maxillary bone. It seems that the Nordrsetur hunters (like modern St. Lawrence Island Inuit) often removed the whole front of the maxilla with both the tusks still embedded, and brought this butchery unit home for tusk extraction. Tusk ivory seems to have been largely reserved for export, and is very rare in the Greenlandic

Table 12.3

Percentage of Walrus Bones Identified in Quantifiable Norse Animal-Bone Collections[a]

Site	Percentage walrus
Eastern Settlement	
Ø17a upper	.60
Ø17a lower	2.33[b]
Ø71 North	.60
Ø71 South	.02
Ø149	.16
Ø167	.75
Western Settlement	
V35	.44
V48 III (late)	.18
V48 II	.17[b]
V48 I (early)	.52
V51 Sandnes	6.93
V52a	3.58
V53c	.62
V53d	1.07
V54	.69
V59	.73[c]
Eastern Settlement (later phases)	
Mean	.43
Standard deviation	.32
N	5
Western Settlement (later phases)	
Mean	1.78
Standard deviation	2.34
N	8

[a]Based on total number of bone fragments. Note the higher mean frequency of walrus bones in the Western Settlement and the relatively greater numbers in the elite farms V51 and V52a. Early phase collections at Ø17a and V48 I contain relatively more walrus fragments than later phases, but further deeply stratified collections are needed to clarify this pattern.

[b]Excluded from summary statistics of later phase collections: note higher percentage of walrus bones in earlier phases.

[c]Data courtesy of J. Møhl (1982).

Norse collections. However, the peglike post canines were retained in Greenland, and were commonly used for craftwork.

Whole walrus skulls were occasionally brought home, apparently as hunting trophies. Nearly complete skulls (some with simple incised decoration) have been found at V51 Sandnes (Roussell 1936) and at V59 in the western settlement. At the cathedral at Gardar in the eastern settlement, between 20 and 30 walrus skulls have been recovered from the churchyard and church interior at various times (Nørlund 1930:138), while a row of five narwhal skulls was found buried together within the cathedral chancel.

The postcranial skeleton of the walrus is rarely found in the settlement areas—with the important exception of the baculum or penis bone. Walrus bacula (often 20 to 30-cm long) are very common finds in both eastern and western settlement sites, and may have served as wall hooks or hafts (Roussell 1941). Curiously, the smaller bacula of the various seal species exploited by the Norse Greenlanders are virtually absent from the Norse collections, though they are fairly common in Greenlandic Inuit bone collections.

The animal-bone collections excavated from the Norse farms in the settlement areas thus suggest several aspects of the Nordrsetur hunt:

1. Initial butchery of both bear and walrus seems to have been sometimes hurried and incomplete.
2. Final finishing of walrus and bear products seems to have taken place on many (if not all) of the Norse farms at one time or another.
3. Most of the bear and walrus carcasses remained at the distant kill site.

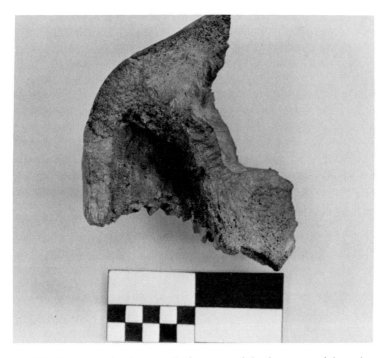

Figure 12.7 Fragment of walrus maxilla from around the deep roots of the tusk, apparently chipped away during final finishing of butchery units brought back from the Nordrsetur. (Collected in 1984 at V51 Sandnes; photograph by T. H. McGovern.)

If walrus and bear meat was brought into the settlement area in any quantity, it must have been largely boneless.

4. Western settlement farmers may have participated in the hunt more frequently or more intensively than eastern settlement farmers. Large church farms may have been the site of the more final finishing of walrus than small farms.

5. The few well-stratified bone collections *seem* to suggest that Norse walrus hunting stabilized or declined in the later phases. More data is needed to clarify this apparent trend.

6. Some of the skeletal elements brought back from the Nordrsetur seem to have been hunting trophies of one sort or another, and may have had some religious/magical significance.

ARTIFACTUAL EVIDENCE

Few artifacts recovered from the Norse farm sites can be unambiguously associated with the Nordrsetur hunt. The most interesting artifacts associated with the Nordrsetur hunt are not weapons but tiny amuletlike figurines. Roussell recovered a bear and a walrus figurine at V51 and V52a, both made from walrus postcanines (Roussell 1936:123). Two additional bear figurines and another walrus were recovered from V54 in 1977 (Andreasen 1980). These figurines are pierced for suspension and may be part of the same complex of Nordrsetur-oriented magic that produced the walrus-skull and penis-bone trophies and the burials at Gardar.

AN ORGANIZATIONAL MODEL FOR THE NORDRSETUR

The varied sources of evidence for the Nordrsetur hunt thus seem rich enough to justify an attempt to model the Nordrsetur hunts' organization and to assess its costs to the Norse Greenlanders. A few Norsemen (like the Kingigtorssuaq rune carvers) may have wintered in the Nordrsetur and might be considered professional hunters. However, the documentary sources and the zooarchaeological evidence suggest that the majority of the participants in the Nordrsetur trips were part-time hunters who spent winters on their home farms in the settlement areas. The wide distribution of the walrus and bear bones in the faunal collections suggests the eventual involvement of the majority of the Norse farmsteads in the hunt and in the final processing of the catch, and is probably the residue of some system of sharing.

Norse sealing and caribou-hunting strategies seem to have involved the targeting of intensive hunting efforts upon seasonal aggregates of prey species. The Norse thus seem to have matched pulses of Arctic resources with time-efficient concentrations of labor and equipment (Jochim 1981). The social mechanisms that concentrated and coordinated communal labor for church building, caribou hunting, migratory seal drives, and probably hay harvesting seem to have been equally effective in overcoming the problems of a dispersed settlement pattern and mobilizing labor for the Nordrsetur hunt.

HUNTING TECHNIQUES

Norse Nordrsetur hunting techniques were thus probably shaped by the ability of the Norse to coordinate labor and by the time constraints of a summer hunt several hundred miles from the permanent settlements. Since walrus were the most consistently aggregated Nordrsetur species, and because they provided some of the most valuable trade goods, it is not surprising that they were a major target of the hunt. Norse hunters probably concentrated their efforts on walrus hauled out on uglit rather than attacking swimming walrus. The Norse lacked harpoons, and studies of recent Inuit hunts of swimming walrus (using both rifles and harpoons) indicate a very low level of time-efficiency and a variable but high kill-to-recovery ratio (Freeman 1969/1970). It seems more likely that Norse walrus hunting resembled the techniques used by the sixteenth-to-eighteenth-century European Arctic whalers. Seventeenth-century whalers in Spitzbergen attacked uglit concentrations from the seaward side, using lances to kill the walrus nearest the surfline and thus creating a barrier to animals further from the water (Perry 1967). Kills of several hundred animals at a time seem to have been regularly obtained by this method. In 1775 Shuldham described a similar method of attack used on uglit of the Magdalen Islands. In this case men with lances as well as dogs were used to divide the herd and to isolate the walrus furthest from the shore. While emphasizing the hazards of such a concerted attack upon a large uglit, Shuldham also reports kills of up to 1500 animals in a single hunt (Shuldham 1775). Since the Norse possessed similar equipment (including large hunting dogs) and similar abilities to coordinate labor, it is likely that they attacked the large medieval uglit of the Nordrsetur in much the same way.

In addition to supplying ample meat for the hunting parties, the piles of skinned walrus carcasses resulting from such massive kills would also attract bear and fox. Seventeenth- and nineteenth-century Spiztbergen hunters regularly returned to walrus kill sites to exploit concentrations of scavenging polar bears (Perry 1967).

If such coordinated attacks on uglit were a feature of the Nordrsetur hunt, then the role of well-built storage structures and centrally located bases becomes clearer. The base camps would have acted as temporary bulking centers as well as secure harbors for wide-ranging hunting parties. A sturdy and spacious skemma would be needed to hold the accumulating hides and tusk butchery units until they could be transported to the settlements at summer's end. Such bear-proof stone buildings might sometimes provide long-term storage for particularly successful hunts and the take of a few year-round hunters.

CONSTRAINTS OF CARGO CAPACITY AND DEMAND

One of the major constraints upon the Nordrsetur hunt must have been the cargo capacity of the Norse six-oared boats. Fragments of boats found in the settlement areas and the wooden model mentioned previously (Roussell 1936:96–101) indicate that these boats must have been part of the long-lived Scandinavian clinker-building tradition. This tradition is well represented by archaeological finds (McGrail 1980) and by modern examples still in use in Atlantic Europe (Henderson 1978; Kristjansson 1980; Morrison 1981). The smaller craft show a good deal of variation in proportions and cargo capacity. The viking-age *faering* of the Gokstad ship and its six-oared companion were light and narrow with a length-to-width ratio of about 5 to 1 (McGrail 1977:250); the medieval Greenlandic six-oared boat was probably longer and broader (the documentary sources specify one man to an oar rather than one to a pair). The V52a boat model is of a four-oared boat and has a length-to-width ratio of about 3 to 1. It is unlikely that the Greenlandic six-oared boat could have been much larger than the Shetlandic *sixern*, which was developed for the offshore fishery of the eighteenth century (Henderson 1978:53) and whose length-to-width ratio was also about 3 to 1. A nineteenth-century sixern crew anticipating rough weather considered their craft prudently laden with about 1179 kg of fish (Morrison 1981). The smallest cargo unit of later medieval Norway was about 1481 kg (Gad 1970:123), so we are probably correct in placing the average cargo capacity of a Greenlandic six-oared boat somewhere in the 1200–1500-kg range.

Table 12.4 presents some possible cargo options based on the lower end of this cargo range. This possible lading breakdown may help to explain the scarcity of postcranial walrus bones in the settlement area. It may also indicate that whole seals or their melted blubber would be a secondary or tertiary cargo option. Zooarchaeological data indicate that Norse farms may have consumed as many as 10–30 seals annually. The western settle-

Table 12.4

Hypothetical Cargo Options for the Six-Oared Boat[a]

Item	Weight (kg)	Number transportable
Adult walrus meat and fat[b]	730	1.6
Large walrus tusk and maxilla	7.5	160
Large walrus tusk/maxilla and hide	52.5	23
Polar-bear meat and fat[b]	220	5
Polar-bear hide (large)	15	80
Adult harp seal meat and fat[b]	73	16
Adult harp seal fat only[b]	40	30

[a] Assumes 1200-kg cargo capacity. Note advantages of cargoes made up largely of butchery units and hides.

[b] After Spiess 1978:58; others based on measurements of museum specimens with allowance for dehydration.

ment's 90 farms would thus have consumed at least 900 seals a year or some 56 boatloads. While some seals were probably taken to fill out a cargo, it seems unlikely that a large proportion of this domestic seal-meat demand was normally satisfied by the Nordrsetur hunt. Unless the Norse Greenlanders possessed a huge fleet of six-oared boats, the constraints of distance and cargo capacity would reject loads of meat for local consumption in favor of loads of hide and tusk for export.

We have no way of estimating the number of six-oared boats available to the Norse Greenlanders, but it is likely that such boats represented a major capital investment at all periods. The documentary sources emphasize the role of the Greenlandic elite in organizing the hunt and in providing the necessary vessels. As in Iceland (Thorlaksson 1978), even the elite may have found it difficult to obtain and repair seagoing boats in a treeless landscape. In 1347 two Icelandic annals reported that a Greenlandic boat on a voyage to Markland (Labrador?) had been blown to Iceland instead. It was noted that this seagoing vessel was small by contemporary Icelandic standards and that baleen lashing was used in place of iron boat nails in its construction (Gad 1970). It would then seem likely that the Norse Greenlanders had no great numbers of such boats at any time, and that they may have become harder to replace as time passed.

It is equally difficult to estimate the yearly demand for the products of the Nordrsetur hunt. The 1327 crusade tithe is the only quantified reference, and it is rather ambiguous. The 1327 exaction was to be the equivalent of six years of tithe income for each (Gad 1970:136–137), so the 653 kg contributed could represent 10% of 6 years' hunt, giving an average yearly kill of about 622 animals (5 boatloads of tusk units, 27 loads of tusk and hide). However, as Gad notes (1970:139), it is more likely that tithe payments were also made to Gardar in other products (hides, wool, dairy produce, etc.) that were then exchanged for walrus ivory for the transatlantic trade. In this case the crusade payment of 653 kg with the Peter's Pence of 15.4 kg might well represent most of the walrus ivory collected in the six years, giving a kill of about 32 animals per year (2 boatloads of tusk and hide). On the other hand, given the irregularity of contact, the payment might simply represent whatever ivory was on hand when the papal collector arrived and may be no reliable indicator of yearly take at all. In any case it is clear that the Norse Nordrsetur hunters could have killed and shipped home at least several hundred walrus annually, providing that at least four to five six-oared boats were available and that their cargoes were mainly tusk.

CONSTRAINTS OF TIME AND LABOR

A reconstruction of a seasonal round in Norse Greenland (McGovern 1980a, 1982) suggests that the brief Arctic summer (mid-June to early September) was packed with subsistence-related activity in the settlement areas. The spring seal hunt, dairying, fodder collection and intensive hay-making, and communal seabird and caribou hunting—all demanded quantities of labor during the summer months. These months were also the navigation season, as the *King's Mirror* relates: "Be sure to have your ship ready when summer begins and do your travelling while the season is best. Keep reliable tackle on shipboard at all times, and never remain out on the sea in late autumn if you can avoid it" (Larsen 1917:84).

Assuming that the hunters would set out in mid-June (after the peak of the harp seal migration in the settlement areas) and begin their return at the end of August, they would have about an 11 week Nordrsetur season. According to the documentary evidence, the western settlement hunters would need about 15 days to reach the Disko Bay hunting grounds (30 days roundtrip), while the eastern settlement hunters would have at least an additional 12 days travel (about 54 days roundtrip). Western settlement hunters would thus have about 7 weeks in the Disko area hunting grounds, and the eastern settlement hunters would have had about 3 weeks in the same area. These estimates may suggest why the western settlement seems to have played a greater role in the Nordrsetur hunting, and why the zoo-archaeological evidence suggests hasty in-field processing of walrus and bear carcasses. It is possible that the constraints of travel time produced a division of hunting territories, with western settlement hunters specializing in the more distant Kroksfjord and the eastern settlement hunters exploiting the nearer Karlsbuthir region.

These estimates of travel time may also suggest that the practical northern limits of the Nordrsetur were somewhere in the modern Upernavik district. As Nansen noted (1911), the garbled account of a 1266 expedition seems to show that the Norse explorers on that occasion penetrated only into Melville Bay, and the account cannot be read as a voyage to Thule or points north without doing violence to the text. While it is possible that the Norse *occasionally* visited the rich polynyas of the Thule–northern Ellesmere region (Schledermann 1980), or even the coast of Baffin Island (McGhee 1982; Sabo and Sabo 1978), constraints of time, distance, and cargo capacity probably restricted *regular* Nordrsetur voyages to Greenland's central west coast.

As in many frontier areas, labor shortage may have been a recurrent problem to the Greenlandic subsistence economy. It is also clear that the Nordrsetur hunt competed directly with summer subsistence activities for a limited pool of active adult males. However, our crudely quantified model may suggest that 4–5 boatloads of hunters might have been enough to allow the hunt to function. This labor force would come to perhaps 30–40 men and could have been entirely supplied from the western settlement's 90 farms if necessary. A more serious problem would be posed by the risk of permanent loss of men in shipwrecks or hunting accidents.

CONSTRAINTS OF HAZARD

Shipwreck hazard is a significant constraint affecting all maritime economies, and it is directly affected by the seamanship and navigational skills of the sailors; the seaworthiness, size, and lading of vessels; the frequency and duration of voyages; distance from safe harbor; the frequency, violence, and predictability of gales; the frequency of dense fog, snowstorms, and drift ice; and the vulnerability of the crew to exposure and hypothermia. The Nordrsetur hunters probably possessed extensive local navigational experience and were undoubtably skilled seamen, but the other factors affecting probability of shipwreck must have weighed heavily against them. Sea voyages in open boats have taken a regular toll of lives from all the communities of the North Atlantic islands. These losses occur both through "normal" attrition and through the occasional catastrophic storm that claims most of a community's active men and scarce boats in a single day (for a Shetlandic example of such catastrophic loss, see Morrison 1981). The hazards of frequent offshore voyages in small boats were well understood by the sixteenth-to-eighteenth-century Icelandic farmers who strongly resisted their landlords attempts to force them into developing commercial fisheries (Gunnarsson 1980). Greenlandic waters are no kinder, and loss at sea is a major cause of death among modern Greenlandic hunter–fishermen.

The various medieval documentary sources mentioned are often garbled and occasionally contradictory, but are unanimous in emphasizing the hazards of the Nordrsetur hunt. Casualties could be expected not only from shipwreck and exposure, but also from the hunt itself. The Nordrsetur prey species include bear and walrus—the two Greenlandic animals with a well-documented history of fatal attacks on humans. The seventeenth-to-eighteenth-century European sources are also united in emphasizing the hazards of attacks on walrus uglit. Shuldham noted that such attacks are "generally looked upon to be a most dangerous process" (1775:250).

It seems likely that the risks as well as the rewards of the Nordrsetur hunt were unequally distributed in Norse Greenland. The distribution of bone fragments suggests that most farms sent one or more men on the Nordrsetur hunt at some time even though the larger church farms (like V51 Sandnes) had several times the labor force of the smaller farms (about 25–30 inhabitants versus about 6–8; see McGovern 1982). The larger farms could more easily spare active men for the summer, and could also more easily absorb their permanent loss through shipwreck or hunting accident.

LABOR MOBILIZATION

The Nordrsetur hunt thus seems to have been relatively expensive to the Norse society in Greenland: it was invariably costly in men and scarce shipping goods diverted from subsistence consumption and occasionally costly in catastrophic loss of life and vessels. In addition, the hunt seems to have contributed little to Norse subsistence. It resulted instead in the accumulation of inedible tusk and hide that could be traded for subsistence-aiding iron tools only after an irregular and often considerable delay (and probably at a grossly unfavorable rate of exchange). The gap between effort expended/hazard endured and the positive reinforcement of the acquisition of new iron tools or the occasional imported luxury would often be quite significant.

Following Jochim's (1981:21–31) model of operant behavioral conditioning of economic strategies, we should expect that some mechanisms should have acted to bridge this gap between effort and positive reinforcement. Positive social reinforcements that placed a high value on participation in the Nordrsetur hunt—perhaps turning it into a sort of male rite of passage—may have been one such mechanism. The Nordrsetur trophies and the bear and walrus amulets may be the remnants of such social rein-forcement. The role of the ecclesiastical elite in sponsoring and sanctifying "Nordrsetur magic" may be seen in mass interments of walrus and narwhal skulls within the sacred precincts of the cathedral at Gardar.

The increasingly stratified political structure of Norse Greenland (Mc-Govern 1981) in the later Middle Ages could also have supplied induce-ments to participation in the Nordrsetur. Walrus and bear products clearly had a high value in external trade and exchange, and presumably had a similar value in internal transactions. By simply making tax, tithe, rent, and fine exactions preferentially payable in Nordrsetur products (as well as in the more usual cloth and dairy produce), Norse elites would provide small farmers with a powerful incentive to acquire tusk and hide. A still more powerful incentive to Nordrsetur participation would be provided by legal outlawry (Foote and Wilson 1970). Outlaws were banished to the wilder-ness (literally "to the forest") for a specified period, and they may well have provided Norse Greenland with many of its specialist hunters. As noted, the documentary sources regularly peopled the Nordrsetur with desperate outlaws.

LOCAL ELITES AND THE EUROPEAN CORE

Readers familiar with Immanuel Wallerstein's influential world-system analysis of sixteenth-century and modern development (Wallerstein 1974, 1979) may already recognize familiar patterns in the apparent behavior of the Greenlandic elite in promoting economic patterns that would never be predicted by an optimization model that considered only Greenlandic re-sources. Central to Wallerstein's model is the ability of core states to manip-ulate the politics of peripheries and to encourage local elites to acquire and collect trade goods and raw materials. Local elites may thus act as more or less conscious agents in a status-conferring economic network mobilizing local labor and facilities to intensify production for export. Despite the irregularity of transatlantic contact and the low bulk—volume of the Green-landic trade, there is evidence that just such a manipulative core—periphery relationship did link elites in Europe with those in Greenland.

The documentary sources indicate that the Greenlandic trade was a royal monopoly after 1262–1264 (Gad 1970), with fines imposed upon traders who failed to secure a royal liscence. The royal agent living in Greenland was to enforce the monopoly, and a law case from 1378 (involving the prosecution of some accidental visitors) suggests that such agents had some effect.

The powerful Greenlandic bishops may also have acted as agents for the

Norwegian trade. Rank–size distributions (Johnson 1977; Paynter 1982; Smith 1976) are commonly used to characterize settlement systems and to provide a measure of their internal economic integration and connection to distant centers. Primate distributions (with the largest site more than three times the size of the next largest) are the product of a number of political and economic processes (Johnson 1977), but are often taken as evidence of a dendritic flow of resources, with the local primate center acting as a bulking point and port of trade for external trading partners. The church farm of Herjolfsnes Ø 111 in the extreme southwest seems to have acted as

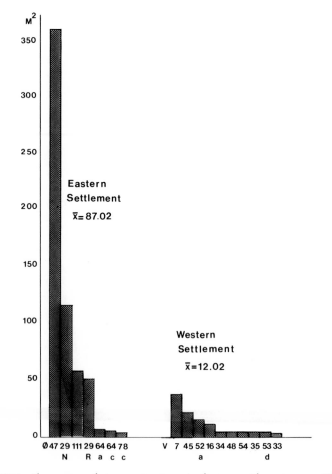

Figure 12.8 Floor areas of storage structures in the two settlement areas. While some measurement errors are probably present, the primacy of the episcopal farm ø47 Gardar is clear.

one entrepot for overseas trade (Nørlund 1924); however, the episcopal manor at Gardar Ø 47 seems to have been the colony's primate center. Gardar is primate with respect to the floor spaces of its byres and barns (McGovern 1982), but is most outstanding in its disproportionately large and numerous storage buildings (Nørlund 1930). While some of this massive storage capacity (Figure 12.8) may have functioned in local-level redistributive networks, it is likely that some structures provided warehouses for the long term storage of Nordrsetur trade goods.

It would thus seem that Greenland's partly ecclesiastical elite was deeply involved in transatlantic trade and acted as *de jure* or *de facto* agents for institutions firmly based in the European core. This elite interest in maintaining transatlantic contact, coupled with the important elite role in local-level subsistence activities and religious ceremonial, may explain the persistence of the Nordrsetur hunt and its apparent ritual importance in Norse society in Greenland. The northern hunt's importance is further underlined by its continued operation in the face of both increasing contact with Thule Inuit and declining contact with the European homeland.

CULTURE CONTACT AND THE NORDRSETUR

When the Norse arrived in Greenland in the 980s, they found only traces of Dorset Paleo-Eskimo and seem to have occupied an abandoned landscape (Gad 1970). This freedom from potential competitors seems to have lasted for about 150–200 years. The Thule-culture Neo-Eskimo migrating eastwards from Alaska reached the rich hunting grounds of northeastern Ellesmere Island and the Thule district in northwest Greenland by about A.D. 1000–1050 (Schledermann 1980; Schledermann and McCullough 1980). Recent archaeological investigations at Tugtulissuaq in Melville Bay (Grønnov and Meldgaard 1980), at Assivissuit near Søndre Strømfjord (M. Meldgaard, personal communication, 1980), and at Kangeq in the outer fjords of Godthaab district (Gulløv 1982) confirm the results of earlier work in the Thule district (Holtved 1944, 1954) and at Sermermiut in Jakobshavn district (Mathiassen 1958). This research presents the impression of a rapid Thule expansion down the west coast, reaching the Disko Bay–Nordrsetur area by about 1200–1250 and the outer fjords of the western settlement by the mid-1300s. It thus would seem that the Norse were in contact with the Neo-Eskimo for over 300 years.

We know frustratingly little about the nature of this long contact period, and we are badly in need of further archaeological evidence for Inuit–Norse interaction. The existing documentary, faunal, and archaeological evidence and a range of speculative contact models have been reviewed elsewhere (H.

Ingstad 1966; Jordan 1979; McGovern 1979b; Meldgaard 1977), so we may limit discussion here to possible effects of the Thule migration on the Nordrsetur hunt.

It may be useful to distinguish between the long-term and the short-term effects of culture contact. In the long term, it is evident that the Inuit replaced the Norse in both the Nordrsetur and the settlement areas. In ecological terms this replacement suggests that the two groups were in competition in some respect, and the rate of replacement suggests that the competition was diffuse and possibly indirect. While the "Inuit invasion model" that envisaged a Norse extermination by waves of Inuit raiders has been largely discredited (McGovern 1979b), it is clear that in the *long* term, the Norse and Inuit did not develop the sort of niche-splitting symbiosis that could have aided the survival of the Norse colony.

The great majority of the European references to Skraeling and Greenlandic Inuit legends about the ancient Kavdlunait recount violent encounters. If relations between groups were even sporadically hostile, the Inuit settlers in the long coastal zone would be well placed to harry small Norse seasonal hunting parties and isolated year-round hunters. Even the occasional raid on caches like the Nugssuaq structure would significantly raise the costs of the Nordrsetur hunt. However, in the short term, we may expect that the relations between cultures were more complex and probably changed as the Skraeling hunters established settlements further and further south. It is probably as unrealistic to characterize the 300 years of Inuit–Norse contact as either wholly hostile or wholly friendly as it would be to similarly label the next 300 years of contact between Europeans and Native Americans in the temperate zone. Instead, it may be more useful to propose a number of possible contact options:

1. unremitting hostility—blood feuds and mutual raids made friendly contact and exchange impossible;
2. limited barter of expendable Norse artifacts for walrus and polar-bear products obtained by the Inuit—relations were a mix of friendly exchange, mutual pilferage, and occasional piracy depending upon opportunity and perceived advantage;
3. significant and regularized trade with a considerable volume of goods changing hands—the Norse shift from active hunting of Nordrsetur species to a middleman role, supplying Greenlandic and possibly Canadian Inuit with European goods in exchange for ivory, hide, and furs;
4. complete integration of Inuit and Norse subsistence economies and overseas trade—the Inuit provide Nordrsetur products and sea mammals and the Norse provide cloth, dairy produce, and access to European markets; and

5. gradual absorption of the Norse (biologically and culturally) by the Inuit.

Some of these options are not mutually exclusive and might represent different stages in a developing contact situation. While my earlier four-phase model for Norse–Inuit contact in Greenland deemphasized the role of barter or more formalized trade (McGovern 1979b), the growing volume of Norse artifacts found in Canadian Inuit sites that are securely dated to the period of Norse occupation (Harp 1974/1975; McCartney and Mack 1973; McGhee 1979, 1982; Sabo and Sabo 1978; Schledermann 1980; Schledermann and McCullough 1980; Sutherland 1981) suggest that a revision of this position is in order. This steadily expanding collection of Norse artifacts in Arctic Canada (especially Schledermann's concentration of Norse iron, cloth, and wood in the Bache Peninsula area of eastern Ellesmere) would seem to indicate the results of exchange as well as plunder. The speed of the Inuit migration down the west coast of Greenland also suggests that the first option of unremitting hostility is improbable. The last contact option, however, seems equally unlikely. Neither analyses of human skeletal collections (Berry 1974; Laughlin and Jørgensen 1966) nor the nearly 50 Norse sites excavated over the past 90 years show any evidence of gradual biological or cultural absorption of the Norse Greenlanders by their Inuit successors.

While the fourth option of economic integration would seem optimum in historical retrospect, it also does not seem to have occurred. Some Inuit stories—recorded under questionable circumstances—(Krogh 1967; McGhee 1982; McGovern 1979b) do describe Inuit servants on Norse farms. One Norse tale describes two Inuit children acting as servants on a large eastern settlement farm (Gad 1970). If some Inuit did act as servants on Norse farms, they are archaeologically invisible. Norse setatite vessels and lamps, hunting technology, and even clothing styles show no admixture of Inuit design; nor have any Inuit tool kits been recovered from the "servants' quarters" of any Norse farm yet excavated. If Inuit hunters did supply the Norse with seals, it is strange that they failed to provide many ringed-seal carcasses (see Table 12.1). This species makes breathing holes in the winter ice and is a mainstay of recent Greenlandic Inuit. Ringed seals do not form seasonal concentrations vulnerable to communal drives, but are best taken with toggling harpoons—an item of Inuit technology conspicuously absent from Norse artifact inventories. As argued elsewhere (McGovern 1979b, 1981), some sort of social barrier seems to have limited the diffusion of Inuit hunting techniques to the Norse.

We, therefore, seem to be limited to a choice between options two and three. The nature of existing documentary and archaeological data makes it impossible to confidently choose one option over the other. However, on the basis of present evidence, I suspect that the second option of limited barter is the more likely. A change of roles from active hunters of Nordrsetur species to middlemen between Inuit hunters and European transatlantic traders would have the advantage of shifting the costs and hazards of the Nordrsetur to the Inuit. However, this would also entail the accumulation of European trade goods (especially metal) in excess of the Norse Greenlanders' own local demands. Since we have evidence that this demand was not being satisfied by the irregular arrival of comparatively small cargos from Europe, such an accumulation of surplus goods for large-scale trade with the Inuit seems unlikely. While the curiosity value of Norse items to Inuit consumers might have allowed a spectacular Norse profit margin initially, the experience of later traders (Gad 1973) suggests that the Inuit would have swiftly learned the value of their own goods and would have held out for more than token payments. While the exchange of archaeologically unrecoverable milk and wool for boneless meat can never be disproven, it is likely that the most profitable exchange for both parties would be ivory for the very metal the Norse were themselves lacking. The larger volume of trade modeled by option three would have been possible if European demand for Greenlandic goods had strengthened and if the rate and volume of transatlantic contact had increased. Instead, both demand and regularity of contact seem to have fatally decreased in the fifteenth century.

DECLINE OF TRANSATLANTIC TRADE

The documentary evidence makes clear that European contact with the Greenland colony became still less regular in the later Middle Ages. The royal "Greenland knarr"—authorized to carry out regular transatlantic voyages—was lost around 1369 and does not seem to have been replaced (Gad 1970:141). Gad's careful documentary research indicated: "towards the end of the 14th century and well into the 15th century, that no single ship intentionally sailed for Greenland" (1970:151). Contact was maintained by accidental visits and probably also by unauthorized visitors who were careful to leave no written record of their voyages. The last reliable record from the colony dates to 1409 and records a proper church wedding at Hvalsey and also notes a recent burning for witchcraft (Gad 1970:149). The presiding churchmen at the wedding (and presumably at the auto-da-fé) were titled officialis (episcopal steward) rather than bishop. (Bishop Alf, originally a Benedictine monk from a monastery near Bergen, had died about 1378.) Though "Bishops of Gardar" continued to be appointed by popes of Rome or Avingnon for several hundred years, none of the later bishops elected to visit his see. Despite recurring papal concern over the continued orthodoxy of the isolated Greenlanders, the see of Gardar had been effectively abandoned by the beginning of the fifteenth century (Gad 1970:136–138).

Part of the waning interest in the Greenland colony may be explained by climatic change. The general cooling of the northern hemisphere during the late medieval "Little Ice Age" is now well documented (Wigley *et al.* 1981; Lamb 1977). One of the effects of this cooling trend was a massive increase of drift ice in Danmark Strait between Iceland and Greenland during the summer sailing season (Oglivie 1981). Medieval documentary sources comment on the increasing drift ice and on the need for a new, more southerly route to Greenland in the mid-fourteenth century (Gad 1970). The hazards of the always-dangerous Greenland voyage were thus seen to increase dramatically.

At the same time, the rewards of a successful voyage to Greenland probably also declined; the royal monopoly and excise fees seem to have discouraged private ventures and decreased profit margins (Gad 1970:146). The extinction of the western settlement around 1350 would have considerably increased the already-significant movement costs of the Greenlanders' Nordrsetur voyages. Unless a large-scale trade with the Inuit was indeed in operation, the Norse Greenlanders may have experienced difficulties in maintaining their stocks of Nordrsetur trade goods. Surplus subsistence produce (cattle and caribou hides, sealskins, woolens, and dairy produce) could have been obtained at lesser risk nearer the European market centers, and would make a poor load for a transatlantic knarr. Finally, European elite tastes seem to have been shifting away from walrus ivory ornaments because colorful enamels came to dominate ecclesiastical and secular decorative arts in the fifteenth century.

Perhaps as significant was the political and economic status of the Norwegian realm (and its North Atlantic periphery) which seems to have shifted in the later Middle Ages. One of the direct ancestors of the sixteenth-century northwest European core of the emergent world system was the Germanic Hanseatic League (Wallerstein 1979). The Hansa's capacious cogs and commercial expertise came to dominate trade in both bulk goods (especially grain and fish) and luxury items in both the Baltic and North seas. Hampered by a cooling climate (Gelsinger 1981) and by the Black Death of the 1340s and 1360s, the Norwegian kingdom was gradually converted into a semiperiphery of the developing Hanseatic core (Wallerstein 1974). The Hansa had alternate sources of Arctic products in northern Russia, and had a vested interest in maintaining and expanding relations with the Russian principalities. They had no such vested interest in Greenland, and may even have seen the sporadic, unpredictable arrival of cargos of Greenlandic ivory on the northwest European market as an annoying disruption of their existing profit structure. As Nørlund (1936) pointed out, the Hanseatics may also have been reluctant to risk their larger, more capital-intensive ships on voyages that might have still attracted owners of smaller and cheaper vessels. In any case, growing English competition in the North Atlantic (Gad 1970:156), increasing Hanseatic involvement in Norwegian trade, and the political integration of Norway into a combined Scandinavian kingdom ruled from Denmark all seem to have reduced Norway's capacity to carry out transatlantic trade with the distant Greenlandic colony by the fifteenth century.

By A.D. 1500 Norse society in Greenland had come to an end. For 500 years the colony had provided Europe with Arctic luxury goods and a toehold in North America; but neither proved indispensable to the medieval homeland. Despite the constraints of distance and limited cargo capacity, the Greenlandic elite seems to have maintained as long as possible the Nordrsetur hunt and the tenuous transatlantic linkage that supplied both technomic and ideotechnic needs: iron tools, stained glass, ship timbers, and church bells. In the end, Greenland seems to have been written off by the European suppliers of both ideological validation and subsistence technology. In many respects, the Greenland colony's economic and political structure prefigured that of many seventeenth- to twentieth-century colonial peripheries. Like many of these successors in marginality, Norse Greenland seems to have payed a high price for its integration into the larger economy. Norse Greenland's eventual extinction was the product of many factors, but one of the more important factors must have been the changing relations of this colony "at the world's rim" with the infant core of the European world system.

ACKNOWLEDGMENTS

I thank all those who worked with me in the Inuit–Norse Project of 1976–1977, Richard Jordan and Claus Andreasen who collaborated in the 1981 Grønlands Landsmuseum Survey Project, and the many in Denmark and the United States who have been so generous with their time and facilities in the analysis of the diverse data from Norse Greenland. I would particularly like to thank Gerald F. Bigelow, Susan Kaplan, Daniel Russell, and the editors of this volume for their aid in the writing and revision of this article. The research reported within was generously supported by National Science Foundation Grants BNS 76-11170 and 8004483, the Research Foundation of the City University of New York, and the Wenner-Gren Foundation for Anthropological Research. Any errors of fact or interpretation remain wholly my responsibility.

REFERENCES

Andreasen, Claus
1980 Nordbosager fra Vesterbygden paa Grønland, *Hikuin* 6:135–146, Moesgaard.

1981 Langhus-ganghus-centraliseret gaard: Nogle betragtninger over de norøne gaardtyper, *Hikuin* 7:179–184, Moesgaard.

1982 Nipaitsoq og Vesterbygden, *Tidsskriftet Grønland* (July).

Barlett, Peggy F. (editor)

1980 *Agricultural decision making: anthropological contributions to rural develeopment,* Academic, New York.

Beresford, G.

1975 *The medieval clay-land village: excavations at Goltho and Barton Blount.* Society for Medieval Archaeology Monograph No. 6, London.

Berglund, J.

1973 Paa den yderste nøgne ø, *Skalk* 4.

Berry, A. C.

1974 The use of non-metrical variations in the study of Scandinavian population movements. *American Journal of Physical Anthropology* 40:345–358.

Bertelsen, R.

1979 Farm mounds in North Norway. *Nor. Arch. Rev.* 12(1):48–57.

Bigelow, Gerald F.

1984 *Subsistence in Late Norse Shetland: An investigation into a Northern Island economy of the Middle Ages.* Unpublished Ph.D. dissertation, University of Cambridge.

Bruemmer, F.

1974 *The Arctic.* Infocor, Montreal.

Bruun, D.

1896 Arkaeologiske Undersogelser i Julianehabs Distrikter. *Meddelelser om Grønland* 16.

1916 Nordboruiner i Godthaabs og Frederikhaabs Distrikter. *Meddelelser om Grønland* 56.

1918 The Icelandic colonization of Greenland. *Meddelelser om Grønland* 57.

1928 Old Norse farms in the eastern and western settlements. *Greenland* 2 (Munksgaard, Copenhagen).

Chisolm, M.

1962 *Rural settlement and land use: an essay in location.* Hutchinson, London.

Christaller, W.

1933 *Die zentralen orte in Soddeutchland,* Jena.

Clarke, David L. (editor)

1977 *Spatial archaeology.* Academic, New York.

Clarke, Helen (editor)

1979 *Iron and man in prehistoric Sweden.* Lys Forlag, Stockholm.

Crumlin-Pedersen, O.

1972 The Vikings and the Hanseatic merchants: 900–1450. In *A history of seafaring based on underwater archaeology,* edited by G. Bass. Walker, New York.

Davis, Ralph

1973 *The rise of the Atlantic economies.* Cornell University Press, Ithaca, New York.

Degerbøl, M.

1929 Animal bones from the Norse ruins at Gardar. *Meddelelser om Grønland* 76(1).

1934 Animal remains from the west settlement in Greenland. *Meddelelser om Grønland* 88(3).

1936 Animal bones from Norse ruins at Brattahlid. *Meddelelser om Grønland* 88(5).

1941 The Osseous material from Austmannadal and Tungmeralik. *Meddelelser om Grønland* 86(3).

1943 Animal remains from inland farms in the Norse eastern settlement. *Meddelelser om Grønland* 90(3).

McGhee, Robert
    1979   *Possible Norse-Eskimo contacts in the eastern Arctic.* Paper delivered at the Con-
            ference on Early European Explorations in North America, St. John's,
            Newfoundland.
    1982   Norsemen and Eskimos in Arctic Canada. In *Vikings in the West,* edited by A.
            Guralnick. Archaeological Institute of North America, Chicago.
McGovern, T. H.
    1979a   *The paleoeconomy of Norse Greenland: adaptation and extinction in a tightly-
            bounded ecosystem.* Ph.D. dissertation, Columbia University. University Micro-
            films, Ann Arbor.
    1979b   Thule-Norse interaction in S.W. Greenland: a speculative model. In *Thule Eskimo
            Culture: an Anthropological Retrospective,* edited by A. P. McCartney. National
            Museum of Man Mercury Series, No. 88, Ottawa.
    1980a   Cows, harp seals, and churchbells: adaptation and extinction in Norse Greenland.
            Human Ecology (8)1.
    1980b   Site catchment and maritime adaptation in Norse Greenland. In *Site Catchment
            Analysis: Essays on Prehistoric Resource Space,* edited by F. Findlow and J.
            Eriksson.
    1980/1981 The Vinland adventure: a North Atlantic perspective. *North American Ar-
            chaeologist* 2(4):285–308.
    1981   The economics of extinction in Norse Greenland. In *Climate and History,* edited by
            T. M. L. Wigley, Cambridge University Press, pp. 404–434.
    1982   *Zooarchaeology and paleoeconomy in Norse Greenland.* Paper presented to the
            Society for Historical Archaeology, Philadelphia.
McGovern, T. H., and G. F. Bigelow
    n.d.   Survival and extinction in Norse Shetland and Greenland. *Scientific American.*
McGovern, Thomas H., P. C. Buckland, Diana Savory, Gudrun Svienbjarnardottir, Claus
Andreasen, and P. Skidmore
    1983   A study of the faunal and floral remains from two Norse farms in the Western
            Settlement, Greenland. *Arctic Anthropology* 20(2):93–120.
McGovern, T. H., and Richard H. Jordan
    1982   Settlement and land use in the inner fjords of Godthaab district, West Greenland.
            Arctic Anthropology 19(1).
McGrail, Sean (editor)
    1977   *Sources and techniques in boat archaeology.* BAR 29.
    1980   Ships, shipwrights, and seamen. In *The Viking World,* edited by J. Graham-Camp-
            bell, pp. 6–59. Ticknor & Fileds, New York.
Meldgaard, Jørgen
    1977   Inuit-Nordbo projektet. *Nationalmuseets Arbejdsmark,* Cop.
Magnusson, M., and H. Palsson (translator)
    1962   *Audun's saga.* Penguin, London.
    1963   *The Vinland sagas.* Penguin, London.
Mansfield, A. W.
    1950   The biology of the Atlantic walrus in the eastern Canadian Arctic. *Fisheries Res.
            Bd. of Canada Publication 653,* Ottawa.
    1966   The walrus in the Canadian Arctic. *Canadian Geographical Journal* 3.
Mathiassen, T.
    1958   The Sermermiut excavations 1958. *Meddelelser om Grønland* 161(3).
Mathiesen, P.
    1981   The Helgøy project. *Norwegian Archaeological Review* 14(2)1–117.

Mendelssohn, K.
1976 *The secret of western domination.* Praeger Publishers Inc., N.Y.
Ministry for Greenland, Fisheries Research Dept.
1954– present *Annual Summary of Catch Statistics.* Copenhagen.
Moltke, E.
1936 Greenland runic inscriptions. In *Sandnes and the Neighboring Farms,* edited by A. Roussell. *Meddelelser om Grønland* 88(2).
Morris, C.
1981 Excavations at the Earls' Bu, Orphir, Orkney. *University of Durham Archaeological Reports 4.*
Morrison, I.
1981 Maritime catastrophes, their archaeological and documentary legacies. *Northern Studies* 18:20–40. (Edinburgh).
Møhl, Jeppe
1982 Ressourceudnyttelse fra norrøne og eskimoisk affaldslag belyst gennem knoglematerialet. *Tidsskrifitet Grønland* (8/9):18–26.
Nansen, F.
1911 *In northern mists.* Hienemann, London.
Nørlund, P.
1924 Buried Norsemen at Herjolfsues. *Meddelelser om Grønland* 67.
1930 Norse ruins at Gardar. *Meddelelser om Grøland* 76.
1936 *Viking Settlers in Greenland.* Munksgaard, Copenhagen.
Nørlund, P., and M. Stenberger
1934 Brattahlid. *Meddelelser om Grønland* 88(1).
Ogilvie, A.
1981 Climate and Economy in Iceland. In *Consequences of Climatic Change,* edited by C. D. Smith and M. Parry, pp. 54–70. Univ. of Nottingham.
Osborne, P. J.
1977 Strandloopers, mermaids and other fairy tales. In *For theory building in archaeology,* edited by L. Binford, pp. 157–197. Academic, New York.
Paynter, Robert
1982 *Models of spatial inequality: settlement patterns in the historical connecticut River Valley.* Academic, New York.
Perlman, S.
1980 An optimum diet model, coastal variability, and hunter–gatherer behavior. In *Recent advances in archaeological method and theory,* (vol. 3), edited by M. Schiffer, pp. 257–310. Academic, New York.
Perry, Richard
1967 *The world of the walrus.* Taplinger, New York.
Petersen, R.
1973 On the variations of settlement pattern and hunting conditions in three districts of Greenland. In *Circumpolar Problems,* edited by G. Berg. Pergamon, New York.
Rink, H.
1877 *Danish Greenland: its people and products.* Hurst, London.
Rosendahl
1961 Grønlandsk jagt og fangstatistik *Geogr. Tidsskr.* 60.
Rosenkrantz, A.
1932 The burning mount of Niaqornat. *Norsk Geografisk Tidsskr.* 4(1–3):40–58.
Roussell, Aage
1936 Sandnes and the Neighboring Farms. *MoG* 88(2) (Copenhagen).

1941 Farms and Churches of the Medieval Norse Settlement in Greenland, *MoG* 89(1) (Copenhagen).

Sabo, D., and G. Sabo
1978 A possible Thule carving of a Viking from Baffin Island, NWT. *Canadian Journal of Anthropology* 2:33–42.

Schledermann, P.
1980 Notes on Norse finds from the east coast of Ellesmere Island, N.W.T. *Arctic* 33(3).

Schledermann, P., and K. McCullough
1980 Western elements in the early Thule culture of the eastern high Arctic. *Arctic* 33(4):833–842.

Scoresby, William
1820 *Arctic regions*. London.

Shuldham, M.
1775 Account of the sea-cow and the use made of it. *Phil. Trans. Royal Soc.* London 65(2):249–251.

Smith, Carol (editor)
1976 *Regional analysis* (Vol. 1). Academic, New York.

Sutherland, P. D.
1981 *Archaeological excavation and survey on northern Ellesmere Island and eastern Axel Heiberg Island, Summer 1980: a preliminary report.* Manuscript on file, Department of Anthropology, McMaster University.

Sveinsson, E. O.
1953 The age of the Sturlungs. *Islandica* 36. Yale University Press.

Thorlaksson, H.
1978 Comments on ports of trade in early medieval Europe. *Norweg. Arch. Rev.* 11(2):112–114.

Thünen, J. H., von
1875 *Der Isolierte Staat in Beziehung auf Landwirtschaft und Nationalokonomie.* Hamburg.

USDMA
1968 et. seq. *Mariner's overseas chart series,* Nos. 38032, 38520, 38500, 38480, 38460, 38440. U.S. Defense Mapping Agency, Washington, D.C.

Vebaek, C. L.
1943a Inland farms in the Norse east settlement. *Meddelelser om Grønland* 90(1).
1943b Nordboforskningen i Grønland. *Geografisk Tidsskrift* 46:101–28.
1952 Vatnahverfi. *National Museum Arbiedsmk* 101(14).
1953a Klostre i de grønlndske Nordbobygder. *Grønland* 5.
1953b Nordbobygdernes kiker. *Grønland* 8.
1953c Vatnahverfi. *Grønland* 6.
1956a Mellembygden. *Grønland* 3.
1956b Ten years of topographic and archaeological investigation in the medieval Norse settlements in Greenland. *32nd International Congress of Americanists,* Copenhagen.
1958 Topographical and archaeological investigation in the medieval Norse settlements in Greenland: a survey of the work of the last ten years. *Third Viking Congress,* Reykjavik.
1962 The climate of Greenland in the 11th and 16th centuries. Paper presented at the Conference on the Climate of the 11th and 16th Centuries, Aspen, Colorado.
1965 An 11th century farmhouse in the Norse colonies in Greenland. *Fourth Viking Congress,* York.
1966 Kirke-topografien i Nordboernes Østerbygd, *Grønland* 6.

1968 The church topography of the medieval Norse eastern settlement in Greenland. *Fifth Viking Congress,* Thorshavn.

Vibe, Chr.
1950 The marine mammals and the marine fauna in the Thule district, N.W. Greenland, with observations on the ice conditions. *Meddl. om Grønland* 150(6).
1956 Walrus west of Greenland. *Proceedings of 5th Technical Meeting, International Union for the Protection of Nature,* pp. 79–84, Copenhagen.
1967 Arctic animals in relation to climatic fluctuations. *Meddelelser om Grønland* 170(5).
1970 The Arctic ecosystem influenced by fluctuations in sun-spots and driftice movements. In *Production and Conservation in the Northern Circumpolar Lands,* ns. 16:115–120.
1978 Cyclic fluctuations in tide related to season as key to some important short and long term fluctuations in climate and ecology in North Atlantic and Arctic Regions. In *Proceedings of the Nordic Symposium on Climatic Changes and Related Problems,* edited by K. Frydendahl. Danish Meteorological Institute No. 4, Copenhagen.

Vita-Finzi, C., and E. S. Higgs
1970 Prehistoric economy in the Mount Carmel area of Palestine: site catchment analysis. *Proceedings Prehistoric Society* 36:1–37.

Wallerstein, I.
1974 *The modern world-system: capitalist agriculture and the European world economy in the 16th century.* Academic, New York.
1979 *The Capitalist World-Economy.* Cambridge University Press, Cambridge.

Wigley, T. M. L. (editor)
1981 *Climate and history.* Cambridge University Press, Cambridge.

Winterhalder, B., and E. A. Smith (editors)
1981 *Hunter–gatherer foraging strategies: ethnographic and archaeological analyses.* University of Chicago Press, Chicago.

CHAPTER 13

Baptists and Boundaries: Lessons from Baptist Material Culture

GORDON BRONITSKY

Department of Anthropology
University of Arizona
Tucson, Arizona

ALAN MARKS

Department of Psychology
University of Texas of the Permian Basin
Odessa, Texas

CINDY BURLESON

Department of Psychology
University of Texas of the Permian Basin
Odessa, Texas

INTRODUCTION

The West Texas Baptist Project was initiated in the fall of 1977 and has continued to the present. The goal has been the study of the relationship between behavior and modern material culture on the one hand, and variables of socioeconomic class and ethnicity on the other. In contrast to archaeological studies that have concentrated on the investigation of symbol systems (e.g., Coe 1972; Furst 1968; Wicke 1971) or world view of extinct societies (e.g., Marshack 1972a,b, 1976, 1979), this project attempts to assess the variability of behavior and material culture expressions within one religious denomination. A major focus is the examination of the ties between material culture in churches and the ethnic composition of the church.

Recent studies in modern material culture have made contributions to archaeology in several areas of interest: in teaching and testing archaeological principles, in doing the archaeology of present-day social systems, and in relating our society to past societies (Rathje 1979:3–4). The potential of modern material-culture studies for testing archaeological principles and assumptions has sparked many ethnoarchaeological studies of nonindustrial, small-scale societies (e.g., Binford 1978; Stanislawski 1969). However, as several archaeologists have pointed out, archaeologists also excavate the remains of more complex societies as well (e.g., Ascher 1974; Salwen 1973). Accordingly, modern material culture studies of our own society may provide opportunities to test the assumptions we make about prehistoric complexity, in particular the effects of behavioral, socioeconomic, and ethnic factors on material culture.

A fundamental assumption in archaeology has been that material culture and the behavior that produces it are systematically patterned (Clarke 1978). All too often, archaeologists and other social scientists have assumed fairly simple, reflexive relationships between behavior and material culture in terms of ethnicity and socioeconomic class, for example, a particular set of grave goods suggests upper-class status (Griffin 1967) or a particular pottery type is correlated with a certain prehistoric society presumed ancestral to an ethnographically known group (see Ford *et al.* 1972 for an example of this approach in reconstructing southwestern prehistory). This view has been criticized from several perspectives, including, for instance, analysis of mortuary remains (Ucko 1969), studies of material cultural similarities in terms of the expression of social relationships rather than simple frequency of interaction (Hodder 1979), studies of ethnicity and material culture (Barth 1969:13), and ceramic analysis (Sears 1973:31; Plog 1980:2).

Human actions are not composed of simple discrete segments that can be neatly mapped onto surviving elements of material culture. Rather, human behavior is a complex integration of cognitive, behavioral, and material elements, all of which must be considered in analysis. Cognitive elements include cultural rules about behavior, along with informant concepts of the behaviors that actually occur as a result of those rules. Behavioral elements include records of observed behavior, along with common "behavioral shorthand concepts" used to group individuals, such as ethnicity and socioeconomic class (Rathje 1979:24). Finally, material elements comprise the quantified measures of the material culture environments. Studies of archaeological entities (Clarke 1978) presumed to have sociocultural dimensions should take this total integration into account.

As an entity with sociocultural dimensions, religion may play a major role as a guide for behavior (Rappaport 1971a,b), a regulator of human–environment interaction (Rappaport 1968), or even as a detailed guide to very specific social ends (Leone 1973). Archaeologists, however, have lacked theoretical and methodological frameworks for dealing with religion and have instead tended to prefer more amenable topics for analysis, such as settlement patterns, faunal analysis, and so on (Marcus 1978:172). Some archaeologists have claimed that there is "surprisingly little" evidence for religion in the archaeological record (Oates 1978:122). Occasionally, archaeologists have used religious and ceremonial behavior as *post hoc* rationalizations to explain items of unclear function, sometimes verging on "personal fantasy" (Marcus 1978:172). Few have focused on the cultural context of religious items (see Drennan 1976; Flannery 1976; Pyne 1976 for exceptions). Instead, much archaeological work has utilized iconographic studies of motif and symbol in order to study ancient religions (e.g., Wicke 1971), concentrating on belief systems rather than behaviors. Although archaeologists have called for examination of the relationships between material and nonmaterial culture (e.g., Deetz 1973:115; Noël Hume 1978:40; Stiles 1979:1) material culture studies of religious items in ongoing sociocultural contexts have been rarer still (see Bronitsky 1980, 1983; Bronitsky and Hamer 1984; Deal 1979; Leone 1973 for exceptions). Even less is understood about the ways in which religious symbolism affects other aspects of life (Myerhoff 1974:230).

CONGREGATIONAL DIVERSITY AND AUTONOMY

The Baptist denomination was selected for study for several reasons. Within the Baptist religion can be found representatives of every socioeconomic class and the major ethnic groups in Texas—black, white, and Mexican–American. Baptists were among the first Anglo-American pioneers in Texas (Matthews *et al.* 1936:viii), and the growth and history of the Baptists in Texas are often regarded as representative of the growth of Protestant Christianity in Texas in general. Since World War II the spectacular growth of the Baptist denomination, particularly the body known as the Southern Baptist Convention, has been one of the more conspicuous trends in American Protestantism (Bailey 1964:152). In 1962 Baptists formed one of the largest denominations in Texas and the United States. The 22 groups calling themselves Baptists make up an estimated 21 million United States Baptists (Rosten 1963). Several factors account for the broad-based public appeal of this particular branch of Protestantism. One is the use of studied promotional techniques, including extensive use of the press, radio, and television, as embodied in Billy Graham—perhaps the best-known Protestant spokesperson today. Another is the willingness and the ability to adapt their religious message and church structure to local conditions, to a degree "seldom possible in hierarchial denominations" (Bailey 1964:152).

The Baptist churches of west Texas provide an ideal setting for the study of the interactions among behavior, material culture, ethnicity, and socioeconomic status within one religious group. The diversity of socioeconomic and ethnic factors and the broad latitude permitted individual congregations allowed, for this study, the greatest possible heterogeneity of church organization and doctrine within the controlling factor of a single denomination. The congregational diversity present in the Baptist faith has its roots in Baptist theology and practice. Traditionally, Baptists have believed that the saving grace of God is available to any individual "without mediation of priest or church or minister or system" (Lipphard 1963:14–21). The membership is therefore seen as a voluntarily organized group of equals: "Each New Testament church is a voluntary organization of repented sinners; each church decides all matters by majority vote" (McConnell 1936:408; see Torbert 1950:24ff. for a discussion of the historical background of Baptist congregational autonomy). Accordingly, not only is church membership voluntary, but the relationship of the church to other churches and to national headquarters (in the form of "conventions" of member churches) is equally voluntary. Texas Southern Baptist Convention churches are grouped into regional associations, containing 17 districts that unite to support a wide variety of institutions, including Baylor and Hardin-Simmons universities, the Southwest Baptist Theological Seminary in Fort Worth, orphanages, hospitals, and so on, in addition to a program of evangelical missionary work (McConnell 1936).

The emphasis on individual access to supernatural grace is further reflected in the ministry. Part of the Baptist appeal to lower-income blacks, whites, or Mexican–Americans is the absence of formal educational prerequisites for the ministry (Pannell 1975); Baptists have "ordained, employed, controlled and discharged clergymen with a freedom denied Methodists and Presbyterians" (Bailey 1964:153). In essence, every church is a law unto itself (Lipphard 1963).

RESEARCH METHODOLOGY

Research was conducted by students in several anthropology classes at the University of Texas of the Permian Basin over a period of three years. Students were assigned to individual churches encompassing the range of socioeconomic and ethnic groups present in west Texas. The project required attendance at the assigned church for at least three Sunday-morning services after obtaining the consent of the minister involved. (It should be noted that all ministers who were asked to participate gave their consent.) An educational goal of the project was to introduce students to techniques of participant observation, so students were given a series of observations to make but were expected to go beyond the basic observations. The series included, first, the physical layout of the service: Where is it held? How is the room arranged? What furniture or other items are present? Is a table for the Lord's Supper present? What kinds of windows and construction materials does the church have? Second, students were directed toward the human dimension of the service. This included observations on number of people in attendance; the relative proportions of male and female, young and old, majority and minority groups; and the clustering of groups by age or sex. A third aspect involved the services themselves including the dress of congregants, minister, and others; the kinds of music and musicians; the specialized personnel; the time of day; and the style of audience participation. Finally, in order to introduce the students to more detailed participant observation, some questions were directed to the minister, such as his reasons for becoming a minister, the nature of his "call" to preach, his education, and so on.

Students then transcribed their observations into an ethnography. The ethnographies were distributed and served as a basis for part of the final examination in which students were asked: Are there differences among these churches? If not, why not? If there are differences, what are they? What factors might account for these differences? These questions enabled students to bring into play knowledge acquired through participant observation and their own background knowledge as members of west Texas society.

Each student was asked to fill out a computer form after completing his or her ethnography. The form employed some 50 variables, going into greater detail in the areas previously mentioned. The data thus provided were later rechecked during visits by the authors to the churches. These forms provided the quantitative data base for the project. At present the data base consists of 21 churches: 12 white, 7 black, and 2 Mexican–American. In terms of socioeconomic status, 5 were labeled "upper income" in terms of attendance and registration, minister's personal estimation, and the estimation of the student (based on types of cars, style of dress, church furnishings, and other general impressions). Twelve were "middle income" by the same standards, and 4 were "lower income." In terms of convention affiliation, 12 were Southern Baptist (including 1 black church), 1 belonged to the National Baptist Convention (the major organization of black Baptist churches), 1 belonged to a black Baptist convention other than the National Baptist, 4 were independent black Baptist churches, 1 white church belonged to the American Baptist Convention, 1 was nonaffiliated, and 1 was a Baptist charismatic church. The latter was included to study the effects of a change in religious belief on behavior. This church had been a member in good standing of the Southern Baptist Convention but had become charismatic (encouraging expression of "gifts of the Holy Spirit," such as speaking in tongues). On this basis, its affiliation with the Southern Baptist Convention was terminated by mutual consent. Its pastor now considered the church closer to traditional Pentecostalism than mainstream Baptist practice.

Since most of the variables listed on the computer form were nominal in nature (see Table 13.1 for a list of variables), methods of analysis were somewhat limited. A series of cluster analyses were performed in which the variables were partitioned into material culture, behavioral, and ministerial sets in order to examine the effects of each set on the total configuration. A cluster analysis was performed for all variables and then for each variable set. The similarity matrices employed in the cluster analyses were based upon the proportion of agreements among each set of variables for each pair of churches. Thus, if two churches had identical codes on all behavioral variables, they received a distance score of 1, indicating maximal closeness; if they had no agreements, they received a distance score of zero, indicating maximal distance. The cluster analyses were performed using Ward's algorithm which minimizes within-cluster variance at each stage of the clustering process (Anderberg 1972). The resultant hierarchical cluster analyses were used to examine the relationships among class and ethnicity to material culture, behavioral, and ministerial variables.

It was immediately apparent that the different dimensions represented by each of the variable sets (material culture, behavior, minister) resulted in very different clusterings of the church groups. The first cluster analysis employed all variables except those explicitly referring to ethnicity and social class in order to determine a general configuration of all the churches. The clusters produced by this analysis clearly reflected socioeconomic and ethnic variability (see Figure 13.1(1)). For instance, all black churches formed a single major discrete cluster. This cluster of black churches, however, did not then join the other churches until the last merge. The white and Mexican–American churches formed three distinct clusters. Since these clusters were ethnically integrated, socioeconomic status was a stronger determinant of cluster membership than ethnicity.

Each data subset was then examined separately to provide information on its role in producing the total configuration. When behavioral variables alone were considered in the analysis, three clusters were formed (see Figure 13.1(2)), and were somewhat less clear-cut than the clusters formed in the

Table 13.1
Baptist Project Variable List

Ethnic/Class Variables
  Financial Status
    No information
    Lower class
    Middle class
    Upper class
    Upper middle class
  Major Ethnic Group Present
    No information
    White
    Mexican–American
    Black
  Others Present
    No information
    White
    Mexican–American
    Black
  Minister Ethnicity
    No information
    White
    Mexican–American
    Black
  Language in Church
    No information
    Informal English
    Formal English
    Spanish
    Bilingual Spanish–English
Behavioral Variables
  Major Age
    No information
    Under 30
    30–50
    Over 50
  Major Sex
    No information
    Male
    Female
    Approximately balanced
  Language in Church
    No information
    Informal English
    Formal English
    Spanish
    Bilingual Spanish–English

Style of Service
  No information
  Informal
  Formal
  Very formal
Participation
  No information
  Amens led by officials
  Handclapping
  Spontaneous amens
  Other interjections
  Several spontaneous interjections
  Spontaneous and led interjections
  None of the above
Sermon Planning
  No information
  Yes
  No
Collection
  No information
  Congregational procession
  Taken by young men
  Taken by young women
  Taken by both
  Taken by deacons or other officials
Collection Counting
  No information
  Public at service
  Private
Seating
  No information
  By sex
  By family
  By age
  By family, with teen clusters
  By family, with organized youth groups
  Mixed
Child Care
  No information
  None
  Provided but not much use
  Provided and used
Ministerial Variables
  Full-time Minister
    No information

(continued)

Table 13.1 (*Continued*)

	Minister Dress in Church
Yes	No information
No	Robe
Other Employment	Casual
No information	Suit
Does not apply	Material Culture Variables
Barber	Male Dress (predominant)
Mail carrier	No information
Minister Ethnicity	Jeans
No information	Casual but not jeans
White	Suits
Black	Casual and suits
Mexican–American	Jeans, casual, suits
Minister Age	Female Dress (predominant)
No information	No information
Under 30	Slacks
30–50	Pantsuits
Over 50	Dresses
Minister Education	Pantsuits and dresses
No information	Slacks, pantsuits, and dresses
High school only	Printed Program
Secular B.A. only	No information
Secular B.A. and theological school	Present
Religious B.A. or equivalent	Absent
Unknown B.A. and theological school	Piano
Call to Preach	No information
No information	Present
Yes	Absent
No	Organ
Age at Call	No information
No information	Present
Under 15	Absent
15–20	Guitar
21–25	No information
26–30	Present
Over 30	Absent
Relatives in Ministry	Drums
No information	No information
None	Present
Sibling	Absent
Cousin	Other Instruments
Father	No information
Mother	Present
Other in parental generation	Absent
Grandparental generation	Choir Robes
More than one of the above	No information

(*continued*)

Table 13.1 (*Continued*)

Present
Absent
Does not apply
Choir Seating
  No information
  Folding chairs—no special structure
  Special structure
  Does not apply
Collection Posting
  No information
  In building
  In printed budget in program
  In printed budget distributed to
    members
Building Exterior
  No information
  Wood
  Concrete/brick veneer
  Concrete block
  Rock
Windows
  No information
  Plain
  Frosted
  Stained/colored
  Plain and frosted
  Plain and stained/colored
  All of the above
Steeple
  No information
  Present
  Absent
Style of Seating
  No information
  Plain wooden pews
  Cushioned pews
  Folding chairs
  Permanent chairs
Baptistry
  No information
  Present and visible
  Present and hidden
Speaking Platform
  No information
  Mobile
  Stationary
  None

Lord's Supper Table
  No information
  Present
  Absent
Sound System
  No information
  None
  Microphone for speaker only
  Microphone for instruments only
  Microphone for speaker and
    instruments
  Elaborate
Flowers
  No information
  None
  Plastic
  Live
  Plastic and Live
Flag
  No information
  American
  Christian
  Both
  Other
  None
Other Decoration
  No information
  Painted depiction of Christ
  Three-dimensional Christ on cross
  Other painting
  Painted depiction and three-dimen-
    sional Christ
  Painted depiction and other painting
  All of the above
  None
Church Layout
  No information
  Cruciform
  Rectangle/square
  Other
Crosses
  No information
  1
  2
  3
  4

(*continued*)

Table 13.1 (*Continued*)

5 or more	Church status
None	No information
Miscellaneous Information	Independent
Church Name	Mission
Denomination	Convention Status
Location	No information
Number of members	Member
Average attendance	Applying for membership
Paid staff	Ex-member
	Does not apply

first analysis. Socioeconomic divisions appeared to be the basis for these clusters since all clusters included both black and white churches. Specifically, the first cluster was primarily middle-income white churches (with one black and one Mexican–American church), the second was primarily lower-income black (with one white church—the charismatic church), and the third mainly upper-income whites (with two black churches). The cluster of lower socioeconomic churches was characterized by a high degree of spontaneity in the service and sermon planning, random seating of members, absence of child care, and an informal service style. The other two clusters were differentiated primarily by the formality of the service style. The middle-income churches, for example, often included spontaneous "amens" and other interjections, but in the upper-income churches these interjections were always under the direction of the minister.

The cluster picture became more complex when analysed by ministerial variables alone. Here the clusters were ethnically homogeneous but socioeconomically diverse (see Figure 13.1(3)). Five clusters were formed—one Mexican–American (with an upper-income white church), one upper-income white cluster, one middle-income white cluster, and two separate clusters of black churches. Black ministers in our sample were generally less likely to be full-time, were generally older when they received a divine call to preach, and had less education, particularly of a secular nature (Moberg 1962:487). In addition, all the black ministers had relatives in the ministry as opposed to only one-half of the white ministers, which may describe a more consistent religious background. The cluster containing the poorest black churches had only part-time ministers who tended to be younger than the full-time ministers of the other slightly more affluent cluster of black churches. The remaining clusters are differentiated less by specific variables than by different configurations of variables. For example, the cluster of upper-income white churches was homogeneous in all respects except minister education.

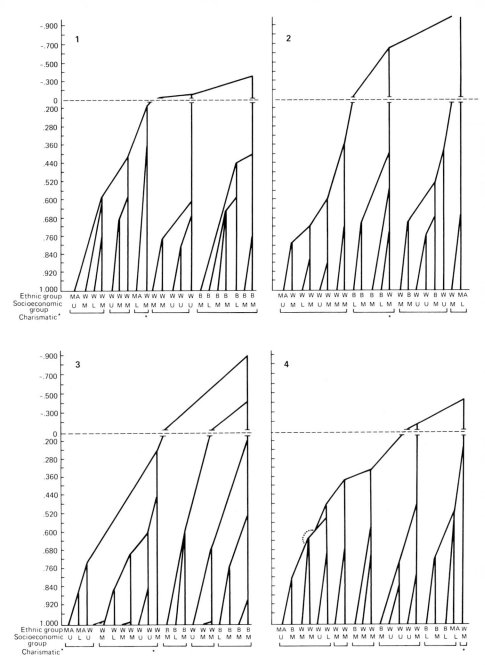

Figure 13.1 1, Clusters by all variables, excluding ethnicity and social class; 2, clusters by behavior variables; 3, clusters by minister variables; 4, clusters by material culture variables; B, black; L, lower income; M, middle income; MA, Mexican-American; U, upper income; W, white.

CONCLUSIONS

With these configurations in mind, we can now consider the patterned relationship of material culture to behavior (see Figure 13.1(4)). Cluster analysis of the subset of material culture data produced churches formed six cultures, with the charismatic church individually isolated from the other five clusters. These clusters appear to be products of church size and socioeconomic class more than of ethnicity, worship style, or other variables. In terms of the clustering process itself, the clusters merged more evenly than for the other two variable sets. This may be an artifact of the greater number of material culture variables incorporated into the analysis, or it may reflect a greater diversity in terms of material goods than in terms of behavioral or ministerial variables.

Only the cluster of lowest-income churches (three black churches, one Mexican–American church) was characterized by the presence or absence of specific variables, such as absence of choir (3 out of 4), absence of organ (2 out of 4), absence of steeple (3 out of 4), absence of microphones for any but the minister (4 out of 4), presence of a wooden church exterior (2 out of 4), presence of plain wooden pews (4 out of 4), presence of visible baptistry (4 out of 4), presence of Lord's Supper table (4 out of 4, which also characterized one of the largely white middle-income clusters as well), presence of plastic flowers only (4 out of 4). The other four clusters were distinguished by a frequency of occurrence of variables (reflecting a continuum of formality/informality) linked to church size and socioeconomic class. In these clusters material culture wealth seemed to correlate with a highly structured organization of possessions—particularly those with symbolic dimensions such as steeples and choir robes.

The multitude of religious functions were reflected differentially in these Baptist data. In the case of the charismatic church, religion had a primarily ideological function—manifested in its break from the mainstream Baptist movement—while it remained socioeconomically and ethnically similar to the church from which it originated. Behaviorally, it approached several of the black churches while remaining quite distinct from all churches in terms of minister and material culture. For the Mexican–American churches, religion seemed to be associated with social mobility, as manifested in behavioral similarity to middle-class white churches. The Mexican–American material culture data were more indicative of present socioeconomic status, since one church was clustered with a lower-income group of black churches and the other was grouped with a predominantly middle-income white group. The ministers of both Mexican–American churches were grouped with the minister of one of the large, wealthy white Baptist churches. The apparent anomaly is resolved when it is realized that these are mission churches originally sponsored by well-to-do white churches. The Baptist movement in Texas had a strong missionary program among Mexican–Americans, providing for the formal training of ministers in this group. This type of mission status and sponsorship was absent for black congregants who were present as early Baptist pioneers in Texas, while the Mexican–Americans were received later as converts from Catholicism.

Any religious denomination in our complex society is a heterogeneous institution, encompassing a wide range of motivations, beliefs, and material culture. The Baptist denomination is especially diverse due to the factors outlined previously—the wide range of socioeconomic classes and ethnic groups it contains, its emphasis on congregational autonomy, and a democratic structure that allows for a great flexibility of response to local conditions. All too often studies of modern material culture have tended to concentrate on narrowly defined links between behavior and object (Schiffer 1978:241ff.). Analysis of ministerial, behavioral, and material culture variables cannot be assumed to link in direct or clear-cut patterns. In this study material culture presented itself as an effective index of socioeconomic class while ethnicity was more clearly reflected in behavior (see Schuyler 1980:644 for a suggestion that archaeologically perceived Afro-American ethnicity may instead be a product of socioeconomic class). In order to understand ethnicity and cultural boundaries past or present, archaeologists must consider the need for interpreting the behavioral correlates of the things we study and move to formulate explicitly testable models of the relationships among behavior, belief, and material culture (Gould 1978:292).

ACKNOWLEDGMENTS

We first thank Cathy Stokes for her suggestion for an earlier title for this chapter, and Michael McCarthy of the University of Arizona for his help with the clustering program. Jeff Eighmy and Stan Green provided helpful criticisms and suggestions. A special note of thanks is due to the cultural anthropology students whose church-going participation, written reports, enthusiasm, and suggestions have laid the basis for this project. Gordon Bronitsky especially thanks Clara Jenkins for teaching him so much about the black experience in west Texas. Finally, this project would not have been possible without the cooperation of Baptist congregations and ministers in Midland, Odessa, Big Spring, and Greenwood, Texas. We appreciate the warmth and hospitality that they have consistently showed us and our students; in a very real sense this essay is theirs.

REFERENCES

Anderberg, M. B.
    1973   *Cluster analysis for applications.* Academic Press, New York.
Ascher, R.
    1974   Tin-can archaeology. *Historical Archaeology* 8:7–16.

Bailey, K. K.
    1964 *Southern white Protestantism in the twentieth century.* Harper & Row, New York.
Barth, F.
    1969 *Ethnic groups and boundaries.* Little, Brown, London.
Binford, L.
    1978 Dimensional analysis of behavior and site structure: learning from an Eskimo hunting stand. *American Antiquity* 43:330–361.
Bronitsky, G.
    1980 *Religion in west Texas: a modern material culture approach.* Paper presented at the 45th Annual Meeting, Society for American Archaeology, Philadelphia.
    1983 Religion in West Texas: Modern material culture and student education. *Southeastern Archeology* 2(1):1–7.
Bronitsky, G. and R. Hamer
    1984 Ethnicity and socioeconomic status: Studies in Baptist material culture. In *Towards an ethnoarcheology of modern America,* R. Gould, ed. Brown University Research Papers in Anthropology, No. 4, pp. 133–141.
Clarke, D. L.
    1978 *Analytical archaeology* (second ed.). Columbia University Press, New York.
Coe, M. D.
    1972 Olmec jaguars and Olmec kings. In *The cult of the Feline,* edited by E. P. Benson, pp. 1–12. Dumbarton Oaks, Washington, D.C.
Deal, M.
    1979 *Recognition of ritual pottery in residential units: an ethnoarchaeological model of the Maya family altar tradition.* Paper presented at the Annual Meeting, Society for American Archaeology, Vancouver, Canada.
Deetz, J.
    1973 Archeology as social science. In *Contemporary archaeology,* edited by M. Leone, pp. 108–112. Southern Illinois University Press, Carbondale.
Drennan, R. D.
    1976 Religion and social evolution formative Mesoamerica. In *The early Mesoamerican village,* edited by K. V. Flannery, pp. 345–367. Academic, New York.
Flannery, K. V.
    1976 Contextual analysis of ritual paraphernalia from formative Oaxaca. In *The early Mesoamerican village,* edited by K. V. Flannery, pp. 333–343. Academic, New York.
Ford, R. I., A. H. Schroder, and S. L. Peckham
    1972 Three perspectives on Puebloan prehistory. In *New perspectives on the Pueblos,* edited by A. Ortiz, pp. 19–39. University of Mexico Press, Albuquerque.
Furst, P. T.
    1968 The Olmec were-jaguar motif in the light of ethnographic reality. In *Dumbarton Oaks conference on the Olmec,* edited by E. P. Benson, pp. 143–175. Dumbarton Oaks, Washington, D.C.
Gould, R. A.
    1978 The anthropology of human residues. *American Anthropologist* 80(4):815–835.
    1979 Beyond analogy in ethnoarchaeology. In *Exploitations in ethnoarchaeology,* edited by R. Gould, pp. 249–293. School of American Research/University of New Mexico, Albuquerque.
Griffin, P. B.
    1967 A high status burial from Grasshopper Ruin, Arizona. *The Kiva* 33:37–53.

Hodder, I.
 1979 Economic and social stress and material culture patterning. *American Antiquity* 44(3):446–454.
Leone, M. P.
 1973 Archeology as the science of technology. In *Research and theory in current archeology*, edited by C. L. Redman, pp. 125–150. Wiley, New York.
Lipphard, W. B.
 1963 What is a Baptist? In *Religion in America*, edited by L. Rosten, pp. 14–21. Simon and Schuster, New York.
McConnell, F.
 1936 The present and the future. In *Centennial Story of Texas Baptists*, edited by H. Matthews, A. Swindell, L. Elliot, pp. 379–414. Baptist General Convention of Texas, Dallas.
Marcus, J.
 1978 Archaeology and religion: a comparison of the Zapotec and Maya. *World Archaeology* 10(2):172–191.
Marshack, A.
 1972a *The roots of civilization*. McGraw-Hill, New York.
 1972b Cognitive aspects of Paleolithic engraving. *Current Anthropology* 13:445–477.
 1976 Some implications of the Paleolithic symbolic evidence for the origin of language. *Current Anthropology* 17:274–282.
 1979 Upper Paleolithic symbol systems of the Russian plain: cognitive and comparative analysis. *Current Anthropology* 20:271–295.
Matthews, J. J., A. Swindell, and L. R. Elliot (editors)
 1936 *Centennial story of Texas Baptists*. Baptist General Convention of Texas, Dallas.
Moberg, D. O.
 1962 *The Church as a social institution*. Prentice-Hall, Englewood Cliffs, N.J.
Myerhoff, B.
 1974 Peyote hunt: *the sacred journey of the Huichol Indians*. Cornell University Press, Ithaca, N.Y.
Noël Hume, I.
 1978 Material culture with the dirt on it: a Virginia perspective. In *Material culture and the study of American life*, edited by I. Quimby, pp. 21–40. Norton, New York.
Oates, J.
 1978 Religion and ritual in sixth millennium B.C. Mesopotamia. *World Archeology* 10(2):117–124.
Pannell, W.
 1975 The religious heritage of blacks. In *The evangelicals*, edited by D. F. Wells and J. D. Woodbridge, pp. 96–121. Abingdon Press, New York.
Plog, S.
 1980 *Stylistic variation in prehistoric ceramics*. Cambridge University Press, Cambridge.
Pyne, N.
 1976 The fire-serpent and were-jaguar in formative Oxaaca. A Contingency Table Analysis. In *The early Mesoamerican village*, edited by K. V. Flannery, pp. 272–282. Academic, New York.
Rappaport, R. A.
 1968 *Pigs for the ancestors: ritual in the ecology of a New Guinea people*. Yale University Press, New Haven, Conn.
 1971a Ritual, sanctity and cybernetics. *American Anthropologist* 73:59–76.

1971b The sacred in human evolution. *Annual Review of Systematics and Ecology* 2:23–44.

Rathje, W. L.
1979 Modern material culture studies. In *Advances in archaeological method and theory* (Vol. 2), edited by M. B. Schiffer, pp. 1–37. Academic, New York.

Rosten, L. (editor)
1963 *Religions in America.* Simon and Schuster, New York.

Salwen, B.
1973 Archeology in Megalopolis. In *Research and theory in current archaeology*, edited by C. L. Redman, pp. 151–163. Wiley, New York.

Schiffer, M.
1978 Methodological issues in ethnoarchaeology. In *Explorations in ethnoarchaeology*, edited by R. Gould, pp. 229–247. School of American Research/University of New Mexico, Albuquerque.

Schuyler, R.
1980 *Review of* In Small things forgotten: the archaeology of early American Life, by J. Deetz. *American Antiquity* 45(3):643–645.

Sears, W.
1973 The sacred and the secular in prehistoric ceramics. In *Variation in anthropology: essays in honor of John C. McGregor,* edited by D. Lathrap and J. Douglas, pp. 31–42. Illinois Archaeological Survey, Urbana, Ill.

Stanislawski, M. B.
1969 The ethno-archaeology of Hopi pottery making. *Plateau* 42:27–33.

Stiles, D.
1979 Paleolithic culture and culture change: experiment in theory and method. *Current Anthropology* 20(1):1–8.

Torbert, R. G.
1950 *A history of the Baptists.* Judson Press, Philadelphia.

Ucko, P.
1969 Ethnography and archaeological interpretation of funerary remains. *World Archaeology* 1(2):262–280.

Wicke, C. R.
1971 *Olmec: an early art style of precolumbian Mexico.* University of Arizona Press, Tucson.

INDEX

STUDIES IN ARCHAEOLOGY

Consulting Editor: Stuart Struever

Department of Anthropology
Northwestern University
Evanston, Illinois

Charles R. McGimsey III. Public Archaeology

Lewis R. Binford. An Archaeological Perspective

Joseph W. Michels. Dating Methods in Archaeology

C. Garth Sampson. The Stone Age Archaeology of Southern Africa

Fred T. Plog. The Study of Prehistoric Change

Patty Jo Watson (Ed.). Archaeology of the Mammoth Cave Area

George C. Frison (Ed.). The Casper Site: A Hell Gap Bison Kill on the High Plains

W. Raymond Wood and R. Bruce McMillan (Eds.). Prehistoric Man and His Environments: A Case Study in the Ozark Highland

Kent V. Flannery (Ed.). The Early Mesoamerican Village

Charles E. Cleland (Ed.). Cultural Change and Continuity: Essays in Honor of James Bennett Griffin

Michael B. Schiffer. Behavioral Archeology

Fred Wendorf and Romuald Schild. Prehistory of the Nile Valley

Michael A. Jochim. Hunter–Gatherer Subsistence and Settlement: A Predictive Model

Stanley South. Method and Theory in Historical Archaeology

Timothy K. Earle and Jonathon E. Ericson (Eds.). Exchange System in Prehistory

Stanley South (Ed.). Research Strategies in Historical Archeology

John E. Yellen. Archaeological Approaches to the Present: Models for Reconstructing the Past

Lewis R. Binford (Ed.). For Theory Building in Archaeology: Essays on Faunal Remains, Aquatic Resources, Spatial Analysis, and Systemic Modeling

James N. Hill and Joel Gunn (Eds.). The Individual in Prehistory: Studies of Variability in Style in Prehistoric Technologies

Michael B. Schiffer and George J. Gumerman (Eds.). Conservation Archaeology: A Guide for Cultural Resource Management Studies

Thomas F. King, Patricia Parker Hickman, and Gary Berg. Anthropology in Historic Preservation: Caring for Culture's Clutter

Richard E. Blanton. Monte Albán: Settlement at the Ancient Zapotec Capital

R. E. Taylor and Clement W. Meighan. Chronologies in New World Archaeology

Bruce D. Smith. Prehistoric Patterns of Human Behavior: A Case Study in the Mississippi Valley

Barbara L. Stark and Barbara Voorhies (Eds.). Prehistoric Coastal Adaptations: The Economy and Ecology of Maritime Middle America

Charles L. Redman, Mary Jane Berman, Edward V. Curtin, William T. Langhorne, Nina M. Versaggi, and Jeffery C. Wanser (Eds.). Social Archeology: Beyond Subsistence and Dating

Bruce D. Smith (Ed.). Mississippian Settlement Patterns

Lewis R. Binford. Nunamiut Ethnoarchaeology

J. Barto Arnold III and Robert Weddle. The Nautical Archeology of Padre Island: The Spanish Shipwrecks of 1554

Sarunas Milisauskas. European Prehistory

Brian Hayden (Ed.). Lithic Use-Wear Analysis

William T. Sanders, Jeffrey R. Parsons, and Robert S. Santley. The Basin of Mexico: Ecological Processes in the Evolution of a Civilization

David L. Clarke. Analytical Archaeologist: Collected Papers of David L. Clarke. Edited and Introduced by His Colleagues

Arthur E. Spiess. Reindeer and Caribou Hunters: An Archaeological Study

Elizabeth S. Wing and Antoinette B. Brown. Paleonutrition: Method and Theory in Prehistoric Foodways

John W. Rick. Prehistoric Hunters of the High Andes

Timothy K. Earle and Andrew L. Christenson (Eds.). Modeling Change in Prehistoric Economics

Thomas F. Lynch (Ed.). Guitarrero Cave: Early Man in the Andes

Fred Wendorf and Romuald Schild. Prehistory of the Eastern Sahara

Henri Laville, Jean-Philippe Rigaud, and James Sackett. Rock Shelters of the Perigord: Stratigraphy and Archaeological Succession

Duane C. Anderson and Holmes A. Semken, Jr. (Eds.). The Cherokee Excavations: Holocene Ecology and Human Adaptations in Northwestern Iowa

Anna Curtenius Roosevelt. Parmana: Prehistoric Maize and Manioc Subsistence along the Amazon and Orinoco

Fekri A. Hassan. Demographic Archaeology

G. Barker. Landscape and Society: Prehistoric Central Italy

Lewis R. Binford. Bones: Ancient Men and Modern Myths

Richard A. Gould and Michael B. Schiffer (Eds.). Modern Material Culture: The Archaeology of Us

Muriel Porter Weaver. The Aztecs, Maya, and Their Predecessors: Archaeology of Mesoamerica, 2nd edition